Hands-on Application Development using Spring Boot

Building Modern Cloud Native Applications by Learning RESTFul API, Microservices, CRUD Operations, Unit Testing, and Deployment

Shagun Bakliwal

www.bpbonline.com

FIRST EDITION 2022

ISBN: 978-93-91030-22-3

LIMITS OF LIABILITY AND DISCLAIMER OF WARRANTY

Distributors:

BPB PUBLICATIONS
20, Ansari Road, Darya Ganj
New Delhi-110002
Ph: 23254990/23254991

MICRO MEDIA
Shop No. 5, Mahendra Chambers,
150 DN Rd. Next to Capital Cinema,
V.T. (C.S.T.) Station, MUMBAI-400 001
Ph: 22078296/22078297

DECCAN AGENCIES
4-3-329, Bank Street,
Hyderabad-500195
Ph: 24756967/24756400

BPB BOOK CENTRE
376 Old Lajpat Rai Market,
Delhi-110006
Ph: 23861747

To View Complete BPB Publications Catalogue Scan the QR Code:

Published by Manish Jain for BPB Publications, 20 Ansari Road, Darya Ganj, New Delhi-110002 and Printed by him at Repro India Ltd, Mumbai

www.bpbonline.com

Dedicated to

All Tech-Learners and
My Mom, who I always care for.

About the Author

Shagun Bakliwal has six years of work experience developing applications in languages such a Java, Spring Boot, Servlets, JSP, and HTML. He focuses primarily on the client-side and cloud technologies. He has worked with multiple MNCs based in India and currently lives in the city of dreams - Mumbai. If he isn't around his friends and family, then you can find him around his laptop or mobile. As he is very tech-savvy, he has cracked most interviews with the help of deep knowledge in Java and Spring Boot.

Prior to writing this book, he was also a technical reviewer for one of the publishers for Cloud Native Application. He is certified in many courses like MongoDB Basics, Google Analytics for Beginners, EMC Academic Associate, Cloud Infrastructure and Services and Predix developer. Over the years, he has implemented ideas ranging from basics to more complex paradigms and has acquired bounty of knowledge around many software tools that he loves to share.

About the Reviewer

Deepak Dhaka has six years of work experience in Java application development, API development. He has experience creating infra in Microservices architecture, handling security, and overall architecture development using tools like IntelliJ, Eclipse, and STS with programming languages such as Java, JavaScript, and so on, with a framework in Spring Boot. Deepak pursued B. Tech in Computer Science and Engineering from Amity University of Engineering, Amity University, Jaipur. He has worked with companies such as Wipro Technologies, the National Bank of Jamaica, Instant Systems, and HCL. He is currently working as a Senior Software Engineer in SOPHOS, a leading Security Product Company, Bangalore.

Acknowledgments

There are a few people who I want to thank personally for their continued support in my life before and after writing this book. First and foremost, I would like to thank my parents for sending me to an Engineering Institute where I fulfilled my passion for coding.

This book wouldn't have happened if I hadn't had the curiosity and the power about coding which aroused when I met Prof. Praful Kelkar. He always taught to aim higher and stand different in crowd based on the skills few can have.

Along the way, we got feedback from several peer reviewers who made sure that the book stayed on target and covered the accurate and latest stuff. Many thanks in particular to Priyanka Deshpande, my Content Development Editor. Thanks to the technical proofer Deepak Dhaka who was thorough, clear and helpful in reviewing the book. Also, much thanks to Shubham Shrivastava and Rajat Sethi for standing with me in happy and sad times throughout the book writing.

Finally, I would like to thank Priyanka Deshpande and Surbhi Saxena at BPB Publications for giving me this opportunity to write my first book for them and staying in contact throughout the book writing.

Preface

Spring is an excellent framework for developing both web and cloud-native applications. This book on application development using Spring Boot simplifies the process of writing boilerplate code for complex software. It allows developers to concentrate on the application's concept rather than on the internal Java configuration.

This book will guide you on how to make the best use of the strength that Spring Boot provides. You'll gain an understanding of how Spring Boot configuration works in conjunction with application development, including auto-configuration and overriding default configurations. You will learn to develop scalable, dependable microservices to accelerate the development lifecycle of a cloud-based application. Each chapter will walk you through the features of Spring Boot as a Software Development Framework, such as performing Create, Read, Update, and Delete (CRUD) operations on a database and securing web services with appropriate logging.

By the end of this book, you will develop, test, and deploy applications ready for production and how to establish them as cloud-based applications. The readers will also gain the expertise of writing unit and integration test cases. Over the 12 chapters in this book, you will learn the following:

Chapter 1 introduces the Spring Boot Framework with the latest version 2.4.3. It will cover the basics, features, advantages of Spring Boot, when to use, when not to use Spring Boot and setting up the workspace with the tools like Spring Tool Suite (STS), Spring Initializer, Maven, and Gradle as build tool. This chapter also explains the 12-Factor App features.

Chapter 2 discusses on how to create a basic Spring Boot Application step by step using Maven and Gradle as build tools. It also explains the Maven and Gradle build file components.

Chapter 3 describes the different Spring Boot Starter dependencies available which are used commonly for developing an application and how those dependencies can be configured by just writing the configurations and enabling them for auto-configuration.

Chapter 4 is a key chapter which discusses in depth the definitions and usage of various annotations used while developing Spring Boot Application so that you will have the idea of using them before developing the application.

Chapter 5 helps you deep dive into application development that interacts with database – H2 and MySQL and caches data that are frequently used.

Chapter 6 helps to create different profiles that can be used to create microservices, the interaction among them using RestTemplate with Eureka Service Discovery and API Gateway. It also includes different actuator endpoints and creating own health check endpoint.

Chapter 7 explains how to enable security in the RESTFul APIs created in Spring Boot Application. It explains concepts of Authentication and Authorization along-with Spring Filters. It also teaches how to implement OAuth 2.0 security.

Chapter 8 helps to understand how to sustain high traffic with different number of same applications running on the same machine so that resiliency of application is taken care by having client-side load balancing. If there is any part of the application that is continuously failing in serving the requests, then implementing the Circuit Breaker gracefully degrades the functionality so that application continues to operate when a related service fails, preventing the failure from cascading and giving the failing service time to recover.

Chapter 9 describes different ways of using logback configuration file for logging events. It also includes the Zipkin for tracing logs with tools like Sleuth, ElasticSearch, Logstash, and Kibana (ELK).

Chapter 10 explains how to document the APIs so that the consumers can consume it easily using Swagger. This chapter also explains how we can generate the Data Transfer Objects classes using YAML specification.

Chapter 11 describes the process of writing test cases in RESTFul Microservices using JUnit and Mockito testing framework. It also shows how to check the code coverage of the test cases developed in addition to automating test cases using Cucumber framework.

Chapter 12 describes the features and creation of docker for running the application in a containerized manner. It also includes the deployment of an application on Heroku Cloud so that its services are available on internet.

Downloading the code bundle and coloured images:

Please follow the link to download the
Code Bundle and the ***Coloured Images*** of the book:

https://rebrand.ly/75ee5f

Errata

We take immense pride in our work at BPB Publications and follow best practices to ensure the accuracy of our content to provide with an indulging reading experience to our subscribers. Our readers are our mirrors, and we use their inputs to reflect and improve upon human errors if any, occurred during the publishing processes involved. To let us maintain the quality and help us reach out to any readers who might be having difficulties due to any unforeseen errors, please write to us at:

errata@bpbonline.com

Your support, suggestions and feedbacks are highly appreciated by the BPB Publications' Family.

BPB is searching for authors like you

If you're interested in becoming an author for BPB, please visit **www.bpbonline.com** and apply today. We have worked with thousands of developers and tech professionals, just like you, to help them share their insight with the global tech community. You can make a general application, apply for a specific hot topic that we are recruiting an author for, or submit your own idea.

The code bundle for the book is also hosted on GitHub at **https://github.com/bpbpublications/Hands-on-Application-Development-using-Spring-Boot**. In case there's an update to the code, it will be updated on the existing GitHub repository.

We also have other code bundles from our rich catalog of books and videos available at **https://github.com/bpbpublications**. Check them out!

PIRACY

If you come across any illegal copies of our works in any form on the internet, we would be grateful if you would provide us with the location address or website name. Please contact us at **business@bpbonline.com** with a link to the material.

If you are interested in becoming an author

If there is a topic that you have expertise in, and you are interested in either writing or contributing to a book, please visit **www.bpbonline.com**.

REVIEWS

Please leave a review. Once you have read and used this book, why not leave a review on the site that you purchased it from? Potential readers can then see and use your unbiased opinion to make purchase decisions, we at BPB can understand what you think about our products, and our authors can see your feedback on their book. Thank you!

For more information about BPB, please visit **www.bpbonline.com**.

Table of Contents

CHAPTER 1
Getting Started with Spring Boot

As the web application development has changed from **Java Server Pages (JSPs)**, Servlets to Spring, many problems of the boiler plate code have reduced. **Spring** has really reduced the boilerplate code to an extent. The Spring team has developed **Spring Boot** on the top of the Spring framework that eliminated boilerplate configurations required for Spring applications. This chapter will introduce you to the **Spring Boot Framework** with the latest *version 2.4.3*. It will cover the basics of setting up the Spring Boot workspace with tools like **JDK 8**, **Spring Tool Suite (STS)**, **Spring Initializr**, and **Apache Maven** and **Gradle** as build tools.

Structure

In this chapter, we will discuss the following topics:

- Introduction to Spring Boot
- Features of Spring Boot
- Advantages of Spring Boot
- Breaking the monolithic way of developing software
- When to start using microservices?
- When not to start using microservices?
- System requirements

- Setting up the environment
- The 12-factor app
- Spring Initializr

Objectives

After studying this unit, you should be able to understand the concept of Spring Boot. You can set up your development environment and learn the **12-factor app** that an application should have.

Introduction to Spring Boot

On October 17, 2012, *Mike Youngstrom* opened a JIRA ticket with the Spring framework team asking for the support for container less web application architectures. As the developers would be more interested in adopting a simpler framework, there should be a mechanism that would allow the developers not to remember both configurations for the Spring model as well as the servlet container on which they are executing their application. There were few items within the older architecture of Spring core that was configured in an inconsistent non-unified way that the developers have to first learn the servlet container on which they are going to deploy in addition to the Spring's own configuration model.

He proposed an idea for having the servlet container and related tools as a part of the Spring component by embedding and unifying the configuration of those common web container services with the Spring container that can be bootstrapped from the `main()` method.

This issue was addressed by *Phil Webb* and from there the Spring Boot started evolving in 2013. On April 1, 2014, the first Spring Boot 1.0 **Globally Available** (**GA**) was released which addressed the preceding concern in addition to the issues.

Spring Boot is now an open-source Java-based framework used to create standalone microservices with production-ready features. It is heavily maintained by the Pivotal Team. Microservices is an architectural design that creates scalable, loosely coupled, and testable applications which have a single function module with well-defined interfaces. The microservices hence created by using Spring Boot can be owned and maintained by a small team; unlike it used to be while creating APIs by older technologies like Java web services that required a team of a larger size. This microservice design is adapted by many enterprises in recent years as they look to have their software development delivery in the Agile manner where they can continuously develop, test, and deliver.

Features of Spring Boot

Why the Spring team developed Spring Boot? How is it beneficial for developers to build their application on Spring Boot and not Spring? How are configurations managed? All features of Spring Boot would be explained in this and upcoming chapters. Few of them are listed as follows:

- Faster way of developing applications by reducing the boilerplate configurations.
- Loosely coupled dependencies.
- Starter packs available as part of dependency for simplifying builds and configuration.
- Creating production-ready microservices with actuator health endpoints such as **`health`**, **`httptrace`**, **`mappings`**, **`metrics`**, **`info`**, **`configprops`**, **`env`**, and so on.
- Embedded container server support. By default, Tomcat is used.
- Auto-configuration for dependencies; once the dependency is loaded into the class path, Spring Boot manages the class instantiations, when needed.
- Externalized configurations with the help of **`.properties`** and **`.yml`** files and **Spring Cloud Config**.
- Live reload for the application during the development phase.
- Ability to exclude/change the dependency version before deployment.

Advantages of Spring Boot

Spring Boot helps you to create stand-alone Spring-based applications with production-ready features that you can execute on the local workspace and the cloud platform which has the **Java Virtual Machine (JVM)** installed. By using Spring Boot as the development platform, you can get started with the creation of an application with minimum code setup with less development time, so that the focus will be in contract with the features that you want to imply in the application. This allows the developer to focus on the idea that evolves during the initial phase of the requirement and then it is the magic of Spring Boot that helps you to bootstrap your application, its external dependencies on the resources like accessing the database and managing the external calls to other applications that consume the data in the prescribed format. Mostly, Spring Boot applications need less Spring configuration.

After you build your Spring Boot application, it can be executed by **`java -jar <jar name>`** just like any other Java project that builds a **`jar`** file. The Spring Boot application can also be started by running the `mvn spring-boot:run` command on the root directory which contains the `src` folder.

Breaking the monolithic way of developing software

Since years the software development used to happen in a monolithic architecture. The developer or the business analyst or even the product owner of the software receives a big requirement at once and then after getting the details of the requirements, the team starts to work on. This leads to the waterfall model of developing a software which is good to release a **Minimal Viable Product** (**MVP**) that is a single release to showcase about what the product is. This single release is created in a single application containing all codes to resolve the user problem. Problem arises when the requirements are portrayed in such a way that the code already developed is duplicated to fulfill another requirement, that is, chunks of code can be repeated which leads to bad quality of code.

Now imagine for that requirement, all we need to repeat all sorts of regression and stress testing which was already done previously before releasing the product. *Why should all codes be tested even if that single enhancement may not be related to test the whole application?*

Since then, business capabilities are delivered using microservices. Now, selecting the microservice architecture over the monolithic architecture can have many reasons and may not be limited to the features of microservices as follows:

- Each service can have a single functionality, single data repository.
- Each service is independent of each other so that the change in one service doesn't impact the whole application.
- Each service can communicate with each other using **Inter Process Communication** (**IPC**) calls via web services/APIs. This also leads to access data that is owned by another service.
- Each service can be tested independently unlike the monolithic application which may require full testing even if few parts of the application is not in scope.
- Deploying each application independently in an isolated environment which can share different external services.

When to start using microservices?

Since microservices have a lot of advantages, one cannot limit to the following:

- Migrate legacy applications to the new technology.
- Changing technology stack for one service would not affect the whole application.
- Create high-performance and scalable services which only serves the single purpose that requires high computation/memory/resources.
- Experiment with the Agile methodology where requirements come in periodic intervals and the same can be delivered in a short span of time unlike monolithic where all the bundles are installed at once.

When not to start using microservices?

Apart from the various advantages of microservices, there can be few drawbacks as listed for not using the microservice architecture:

- Cost increased since each microservice runs in isolated virtual machines.
- If the development team is of small size, then it must manage all independent small size services which may lead to big changes in the capacity and productivity of the team. This can put a strain on all the operating units and the developers of that particular service.
- If the requirement is that tiny, then it cannot be further broken into different service creations.
- Some support of tools in legacy applications may not be supported in the microservice architecture because of tool limitation.

System requirements

Spring Boot *2.4.3* minimum requires Java 8 or its higher versions. The Spring framework *5.3.4* will automatically be downloaded if you include **`spring-boot-starter-parent`** with version *2.4.3*. The Spring team changed the naming conventions of their release versions after releasing the **`2.3.9.RELEASE`** version. After **`2.3.9.RELEASE`**, they formalized their naming convention to remove **`RELEASE`** from the starter packs.

While developing the Spring Boot application, you may require the following tools:

Tool	Version
Java	8 and higher
Apache Maven Gradle	3.3 and higher 6.3 and higher
Spring Tool Suite	3.9.4.RELEASE and higher

***Table 1.1**: Development tools and versions*

Setting up the environment

Spring Boot requires Java 8 and higher version and any of the build tools, that is, Apache Maven or Gradle. The next step is to install Java 8, Apache Maven, Gradle, and **Spring Tool Suite** (**STS**) for Spring Boot application development.

The following steps will explain how to download and install Java Development Kit 8, Apache Maven, Gradle, and Spring Tool Suite 4.

Installing Java Development Kit 8 (jdk-8u261-windows-x64)

Perform the following steps:

1. Browse the following link on Chrome for downloading Java 8:

   https://www.oracle.com/in/java/technologies/javase/javase-jdk8-downloads.html

2. Click on **`jdk-8u261-windows-x64.exe`**.
3. Click on the checkbox as mentioned in the following screenshot to accept the license agreement and then click on the **`Download jdk-8u261-windows-x64.exe`** button:

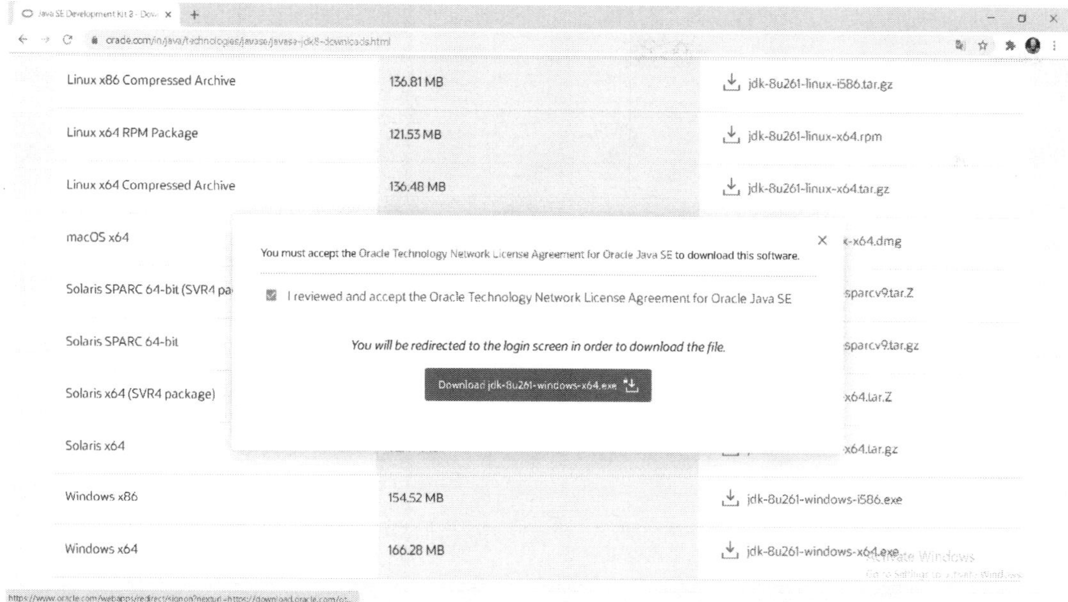

***Figure 1.1:** Download Java Development Kit 8*

4. Sign in to your Oracle account. If you do not have one, create an Oracle account and come back to this page for downloading Java 8. The **`Oracle account sign in`** page looks like the following screenshot:

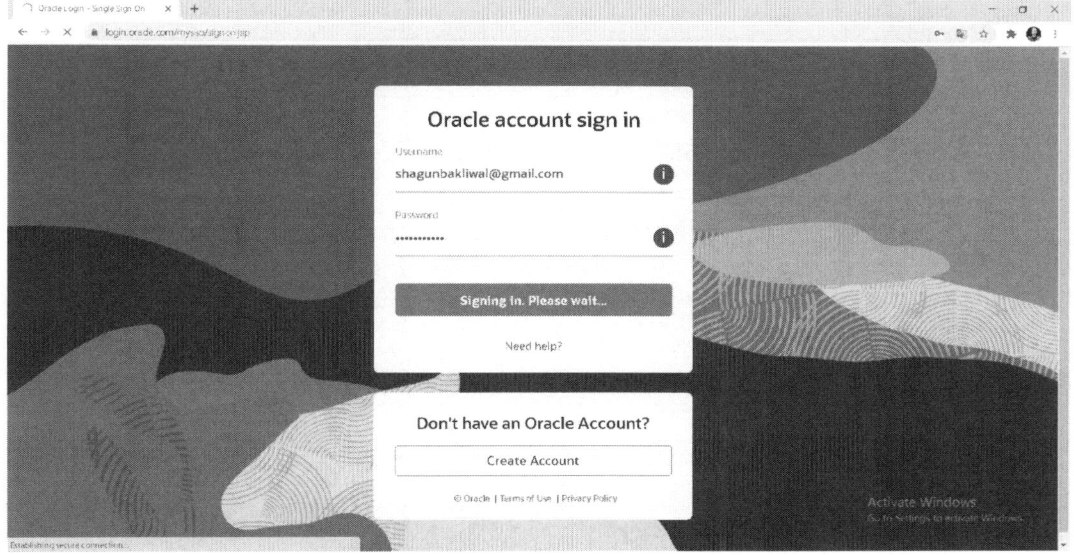

***Figure 1.2:** Sign into Oracle account*

5. On executing the Java installation file, you will see the following dialog box. Click on **`Next`** to select the Java directory:

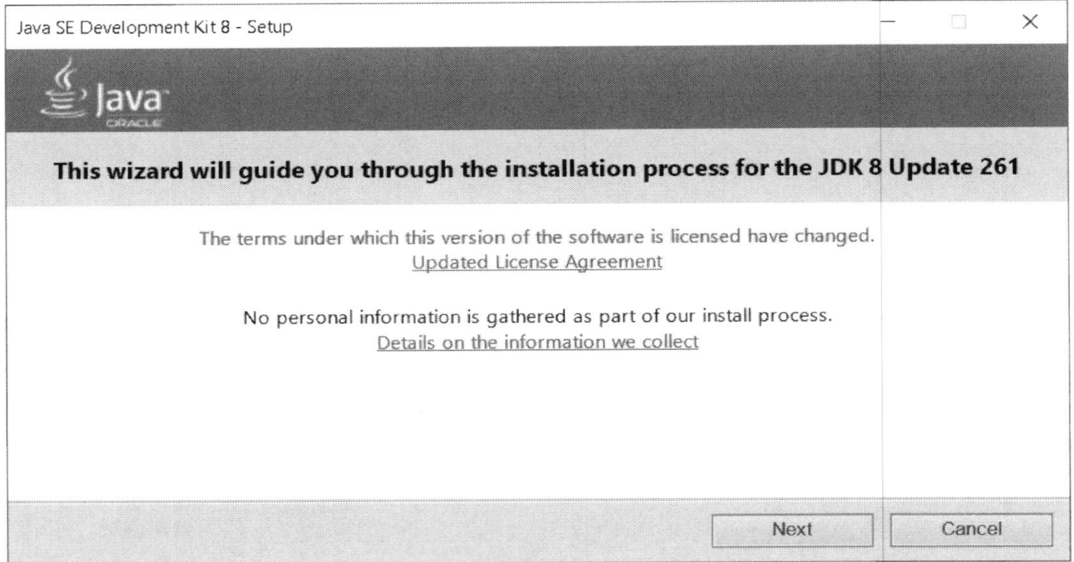

Figure 1.3: *Installation wizard for JDK 8*

6. Verify the directory where you wish to install the **Java Development Kit (JDK)**. For simplicity, install it in the default directory as shown in the following screenshot:

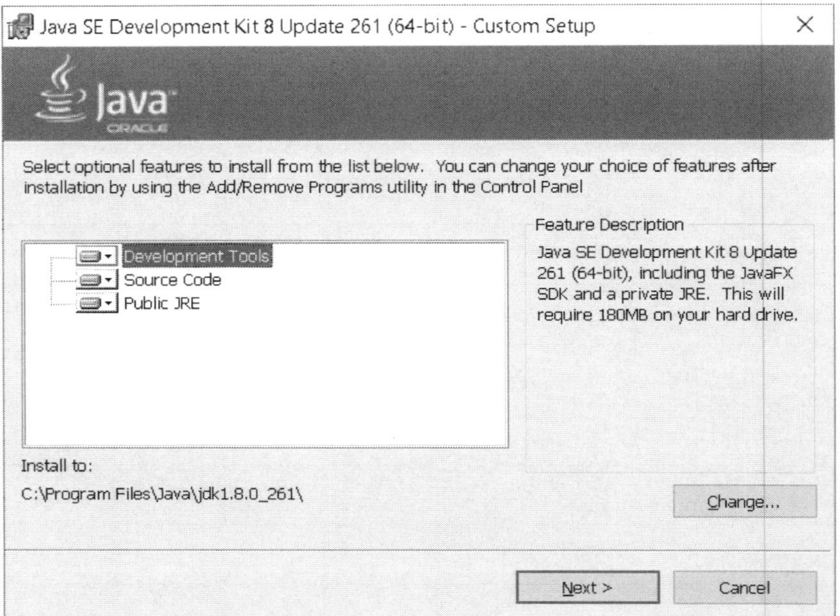

Figure 1.4: *Selecting JDK directory for installation*

7. In middle of the installation, the setup will ask to install JRE 8. Keep it in the same folder where the JDK is installed. For simplicity, keep it in the default directory as shown in the following screenshot:

It is always better to use the latest versions of tools. Spring Boot keeps on upgrading versions with new features. If you avoid upgrades, then you may miss out important features that might be helpful for the state of your application. In addition, if you upgrade later, then you may end up with doing a lot of regression testing when you actually go for an upgrade.

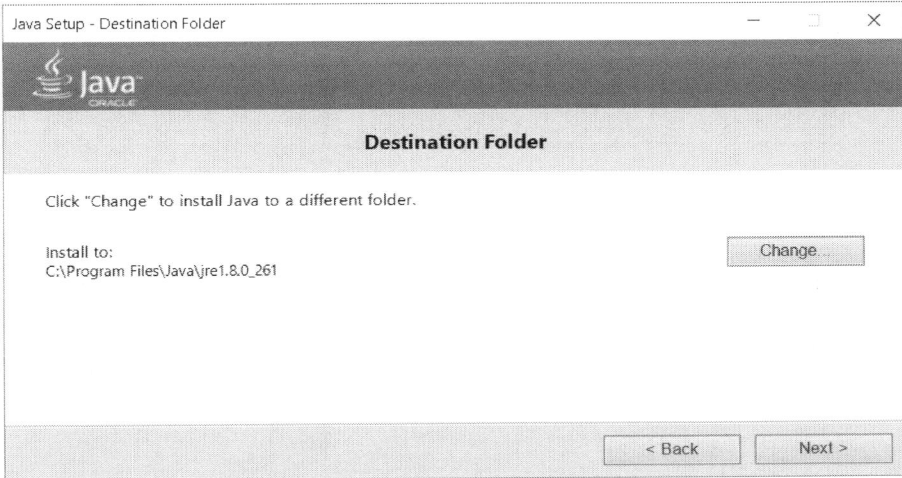

Figure 1.5: *Selecting JRE directory for installation*

8. Click on **`Next`** to install JRE 8:

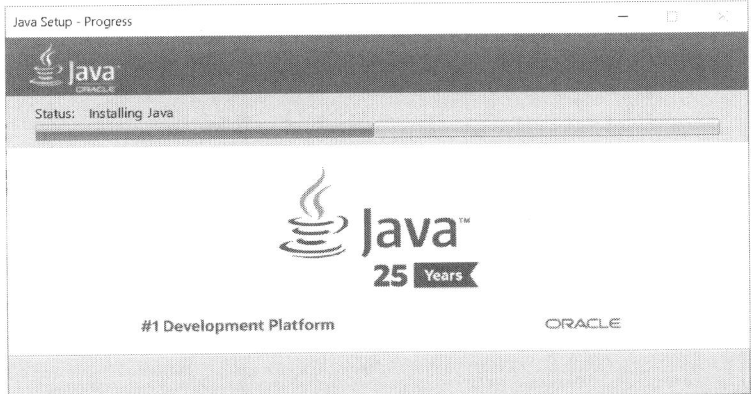

Figure 1.6: *Installing JRE*

9. After JRE is installed, the focus would be to switch back to continue with the JDK installation:

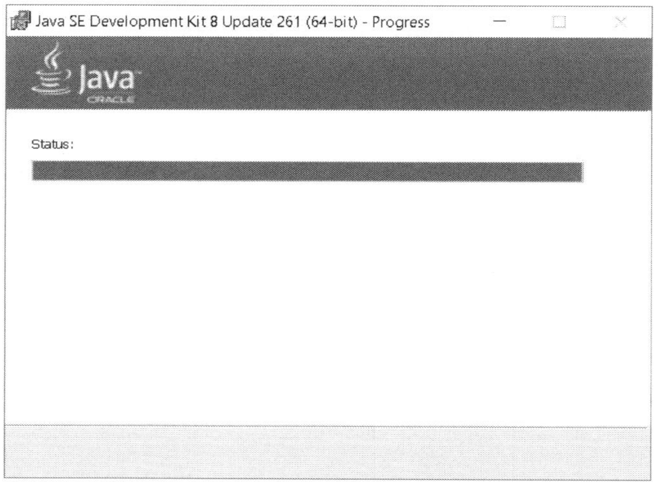

Figure 1.7: *Installing JDK*

10. If you see the following dialog box, Java would be installed correctly in the specified path:

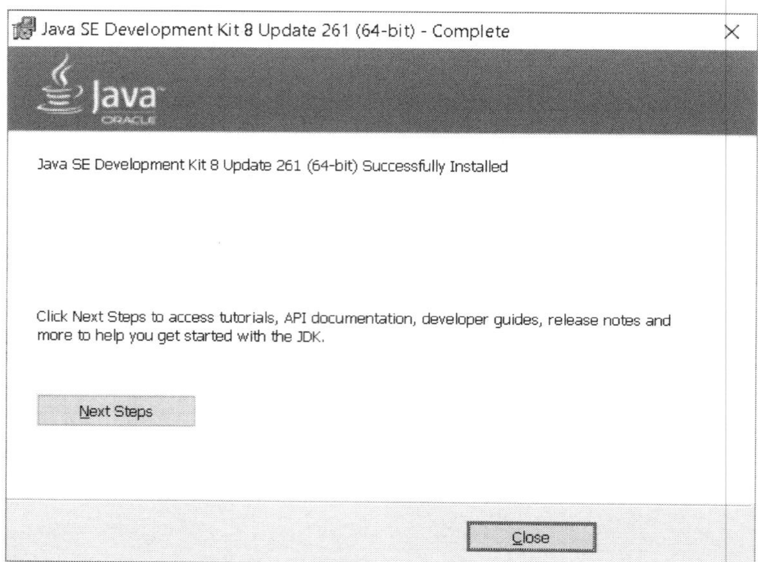

Figure 1.8: *Installation success for Java*

11. Click on **`Close`** to exit the setup window.

You have now installed Java successfully.

Installing Apache Maven (apache-maven-3.6.3)

Perform the following steps:

1. Browse the following link on Chrome to download Apache Maven:

   https://maven.apache.org/download.cgi

2. Alternatively, you can download Apache Maven from the following link for Windows:

   https://mirrors.estointernet.in/apache/maven/maven-3/3.6.3/binaries/apache-maven-3.6.3-bin.zip

3. Extract files to the **`C:\maven`** directory or any desired directory for the installation of Apache Maven.

You have now installed Apache Maven successfully.

Installing Gradle (gradle 6.6)

Perform the following steps:

1. Browse the following link on Chrome to download Gradle for Windows:

   https://gradle.org/releases

2. Alternatively, you can download Gradle from the following link for Windows:

   https://services.gradle.org/distributions/gradle-6.6-bin.zip

3. Extract files to the **`C:\gradle`** directory or any desired directory for the installation of Gradle.

You have now installed Gradle successfully.

After installation of Java, Maven, and Gradle, you need to add **Environment User Variables** named as **`MAVEN_HOME`**, **`JAVA_HOME`**, **`GRADLE_HOME`** which will have the path value to the **`root`** folder of the software.

For instance:

```
JAVA_HOME= C:\Program Files\Java\jdk1.8.0_261

MAVEN_HOME=C:\maven

GRADLE_HOME=C:\gradle
```

The following screenshot shows the keys and values for environment variables:

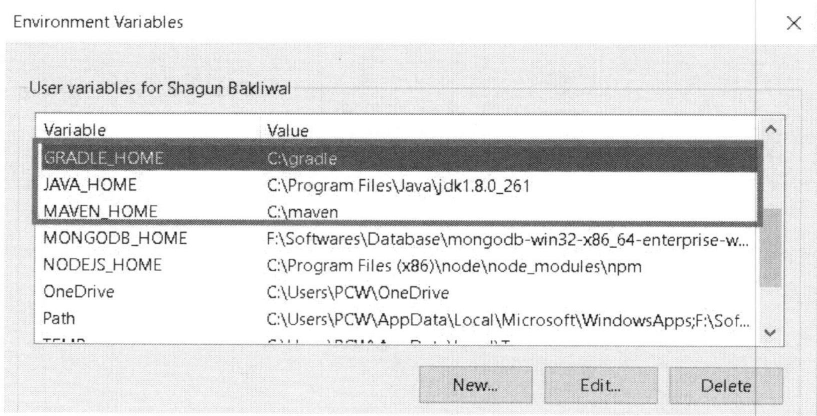

***Figure 1.9:** Setting up user variables for tools*

After setting up these values, set the path to these folders in the environment path variable by suffixing `\bin` to each of these tools as shown in the following screenshot:

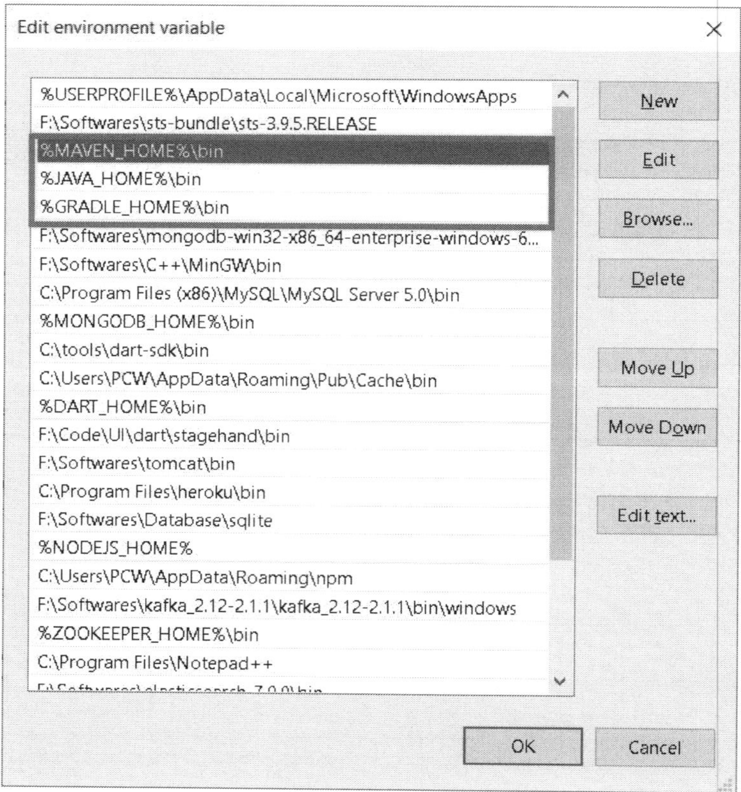

***Figure 1.10:** Setting up path variables for tools*

The next step is to check for the version for each of these by executing the following command.

In the following screenshot, you can verify the version of Java installed after executing **java -version** on Windows terminal:

```
C:\Users\PCW>java -version
java version "1.8.0_261"
Java(TM) SE Runtime Environment (build 1.8.0_261-b12)
Java HotSpot(TM) 64-Bit Server VM (build 25.261-b12, mixed mode)
```

Figure 1.11: *Verifying Java installation*

In the following screenshot, you can verify the version of Apache Maven installed after executing **mvn -version** on Windows terminal:

```
C:\Users\PCW>mvn -version
Apache Maven 3.6.3 (cecedd343002696d0abb50b32b541b8a6ba2883f)
Maven home: C:\maven\bin\..
Java version: 1.8.0_261, vendor: Oracle Corporation, runtime: C:\Program Files\Java\jdk1.8.0_261\jre
Default locale: en_US, platform encoding: Cp1252
OS name: "windows 10", version: "10.0", arch: "amd64", family: "windows"
```

Figure 1.12: *Verifying Apache Maven installation*

In the following screenshot, you can verify the version of Gradle installed after executing **gradle -v** on Windows terminal:

```
C:\Users\PCW>gradle -v

------------------------------------------------------------
Gradle 6.6
------------------------------------------------------------

Build time:   2020-08-10 22:06:19 UTC
Revision:     d119144684a0c301aea027b79857815659e431b9

Kotlin:       1.3.72
Groovy:       2.5.12
Ant:          Apache Ant(TM) version 1.10.8 compiled on May 10 2020
JVM:          1.8.0_261 (Oracle Corporation 25.261-b12)
OS:           Windows 10 10.0 amd64

C:\Users\PCW>
```

Figure 1.13: *Verifying Gradle installation*

Installing Spring Tool Suite (STS 4)

Perform the following steps:

1. Browse the following link on Chrome to download STS for Windows:

   https://spring.io/tools

2. Alternatively, you can download Gradle from the following link for Windows:

   https://download.springsource.com/release/STS4/4.7.1.RELEASE/dist/e4.16/spring-tool-suite-4-4.7.1.RELEASE-e4.16.0-win32.win32.x86_64.self-extracting.jar

3. Move the `jar` file to any desired folder where you want to install STS and double click on the `jar` file. The `jar` file itself unpacks all files in the current directory. The application file is named as `SpringToolSuite4.exe`.

You have now installed STS successfully.

Any Integrated Development Environment (IDE) can be used to develop a Spring Boot application. However, it is suggested to have Spring tool suite or IntelliJ for developing Spring Boot applications. These tools have wide support and variety of plugins.

The 12-factor app

Any developer, who builds the application that runs as a service, should incorporate the 12-factors in their application. These factors can be referred from **https://12factor.net** and are listed as follows:

- **Codebase**: One codebase is tracked in revision control; many deploys.

  There is a single repository for a functional module that can be managed by Source Code Management Tool (SCM) like GitHub and BitBucket for managing the versions of the source code. Once the source code is committed, it can be deployed using any CI/CD tool like Jenkins.

- **Dependencies**: Explicitly declare and isolate dependencies.

  A dependency in a Spring Boot application is maintained by `pom.xml` which comprises various dependencies (external libraries) which have their own version. The advantage of these dependencies is to include them as a separate component and not the whole library. This makes them a reusable component for other applications.

- **Config**: Store config in the environment.

  All the configurations can be made environment-specific and can be called by running the Spring Boot application with the specific profile. The configurations can be stored in GIT and later referenced by the Spring Boot dependency.

- **Backing services**: Treat backing services as attached resources.

  Your application may use the external resources like database, network firewalls, and caching tools like Redis. Spring Boot ensures that these services are managed with the correct set of configurations required so that it would be just a matter of configuration, if the application migrated from one geographical location to other geographical location. It may also happen that the application is transitioned between data centers.

- **Build, release, run**: Strictly separate build and run stages.

  With defined `pom.xml`, you can upload your release build to the artifact repository. By simple build commands, you can build and deploy your applications.

- **Processes**: Execute the app as one or more stateless processes.

  Spring Boot allows your application to run independently. By creating Restful APIs, you can develop the services that don't require maintaining states of the process.

- **Port binding**: Export services via port binding.

  All web applications built using Spring Boot have the capability to use the embedded **Tomcat** server by default exposing the port **`8080`** so that the services can be consumed by other applications. This also helps the developer to test their applications using any of the web clients (**Browser**, **Postman**, **JMeter**, and so on).

- **Concurrency**: Scale out via the process model.

  The applications can also be scaled up and scaled down depending on the users hitting the environment. When applications are deployed into the cloud environment, their auto-scale services can be used so that the metrics like CPU, memory, and HTTP throughput, when crosses a certain threshold, the applications can be scaled up and down. The distributed services used in the applications should be defined in such a way that scaling up and down does not affect the functionality.

- **Disposability**: Maximize robustness with fast startup and graceful shutdown.

  The Spring Boot applications have the minimum startup time ranging from 8 secs to few minutes. When the application is integrated with the web server, that is, using embedded servers like Tomcat, it allows the application to be shut down gracefully so that any request that comes in during the shutdown process may be fulfilled successfully.

- **Dev/prod parity**: Keep developing, staging, and production as similar as possible.

It is essential to have the similar states of the environment on which the applications are running. This helps us to identify the errors coming to the lower environments and fix them before promoting the applications to the production environment. The developers use the development environment; staging used by the UAT testers; sometimes clients, and production is exposed to the customers or users who would be using your application.

- **Logs**: Treat logs as event streams.

  The application logs can be sent out as the stream to the log aggregator tools like **Splunk**, which indexes the logs based on the applications. This helps the team to go through the logs in case of any issues. Various patterns like total time taken for making external calls to the other applications and accessing the database can be drawn out for analysis. This proactive approach can be followed so that it would be easier for a developer to rectify an issue, be it business related or the deviation of the workflow.

- **Admin processes**: Run admin/management tasks as one-off processes.

  There can be few APIs exposed as REST endpoints, which can be only used by the users who have **ADMIN** roles. This ADMIN role can be set up by a system within the application and then roles can be validated once the API is being requested. In the same way, there can be multiple roles created for given users and then they can be mapped to the APIs so that they are the only consumers.

Spring Initializr

One of the best ways to create a Spring Boot application is to generate the skeleton project from **Spring Initializr**. Browse the following link:

https://start.spring.io/

This is the tool provided by the Spring team that acts like a kickstart for the development of any Spring Boot application. It has many configurations in terms of selecting the language, building the tool type, Spring Boot version, project metadata, packaging type, and Java version that will store all the details related to the project in the form of artifacts and group IDs. Commonly used dependencies for creating a web application can also be added at this stage. The following is the screenshot for creating a Spring Boot project using Spring Initializr:

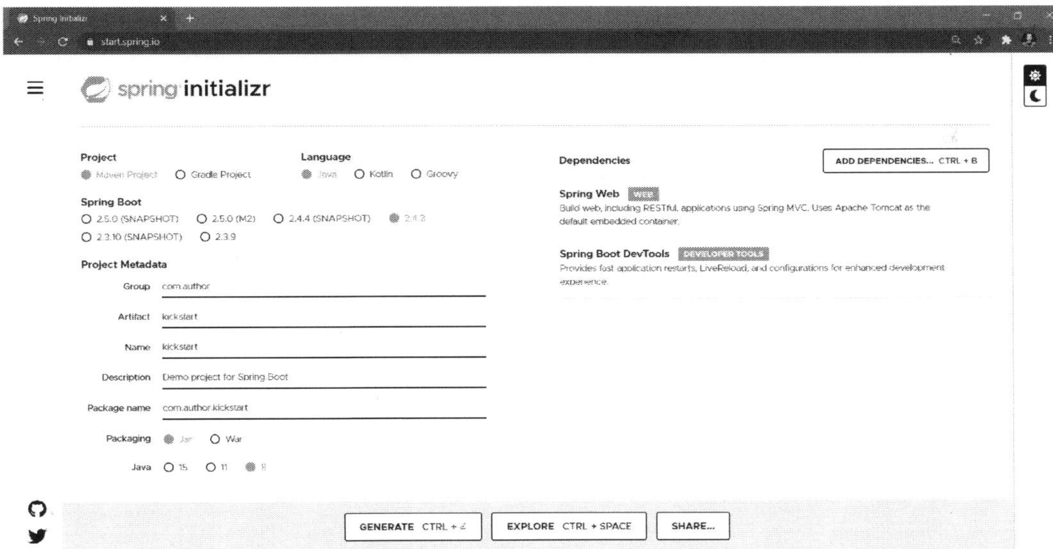

Figure 1.14: Spring Initializr

After clicking on the **GENERATE** button, it will download a **.zip** file containing the skeleton of the code. Another way of creating a Spring Boot project in STS could be by going to **File** -> **New** -> **Project,** or if there are no STS built projects in the workspace, then click on **Create a project...** in project explorer and select **Spring Starter Project** as shown in the following screenshot:

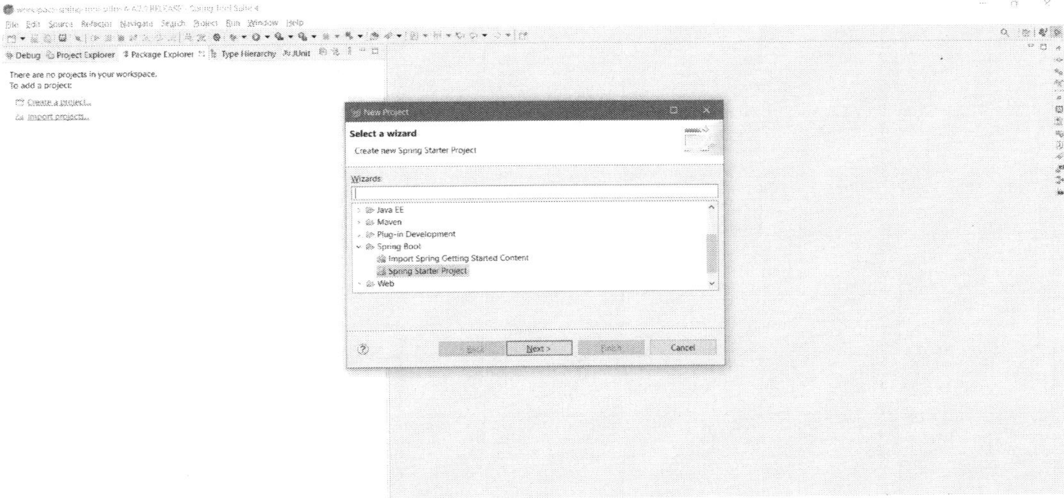

Figure 1.15: Creating Spring Project in STS

Conclusion

By now you must have got some idea about what Spring Boot is, how it evolved, its features, advantages, and tools required for developing Spring Boot applications. In addition to Spring Boot, we also learned how to use the features of 12-factor app to build applications. The next chapter would be more of a hands-on experience with Spring Boot applications by using Spring Initializr for our first Spring Boot application.

Points to remember

- Always use the latest versions of tools, Spring libraries, and other dependencies.
- Spring Boot is a comprehensive way of developing production-ready applications focusing on single functionality.

Questions

1. What is Spring Boot?
2. List out features of Spring Boot.
3. Which tools are required to build an application in Spring Boot?
4. List out the features of the 12-factor app.

CHAPTER 2
Developing Your First Spring Boot Application

In the previous chapter we learned about **Spring Boot**, its history, its features, advantages, and tools required to develop a Spring Boot application. Now, it's the time to develop our first Spring Boot application. In this chapter, we will discuss how to create a basic Spring Boot application and the different uses of the Spring framework annotations.

Structure

In this chapter, we will discuss the following topics:

- Starting with Spring Initializr
- Build tools – Maven and Gradle
- Understanding **`pom.xml`**
- Understanding **`build.gradle`**
- Building an application using Maven
- Building an application using Gradle
- Understanding the entry point class and **`SpringBootApplication`** annotation
- Bootstrap **`ApplicationContext`**

Objectives

After studying this unit, you should be able to use **Spring Initializr** to create a Spring Boot skeleton. This chapter will help you understand the `pom.xml` file and its components, compile the project using Maven and Gradle, and execute the application and see logs in the console.

Starting with Spring Initializr

For developing the Spring Boot application from scratch, you can use the Spring Initializr tool provided by the Spring team that offers you the most commonly used dependencies and you can set up with those dependencies. In this chapter, we will develop one web-based application with one REST endpoint. This will help you understand how to use the Spring Initializr tool and test that endpoint from any web client such as **Browser**, **Postman**, **JMeter**, and so on.

To start with Spring Initializr, follow the given steps:

1. Browse the following website on Chrome:

   https://start.spring.io

   The following screenshot shows the Spring Initializr tool setting up our first application:

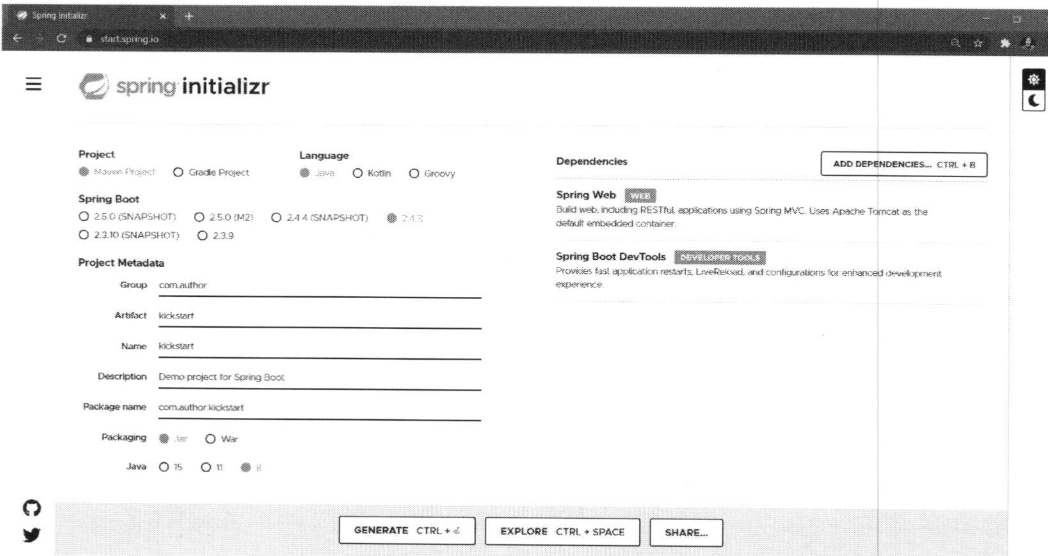

Figure 2.1: Spring Initializr

2. Select the `Project` type as `Maven Project`.

3. Select the language as **`Java`**.
4. Select the Spring Boot version. Here, we will use **`2.4.3`** which is the latest version. You can also use the snapshot versions of the later versions, but it is recommended that you use the stable version as the snapshot is the beta version rolled out for a developer's testing.
5. Provide a suitable project metadata – group ID, artifact ID, name of the project, project description, and package name. Definitions of each of them will be explained at the end of this chapter.
6. Select **`Packaging`** as **`Jar`**.
7. Select **`Java`** as **`8`**.
8. Add dependencies – **`Spring Web`** and **`Spring Boot DevTools`**.
9. Click on the **`Generate`** button.

This will now download the **`.zip`** file with the structure that can be understood by the Maven tool. Extract the **`.zip`** file to your workspace.

To continue with another way to create a Spring Boot application as discussed in *Chapter 1, Getting Started with Spring Boot,* we need to provide the same metadata as shown in the previous section in the dialog-box as shown in the following screenshot:

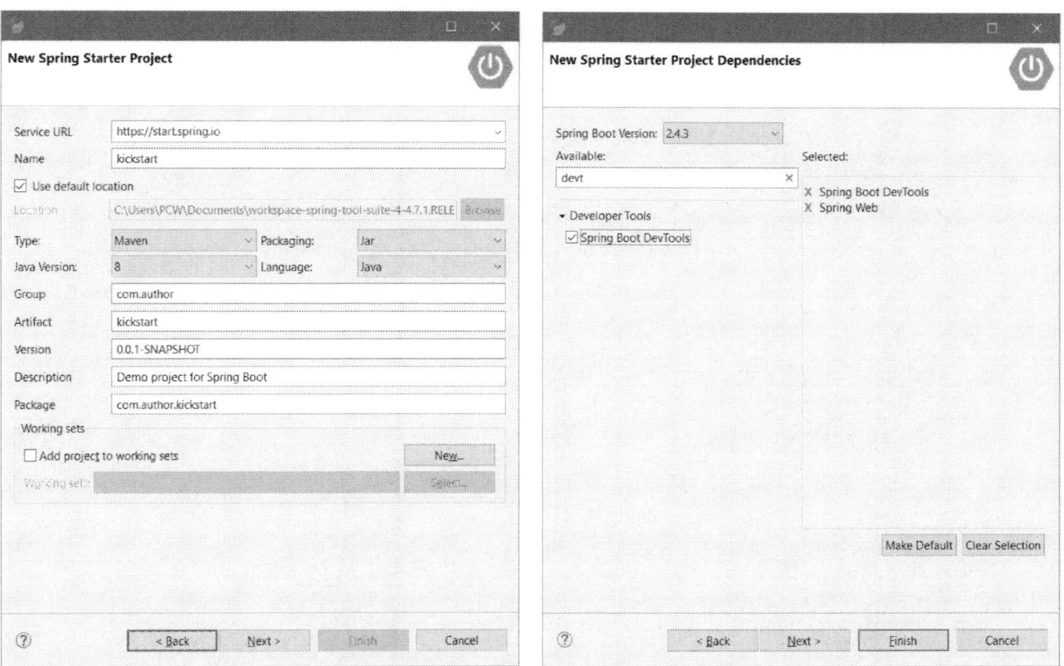

Figure 2.2: *Creating Spring Boot project in STS*

After feeding inputs, click on **Finish**. Spring Tool Suite will create related files by downloading them from Spring Initializr. To know how the files get downloaded, you may skip the **Finish** button and click on the **Next** button.

Build tools – Maven and Gradle

For building heavy projects, there is a need of segregating codes into components so that they can be reused again within the same project or by other projects. Here, the project is the build module for an application. For using these components in the project, we need to add components into our classpath so that our project gets these components and the build is successful. As there would be a large number of such components adding to the classpath for building and execution of the project, there are build tools available on the Internet which can be used by developers. The famous build tools are **Maven** and **Gradle**.

The components are stored in a location called **repository**. These components can be referred to as the artifacts when we talk in terms with any build tool. The build tools are explained as follows:

- **Maven** is the project management build tool developed by **Apache Org** which adds the functionalities of Java libraries through dependencies. Developers can create their own dependencies for the purpose of modularity. They can also use the dependencies stored in the repository. Maven is a stage-driven build tool and its lifecycle is divided into stages such as **validate**, **compile**, **test**, **package**, **verify**, **install,** and **deploy**. The core component of the Maven project is **pom.xml**.
- **Gradle** is an open-source build tool which adds functionalities of Java libraries through plugins. You can also create custom plugins to have your own functionality. Gradle is task-driven; the core model of the gradle decides the lists of tasks for a build cycle and bundles them in order for execution. The lifecycle of the gradle build is divided into phases such as **initialization**, **configuration,** and **execution**. The core component of the Gradle project is the **build.gradle** file.

However, it is up to the developer to decide the build tool for building their applications. The factors for decision may vary from developer to developer and may not be limited to the size of the project, the build platform, flexibility, performance, user experience, and dependency management.

Now, let's understand the pom.xml which is the primary component of the Maven project.

Understanding the pom.xml

The first file which we should be looking into after creating the first project or enhancing the already developed Spring application is **pom.xml**.

pom.xml is called the **project object model** where it stores the project-related metadata. This file is used by the Maven build tool to download the dependencies required to build the project.

The contents of **pom.xml** are as follows:

```
<?xml version="1.0" encoding="UTF-8"?>
<project xmlns="http://maven.apache.org/POM/4.0.0" xmlns:xsi="http://www.w3.org/2001/XMLSchema-instance"
    xsi:schemaLocation="http://maven.apache.org/POM/4.0.0 https://maven.apache.org/xsd/maven-4.0.0.xsd">
    <modelVersion>4.0.0</modelVersion>
    <parent>
        <groupId>org.springframework.boot</groupId>
        <artifactId>spring-boot-starter-parent</artifactId>
        <version>2.4.3</version>
        <relativePath/> <!-- lookup parent from repository -->
    </parent>
    <groupId>com.author</groupId>
    <artifactId>kickstart</artifactId>
    <version>0.0.1-SNAPSHOT</version>
    <name>kickstart</name>
    <description>Demo project for Spring Boot</description>

    <properties>
        <java.version>1.8</java.version>
    </properties>

    <dependencies>
        <dependency>
            <groupId>org.springframework.boot</groupId>
```

```
            <artifactId>spring-boot-starter-web</artifactId>
        </dependency>

        <dependency>
            <groupId>org.springframework.boot</groupId>
            <artifactId>spring-boot-devtools</artifactId>
            <scope>runtime</scope>
            <optional>true</optional>
        </dependency>
        <dependency>
            <groupId>org.springframework.boot</groupId>
            <artifactId>spring-boot-starter-test</artifactId>
            <scope>test</scope>
        </dependency>
    </dependencies>

    <build>
        <plugins>
            <plugin>
                <groupId>org.springframework.boot</groupId>
                <artifactId>spring-boot-maven-plugin</artifactId>
            </plugin>
        </plugins>
    </build>

</project>
```

Let's discuss several tags that are present in the basic Spring Boot application:

- **<parent>:** The **<parent>** tag is the most important tag within the **pom.xml** file. It's the decision maker of skills and knowledge of its dependencies the project will be inheriting which also means that once a new version of Spring Boot is released, it will change all the dependency versions, its metadata, and versioning throughout the project through a technique known as **Bill of Materials** (**BOM**). The following snippet is a sample structure of the **<parent>** tag:

```
<parent>
    <groupId>org.springframework.boot</groupId>
    <artifactId>spring-boot-starter-parent</artifactId>
    <version>2.4.3</version>
    <relativePath/> <!-- lookup parent from repository -->
</parent>
```

It is necessary for a parent artifact to be packaged as **pom** and not **.jar**. This is specified in the **pom.xml** file of the parent which we would be using under the **<packaging>** tag. Here, we will use the Spring Boot starter parent. The artifact **spring-boot-starter-parent** means we are using the library with the name **spring-boot-starter-parent**. Spring Boot has many such starters dependencies called **starter packs**.

Every Maven dependency is associated with **groupId** and **artifactId**. **groupId** describes the group of the artifact where it belongs. Every artifact that we use should have the version. There can be many versions for a given artifact. It is recommended to use the latest one.

- **<groupId>**, **<artifactId>**, **<version>**, **<name>**, **<description>** tags: The following snippet describes the **artifact** and **group** to which our project belongs to:

```
<groupId>com.author</groupId>
<artifactId>kickstart</artifactId>
<version>0.0.1-SNAPSHOT</version>
<name>kickstart</name>
<description>Demo project for Spring Boot</description>
```

  The **<version>** tag specifies the version of the artifact that we would be creating. If this is not specified, it will inherit the version of its parent dependency.

  <name> and **<description>** are the optional fields to describe the name of the project and its description.

- **<properties>**: The following snippet contains the properties that can be understood by the project:

```
<properties>
    <java.version>1.8</java.version>
</properties>
```

It can be a placeholder to store the version for the dependencies used in the latter part of the **pom.xml** file. It can also have the version of Java as described earlier to mark the project to use Java 1.8 throughout its lifecycle. Moreover, it can store externalized values that can be used within the application. For example:

```
<maven.compiler.source>${java.version}</maven.compiler.source>
<maven.compiler.target>${java.version}</maven.compiler.target>
```

- **<dependency>** and **<dependencies>**: The **<dependency>** tag has **groupId** and **artifactId**. The following snippet is enclosed within **</dependencies>**:

```
<dependencies>
    <dependency>
        <groupId>org.springframework.boot</groupId>
        <artifactId>spring-boot-starter-web</artifactId>
    </dependency>

    <dependency>
        <groupId>org.springframework.boot</groupId>
        <artifactId>spring-boot-devtools</artifactId>
        <scope>runtime</scope>
        <optional>true</optional>
    </dependency>
    <dependency>
        <groupId>org.springframework.boot</groupId>
        <artifactId>spring-boot-starter-test</artifactId>
        <scope>test</scope>
    </dependency>
</dependencies>
```

This block will have all the dependencies which we will use to develop our project under the **<dependency>** tag. The dependencies may be scalar or composite. The scalar dependency has the single dependency in its project. The scalar dependency has no external dependency; whereas, the composite dependency like any of the starter packs of Spring has a combination of multiple dependencies. Composite dependency follows the nested dependencies architecture. These nested dependencies can be called **transitive dependencies** as they are placed into the parent dependency. To get the information of all dependencies used within **pom.xml,** they can be listed out by executing the **mvn dependency:tree** command.

- **<scope>**: The **<scope>** tag describes when that dependency will be used. Examples of various scopes are **compile**, **runtime**, **test**, **provided**, **system,** and **import**.
- **compile**: It is used during the compilation process. This is the default scope unless provided. This ensures that the dependency is available on classpath for building the project and used in sub-modules of the project.
- **runtime**: It is used when we need that dependency during the execution of the project and not during the compilation process.
- **test**: It is used when we need that dependency during test runs.
- **provided**: It is used when we need the dependency that should be provided by JDK at runtime.
- **system**: It is used when we want to specify the dependency path within our workspace.
- **import**: It is used when we want to override all dependencies which are effectively declared in **pom.xml**.
- **<exclusions>**: The **<exclusions>** tag is used within a dependency to exclude the specified dependency from the dependency. This is useful when we are using a dependency which already has other dependencies. An example of such a tag could be removing **junit-vintage-engine** from **spring-boot-starter-test** as it is no longer present under **spring-boot-starter-test** from *Spring Boot 2.4.0*. If you still use the older version and want to exclude this dependency, then the following snippet removes the dependency:

```
<dependency>
  <groupId>org.springframework.boot</groupId>
  <artifactId>spring-boot-starter-test</artifactId>
  <scope>test</scope>
  <exclusions>
    <exclusion>
      <groupId>org.junit.vintage</groupId>
      <artifactId>junit-vintage-engine</artifactId>
    </exclusion>
  </exclusions>
</dependency>
```

- **<build>** and **<plugins>**: The following snippet describes the plugins that we will use during the build process. The plugins are enclosed within the **<build>** tag:

```
<build>
    <plugins>
        <plugin>
            <groupId>org.springframework.boot</groupId>
            <artifactId>spring-boot-maven-plugin</artifactId>
        </plugin>
    </plugins>
</build>
```

Specifically, **spring-boot-maven-plugin** provides Spring Boot support in Maven. It is used when we want to package our build in the **.jar** or **.war** file.

Understanding build.gradle

For Maven, we need **pom.xml** and the build command is **mvn clean install**. While using the gradle tool for building the project, we need to have the **build.gradle** file.

The contents of the **build.gradle** file are as follows:

```
plugins {
    id 'org.springframework.boot' version '2.4.3'
    id 'io.spring.dependency-management' version '1.0.11.RELEASE'
    id 'java'
}

group = 'com.author'
version = '0.0.1-SNAPSHOT'
sourceCompatibility = '1.8'

repositories {
    mavenCentral()
}
```

```
dependencies {
    implementation 'org.springframework.boot:spring-boot-starter-web'
    developmentOnly 'org.springframework.boot:spring-boot-devtools'
   testImplementation'org.springframework.boot:spring-boot-starter-test'


}


test {
    useJUnitPlatform()
}
```

Let's understand the structure of the **build.gradle** file:

- **plugins**: A plugin is any class that implements the **Plugin** interface. Gradle provides core plugins as part of its distribution library through which they are automatically resolved. For example, **plugin: java**.

  Gradle also provides another type of plugin that is the binary plugin. This plugin needs to be resolved, that is, they don't come along with the distribution.

  For example, **plugin: org.springframework.boot, io.spring.dependency-management**.

  For multiple plugins, you need to configure each of them using the **id** tag and the **version** tag.

  For instance:

  ```
  plugins {
      id 'org.springframework.boot' version '2.4.3'
      id 'io.spring.dependency-management' version '1.0.11.RELEASE'
      id 'java'
  }
  ```

  The **java** plugin builds the **.jar** file as the output file of the build process. You can also generate the **.war** file through gradle by replacing **java** with **war** as follows:

  ```
  plugins {
      id 'org.springframework.boot' version '2.4.3'
      id 'io.spring.dependency-management' version '1.0.11.RELEASE'
      id 'war'
  ```

```
}
```

The **`java`** plugin doesn't require **`version`** here. The **`version`** of **`java`** is maintained with the **`sourceCompatibility`** and **`targetCompatibility`** tags.

- **`group and version`**: The following are the attributes that are used to define the **`group`** and **`version`** of the artifact:

  `group:` It describes the group of the artifact where it belongs:

  ```
  group = 'com.author'
  ```

  `version:` It can be specified as shown in the following snippet:

  ```
  version = '0.0.1-SNAPSHOT'
  ```

- **`sourceCompatibility`** and **`targetCompatibility:`** **`sourceCompatibility`** decides the base version of Java for the source code.

  `targetCompatibility` decides the output version of Java for the compiled code. **`targetCompatibility`** is optional.

  Here is the syntax:

  ```
  sourceCompatibility = '1.8'
  targetCompatibility = '1.8'
  ```

- **`repositories`**: The dependencies are resolved from the repository. For instance, commonly used dependencies are available at the **maven** repository. Here, we would be downloading them from maven central and the syntax for repositories is as follows:

  ```
  repositories {
      mavenCentral()
  }
  ```

- **`dependencies`**: This section comprises the dependencies used within the project having different scopes such as **`implementation`**, **`developmentOnly`**, and **`testImplementation`**.

  These can be related to scopes of maven such as **`compile`**, **`runtime,`** and **`test,`** respectively. All the dependencies are quoted in single quotes. If you want to exclude a particular dependency from a composite dependency, you can use **`exclude group`** along with the **`module`** name. For example:

  ```
  dependencies {
      implementation 'org.springframework.boot:spring-boot-starter-
      web'
      developmentOnly 'org.springframework.boot:spring-boot-
      devtools'
  ```

```
    testImplementation 'org.springframework.boot:spring-boot-
    starter-test'
}
```

- `test`: This section describes the test platform which we can use to execute our test cases. Here, we will use **`Junit`** for our unit testing. The following snippet can be used to provide **`Junit`** as the **`test`** platform:

```
test {
    useJUnitPlatform()
}
```

Now, let's build the application using build tools such as Maven and Gradle.

Building an application using Maven

Perform the following steps:

1. Now, you can launch the **`SpringToolSuite4.exe`** application from the directory where you have installed STS. The following screenshot displays the launch screen:

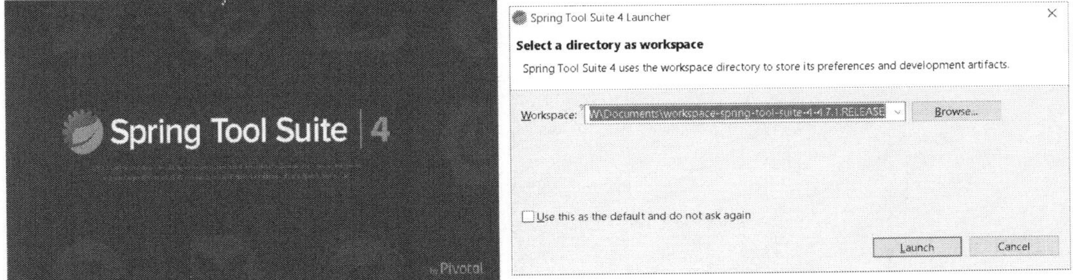

Figure 2.3: *Selecting workspace in STS 4*

2. Select the desired directory for storing the metadata for STS and click on **`Launch`**. Then, click on **`File -> Import Project from File System`** or **`Archive`**. Paste the folder path of the project where **`pom.xml`** resides as shown in the following screenshot and click on **`Finish`**:

> **Prior to Spring Boot 2.0, that is, `spring-boot-starter-parent 2.0.0.RELEASE`, the `@SpringBootApplication` consisted of three annotations such as `@Configuration`, `@EnableAutoConfiguration`, and `@ComponentScan`.**

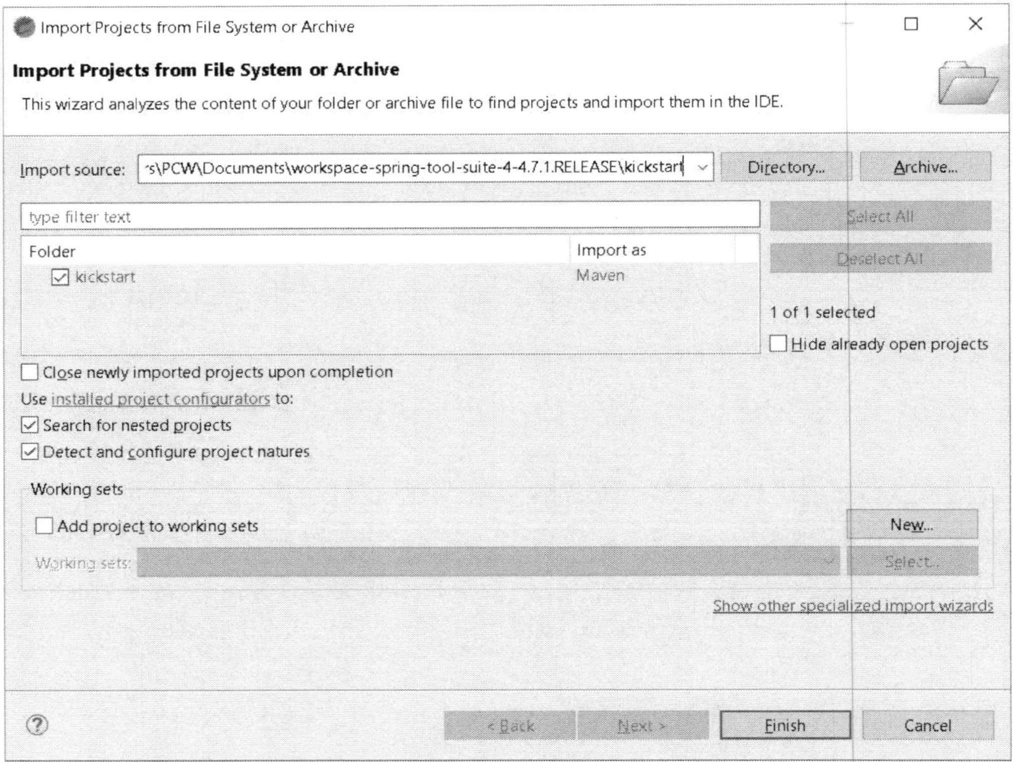

Figure 2.4: Import project

3. Now, you will see the package explorer on the left-hand side of the STS. This describes your files in the project. Please make sure you have a good Internet connection for downloading the dependencies. The package explorer looks like the following screenshot:

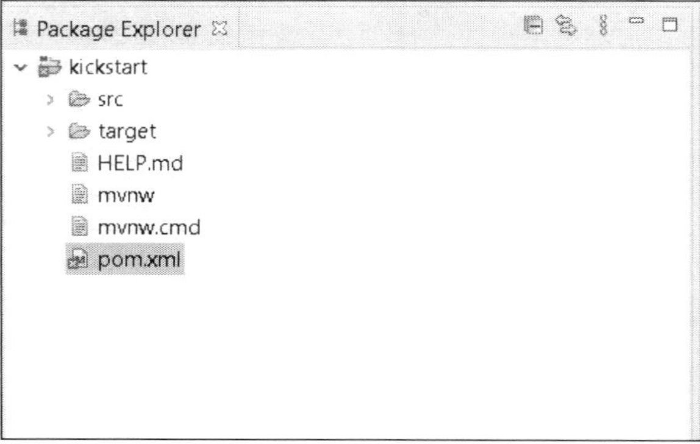

Figure 2.5: Package explorer

4. The cross mark in the **pom.xml** file shows that there is something wrong with the file. As soon as you open the project, the automatic build will start to download the dependencies. If it does not start, then you can build the project manually by following the given steps:
   a) Right click on the project and go to **Run As.**
   b) Now, select the **Maven build** option as shown in the following screenshot:

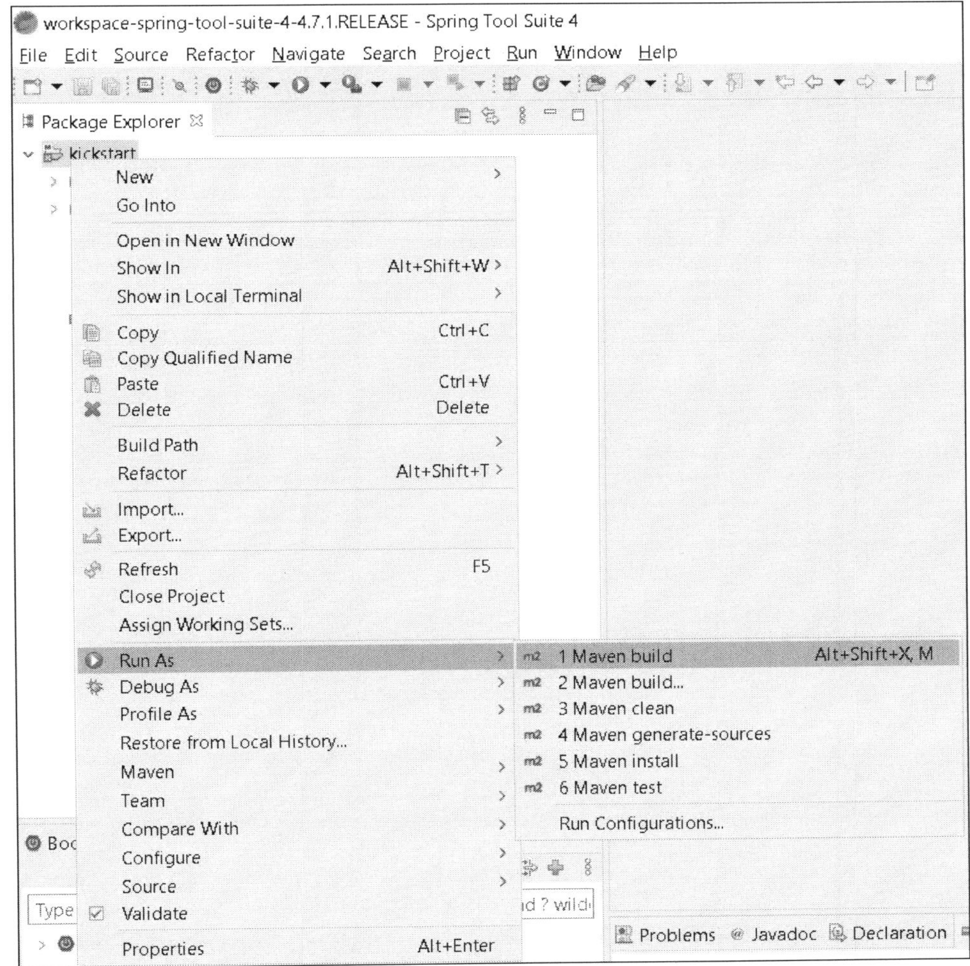

Figure 2.6: *Run as Maven build*

5. Now, set the goal as clean install. Alternatively, if you are using any terminal window for building the Maven project, execute the **mvn clean install** command. For now, we will build the project in STS and click on **Run**:

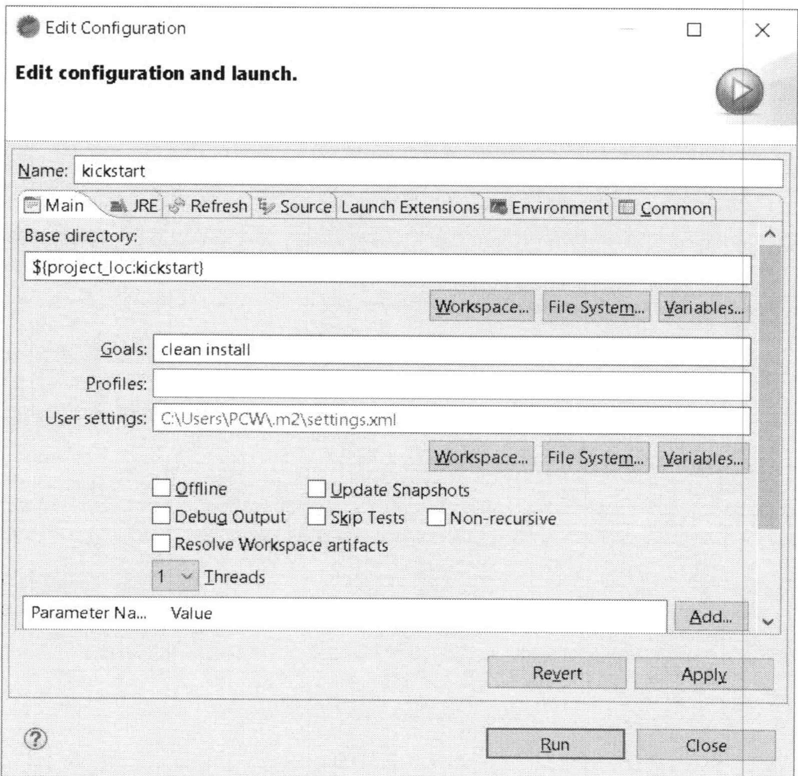

Figure 2.7: Executing Maven build

6. For the first time, if you are getting a compilation error on the console **`No compiler is provided in this environment. Perhaps you are running on a JRE rather than a JDK?`**, then you need to set up JDK in STS from the **`Java Installed JRE`** option in the **`Preferences`** menu item under the **`Window`** menu. Please follow the given steps:

   a) On the **`Installed JRE`** screen, click on **Add** to select the JRE type **`JDK HOME`** directory.

   b) Select the **`Standard VM`** on **`JRE type`** selection. After selecting the correct **`JDK HOME`** directory, you will see the following **`JRE system libraries`**. If you see the following screen, then the JDK has been set up successfully:

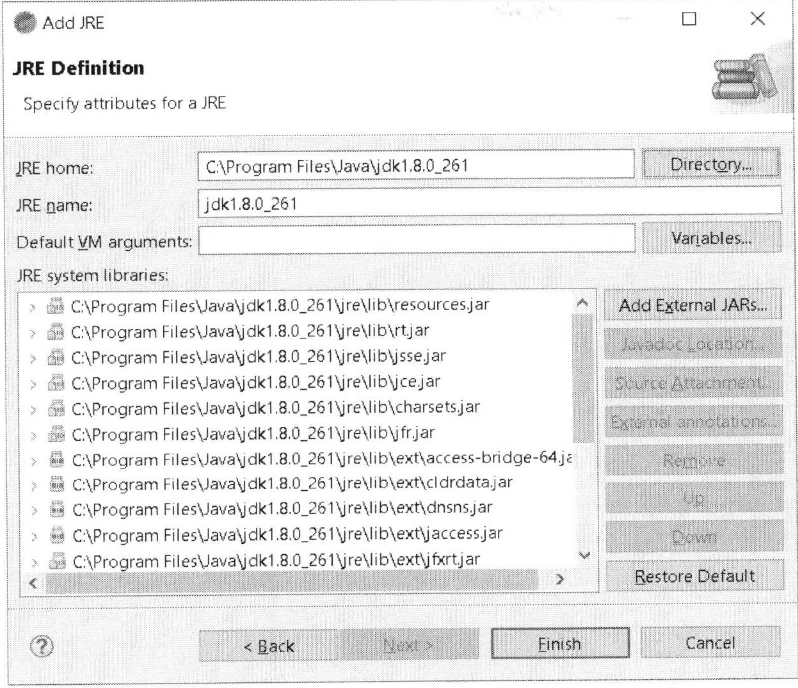

Figure 2.8: Add JRE definition

7. Click on Finish and select the newly added JDK.
8. Now, re-run the maven build.

You will now see the following screen when the build is successful:

```
Console  Problems  Progress  Debug Shell  Search  Terminal  Call Hierarchy  Coverage
<terminated> kickstart [Maven Build] C:\Program Files\Java\jdk1.8.0_261\bin\javaw.exe (Mar 11, 2021 4:34:55 PM – 4:35:20 PM)
[INFO] --- maven-jar-plugin:3.2.0:jar (default-jar) @ kickstart ---
[INFO] Building jar: C:\Users\PCW\Documents\workspace-spring-tool-suite-4-4.7.1.RELEASE\kickstart\target\kickstart-0.0.1-SNAPSHOT.jar
[INFO]
[INFO] --- spring-boot-maven-plugin:2.4.3:repackage (repackage) @ kickstart ---
[INFO] Downloading from : https://repo.maven.apache.org/maven2/org/springframework/boot/spring-boot-buildpack-platform/2.4.3/spring-boot-build
[INFO] Downloaded from : https://repo.maven.apache.org/maven2/org/springframework/boot/spring-boot-buildpack-platform/2.4.3/spring-boot-buildp
[INFO] Downloading from : https://repo.maven.apache.org/maven2/org/springframework/boot/spring-boot-loader-tools/2.4.3/spring-boot-loader-tool
[INFO] Downloaded from : https://repo.maven.apache.org/maven2/org/springframework/boot/spring-boot-loader-tools/2.4.3/spring-boot-loader-tools
[INFO] Downloading from : https://repo.maven.apache.org/maven2/org/springframework/boot/spring-boot-buildpack-platform/2.4.3/spring-boot-build
[INFO] Downloading from : https://repo.maven.apache.org/maven2/org/springframework/boot/spring-boot-loader-tools/2.4.3/spring-boot-loader-tool
[INFO] Downloaded from : https://repo.maven.apache.org/maven2/org/springframework/boot/spring-boot-buildpack-platform/2.4.3/spring-boot-buildp
[INFO] Downloaded from : https://repo.maven.apache.org/maven2/org/springframework/boot/spring-boot-loader-tools/2.4.3/spring-boot-loader-tools
[INFO] Replacing main artifact with repackaged archive
[INFO]
[INFO] --- maven-install-plugin:2.5.2:install (default-install) @ kickstart ---
[INFO] Installing C:\Users\PCW\Documents\workspace-spring-tool-suite-4-4.7.1.RELEASE\kickstart\target\kickstart-0.0.1-SNAPSHOT.jar to C:\Users
[INFO] Installing C:\Users\PCW\Documents\workspace-spring-tool-suite-4-4.7.1.RELEASE\kickstart\pom.xml to C:\Users\PCW\.m2\repository\com\auth
[INFO] ------------------------------------------------------------------------
[INFO] BUILD SUCCESS
[INFO] ------------------------------------------------------------------------
[INFO] Total time:  20.601 s
[INFO] Finished at: 2021-03-11T16:35:19+05:30
[INFO] ------------------------------------------------------------------------
```

Figure 2.9: Build successful

Once all the dependencies are downloaded, the cross sign on **`pom.xml`** vanishes. You will also notice the **`jar`** file created in the **`target`** folder. You will see the project explorer as shown in the following screenshot:

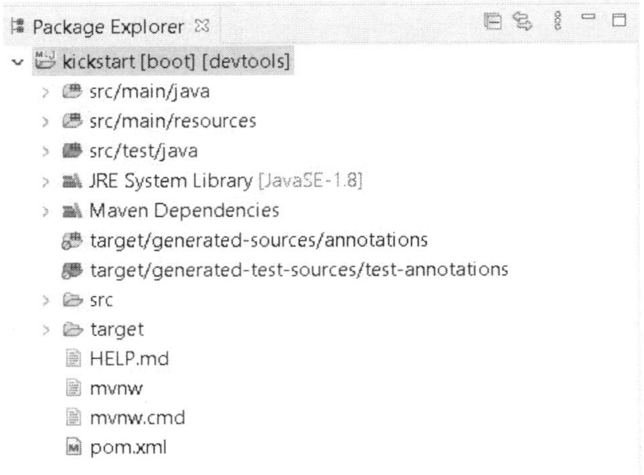

Figure 2.10: *Package explorer*

The screenshot on the left-hand side depicts that the project is now recognized as the maven project. Moreover in its title, it has words like **`boot`** and **`devtools`**. Now, we can say that it's a Spring Boot project. The devtools is because of the dependency which we selected in Spring Initializr.

Now, we have understood how to build the project using Maven. Let's dive into the other build tool - **Gradle**.

Building an application using Gradle

For building a project using Gradle, we need to configure the **`build.gradle`** file as mentioned in *Understanding build.gradle* section. Once the Gradle file is configured, you can execute the **`gradle build`** command from the command line to build the project. It will download the dependencies and plugins. When you start building the project, you will see the following screen:

```
kickstart (shagun-pc)

C:\Users\PCW\Documents\workspace-spring-tool-suite-4-4.7.1.RELEASE\kickstart-gradle\kickstart>gradle build
Starting a Gradle Daemon (subsequent builds will be faster)
<-------------> 0% INITIALIZING [6s]
> Evaluating settings
```

Figure 2.11: *Build project using Gradle*

After the build is successful, you will see the following screen:

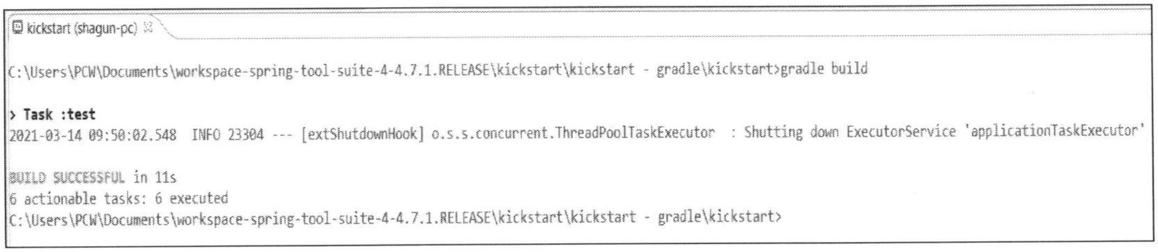

```
kickstart (shagun-pc)

C:\Users\PCW\Documents\workspace-spring-tool-suite-4-4.7.1.RELEASE\kickstart\kickstart - gradle\kickstart>gradle build

> Task :test
2021-03-14 09:50:02.548  INFO 23304 --- [extShutdownHook] o.s.s.concurrent.ThreadPoolTaskExecutor  : Shutting down ExecutorService 'applicationTaskExecutor'

BUILD SUCCESSFUL in 11s
6 actionable tasks: 6 executed
C:\Users\PCW\Documents\workspace-spring-tool-suite-4-4.7.1.RELEASE\kickstart\kickstart - gradle\kickstart>
```

Figure 2.12: *Build successful using Gradle*

When you build the project with Gradle, the **`.jar`** files will be placed in the **`\build\libs`** folder.

All the external libraries can be placed there in order to execute the **`jar`** file. The external libraries can be put into the classpath while executing the application.

Understanding the entry point class and SpringBootApplication annotation

The following snippet is the entry point class with the main function:

```
package com.author.kickstart;

import org.springframework.boot.SpringApplication;

import org.springframework.boot.autoconfigure.SpringBootApplication;


@SpringBootApplication

public class KickstartApplication {


    public static void main(String[] args) {

        SpringApplication.run(KickstartApplication.class, args);

    }


}
```

The main function of the class is calling the run function of the **`SpringApplication`** class. When this is called during runtime, it loads all the dependencies which are there in the classpath and in the background, there are numerous activities performed to make all the dependencies useful.

The **@SpringBootApplication** annotation describes the class where it is used in a Spring Boot application. This annotation is a combination of the following annotations:

- **@SpringBootConfiguration**
- **@EnableAutoConfiguration**
- **@ComponentScan**

These annotations will be explained in the upcoming chapters. Let's build the application using Maven and Gradle:

1. Let's now execute the application. Right click on the **KickstartApplication.java** or the project and select **Run As | Spring Boot App** as shown in the following screenshot:

   > **You can also execute the project by running build commands from the terminal and then navigating to the target folder and executing the command java -jar <filename>.**

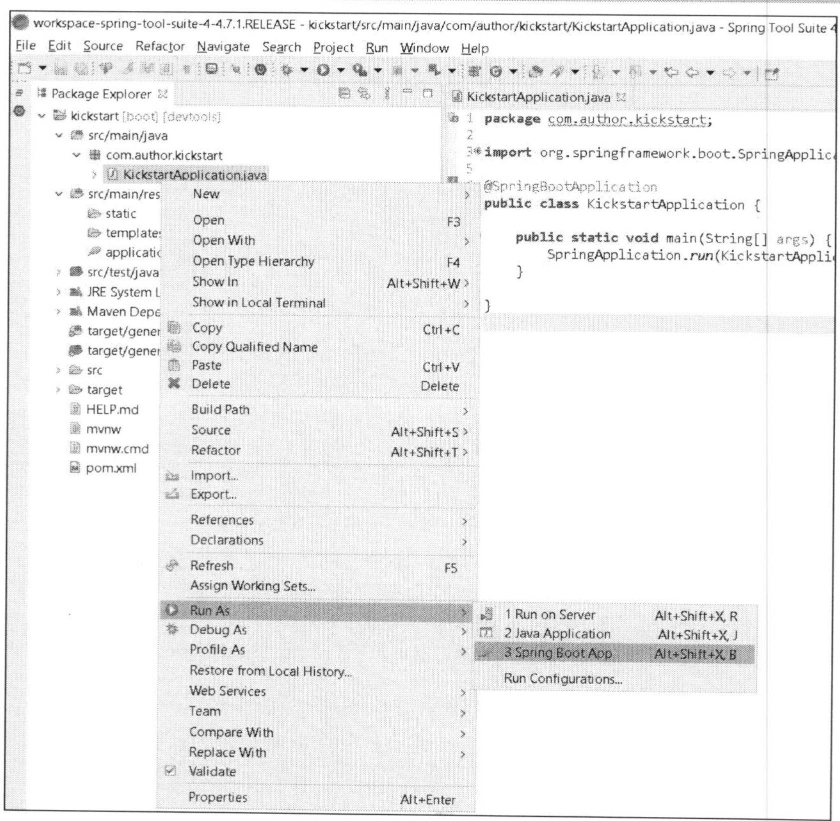

Figure 2.13: Running the Spring Boot app

Now, you should be able to see the following screen:

Figure 2.14: Console for the started app

2. You will see that the application has started at port **8080**. You will also see the following message on the console:

```
2020-08-28 19:47:51.484  INFO 8712 --- [  restartedMain] c.author.
kickstart.KickstartApplication  : Started KickstartApplication in
3.142 seconds (JVM running for 4.241)
```

> **The higher number of dependencies you add in your project, the larger will be the startup time for the application. You can anytime check the transitive dependencies used in your application by executing `mvn dependency:tree`.**

3. If you see the following logs, then you need to change the port of the application:

```
***************************

APPLICATION FAILED TO START

***************************


Description:
Web server failed to start. Port 8080 was already in use.
```

```
Action:

Identify and stop the process that's listening on port 8080 or configure this application to listen on another port.
```

4. The port can be changed by putting **server.port=8081** in **application.properties**.

   Yes, now you would have understood correctly. This **application.properties** is the file where you can manage the configuration. There's another convention that can be adopted which is using **application.yml.**

   If you use both, then preference would be given to **application.properties.** Let's discuss the convention of this application configuration file.

5. A snippet of the configuration in **application.yml** is shown here:

   ```
   server:
     port: 8081
   ```

   A snippet of the configuration in **application.properties** is shown as follows:

   ```
   application.properties
     server.port=8081
   ```

   The **application.yml** file follows the indentation methodology. If there are nested attributes, then they are specified one under another with proper indentation. Whereas the **application.properties** follows a single line configuration.

   In the upcoming chapters, we will understand how to create environment-specific property files.

Bootstrap ApplicationContext

You can also take advantage of getting the configurations and using the objects by having your own **ApplicationContext**.

The run method of the **SpringApplication** class returns an instance of **ConfigurableApplicationContext** as shown here:

```
ConfigurableApplicationContext applicationContext = SpringApplication.run(KickstartApplication.class, args);
```

You may use this instance for the following purposes with the following code snippets:

- Get the application name:

  ```
  String applicationName = applicationContext.getApplicationName();
  ```

- Get the beans named after a particular text:

  ```
  KickstartApplication kickstartApplication = (KickstartApplication)
  applicationContext.getBean("kickstartApplication");
  ```

- The beans those are annotated with some annotation:

  ```
  Map<String, Object> classWithAnnotations = applicationContext.
  getBeansWithAnnotation(SpringBootApplication.class);
  ```

- Get active and default profiles on which the application is running:

  ```
  ConfigurableEnvironment environment = applicationContext.
  getEnvironment();
  System.out.println(Arrays.asList(environment.
  getDefaultProfiles()));
  ```

There are many methods in **`ConfigurableApplicationContext`** which will help to dig out bean details, register **ApplicationListeners**, get startup date, and so on.

However, you can also retrieve bean definitions using the following approaches:

Java configuration

The Java configuration class needs to be public in order to get the bean details.

For example:

```
AnnotationConfigApplicationContext applicationContext = new
AnnotationConfigApplicationContext(KickstartApplication.class);
```

XML configuration

If you have any XML configuration, you can also use it by providing the XML file name. The file should already be loaded into the classpath in order to get the **`ApplicationContext`**.

For example:

```
ClassPathXmlApplicationContext applicationContext = new
ClassPathXmlApplicationContext("applicationContext.xml");
```

Annotation configuration

You can also get the **ApplicationContext** for the beans annotated with **@Component** located in the **com.author.kickstart** package by the given snippet:

```
AnnotationConfigApplicationContext applicationContext = new
AnnotationConfigApplicationContext();

applicationContext.scan("com.author.kickstart");

System.out.println(applicationContext.getEnvironment().
getDefaultProfiles()[0]);
```

We will learn annotations like **@Component, @SpringBootApplication, @Configuration, @EnableAutoConfiguration,** and **@ComponentScan** in *Chapter 4, Spring Boot Annotations,* along with other annotations used within Spring Boot.

Conclusion

We learned how to create a Spring Boot application using Spring Initializr, use the **pom.xml** file with the project type maven, and build a project using Maven and Gradle compilation tools. We later discussed how to bootstrap the **ApplicationContext**, get **ApplicationContext** with different configuration methods like Java, XML, and annotation.

In the next chapter, we will learn about the different starter packs provided in Spring Boot and see how they can be configured.

Points to remember

- Try to use *Spring Boot 2.x.x* versions for developing applications.
- The Spring Initializr tool provided by the Spring team is available online on the following website:

  https://start.spring.io

Questions

1. What is the parent dependency of a Spring Boot application?
2. Which annotations are included in **@SpringBootApplication**?
3. Describe the ways in which you can get the **ApplicationContext**.
4. What is transitive dependency and how can you capture all dependencies in a project?

CHAPTER 3

Spring Boot Starter Dependencies and Auto-Configuration

Congratulations! We just created a basic Spring Boot application with the **Spring Initializr** tool in *Chapter 2, Developing Your First Spring Boot Application*. Now, it's time to understand the different starter dependencies called starter packs provided within the Spring Boot framework. This chapter describes the different Spring Boot starter dependencies available which are used commonly for developing an application and how those dependencies can be configured by just writing the configurations.

Structure

In this chapter, we will discuss the following topics:

- Spring Boot starters
- Spring Boot starter dependencies and their configurations
- Understanding auto-configuration

Objectives

After studying this unit, you should be able to understand the different starter packs. You can configure starter packs and learn how auto-configuration works.

Spring Boot starters

Spring Boot provides a number starter packs which can be used while developing an application. These starter packs when loaded into **classpath** get into action. This auto action is due to auto-configuration done under the hood due to inclusion of **`spring-boot-autoconfigure.jar`**. This dependency has few annotations like **`@ConditionalOnClass`**, **`@ConditionalOnMissingBean`**, **`@ConditionalOnMissingClass`**, **`@ConditionalOnResource`**, **`@ConditionalOnProperty`**, and so on.

The Spring Boot framework follows the **`spring-boot-starter-*`** pattern for all its starter packs where `*` can be replaced with any of its utility provided. For example, for **`web-spring-boot-starter-web`**, for **`JPA-spring-boot-starter-data-jpa`**.

These starters resolve the problem of hunting different code snippets for configuring your application related to the utility or technology. Starter packs are the starter POMs just like any other pom managed by the Spring Boot framework which has a set of dependency descriptors.

Let's start understanding the first starter pack – **`spring-boot-starter`**:

- **`spring-boot-starter`** is the core component of the Spring Boot framework. It is used for the core support which also includes auto-configuration support, logging events, and YAML. It includes the following dependencies:

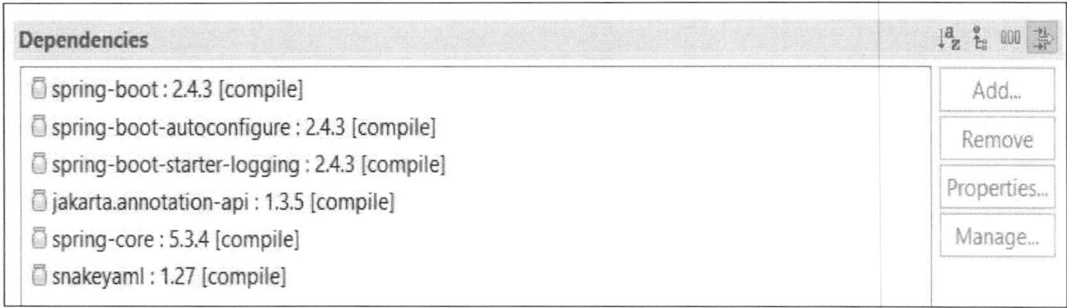

***Figure 3.1:** Dependencies for spring-boot-starter*

- These dependencies have the scope of compile, that is, they are loaded when the project is under the compilation mode. Usually, all spring-related dependencies follow the same version as that of **`spring-boot-starter-parent`**.

  Now the question arises, *from where do we get this list of dependencies? How have we reached to spring-boot-starter straight from what we knew earlier – `spring-boot-starter-parent`?* Well, you can get this understanding from following the top-to-bottom approach within any IDE. Here, we will use STS. So let's understand the mechanism of knowing the structure of any dependency.

- In *Chapter 2, Developing Your First Spring Boot Application,* we looked at the **pom.xml** structure. In **pom.xml,** we have the **<parent>** tag which has a **groupId** and **artifactId** similar to the following syntax:

```
<parent>
        <groupId>org.springframework.boot</groupId>
        <artifactId>spring-boot-starter-parent</artifactId>
        <version>2.4.3</version>
        <relativePath /> <!-- lookup parent from repository -->
</parent>
```

- This parent is packaged with the packaging type as **pom**. To know what's there inside, place the cursor on the artifact name and click on the control button from the keyboard and left click together. It will open a new tab containing the **pom** file for the artifact.
- The tab name is **org.springframework.boot:spring-boot-starter-parent:2.4.3.pom**. It follows the naming convention as **groupId:artifactId:version.pom**. Now take a look at the following syntax:

```
<?xml version="1.0" encoding="UTF-8"?>
<project xmlns="http://maven.apache.org/POM/4.0.0" xsi:schemaLo-
cation="http://maven.apache.org/POM/4.0.0 http://maven.apache.
org/xsd/maven-4.0.0.xsd" xmlns:xsi="http://www.w3.org/2001/XM-
LSchema-instance">
  <modelVersion>4.0.0</modelVersion>
  <parent>
    <groupId>org.springframework.boot</groupId>
    <artifactId>spring-boot-dependencies</artifactId>
    <version>2.4.3</version>
  </parent>
  <artifactId>spring-boot-starter-parent</artifactId>
  <packaging>pom</packaging>
  <name>spring-boot-starter-parent</name>
 <description>Parent pom providing dependency and plugin management
for applications built with Maven</description>
```

Notice that this file has another **<parent>** tag and the **artifactId** tag is the one which we just clicked. Also, notice that the packaging type is **pom**.

So, in this way, you can dive deeper into the structure of any dependency used within the project.

- Similarly, place the cursor on the **artifactId spring-boot-dependencies** and press *ctrl* + left click, and the window will open another tab. Here is the code snippet that is there in the **org.springframework.boot:spring-boot-dependencies:2.4.3.pom** file:

```
<?xml version="1.0" encoding="UTF-8"?>
<project xmlns="http://maven.apache.org/POM/4.0.0" xsi:schemaLocation="http://maven.apache.org/POM/4.0.0 http://maven.apache.org/xsd/maven-4.0.0.xsd" xmlns:xsi="http://www.w3.org/2001/XMLSchema-instance">
  <modelVersion>4.0.0</modelVersion>
  <groupId>org.springframework.boot</groupId>
  <artifactId>spring-boot-dependencies</artifactId>
  <version>2.4.3</version>
  <packaging>pom</packaging>
  <name>spring-boot-dependencies</name>
  <description>Spring Boot Dependencies</description>
```

By this time, you will see the following screen having all the tabs opened and in order of **kickstart/pom.xml** till **org.springframework.boot:spring-boot-starter:2.4.3.pom**:

```
kickstart/pom.xml   org.springframework.boot:spring-boot-starter-parent:2.4.3.pom   org.springframework.boot:spring-boot-dependencies:2.4.3.pom   org.springframework.boot:spring-boot-starter:2.4.3.pom
<?xml version="1.0" encoding="UTF-8"?>
<project xsi:schemaLocation="http://maven.apache.org/POM/4.0.0 http://maven.apache.org/xsd/maven-4.0.0.xsd" xmlns="http:
    xmlns:xsi="http://www.w3.org/2001/XMLSchema-instance">
  <!-- This module was also published with a richer model, Gradle metadata,  -->
  <!-- which should be used instead. Do not delete the following line which  -->
  <!-- is to indicate to Gradle or any Gradle module metadata file consumer  -->
  <!-- that they should prefer consuming it instead. -->
  <!-- do_not_remove: published-with-gradle-metadata -->
  <modelVersion>4.0.0</modelVersion>
  <groupId>org.springframework.boot</groupId>
  <artifactId>spring-boot-starter</artifactId>
  <version>2.4.3</version>
  <name>spring-boot-starter</name>
```

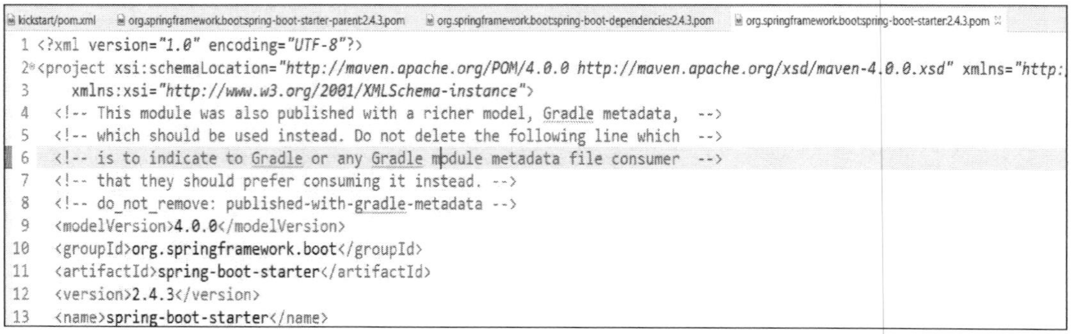

Figure 3.2: Traversing to spring-boot-starter dependency

Spring Boot starter dependencies and their configuration

For all the Spring Boot starters dependencies, the following is the syntax for using them in the Maven project:

```
<dependency>
  <groupId>org.springframework.boot</groupId>
  <artifactId>spring-boot-starter-*</artifactId>
</dependency>
```

Here is the syntax for using them in the Gradle project:

```
dependencies {
    implementation 'org.springframework.boot:spring-boot-starter-*'
}
```

The asterisk (*) denotes the utility such as **parent**, **web**, **data-jpa**, **test**, **security**, and so on. We will discuss the following starter dependencies that can be used for developing an application:

- **spring-boot-starter-parent**
- **spring-boot-starter-web**
- **spring-boot-starter-data-jpa**
- **spring-boot-starter-test**
- **spring-boot-starter-security**
- **spring-boot-starter-actuator**
- **spring-boot-starter-logging**
- **spring-boot-starter-cache**
- **spring-boot-starter-aop**

spring-boot-starter-parent

It is the parent **pom** providing dependency and plugin management for applications built with the Maven build tool. It has a packaging type of **pom**. This **pom** decides the version of Java that will be used in the project for doing compilation of source code and creating the target file with the version. It's preferred to have the source and target version of Java to be the same.

The following properties are present in **spring-boot-starter-parent**:

```
<properties>
  <java.version>1.8</java.version>
  <resource.delimiter>@</resource.delimiter>
  <maven.compiler.source>${java.version}</maven.compiler.source>
  <maven.compiler.target>${java.version}</maven.compiler.target>
  <project.build.sourceEncoding>UTF-8</project.build.sourceEncoding>
  <project.reporting.outputEncoding>UTF-8</project.reporting.
outputEncoding>
</properties>
```

To prevent the warning message **"[WARNING] Using platform encoding (Cp1252 actually) to copy filtered resources, i.e. build is platform dependent!"** or such kind of warning messages, you need to set **<project.build.sourceEncoding>UTF-8</project.build.sourceEncoding>** in the Maven project properties. This is auto-handled in spring-boot-starter-parent pom. The same is the case for the output encoding for the reporting purposes **<project.reporting.outputEncoding>UTF-8</project.reporting.outputEncoding>** when added, and then it will handle special characters in the site folder of the target.

In *Chapter 2, Developing Your First Spring Boot Application,* we discussed about the **application.properties** and **application.yml** configuration files for the project. *Have you wondered how Spring knows to load these files automatically?* Well, the answer lies in the **<build>** tag of **spring-boot-starter-parent**. The following is the syntax of the **<build>** tag:

```
<build>
    <resources>
      <resource>
          ...
      </resource>
    </resources>
    <pluginManagement>
      <plugins>
        <plugin>
          ...
        </plugin>
```

```
    </pluginManagement>
  </build>
```

Here is the code snippet from the **<build>** section of **spring-boot-starter-parent**:

```
<build>
    <resources>
      <resource>
        <directory>${basedir}/src/main/resources</directory>
        <filtering>true</filtering>
        <includes>
          <include>**/application*.yml</include>
          <include>**/application*.yaml</include>
          <include>**/application*.properties</include>
        </includes>
      </resource>
      <resource>
        <directory>${basedir}/src/main/resources</directory>
        <excludes>
          <exclude>**/application*.yml</exclude>
          <exclude>**/application*.yaml</exclude>
          <exclude>**/application*.properties</exclude>
        </excludes>
      </resource>
    </resources>
```

From here, the Spring recognizes the files named as **application*.yaml**, **application*.yml,** and **application*.properties**. The asterisks (*****) here mean that the file can have any name convention prefixed with the application. This wildcard will be used to load configuration files based on the environment. For example, **application-prod.properties** can be loaded only when the profile selected in the execution is specified as prod. With *Spring Boot 2.4,* there have been changes around the way the different application properties files are processed. If you still want to continue with the older technique, then we need to set **spring.config.use-legacy-processing** to **true**.

We used plugins in our kickstart project in *Chapter 2, Developing Your First Spring Boot Application,* where it had **spring-boot-maven-plugin**. **spring-boot-starter-parent** has more plugins preconfigured so they are not required to be loaded each time with a new project. These plugins are as follows:

- **org.jetbrains.kotlin:kotlin-maven-plugin**
- **org.apache.maven.plugins:maven-compiler-plugin**
- **org.apache.maven.plugins:maven-failsafe-plugin**
- **org.apache.maven.plugins:maven-jar-plugin**
- **org.apache.maven.plugins:maven-war-plugin**
- **org.apache.maven.plugins:maven-resources-plugin**
- **pl.project13.maven:git-commit-id-plugin**
- **org.springframework.boot:spring-boot-maven-plugin**
- **org.apache.maven.plugins:maven-shade-plugin**

Each of these plugins have their own set of <configuration> and <executions> tags.

The following is the code snippet of **spring-boot-starter-parent** plugins:

```
<pluginManagement>
      <plugins>
        <plugin>
          <groupId>org.jetbrains.kotlin</groupId>
          <artifactId>kotlin-maven-plugin</artifactId>
          <version>${kotlin.version}</version>
          <configuration>...</configuration>
          <executions>...</executions>
        </plugin>
        <plugin>
          <groupId>org.apache.maven.plugins</groupId>
          <artifactId>maven-compiler-plugin</artifactId>
          <configuration>...</configuration>
        </plugin>
        <plugin>
          <groupId>org.apache.maven.plugins</groupId>
          <artifactId>maven-failsafe-plugin</artifactId>
```

```
            <executions>...</executions>
            <configuration>...</configuration>
        </plugin>
        <plugin>
            <groupId>org.apache.maven.plugins</groupId>
            <artifactId>maven-jar-plugin</artifactId>
            <configuration>...</configuration>
        </plugin>
            ...
    </plugins>
</pluginManagement>
```

spring-boot-starter-web

The **`spring-boot-starter-web`** starter pack is well constructed to build a web application, including RESTful services, applications using Spring MVC. It also uses Tomcat as the default embedded container. This starter pack has nested dependencies as shown in the following screenshot:

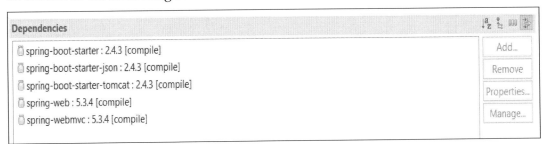

Figure 3.3: *Dependencies for spring-boot-starter-web*

These nested dependencies can be identified from the **`Dependencies`** tab present next to the **`Overview`** tab (tabs where **`pom.xml`** is shown).

Notice that the version of dependencies whose **`groupId`** is **`org.springframework.boot`** has version **`2.4.3`** whereas for **`groupId org.springframework,`** the version is **`5.3.4`**. This is because of the Spring architecture defining the versions of the Spring framework and Spring Boot framework. If you want to load different embedded containers other than the default Tomcat, then you can exclude the tomcat dependency by the following code snippet:

```
<dependency>
```

```
    <groupId>org.springframework.boot</groupId>
    <artifactId>spring-boot-starter-web</artifactId>
    <exclusions>
        <exclusion>
            <groupId>org.springframework.boot</groupId>
            <artifactId>spring-boot-starter-tomcat</artifactId>
        </exclusion>
    </exclusions>
</dependency>
```

When we execute the application, the console will contain the following logs:

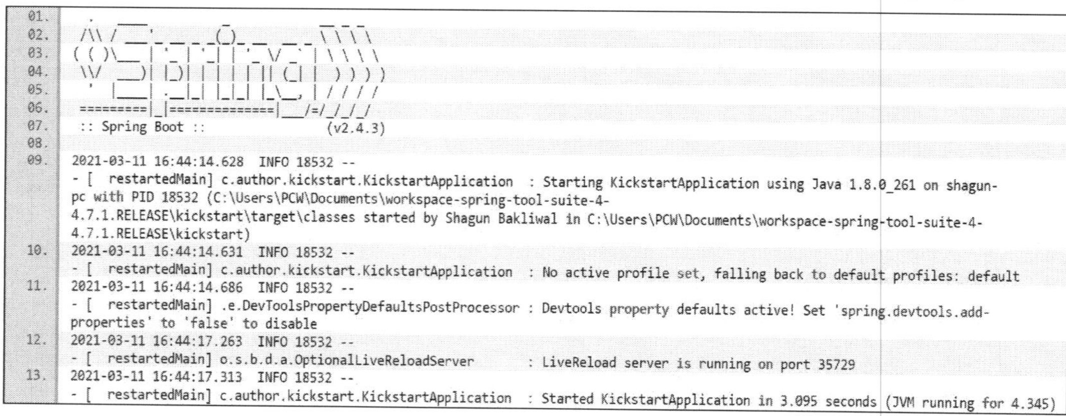

***Figure 3.4:** Console Logs without Tomcat*

As soon as the application starts, after the *Started* log, the application will stop as there is no web servlet container which will keep the application running on the port.

So, *what if you want to use servlet container other than Tomcat?* You can also use other web servlet containers like **`jetty`** by putting the following syntax in **`pom.xml`**:

```
<dependency>
    <groupId>org.springframework.boot</groupId>
    <artifactId>spring-boot-starter-web</artifactId>
    <exclusions>
        <exclusion>
            <groupId>org.springframework.boot</groupId>
```

```
            <artifactId>spring-boot-starter-tomcat</artifactId>
        </exclusion>
    </exclusions>
</dependency>
<dependency>
    <groupId>org.springframework.boot</groupId>
    <artifactId>spring-boot-starter-jetty</artifactId>
</dependency>
```

Here, we are excluding **spring-boot-starter-tomcat** from **spring-boot-starter-web dependency** and adding **spring-boot-starter-jetty** as our web servlet container. As you start compiling and executing your application, you will see the following logs:

```
  .   ____          _            __ _ _
 /\\ / ___'_ __ _ _(_)_ __  __ _ \ \ \ \
( ( )\___ | '_ | '_| | '_ \/ _` | \ \ \ \
 \\/  ___)| |_)| | | | | || (_| |  ) ) ) )
  '  |____| .__|_| |_|_| |_\__, | / / / /
 =========|_|==============|___/=/_/_/_/
 :: Spring Boot ::                (v2.4.3)

2021-03-11 17:26:29.580  INFO 9124 --- [  restartedMain] c.author.kickstart.KickstartApplication  : Starting KickstartApplication using Java 1.8.0_261 on shagun-
pc with PID 9124 (C:\Users\PCW\Documents\workspace-spring-tool-suite-4-
4.7.1.RELEASE\kickstart\target\classes started by Shagun Bakliwal in C:\Users\PCW\Documents\workspace-spring-tool-suite-4-4.7.1.RELEASE\kickstart)
2021-03-11 17:26:29.593  INFO 9124 --- [  restartedMain] c.author.kickstart.KickstartApplication  : No active profile set, falling back to default profiles: default
2021-03-11 17:26:29.707  INFO 9124 --- [  restartedMain] .e.DevToolsPropertyDefaultsPostProcessor : Devtools property defaults active! Set 'spring.devtools.add-
properties' to 'false' to disable
2021-03-11 17:26:29.707  INFO 9124 --
- [  restartedMain] .e.DevToolsPropertyDefaultsPostProcessor : For additional web related logging consider setting the 'logging.level.web' property to 'DEBUG'
2021-03-11 17:26:30.854  INFO 9124 --- [  restartedMain] org.eclipse.jetty.util.log               : Logging initialized @4174ms to org.eclipse.jetty.util.log.Slf4jLog
2021-03-11 17:26:31.117  INFO 9124 --- [  restartedMain] o.s.b.w.e.j.JettyServletWebServerFactory : Server initialized with port: 8080
2021-03-11 17:26:31.120  INFO 9124 --- [  restartedMain] org.eclipse.jetty.server.Server          : jetty-9.4.36.v20210114; built: 2021-01-
14T16:44:28.689Z; git: 238ec6997c7806b055319a6d11f8ae7564adc0de; jvm 1.8.0_261-b12
2021-03-11 17:26:31.146  INFO 9124 --- [  restartedMain] o.e.j.s.h.ContextHandler.application     : Initializing Spring embedded WebApplicationContext
2021-03-11 17:26:31.146  INFO 9124 --- [  restartedMain] w.s.c.ServletWebServerApplicationContext : Root WebApplicationContext: initialization completed in 1435 ms
2021-03-11 17:26:31.242  INFO 9124 --- [  restartedMain] org.eclipse.jetty.server.session         : DefaultSessionIdManager workerName=node0
2021-03-11 17:26:31.243  INFO 9124 --- [  restartedMain] org.eclipse.jetty.server.session         : No SessionScavenger set, using defaults
2021-03-11 17:26:31.244  INFO 9124 --- [  restartedMain] org.eclipse.jetty.server.session         : node0 Scavenging every 600000ms
2021-03-11 17:26:31.256  INFO 9124 --- [  restartedMain] o.e.jetty.server.handler.ContextHandler  : Started o.s.b.w.e.j.JettyEmbeddedWebAppContext@530a36bd{application,/,
[file:///C:/Users/PCW/AppData/Local/Temp/jetty-docbase.8080.5469633629945251128/],AVAILABLE}
2021-03-11 17:26:31.256  INFO 9124 --- [  restartedMain] org.eclipse.jetty.server.Server          : Started @4578ms
2021-03-11 17:26:31.398  INFO 9124 --- [  restartedMain] o.s.s.concurrent.ThreadPoolTaskExecutor  : Initializing ExecutorService 'applicationTaskExecutor'
2021-03-11 17:26:31.612  INFO 9124 --- [  restartedMain] o.s.b.d.a.OptionalLiveReloadServer       : LiveReload server is running on port 35729
2021-03-11 17:26:31.646  INFO 9124 --- [  restartedMain] o.e.j.s.h.ContextHandler.application     : Initializing Spring DispatcherServlet 'dispatcherServlet'
2021-03-11 17:26:31.646  INFO 9124 --- [  restartedMain] o.s.web.servlet.DispatcherServlet        : Initializing Servlet 'dispatcherServlet'
2021-03-11 17:26:31.647  INFO 9124 --- [  restartedMain] o.s.web.servlet.DispatcherServlet        : Completed initialization in 1 ms
2021-03-11 17:26:31.678  INFO 9124 --- [  restartedMain] o.e.jetty.server.AbstractConnector       : Started ServerConnector@7b3175d5{HTTP/1.1, (http/1.1)}{0.0.0.0:8080}
2021-03-11 17:26:31.680  INFO 9124 --- [  restartedMain] o.s.b.web.embedded.jetty.JettyWebServer  : Jetty started on port(s) 8080
2021-03-11 17:26:31.701  INFO 9124 --- [  restartedMain] c.author.kickstart.KickstartApplication  : Started KickstartApplication in 2.545 seconds (JVM running for 5.022)
```

Figure 3.5: *Jetty logs*

spring-boot-starter-data-jpa

This starter pack has the capability to interact with the database using Spring Data **Java Persistence API (JPA)** with Hibernate. JPA is one of the well-known mechanisms for accessing the database by dealing with repositories. This starter pack has the following dependencies:

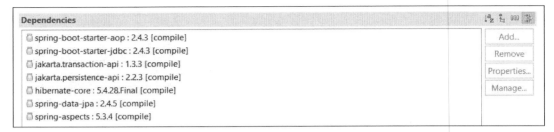

Figure 3.6: *Dependencies for spring-boot-starter-data-jpa*

Now if you start the application that uses this dependency, it will throw the following error messages:

```
Error starting ApplicationContext. To display the conditions report re-run your application with 'debug' enabled.
2021-03-11 17:31:48.877 ERROR 16816 --- [  restartedMain] o.s.b.d.LoggingFailureAnalysisReporter   :

***************************
APPLICATION FAILED TO START
***************************

Description:

Failed to configure a DataSource: 'url' attribute is not specified and no embedded datasource could be configured.

Reason: Failed to determine a suitable driver class


Action:

Consider the following:
    If you want an embedded database(H2, HSQL or Derby), please put it on the classpath.
    If you have database settings to be loaded from a particular profile you may need to activate it (no profiles are currently active).
```

Figure 3.7: *spring-boot-starter-data-jpa requires suitable driver*

This error message is due to the unavailability of the database for which the data source object could not be configured. The resolution of this error will be explained in detail in *Chapter 5, Working with Spring Data JPA and Caching*.

spring-boot-starter-test

This starter pack is used when we want to have some unit testing to be executed for the Java source code. Test cases may extend from the normal public method test to the REST endpoint test by mocking requests and responses. The following is the syntax:

```
<dependency>
    <groupId>org.springframework.boot</groupId>
    <artifactId>spring-boot-starter-test</artifactId>
    <scope>test</scope>
</dependency>
```

The following are the dependencies declared inside **`spring-boot-starter-test`**:

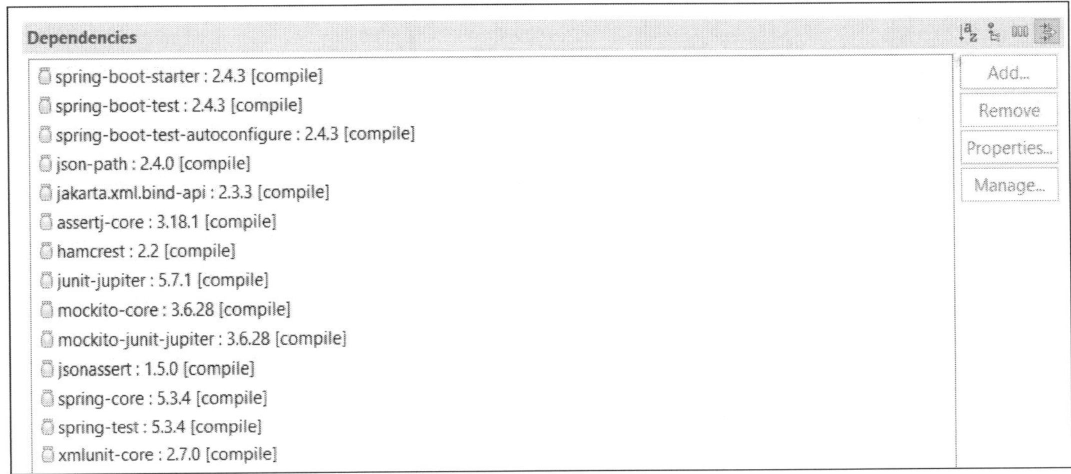

Figure 3.8: *Dependencies for spring-boot-starter-test*

spring-boot-starter-security

This starter pack takes care of the access to the application by including Spring Security in the classpath. The authentication and authorization for an application is managed by the following dependencies:

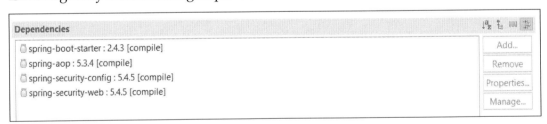

Figure 3.9: *Dependencies for spring-boot-starter-security*

When this dependency is successfully loaded into the application, you will see the following logs in the console:

```
2021-03-11 17:38:58.137  INFO 8340 --- [  restartedMain] .s.s.UserDetailsServiceAutoConfiguration :

Using generated security password: c13f7578-1802-436e-98ca-b1bfbe6f603e

2021-03-11 17:38:58.383  INFO 8340 --
- [  restartedMain] o.s.s.web.DefaultSecurityFilterChain     : Will secure any request with [org.springframework.securi
```

Figure 3.10: *Console log*

It generates a default security password that is a random UUID generated from **`SecurityProperties`** in the **`UserDetailsServiceAutoConfiguration`** class. When you browse `http://localhost:8082` on any client (browser, Postman), it will redirect the request to **`/login`** where it will ask the user to enter the username and password to access the original resource requested. The following screenshot displays the login screen when you try to access the server from browser:

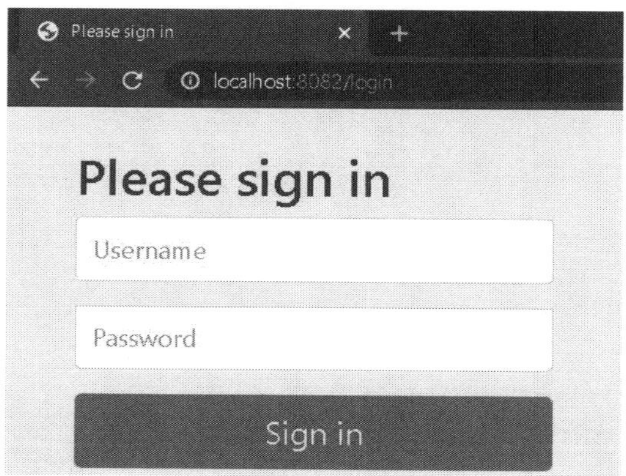

Figure 3.11: *Login screen*

When you enter the username as **`user`** and the password as the one present in the console logs for example, using the generated security password: **`c13f7578-1802-436e-98ca-b1bfbe6f603e`**, you will get access to the URL. The username **`user`** is preconfigured in the **`SecurityProperties`** class.

Security dependency and its implementation in our application will be explained in the upcoming chapters.

spring-boot-starter-actuator

This starter pack gives out the production-ready features to help you monitor and manage your application by using Spring Boot's actuator. The following dependencies are used with this starter pack:

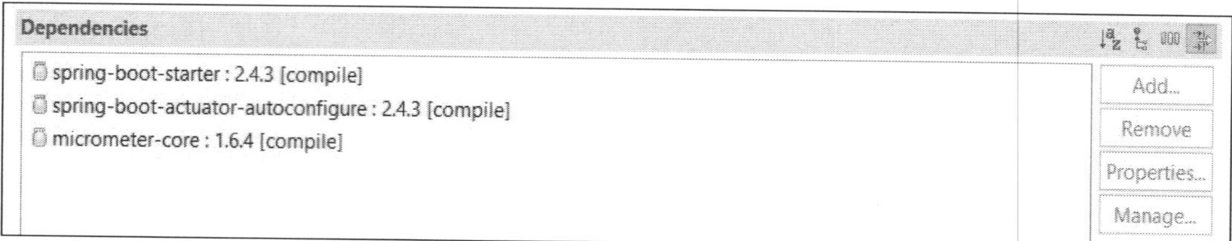

Figure 3.12: *Dependencies for spring-boot-starter-actuator*

When this dependency is loaded into the classpath and application starts, you will see the log **`Exposing 2 endpoint(s) beneath base path '/actuator'`** in the console.

The following is the response of the actuator endpoint **`http://localhost:8082/actuator`**:

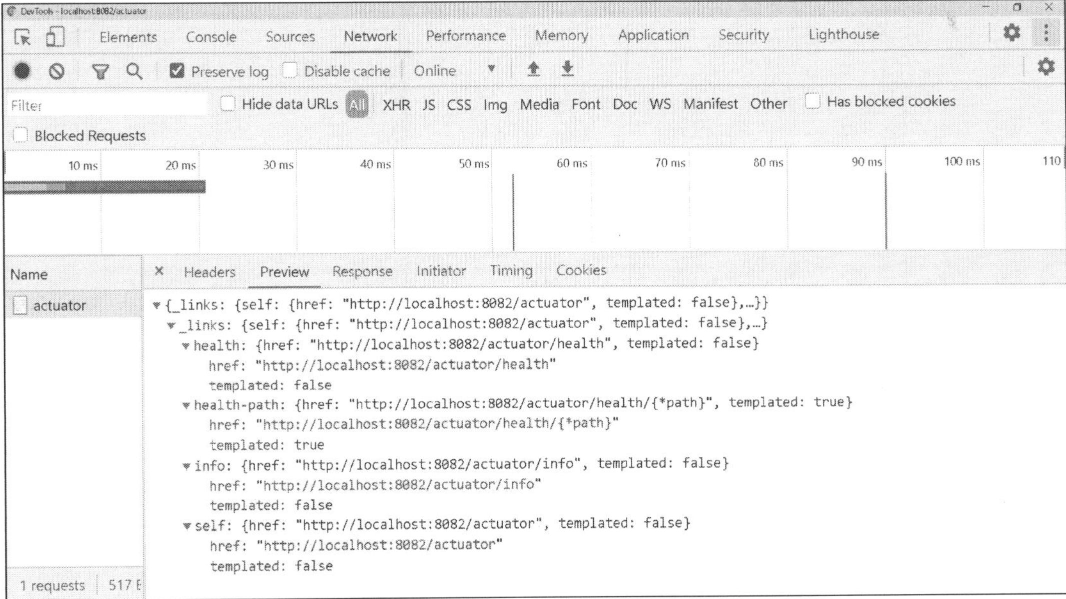

Figure 3.13: *Actuator endpoint response*

The actuator endpoints **`/actuator`**, **`/info`** and **`/health`** are enabled by default as they do not contain sensitive information. The other actuator endpoints will be discussed in the upcoming chapters when needed by adding the following configuration in **`application.yml`**:

```
server:
  port: 8082
management:
  endpoints:
    web:
      exposure:
        include: "*"
```

The same can be configured in **`application.properties`**:

```
server.port: 8082
management.endpoints.web.exposure.include: *
```

spring-boot-starter-logging

This is the default logging starter pack for logging using **logback**. It uses the following dependencies:

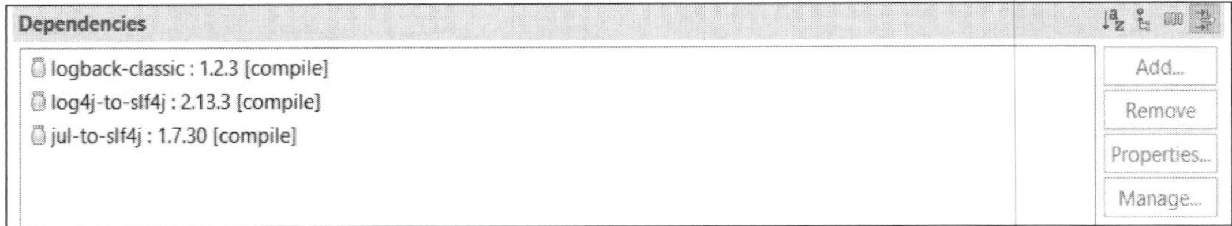

Figure 3.14: *Dependencies for spring-boot-starter-logging*

The understanding behind the logging and **logback** will be explained in *Chapter 9, Logging*.

spring-boot-starter-cache

This starter pack is provided for using Spring Framework's **caching support**. Caching is a temporary part of RAM where the data is stored so that it can be accessed faster as compared with secondary memory. It is recommended to store static data or frequently used data.

In Spring Boot, we will use caching techniques - **in-memory** and **database**. Examples of these techniques could be Redis and Hibernate, respectively. This dependency includes two dependencies – **spring-boot-starter** and **spring-context-support**. More hands-on on caching will be discussed in *Chapter 5, Working with Spring Data JPA and Caching*.

spring-boot-starter-aop

This starter pack is for aspect-oriented programming with **Spring AOP** and **AspectJ**. This is used for using common behavior across methods, classes, object hierarchies, and REST endpoints. It manages the cross-cutting concerns for an application. This starter pack uses the following dependencies:

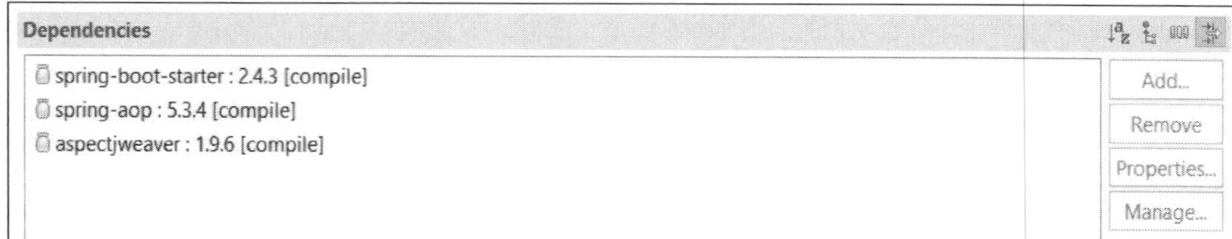

Figure 3.15: *Dependencies for spring-boot-starter-aop*

Now that we have discussed few starter packs, we will be discussing the auto-configuration part of the Spring Boot.

Understanding auto-configuration

Spring Boot automatically configures a Spring application based on the dependencies included in the classpath. By doing this, it makes the development easier for the developer for creating beans explicitly and using them. By beans, we mean Spring Beans which are the objects created and managed by Spring Core specifically **`ApplicationContext`**.

So *how does Spring know when to do the configuration automatically once the dependency is loaded?* The answer to this lies in the usage of **`@EnableAutoConfiguration`**. This annotation is present in the autoconfigure dependency under the package **`org.springframework.boot.autoconfigure`**. Now, there can be many classes or beans that can be auto-configured together, but *how to set the order for them?* This can be sorted by using **`@AutoConfigureOrder`** or **`@AutoConfigureAfter`** where **`@AutoConfigureOrder`** allows auto-configuration classes to be ordered among themselves without affecting the order of configuration classes passed to **`AnnotationConfigApplicationContext`**. The default order is **`0`**, but can be changed by adding **`Ordered.HIGHEST_PRECEDENCE`** while using annotation. **`@AutoConfigureAfter`** is used when we want the auto-configuration to be applied after other specified auto-configuration classes.

Now, the third step for doing auto-configuration is to annotate the methods and classes with the **`@Conditional`** annotation that means the class or bean will be auto-configured if the same is not present in **`ApplicationContext`**.

The following are few types of conditional auto-configurations:

- Conditional on class
- Conditional on bean
- Conditional on property

Conditional on class

It allows Spring to create and load the class if the class is present in the context with the usage of the **`@ConditionalOnClass`** annotation. For example, **`HibernateJpaAutoConfiguration`** is annotated with the **`@ConditionalOnClass`** annotation:

```
@Configuration(proxyBeanMethods = false)
```

```
@ConditionalOnClass({ LocalContainerEntityManagerFactoryBean.class,
EntityManager.class, SessionImplementor.class })
@EnableConfigurationProperties(JpaProperties.class)
@AutoConfigureAfter({ DataSourceAutoConfiguration.class })
@Import(HibernateJpaConfiguration.class)
public class HibernateJpaAutoConfiguration {


}
```

By looking into the preceding snippet, it is clear that when **LocalContainerEntityManagerFactoryBean.class**, **EntityManager.class**, and **SessionImplementor.class** are present in the context, and then create the bean for the **HibernateJpaAutoConfiguration** class. Also, note that it is annotation with **@Configuration**. These two annotations - **@Configuration** and **@ConditionalOnClass** are required for the classes to get themselves auto-configured.

If we want to auto-configure the class when some class is missing, then **@ConditionalOnMissingClass** can be used.

Conditional on bean

It allows Spring to create and load the bean if the bean is present in the context with the usage of the **@ConditionalOnBean** annotation. For example, if you use **spring-boot-devtools**, then the **DevToolsDataSourceAutoConfiguration** class is loaded and it is uses **@ConditionalOnBean** for loading **DatabaseShutdownExecutorEntityManagerFactoryDependsOnPostProcessor** if **AbstractEntityManagerFactoryBean** is present. The following is the snippet of the **DevToolsDataSourceAutoConfiguration** class:

```
@AutoConfigureAfter(DataSourceAutoConfiguration.class)
@Conditional({ OnEnabledDevToolsCondition.class, DevToolsDataSourceCon-
dition.class })
@Configuration(proxyBeanMethods = false)
@Import(DatabaseShutdownExecutorEntityManagerFactoryDependsOnPostProces-
sor.class)
public class DevToolsDataSourceAutoConfiguration {
```

```
@Bean
NonEmbeddedInMemoryDatabaseShutdownExecutor inMemoryDatabaseShut-
downExecutor(DataSource dataSource,
        DataSourceProperties dataSourceProperties) {
    return new NonEmbeddedInMemoryDatabaseShutdownExecutor(data-
    Source, dataSourceProperties);
}

/**
 * Post processor to ensure that {@link javax.persistence.EntityMan-
 agerFactory} beans
 * depend on the {@code inMemoryDatabaseShutdownExecutor} bean
 */
@ConditionalOnClass(LocalContainerEntityManagerFactoryBean.class)
@ConditionalOnBean(AbstractEntityManagerFactoryBean.class)
static class DatabaseShutdownExecutorEntityManagerFactoryDependsOn-
PostProcessor
        extends EntityManagerFactoryDependsOnPostProcessor {

    DatabaseShutdownExecutorEntityManagerFactoryDependsOnPostProces-
    sor() {
        super("inMemoryDatabaseShutdownExecutor");
    }

}
```

If we want to auto-configure the class when some bean is missing, then **@ConditionalOnMissingBean** can be used.

Conditional on property

It allows Spring to create and load the class or bean if the property is specified in the application configuration file. If the class or bean is annotated with the **@ConditionalOnProperty** annotation, then the class will be loaded. For example, **H2ConsoleAutoConfiguration** uses **@ConditionalOnProperty** to check whether the property **spring.h2.console.enabled** is present or not with value as **true**. The following is the snippet of the **H2ConsoleAutoConfiguration** class:

```
@Configuration(proxyBeanMethods = false)

@ConditionalOnWebApplication(type = Type.SERVLET)

@ConditionalOnClass(WebServlet.class)

@ConditionalOnProperty(prefix = "spring.h2.console", name = "enabled",
havingValue = "true", matchIfMissing = false)

@AutoConfigureAfter(DataSourceAutoConfiguration.class)

@EnableConfigurationProperties(H2ConsoleProperties.class)

public class H2ConsoleAutoConfiguration {


 private static final Log logger = LogFactory.getLog(H2ConsoleAutoConfiguration.
class);
```

Now, the question arises, *what if you do not need the class to be auto-configured even though they are annotated?* To resolve this question, you can exclude the class in the **@EnableAutoConfiguration** annotation. For instance, **@EnableAutoConfiguration(exclude={DataSourceAutoConfiguration.class})**.

Wonder *where this **@EnableAutoConfiguration** annotation is used?* It is included in the **@SpringBootApplication** annotation present in our main class from where we call run the method of **SpringApplication**.

By now, you have understood how **@EnableAutoConfiguration** is used under the hood and how Spring is doing auto-configuration for us.

Conclusion

In this chapter, we learned most of the starter packs that can be used to develop an application. We also took a look at how the classes or beans are autoconfigured automatically by the Spring feature of auto-configuration. In the next chapter, we will learn different annotations that are provided by Spring and the Spring Boot framework.

Points to remember

- For creating custom beans to be configured automatically, make sure those are loaded in the correct order.
- While using **`application.yml`**, make sure the indentation of attributes is correct.

Questions

1. What are the different starter packs provided by Spring Boot?
2. How can we use the starter packs with maven and gradle configurations?
3. How to get the dependencies used within the starter pack?
4. How to exclude the embedded Tomcat container and include **`jetty`** while using web dependency?
5. How does Spring know how to load the configurations from **`application.properties`**?
6. How to enable auto configuration?
7. How can we create our own auto-configuration classes?

CHAPTER 4
Spring Boot Annotations

Now that we have understood the different starter packs provided by Spring Boot and auto-configuration under the hood, we will learn annotations created in the Spring Boot framework which favors the developer to save time in writing the configurations in the old convention – **XML Configurations**. This chapter will bring out all the annotations used with a Spring Boot application so that you can have an idea of using them before developing an application.

Structure

In this chapter, we will discuss the following topics:

- Java annotations
- Existence of Spring annotations
- Spring and Spring Boot annotations

Objectives

After studying this unit, you should be able to understand the need of annotations and the usage of Spring Boot annotations.

Java annotations

Java annotations are used to provide some kind of metadata to the Java compiler and JVM. They are embedded within the source code which tells the compiler about the behavior of the field, class, interface, or method. The annotation starts with the symbol `@` followed by the name of the annotation. The following are few built-in annotations introduced in Java 1.5:

- `@Override`: It is used when the child class is overriding methods of its parent class to change the behavior. The use of this annotation is necessary so that it makes the code readable and avoids any type of compilation issues if the signature of the method doesn't match with the signature of the parent class method.
- `@Deprecated`: It is used to denote the class, method, or field that should no longer be referenced in the source code. If it is used, then the Java compiler generates a warning message. For the preceding entities, if you are deprecating, then it should also be documented with `@deprecated` with reasons.
- `@SuppressWarnings`: It is used when the deprecated methods, classes, or fields are used and we don't want the compiler to generate a warning message.

Existence of Spring annotations

The Spring framework is designed to expand the principle of **Inversion of Control** (**IOC**) or **Dependency Injection** (**DI**) which allows a developer to have loosely coupled components and applications so that components can be prepared for unit testing easily. Prior to Spring Boot, all the Spring managed objects were called **beans** and their dependencies were managed by XML-based configurations and also by the Java-based code, but this increases configuration in `pom.xml` just for managing beans.

There's an alternate way of managing these beans in Spring by writing the Java-based configuration. Let's now understand the different annotations in Spring Boot.

Spring and Spring Boot annotations

Let's dive deeper into different annotations provided by the Spring framework and Spring Boot which can be broadly classified into the following:

- Core Spring framework annotations
- Spring framework stereotype annotations

- Spring Boot annotations
- Spring task execution annotations
- Spring profiles annotations

Core Spring framework annotations

The following are few annotations that can be categorized under the Core Spring framework:

@Bean

@Bean is an annotation that is used on the top of a method and can act as a replacement of the XML **<bean/>** element. The annotation supports most of the attributes offered by **<bean>** such as **initMethod, destroyMethod,** and **autowireCandidate**. To declare a bean, simply annotate the method with the **@Bean** annotation. When **JavaConfig** notices this annotation, it calls the method and registers the return value as a bean within **BeanFactory. Bean** name is the method name by default unless specified. For example:

```
package com.author.kickstart.configuration;


import org.springframework.context.annotation.Bean;

import org.springframework.context.annotation.Configuration;


import com.author.kickstart.model.CPU;


@Configuration

public class Config {

    @Bean("cpu")

    public CPU createCpu() {

        return new CPU("i5", 7);

    }

}
```

After the bean is created, it is injected to a class by autowiring the bean.

@Autowired

It is used to mark a constructor, field, or setter method to get autowire by Spring DI. **Dependency Injection** is a technique that removes the dependency of a component from the source code so that our source code is loosely coupled with the component. This also makes the unit testing possible. The Spring framework provides two ways of dependency injection – **constructor** and **setter method**.

The following are the autowiring types:

- **Autowired constructor:** Only one constructor can be autowired within a class. If multiple constructors are declared with **`@Autowired`**, then they are considered as options for autowiring and the constructor with the greatest number of dependencies that can satisfy matching beans in the Spring container will be chosen. If no constructor satisfies, then the default constructor will be used if present. Also note, if a class declares multiple constructors but none of them is annotated with **`@Autowired`**, then a default constructor will be used if present.

  For example:

```
package com.author.kickstart.model;

import org.springframework.beans.factory.annotation.Autowired;

import org.springframework.stereotype.Component;

@Component

public class CPU {

    private Harddisk harddisk;

    @Autowired

    public CPU(Harddisk harddisk) {

        this.harddisk = harddisk;

    }

}
```

- **Autowired fields**: Fields are autowired after the bean of the class is created. This bean is created and managed by the Spring container. Generally, the autowired fields are not set to public. For instance:

```
package com.author.kickstart.model;

import org.springframework.beans.factory.annotation.Autowired;
```

```
import org.springframework.stereotype.Component;
@Component
public class CPU {

    @Autowired
    private Harddisk;
}
```

- **Autowired setters:** When the **@Autowired** annotation is used at the top of a setter method for a field, Spring injects the dependency of the field while creating the bean of the class. For example:

```
package com.author.kickstart.model;
import org.springframework.beans.factory.annotation.Autowired;
import org.springframework.stereotype.Component;
@Component
public class CPU {

    private Harddisk;

    @Autowired
    public void setHarddisk(Harddisk harddisk) {
        this.harddisk = harddisk;
    }

}
```

- **Autowired collections, arrays, and maps:** Even collections, arrays, maps, string, or any datatype can be autowired by creating the bean first. For example, create the **HarddiskConfig** class as follows:

```
package com.author.kickstart.configuration;
import java.util.HashMap;
import java.util.Map;
import org.springframework.context.annotation.Bean;
import org.springframework.context.annotation.Configuration;
@Configuration
public class HarddiskConfig {
```

```
    @Bean
    public Map<String, String> map() {
        Map<String, String> map = new HashMap<>();
        map.put("partitionSize", "500MB");
        return map;
    }

}
```

Create the **CPUConfig** class as follows:

```
package com.author.kickstart.configuration;
import java.util.Map;
import org.springframework.context.annotation.Configuration;
@Configuration
public class CPUConfig {
    CPUConfig(Map<String, String> map) {
            System.out.println(map.keySet().iterator().next()); //
gives output as partitionSize
    }
}
```

@ComponentScan

The most important annotation used within the **@SpringBootApplication** is the **@ComponentScan**. This annotation looks for components defined in the directories and allows them to configure to the Spring container. It uses source code packages for searching beans; if a specific package is not defined, then scanning will occur from the package of the class where this annotation is used. For instance, when the **@SpringBootApplication** is used, the Spring container looks for the beans in the same package and sub-packages where the **@SpringBootApplication** is used. For applications, where **@SpringBootApplication** cannot be used, then simply scanning for beans can be done by using **@ComponentScan(value = "com.author")** where **value** can be any base package.

For example:

```
package com.author.kickstart.configuration;
```

```
import org.springframework.context.annotation.ComponentScan;
import org.springframework.context.annotation.Configuration;
@Configuration
@ComponentScan(value = "com.author")
public class HarddiskConfig {
    // some methods which uses beans created in basePackage: com.author
}
```

@Configuration

This indicates that the class has one or more beans that can be used throughout the project and can be processed by the Spring container to generate other bean definitions. For instance:

```
package com.author.kickstart.configuration;
import java.util.HashMap;
import java.util.Map;
import org.springframework.context.annotation.Bean;
import org.springframework.context.annotation.Configuration;
@Configuration
public class HarddiskConfig {

    @Bean
    public Map<String, String> map() {
        Map<String, String> map = new HashMap<>();
        map.put("partitionSize", "500MB");
        return map;
    }

}
```

@ConfigurationProperties

This is an advanced way of using the configuration defined in properties or **`yml`** files while comparing the way it used to be while using **`@Value`** for fetching properties. For instance, let's have the configuration defined in the following **`application.yml`** file:

```
harddisk:
  config:
    size: 2TB
    brand: Seagate
    price: 6300

server:
  port: 8081
```

Then, the configuration class **HarddiskConfig.java** for using these values can be created as follows:

```
package com.author.kickstart.configuration;
import   org.springframework.boot.context.properties.ConfigurationProper-
ties;
import org.springframework.context.annotation.Configuration;
@Configuration
@ConfigurationProperties(prefix = "harddisk.config")
public class HarddiskConfig {

    private String size;
    private String brand;
    private double price;

    public String getSize() {
        return size;
    }

    public void setSize(String size) {
        this.size = size;
    }

    public String getBrand() {
        return brand;
    }
```

```
    public void setBrand(String brand) {
        this.brand = brand;
    }

    public double getPrice() {
        return price;
    }

    public void setPrice(double price) {
        this.price = price;
    }

}
```

For **@ConfigurationProperties** to work for the attributes, it is necessary to have getters and setters for the attributes or else you will face a compilation error asking for methods.

@TestPropertySource

While writing **JUnits** for integration testing, one may configure the runtime properties for the classes which are fetching values from property files. With the use of **@TestPropertySource**, you can specify the configuration file location and these configurations have higher precedence than any other configurations specified throughout the project. Consider the following configuration code that fetches the value from **application.yml**:

```
package com.author.kickstart.configuration;
import org.springframework.beans.factory.annotation.Value;
import org.springframework.context.annotation.Configuration;
@Configuration
public class MyConfiguration {
    @Value("${complex.values}")
    private String[] complexValues;

    public String[] getComplexValues() {
```

```
        return complexValues;
    }


}
```

And **application.yml** contains:

```
server:
  port: 8081


complex:
  values: 1,2,3,4,5
```

To write JUnit for this class, we can override the values for **complexValues** by using **@TestPropertySource**. Create the **MyConfiguration.properties** file in the **src/test/resources** folder which will have configurations to be provided while running integration tests. The contents for the properties file are described as follows:

```
complex.values=6,7,8,9,10
```

And now, we will use this configuration to provide or override existing values. The JUnit class is shown as follows:

```
package com.author.kickstart.configuration;
import static org.assertj.core.api.Assertions.assertThat;
import org.junit.jupiter.api.Test;
import org.junit.jupiter.api.extension.ExtendWith;
import org.springframework.beans.factory.annotation.Autowired;
import org.springframework.test.context.ContextConfiguration;
import org.springframework.test.context.TestPropertySource;
import org.springframework.test.context.junit.jupiter.SpringExtension;


@ExtendWith(SpringExtension.class)
@ContextConfiguration(classes = MyConfiguration.class)
@TestPropertySource(locations = "/MyConfigurationTest.properties")
public class MyConfigurationTest {
    @Autowired
    MyConfiguration configuration;
```

```
    @Test
    public void testValues() {
        String[] output = configuration.getComplexValues();
        assertThat(output).contains("6", "7", "8", "9", "10");
    }
}
```

We will learn how to write test cases in *Chapter 11, Testing a Spring Boot Application.*

@Lazy

This annotation is used to specify that the bean can be initialized later when used. This annotation can be used within a class that is annotated with **`@Component`**. This annotation can flip the laziness by changing the default value from true to false. Without this annotation, as usual, there would be eager initialization of the bean. If the value is flipped to true or the annotation is used, then the parent bean or the component will not be initialized until the bean on which the **`@Lazy`** annotation is there is fully initialized and available in **`BeanFactory`**. The **`@Lazy`** annotation can be used with **`@Configuration`** and **`@Autowired`**. For instance, the following snippet shows the usage of **`@Lazy`** at the class level in conjunction with **`@Configuration`**:

```
package com.author.kickstart.configuration;
import org.springframework.context.annotation.Bean;
import org.springframework.context.annotation.Configuration;
import org.springframework.context.annotation.Lazy;
import com.author.kickstart.model.CPU;

@Configuration
@Lazy
public class Config {
    @Bean
    public CPU cpu() {
        System.out.println("CPU is initializing");
        return new CPU();
    }

}
```

This indicates that all the **@Bean** methods should be loaded lazily into **BeanFactory**. When the application is booting up, the CPU bean will not be created immediately until the CPU bean is injected into the other part of the application. When the CPU bean is explicitly autowired like the following snippet, then the CPU bean gets created.

```
package com.author.kickstart.configuration;
import org.springframework.beans.factory.annotation.Autowired;
import org.springframework.context.annotation.Configuration;
import com.author.kickstart.model.CPU;

@Configuration
public class AppConfig {

    @Autowired
    CPU cpu;
}
```

In the preceding example, the beans were lazily created due to the **@Lazy** annotation applied on the class, but as soon as the CPU class is autowired, the bean was created immediately. Now, we will understand the usage of **@Lazy** with the **@Autowired** annotation. Let's have a method **getInfo()** in the CPU class so that it can be invoked from outside the class:

```
package com.author.kickstart.model;
public class CPU {

    public String getInfo() {
        return "info";
    }
}
```

Keeping the **Config.java** class same where the class is using the **@Lazy** annotation, we will modify the **AppConfig.java**:

```
package com.author.kickstart.configuration;
import javax.annotation.PostConstruct;
import org.springframework.beans.factory.annotation.Autowired;
```

```
import org.springframework.context.annotation.Configuration;
import org.springframework.context.annotation.Lazy;
import com.author.kickstart.model.CPU;

@Configuration
public class AppConfig {

    @Lazy
    @Autowired
    CPU cpu;

    @PostConstruct
    public void callAfterBeanCreation() {
        cpu.getInfo();
    }
}
```

In the preceding code snippet, the CPU is autowired lazily. This means that at the time of startup, the CPU bean will not be available as we used the **@Lazy** annotation while autowiring. The bean will be actually referenced when we call any of the method from the CPU class. Here, we will use the **@PostConstruct** annotation on a method which will be invoked just after all the beans are initialized for the **AppConfig** class into **BeanFactory**. As soon **AppConfig** is created in the Spring container, it calls **callAfterBeanCreation()** and then the lazy loading of CPU bean is done.

@Qualifier

There would be scenarios where there are multiple beans inheriting the same parent class. It's up to the developer to select the bean for autowiring. We saw that the bean is created with the same name as that of the method in the preceding section. The **@ Qualifier** annotation requires the same bean name for autowiring or injecting into the target class. Let us understand how to define bean:

1. Let's have an interface which is extended by two classes and then the interface is autowired for using the features of any of the two classes. The interface is declared as follows with the **getWheels()** method:

   ```
   package com.author.kickstart.interfaces;
   ```

```
public interface Vehicle {
    public int getWheels();
}
```

2. Now, we will implement **Vehicle** in two classes – **Car** and **Bike**:

   The following is the snippet of **Car.java**:

```
package com.author.kickstart.interfaces.impl;
import com.author.kickstart.interfaces.Vehicle;
public class Car implements Vehicle {

    @Override
    public int getWheels() {
        return 4;
    }

}
```

   The following is the snippet of **Bike.java**:

```
package com.author.kickstart.interfaces.impl;
import com.author.kickstart.interfaces.Vehicle;
public class Bike implements Vehicle {

    @Override
    public int getWheels() {
        return 2;
    }

}
```

3. Let's have another class **VehicleService** with **Vehicle** autowired:

```
package com.author.kickstart.service;
import org.springframework.beans.factory.annotation.Autowired;
import org.springframework.context.annotation.Configuration;
import com.author.kickstart.interfaces.Vehicle;
```

```
@Configuration
public class VehicleService {
    @Autowired
    Vehicle vehicle;


}
```

4. Notice that we don't have the beans created for **Car** and **Bike**. While executing the application, we will end up with the following error:

```
***************************
APPLICATION FAILED TO START
***************************

Description:

Field vehicle in com.author.kickstart.VehicleService required a bean of type 'com.author.kickstart.interfaces.Vehicle' that could not be found.

The injection point has the following annotations:
    - @org.springframework.beans.factory.annotation.Autowired(required=true)

Action:

Consider defining a bean of type 'com.author.kickstart.interfaces.Vehicle' in your configuration.
```

From the preceding message in action, we can now understand that the application requires a bean for **Vehicle** for autowiring.

To resolve this issue, let's create the bean either by the **@Bean** annotation or the **@Configuration** annotation. We will use the **@Configuration** annotation for simplicity. The following is the snippet which looks like after the **@Configuration** annotation is in use:

Bike.java

```
package com.author.kickstart.interfaces.impl;
```

```
import org.springframework.context.annotation.Configuration;
import com.author.kickstart.interfaces.Vehicle;
@Configuration
public class Bike implements Vehicle {

    @Override
    public int getWheels() {
        return 2;
    }

}
```

Car.java

```
package com.author.kickstart.interfaces.impl;
import org.springframework.context.annotation.Configuration;
import com.author.kickstart.interfaces.Vehicle;

@Configuration
public class Car implements Vehicle {

    @Override
    public int getWheels() {
        return 4;
    }

}
```

And now when we execute the application, we run into another error:

```
***************************
APPLICATION FAILED TO START
***************************

Description:
```

```
Field vehicle in com.author.kickstart.service.VehicleService re-
quired a single bean, but 2 were found:
    - bike: defined in file [C:\Users\PCW\Documents\workspace-spring-
tool-suite-4-4.7.1.RELEASE\kickstart-maven\kickstart\target\
classes\com\author\kickstart\interfaces\impl\Bike.class]
    - car: defined in file [C:\Users\PCW\Documents\workspace-spring-
tool-suite-4-4.7.1.RELEASE\kickstart-maven\kickstart\target\
classes\com\author\kickstart\ interfaces\impl\Car.class]


Action:


Consider marking one of the beans as @Primary, updating the consumer
to accept multiple beans, or using @Qualifier to identify the bean
that should be consumed
```

From the preceding error message, we notice that it requires one bean for the **`Vehicle`** class but it found two, that is, **`Car`** and **`Bike`**. Now, we will use the **`@Qualifier`** annotation while autowiring the **`Vehicle`** interface:

```
package com.author.kickstart.service;
import javax.annotation.PostConstruct;
import org.springframework.beans.factory.annotation.Autowired;
import org.springframework.beans.factory.annotation.Qualifier;
import org.springframework.context.annotation.Configuration;
import com.author.kickstart.interfaces.Vehicle;


@Configuration
public class VehicleService {
    @Autowired
    @Qualifier("car")
    Vehicle vehicle;


    @PostConstruct
    public void service() {
        System.out.println("Wheels for vehicle:" + vehicle.get-
        Wheels());
```

```
        }


    }
```

Once we decide to use which bean, we can have the name of the bean in the **@Qualifier** annotation. Here, we will use car as the bean name which will only autowire the **Car** bean. Hence, the result after the **VehicleService** is created, invokes the method, and prints the wheel for the **Car** vehicle.

There is another way of using the bean of our choice, without using **@Qualifier** that is, marking the bean as primary to identify the bean that should be consumed.

@Primary

This indicates that a bean should be given preference when multiple candidates are qualified to autowire a single-valued dependency. If exactly one *primary* bean exists among the candidates, it will be the autowired value.

Considering the preceding scenario where we used **@Qualifier**, we will remove the **@Qualifier** while autowiring vehicle and we will also add the **@Primary** annotation at the top of Bike as follows:

Bike.java

```
package com.author.kickstart.interfaces.impl;
import org.springframework.context.annotation.Configuration;
import org.springframework.context.annotation.Primary;
import com.author.kickstart.interfaces.Vehicle;

@Configuration
@Primary
public class Bike implements Vehicle {
```

VehicleService.java

```
package com.author.kickstart.service;
import javax.annotation.PostConstruct;
import org.springframework.beans.factory.annotation.Autowired;
import org.springframework.context.annotation.Configuration;
import com.author.kickstart.interfaces.Vehicle;
```

```
@Configuration
public class VehicleService {
    @Autowired
    Vehicle vehicle;

    @PostConstruct
    public void service() {
        System.out.println("Wheels for vehicle:" + vehicle.getWheels());
    }

}
```

As a result, we will get the Bike bean that gets autowired for **`Vehicle`**.

@Value

The **`@Value`** annotation is used to pick up the values from the **`application*.properties`** or **`application*.yml`** files. It can be used as the field or method/constructor parameter level that stores the default values present in properties. The value expression such as **`#{systemProperties.myProp}`** or property placeholder such as **`${server.port}`** can be stored to a variable. The usage of **`@Value`** is shown as follows to fetch the port on which server is running:

```
package com.author.kickstart.service;
import javax.annotation.PostConstruct;
import org.springframework.beans.factory.annotation.Value;
import org.springframework.stereotype.Service;

@Service
public class MyService {
    @Value("${server.port}")
    private int serverPort;

    @PostConstruct
    public void postConstruct() {
        System.out.println(serverPort);
    }
}
```

Wonder *how to provide multi-valued attributes from properties?* The answer to this can be given by having a multi-valued property in **application.yml** which has comma separated values as follows:

```
server:
  port: 8081

complex:
  values: 1,2,3,4,5
```

And these values can be accessed in **MyService** by writing the following code:

```
package com.author.kickstart.service;
import java.util.Arrays;
import javax.annotation.PostConstruct;
import org.springframework.beans.factory.annotation.Value;
import org.springframework.stereotype.Service;

@Service
public class MyService {
    @Value("${server.port}")
    private int serverPort;

    @Value("${complex.values}")
    private int[] complexValues;

    @PostConstruct
    public void postConstruct() {
        System.out.println(serverPort);
        System.out.println(Arrays.toString(complexValues));
    }
}
```

This generates the output as follows:

```
8081
[1, 2, 3, 4, 5]
```

So far, we took the core annotation provided in Spring for understanding basic annotations used. Let's now understand the stereotype annotations.

Spring framework stereotype annotations

Stereotype annotations are the annotations that denote the roles of types or methods in the overall architecture (at a conceptual, rather than implementation, level).

These annotations are used at the class level. Here are the stereotype annotations:

@Component

This indicates that an annotated class is a **component**. Such classes are considered as candidates for auto-detection when using annotation-based configuration and classpath scanning. This is the basic annotation used on the top of all **stereotype annotations**. The syntax for using the annotation is as follows:

```
package com.author.kickstart.service;
import org.springframework.stereotype.Component;


@Component
public class MyComponent {


}
```

@Controller

This indicates that an annotated class is a **controller**. This annotation serves as a specialization of **`@Component`** that allows you to implement classes to be autodetected through classpath scanning. It is used with **`@RequestMapping`** and **`@ResponseBody`** annotations for developing web APIs. The syntax for this annotation is as follows:

```
package com.author.kickstart.controller;
import org.springframework.stereotype.Controller;
import org.springframework.web.bind.annotation.RequestMapping;
import org.springframework.web.bind.annotation.RequestMethod;
import org.springframework.web.bind.annotation.ResponseBody;


@Controller
```

```
public class MyController {

    @RequestMapping(method = RequestMethod.GET, value = "/")
    @ResponseBody
    public String doSomething() {
        return "Hello";
    }
}
```

When requested for **`http://localhost:8081/`** on the browser, it returns **`Hello`**.

@Repository

This indicates that the annotated class is a **repository**. This is used when the application involves retrieval, storage, or search on the database or collection of objects. We will use this annotation with Spring Data JPA in *Chapter 5, Working with Spring Data JPA and Caching*. The syntax for this annotation is as follows:

```
package com.author.kickstart.repository;
import org.springframework.data.repository.CrudRepository;
import org.springframework.stereotype.Repository;
import com.author.kickstart.interfaces.impl.Car;

@Repository
public interface MyRepository extends CrudRepository<Car, String> {

}
```

@Service

This indicates that an annotated class is a **service**. The syntax for this annotation is as follows:

```
package com.author.kickstart.service;
import org.springframework.stereotype.Service;

@Service
public class MyService {
}
```

All stereotype annotations when used create the object for the class and are managed by the Spring container for their lifecycle. The objects hence created are named as the class name where the annotation is used. This can be modified by providing the value-to-value attribute of these annotations.

For the best fit, use **`@Service`** when you are interacting with a database via an interface or having calculations. Use **`@Repository`** when you have a database where you need to perform **Create, Retrieve, Update, and Delete** (**CRUD**) operations as internally any interface annotated with **`@Repository`** injects the database handling code and throws database-related runtime exceptions. **`@Controller`** can be used in conjunction with **`@ResponseBody`** for creating APIs and making them accessible to use services provided by an application.

Spring Boot annotations

In addition to the annotations in the Spring framework, Spring Boot also provides few annotations as follows:

@EnableAutoConfiguration

This annotation is very useful in terms of the working of Spring Boot under the hood. This annotation enables auto-configuration of the Spring application context which detects all the beans which you want to use within the application for which the dependency is included. Auto-configuration classes are usually applied on the classes that are included in the class path and the beans which you have created. In *Chapter 3, Spring Boot Starter Dependencies and Auto-Configuration*, we have seen examples where we learned about **`spring-boot-starter-web`** and **`spring-boot-starter-data-jpa`**. *How does the Spring Framework know that few classes or beans needs to be instantiated?* If we use **`starter-web`**, *how does it know how to create a web server for Tomcat?*

The answer lies in the auto-configuration which got active due to this annotation and created a bean of the **`TomcatServletWebServerFactory`** class and stored it in the **`ServletWebServerFactory`** instance.

Taking another example of **`spring-boot-starter-data-jpa`**, the application failed with the console logs stating that **`Failed to determine a suitable driver class`**. The reason for this error lies where Spring tries to create **`DataSourceConfiguration`** when the **`DataSource`** bean is not available and hence, the error is thrown from the **`org.springframework.boot.autoconfigure.jdbc.DataSourceProperties.deter-`**

mineDriverClassName() method where it doesn't find the driver class name for loading into the classpath.

Auto-configuration tries to be as intelligent as possible and will back away for the errors once we start giving proper configurations. The **@EnableAutoConfiguration** annotation is packaged along with the **@SpringBootApplication** annotation by default. It is recommended that you use the **@EnableAutoConfiguration** annotation at the root of project in order to scan all the packages and sub-packages in search of beans.

The auto-configuration will easily understand that the beans that are loaded into the application where the annotations such as **@Conditional** (**@ConditionOnClass**, **@ConditionOnClass**, **@ConditionOnBean**, **@ConditionOnMissingBean,** and so on) are configured.

@SpringBootApplication

This annotation is a combination of three annotations: **@EnableAutoConfiguration**, **@SpringBootConfiguration**, and **@ComponentScan**. This makes it easier to use the preceding annotations by using a single annotation. This indicates a **@Configuration** class that has one or more **@Bean** methods and also triggers **@EnableAutoConfiguration** and **@ComponentScan**. This annotation should be used only once and should be present at the root of the source code to enable scanning to all packages and sub-packages in search of beans.

The snippet for **@SpringBootApplication** is as follows:

```
@Target(ElementType.TYPE)
@Retention(RetentionPolicy.RUNTIME)
@Documented
@Inherited
@SpringBootConfiguration
@EnableAutoConfiguration
@ComponentScan(excludeFilters = { @Filter(type = FilterType.CUSTOM, classes = TypeExcludeFilter.class),
        @Filter(type = FilterType.CUSTOM, classes = AutoConfiguration
        ExcludeFilter.class) })
public @interface SpringBootApplication {
 //some methods
}
```

@SpringBootConfiguration

This is a specialized **@Configuration** annotation that can be used above **SpringBootApplication**. It should be also used only once throughout the source code. After the global release of *Spring Boot 1.4*, the **@Configuration** in the **@SpringBootApplication** annotation got replaced with the **@SpringBootConfiguration** annotation.

Spring task execution annotations

The following are the few annotations that are used for scheduling tasks and taking the decision to create a separate thread for its execution:

@Async

This annotation is used to mark a method to start a separate thread for its asynchronous execution. The return type for the **@Async** methods are restricted to have **void** or **Future**. The @**Async** is not supported on methods that are declared within a @**Configuration** class. To understand this with a simple async call to a service, let's create two classes named as **AsyncService.java** and **TService.java**.

The snippet for **AsyncService.java** is as follows:

```
package com.author.kickstart.service;
import java.util.concurrent.CompletableFuture;
import java.util.concurrent.Future;
import org.slf4j.Logger;
import org.slf4j.LoggerFactory;
import org.springframework.scheduling.annotation.Async;
import org.springframework.stereotype.Service;

@Service
public class AsyncService {
    private static final Logger log = LoggerFactory.getLogger(AsyncSer-
    vice.class);

    @Async
    public Future<String> doSomethingAsync() {
```

```
        log.info("Async Method called");
        return CompletableFuture.completedFuture("Completed");
    }
}
```

In the preceding source code for **AsyncService.java,** we will use **SLF4J logger** for logging purpose. We also created a method **doSomethingAsync()** which has some operations that are required to be executed asynchronously. Here, we will log the message and return a future type of response which contains a String.

We will call the **doSomethingAsync()** method from the **TService** class by autowiring the **AsyncService** class. The snippet for the same is as follows:

```
package com.author.kickstart.service;
import java.util.concurrent.Future;
import org.slf4j.Logger;
import org.slf4j.LoggerFactory;
import org.springframework.beans.factory.annotation.Autowired;
import org.springframework.boot.CommandLineRunner;
import org.springframework.stereotype.Service;

@Service
public class TService implements CommandLineRunner {
     private static final Logger log = LoggerFactory.getLogger(TService.
       class);
    @Autowired
    AsyncService asyncService;

    @Override
    public void run(String... args) throws Exception {
        Future<String> future = asyncService.doSomethingAsync();
        log.info(future.get());
    }

}
```

The **TService** class implements the **CommandLineRunner** interface for which we need to override the **run()** method. This **run()** methods gets executed after the beans are created successfully. In the definition of the **run()** method, we will call the **doSomethingAsync()** method of **AsyncService** and store the response in the **Future** type. We will also log the response of **Future** in the same class. Let's now build the application and execute the **SpringBootApplication**. The following console log will be seen after the successful startup:

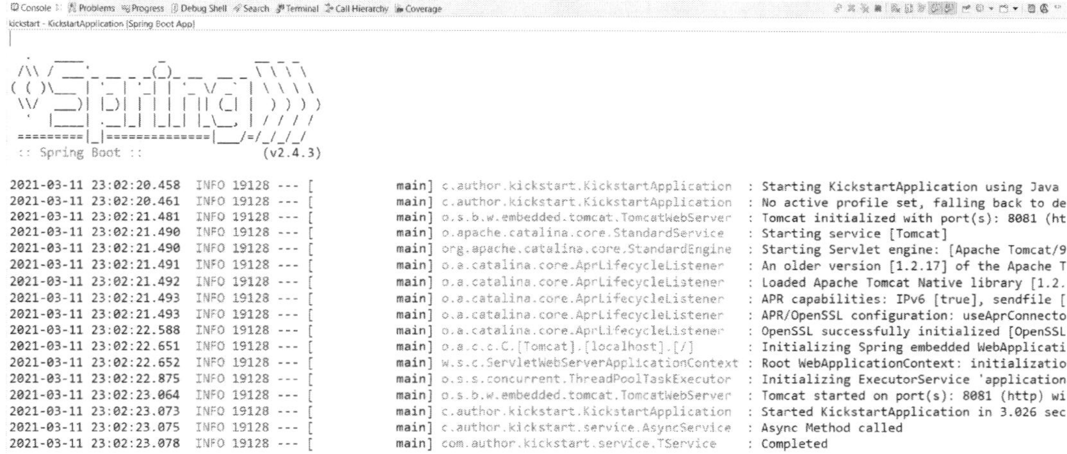

Figure 4.1: *Console logs for Async method*

Congrats, we just executed the async method in our application! Wait a second, *is there something wrong?*

Notice that the logs for **AsyncService** are in the **main** thread. However, this is not called asynchronously. It started its execution on the main thread. But don't worry this can be executed on a separate thread by enabling async operations wherever async methods are called. For this to accomplish, use the **@EnableAsync** annotation in the **TService** class as follows:

```
package com.author.kickstart.service;
import java.util.concurrent.Future;
import org.slf4j.Logger;
import org.slf4j.LoggerFactory;
import org.springframework.beans.factory.annotation.Autowired;
import org.springframework.boot.CommandLineRunner;
import org.springframework.scheduling.annotation.EnableAsync;
import org.springframework.stereotype.Service;
```

```
@Service
@EnableAsync
public class TService implements CommandLineRunner {
```

And rebuild the application and start the **SpringBootApplication**:

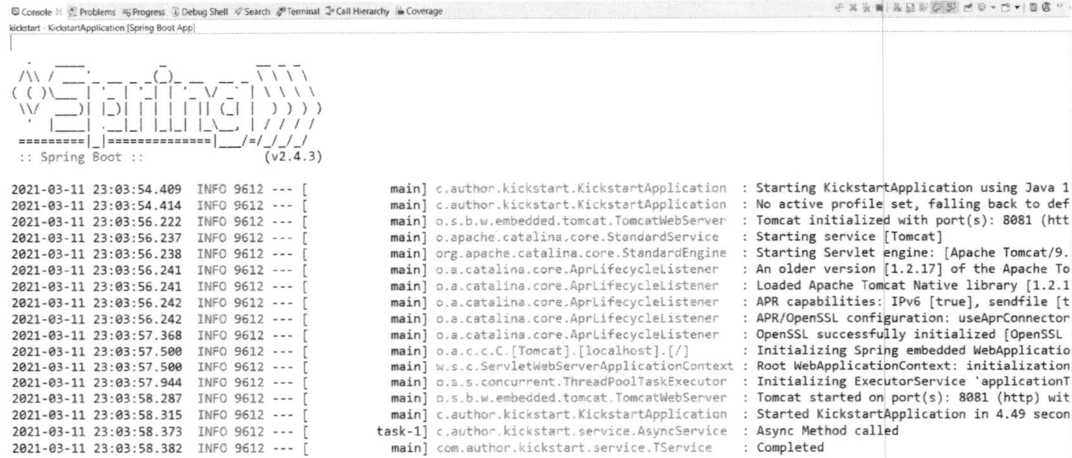

Figure 4.2: Console logs for Async method with EnableAsync

Now notice the thread for **AsyncService**. It starts the execution of the async method on a different thread other than the main thread.

Now we are able to understand the async method executions. The thread name **task-1** can be customized according to our needs and this logging pattern would be understood in *Chapter 9, Logging*.

@EnableScheduling

It enables the Spring's task execution capability. In Spring, you can schedule a task to run on periodic timings automatically. The **@EnableScheduling** annotation enables detection of any **@Scheduled** annotations used. All the scheduled tasks are invoked on separate threads so that it does not interrupt the execution for running threads. There can be two uses of this annotation as shown in the following examples:

- Combination of **@Configuration** and **@EnableScheduling** in conjunction with the **@Scheduled** task. The following is the code for **MTask.java**:

  ```
  package com.author.kickstart.tasks;
  import java.util.Date;
  ```

```
import org.slf4j.Logger;
import org.slf4j.LoggerFactory;
import org.springframework.scheduling.annotation.Scheduled;

public class MTask {
    private static final Logger log = LoggerFactory.getLogger(MTask.
    class);

    @Scheduled(fixedDelay = 1 * 60 * 1000)
    public void doSomethingPeriodically() {
        log.info("Task Executed at:" + new Date());
    }

}
```

And now create **AppConfig.java** as follows:

```
package com.author.kickstart.configuration;
import org.springframework.context.annotation.Bean;
import org.springframework.context.annotation.Configuration;
import org.springframework.scheduling.annotation.EnableScheduling;
import com.author.kickstart.tasks.MTask;

@Configuration
@EnableScheduling
public class AppConfig {
    @Bean
    public MTask mTask() {
        return new MTask();
    }
}
```

When we compile this code and start the execution of the Spring Boot application, the following logs will be displayed in the console:

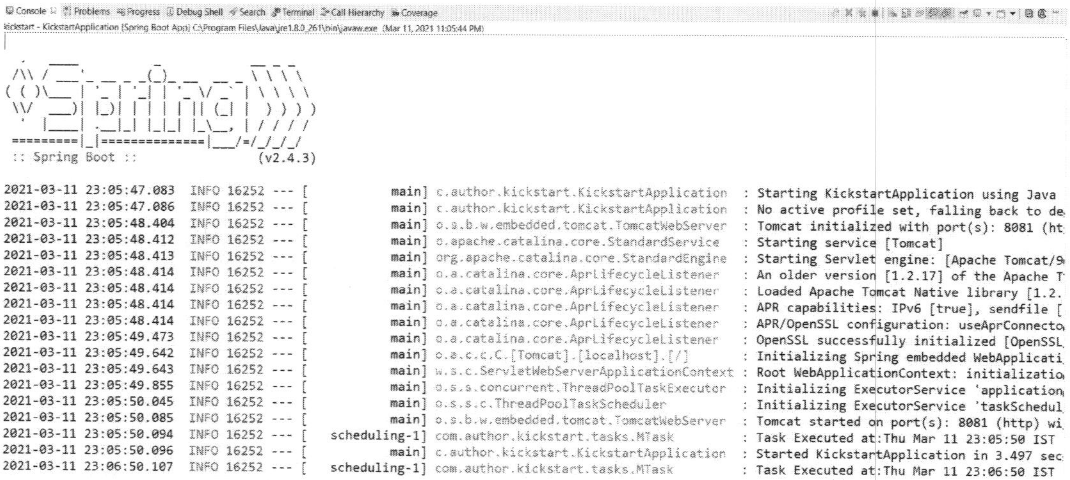

```
Console  Problems  Progress  Debug Shell  Search  Terminal  Call Hierarchy  Coverage
kickstart - KickstartApplication [Spring Boot App] C:\Program Files\Java\jre1.8.0_261\bin\javaw.exe (Mar 11, 2021 11:05:44 PM)

  .   ____          _            __ _ _
 /\\ / ___'_ __ _ _(_)_ __  __ _ \ \ \ \
( ( )\___ | '_ | '_| | '_ \/ _` | \ \ \ \
 \\/  ___)| |_)| | | | | || (_| |  ) ) ) )
  '  |____| .__|_| |_|_| |_\__, | / / / /
 =========|_|==============|___/=/_/_/_/
 :: Spring Boot ::                (v2.4.3)

2021-03-11 23:05:47.083  INFO 16252 --- [           main] c.author.kickstart.KickstartApplication  : Starting KickstartApplication using Java
2021-03-11 23:05:47.086  INFO 16252 --- [           main] c.author.kickstart.KickstartApplication  : No active profile set, falling back to de
2021-03-11 23:05:48.404  INFO 16252 --- [           main] o.s.b.w.embedded.tomcat.TomcatWebServer  : Tomcat initialized with port(s): 8081 (ht
2021-03-11 23:05:48.412  INFO 16252 --- [           main] o.apache.catalina.core.StandardService   : Starting service [Tomcat]
2021-03-11 23:05:48.413  INFO 16252 --- [           main] org.apache.catalina.core.StandardEngine  : Starting Servlet engine: [Apache Tomcat/9
2021-03-11 23:05:48.414  INFO 16252 --- [           main] o.a.catalina.core.AprLifecycleListener   : An older version [1.2.17] of the Apache T
2021-03-11 23:05:48.414  INFO 16252 --- [           main] o.a.catalina.core.AprLifecycleListener   : Loaded Apache Tomcat Native library [1.2.
2021-03-11 23:05:48.414  INFO 16252 --- [           main] o.a.catalina.core.AprLifecycleListener   : APR capabilities: IPv6 [true], sendfile [
2021-03-11 23:05:48.414  INFO 16252 --- [           main] o.a.catalina.core.AprLifecycleListener   : APR/OpenSSL configuration: useAprConnecto
2021-03-11 23:05:49.473  INFO 16252 --- [           main] o.a.catalina.core.AprLifecycleListener   : OpenSSL successfully initialized [OpenSSL
2021-03-11 23:05:49.642  INFO 16252 --- [           main] o.a.c.c.C.[Tomcat].[localhost].[/]       : Initializing Spring embedded WebApplicati
2021-03-11 23:05:49.643  INFO 16252 --- [           main] w.s.c.ServletWebServerApplicationContext : Root WebApplicationContext: initializatio
2021-03-11 23:05:49.855  INFO 16252 --- [           main] o.s.s.concurrent.ThreadPoolTaskExecutor  : Initializing ExecutorService 'application
2021-03-11 23:05:50.045  INFO 16252 --- [           main] o.s.s.c.ThreadPoolTaskScheduler          : Initializing ExecutorService 'taskSchedul
2021-03-11 23:05:50.085  INFO 16252 --- [           main] o.s.b.w.embedded.tomcat.TomcatWebServer  : Tomcat started on port(s): 8081 (http) wi
2021-03-11 23:05:50.094  INFO 16252 --- [   scheduling-1] com.author.kickstart.tasks.MTask         : Task Executed at:Thu Mar 11 23:05:50 IST
2021-03-11 23:05:50.096  INFO 16252 --- [           main] c.author.kickstart.KickstartApplication  : Started KickstartApplication in 3.497 sec
2021-03-11 23:06:50.107  INFO 16252 --- [   scheduling-1] com.author.kickstart.tasks.MTask         : Task Executed at:Thu Mar 11 23:06:50 IST
```

Figure 4.3: *Console logs for scheduled task*

- Combination of **@Configuration** and **@EnableScheduling** with the **@Scheduled** task. The following is the code for **AppConfig.java**:

```
package com.author.kickstart.configuration;
import java.util.Date;
import org.slf4j.Logger;
import org.slf4j.LoggerFactory;
import org.springframework.context.annotation.Configuration;
import org.springframework.scheduling.annotation.EnableScheduling;
import org.springframework.scheduling.annotation.Scheduled;

@Configuration
@EnableScheduling
public class AppConfig {
    private static final Logger log = LoggerFactory.getLogger(AppConfig.
    class);

    @Scheduled(fixedDelay = 1 * 60 * 1000)
    public void doSomethingPeriodically() {
        log.info("Task Executed at:" + new Date());
    }
```

```
}
```

Here, there will be no need to create tasks separately. The output of the preceding snippet is as follows:

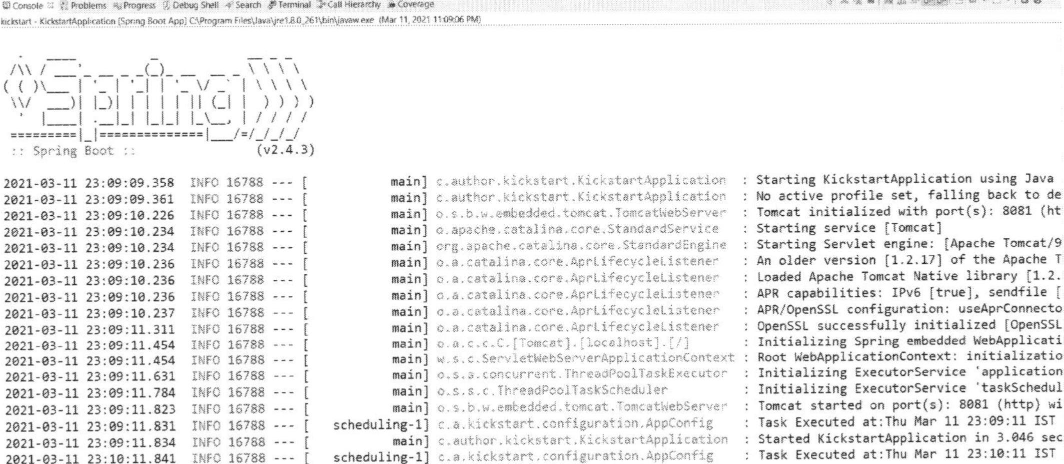

Figure 4.4: Console logs for scheduled task in same config class

@Scheduled

This annotation is used to mark the method to be scheduled at a given period of time. There are several attributes for triggering the task and any one of them should be used at a time. For example, **`cron`**, **`fixedDelay`**, and **`fixedRate`**. The method annotated with **`@Scheduled`** will not return anything and does not take any argument. All the scheduled tasks are registered in **`ScheduledAnnotationBeanPostProcessor`** manually or by having the **`@EnableScheduling`** annotation. The several attributes which the **`@Scheduled`** annotation takes are as follows:

- **`cron`**: It takes a **`cron`** string expression which is similar to UNIX-based **`cron`** in the format of the second, minute, hour, day of month, month, and day of week. The format is read from left to right. For example, **`@Scheduled(cron = "0 * * * * MON-FRI")`** means once per minute on weekdays at **`0`**th second.
- **`zone`**: This attribute is used to define the time zone when the task should be invoked. It takes the value of **`TimeZone`**. By default, it's the server time zone.
- **`fixedDelay`**: It executes the method with a fixed period of time in milliseconds between the end of the last invocation and the start of the next. For example, **`@Scheduled(fixedDelay = 5 * 60 * 1000)`** will execute in every 5 minutes of the interval.

- **fixedDelayString**: It is the same as **fixedDelay** but differs in the value which is provided as the String. For example, **@Scheduled(fixedDelayString = "10000")** will execute in every **10** seconds.
- **fixedRate**: It executes the method with a fixed period of time in milliseconds between the invocations, that is, it doesn't wait for the prior task to get completed. For example, **@Scheduled(fixedRate = 5 * 60 * 1000)** will execute in every **5** minutes regardless of the status of the already executed task.
- **fixedRateString**: It is the same as **fixedRate** but differs in the value which is provided as the String. For example, **@Scheduled(fixedRateString = "10000")** will execute in every **10** seconds.
- **initialDelay**: It provides a delay in execution before the first execution of a **fixedRate** or **fixedDelay**. For example, **@Scheduled(fixedRate = 5 * 60 * 1000, initialDelay = 3 * 60 * 1000)** will execute in every **5** minutes but with a starting delay of **3** minutes.

Spring profiles annotations

Going forward to advancement of microservices, the running profile can be changed by managing different profiles in **application*.properties** or **application*.yml** configuration files. These profiles can be selected at runtime depending on the value of **spring.profiles.active**. The following annotations are used for profiling:

@Profile

This annotation takes a string or string array for the names of the environment for which the following class should have its bean created. In other words, if you want to create a production-specific configuration, you can create the production-specific configuration class and annotate with **@Profile("prod").** For example, for using prod-specific configuration, create the following class with annotation:

```
package com.author.kickstart.configuration;

import org.springframework.context.annotation.Profile;

import org.springframework.stereotype.Component;


@Component

@Profile("prod")

public class ProdDatabaseConfig {


}
```

For supporting all kinds of non-prod configurations, you can have the following configuration:

```
package com.author.kickstart.configuration;
import org.springframework.context.annotation.Profile;
import org.springframework.stereotype.Component;

@Component
@Profile({"dev","qa"})
public class NonProdDatabaseConfig {

}
```

By default, Spring follows the naming convention of picking up the configuration files by **`application-*.properties`** or **`application-*.yml`** where * is the name of the environment.

You can always change the environment configuration by overriding the value of **`spring.profiles.active`**. For example, if you want to execute your application in the **`dev`** environment and have **`application-dev.yml`** to be configured at startup, then provide VM level arguments as **`-Dspring.profiles.active=dev`** while starting the application. More hands-on for selecting profiles at runtime would be explained in the upcoming chapters where we will build our REST microservices and deploy them into cloud.

@ActiveProfiles

This annotation takes a string or string array for the names of the environment for which we will run test cases to load those profiles. This annotation takes the decision to load the active bean definition profiles to be used for loading the **`ApplicationContext`** for test classes.

Jakarta annotations

The following are the annotations placed within the **`Jakarta-annotations-api`** library. These annotations are called within the lifecycle of the bean.

@PreDestroy

This annotation when used on top of a method notifies the container to call this method whenever the bean is no longer required to be referenced. Generally, this method contains the logic to release the resources used by the class. For example:

```
package com.author.kickstart.configuration;
import javax.annotation.PreDestroy;
import org.springframework.context.annotation.Profile;
import org.springframework.stereotype.Component;

@Component
@Profile({ "dev", "qa" })
public class NonProdDatabaseConfig {
    //some code

    @PreDestroy
    public void destroy() {
        connection.close();
    }
}
```

@PostConstruct

This annotation when used on top of methods notifies the container to invoke the method whenever the bean instantiation is completed for any initialization to bean properties. This method must be invoked before the class is put into service. In earlier examples, we have seen the usage of **`@Primary`** and **`@Qualifier`**. Here, we used this annotation to get invoked after the bean is created successfully with all of its dependencies injected. Here is the snippet:

```
package com.author.kickstart.service;
import javax.annotation.PostConstruct;
import org.springframework.beans.factory.annotation.Autowired;
import org.springframework.context.annotation.Configuration;
import com.author.kickstart.interfaces.Vehicle;

@Configuration
public class VehicleService {
    @Autowired
    Vehicle vehicle;
```

```
    @PostConstruct
    public void service() {
        System.out.println("Wheels for vehicle:" + vehicle.getWheels());
    }

}
```

Conclusion

In this chapter, we discussed a lot of annotations which we would be surely useful when you develop the Spring Boot application. There will be more set of annotations that would be explained in the upcoming chapters along with the examples. In the next chapter, we will create a Spring Boot application that will be fetch data from the database and cache them using Spring Cache for frequent access.

Points to remember

- For many annotations provided, the Spring framework gets into action by enabling them by the **`@Enable`** annotation. For example, **`@EnableScheduling`**, **`@EnableAsync`**.
- **`@Service`**, **`@Component`**, and **`@Configuration`** can be used interchangeably but it is a practice to use it at appropriate places.

Questions

1. How can you change the name of the bean?
2. How would you know if any keyword is used in an annotation?
3. How do you identify which annotation can be used at the top of class, fields?
4. Which are the stereotype annotations?
5. How do you schedule a Spring job?
6. Does the Spring job support the return type?
7. How does Spring know where to look for beans?

CHAPTER 5
Working with Spring Data JPA and Caching

We hope that you now have the knowledge on the power of Spring Boot. So far, we have understood various annotations that can be used to develop an application using Spring Boot. From now on, we would be actually diving deep into application development. In this chapter, we will create a Spring Boot application which interacts with the database and caches data that is frequently used.

Structure

In this chapter, we will discuss the following topics:

- Accessing relational data using **JdbcTemplate** with the in-memory database
- Accessing relational data using Spring Data JPA with the in-memory database
- MySQL and its installation
- Accessing relational data using Spring Data JPA with MySQL
- Query methods in Spring Data JPA
- Caching

Objective

After studying this unit, you should be able to learn how to interact with the database and understand how cache is the commonly used data.

Accessing relational data using JdbcTemplate with the in-memory database

We will start from the very first step, that is, **Spring Initializr** to create skeletons for the project:

1. Browse the following website:

   https://start.spring.io

   Create a basic project with dependencies - **H2 Database** and **Spring Data JDBC** as shown in the following screenshot:

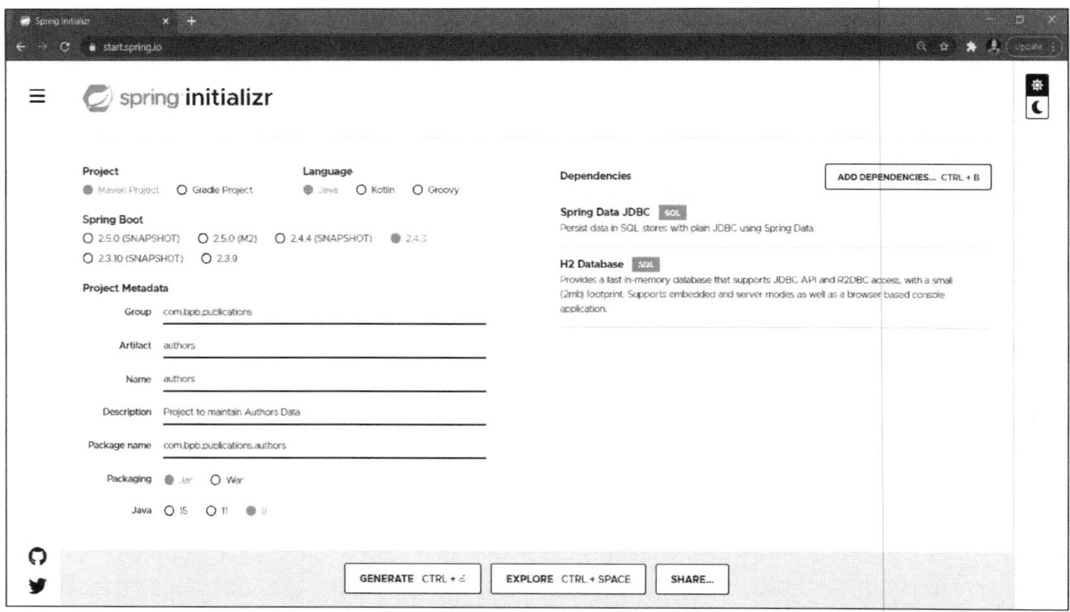

Figure 5.1: *Spring Initializr for H2 database with Spring data JDBC*

2. Once the project configuration is done, as shown in the preceding screenshot, click on `GENERATE` and extract the `.zip` file into your Spring tool suite workspace. Let the workspace get refreshed with dependencies in STS and the project explorer will look like the following screenshot:

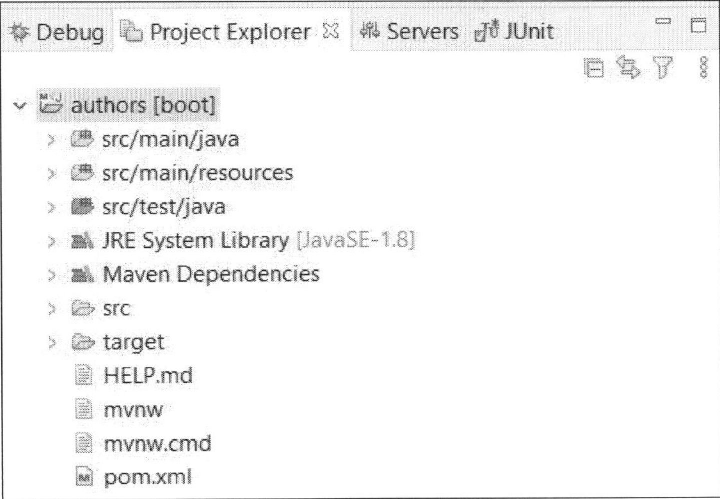

***Figure 5.2**: Project explorer*

You can also add **`spring-boot-devtools`** dependencies if you want to reload the running application after every change in files and classes which are there in classpath.

Here, we will use the H2 database that provides a fast in-memory database that supports JDBC APIs and R2DBC access, with a small footprint. It's an open-source database that supports embedded and server modes and transaction support. It is useful for small applications or can be used to create MVP applications for testing on a small scale.

3. Here is how the **`pom.xml`** file looks like:

```
<?xml version="1.0" encoding="UTF-8"?>
<project xmlns="http://maven.apache.org/POM/4.0.0" xmlns:xsi="http://www.w3.org/2001/XMLSchema-instance"
    xsi:schemaLocation="http://maven.apache.org/POM/4.0.0 https://maven.apache.org/xsd/maven-4.0.0.xsd">
    <modelVersion>4.0.0</modelVersion>
    <parent>
        <groupId>org.springframework.boot</groupId>
        <artifactId>spring-boot-starter-parent</artifactId>
        <version>2.4.3</version>
        <relativePath/> <!-- lookup parent from repository -->
    </parent>
```

```
<groupId>com.bpb.publications</groupId>
<artifactId>authors</artifactId>
<version>0.0.1-SNAPSHOT</version>
<name>authors</name>
<description>Project to maintain Authors Data</description>

<properties>
    <java.version>1.8</java.version>
</properties>

<dependencies>
    <dependency>
        <groupId>org.springframework.boot</groupId>
        <artifactId>spring-boot-starter-data-jdbc</artifactId>
    </dependency>

    <dependency>
        <groupId>com.h2database</groupId>
        <artifactId>h2</artifactId>
        <scope>runtime</scope>
    </dependency>
    <dependency>
        <groupId>org.springframework.boot</groupId>
        <artifactId>spring-boot-starter-test</artifactId>
        <scope>test</scope>
    </dependency>
</dependencies>

<build>
    <plugins>
        <plugin>
            <groupId>org.springframework.boot</groupId>
            <artifactId>spring-boot-maven-plugin</artifactId>
```

```
        </plugin>
    </plugins>
</build>

</project>
```

4. Let us now create the **Author.java** class in the model package and few attributes for the author as shown in the following code:

```
package com.bpb.publications.authors.model;

public class Author {
    private long id;
    private String firstName;
    private String lastName;

    public long getId() {
        return id;
    }

    public void setId(long id) {
        this.id = id;
    }

    public String getFirstName() {
        return firstName;
    }

    public void setFirstName(String firstName) {
        this.firstName = firstName;
    }

    public String getLastName() {
        return lastName;
    }
```

```
    public void setLastName(String lastName) {
        this.lastName = lastName;
    }

    public Author(long id, String firstName, String lastName) {
        super();
        this.id = id;
        this.firstName = firstName;
        this.lastName = lastName;
    }

}
```

5. To store and retrieve the records in the database, we can create a service class which autowires the **JdbcTemplate** object into the **jdbcTemplate** variable and this variable can now access the database. This **jdbcTemplate** now acts as an interface between the Java program and database. The following list of lines for the service class has the code to save and retrieve the record:

```
package com.bpb.publications.authors.service;

import java.util.ArrayList;
import java.util.List;

import javax.annotation.PostConstruct;

import org.slf4j.Logger;
import org.slf4j.LoggerFactory;
import org.springframework.beans.factory.annotation.Autowired;
import org.springframework.jdbc.core.JdbcTemplate;
import org.springframework.stereotype.Service;

import com.bpb.publications.authors.model.Author;

@Service
public class AuthorService {
```

```
    private static final Logger log = LoggerFactory.
    getLogger(AuthorService.class);

    @Autowired
    JdbcTemplate jdbcTemplate;

    @PostConstruct
    public void postConstruct() {
        Author author1 = new Author("Mark", "Shogun");
        Author author2 = new Author("Ruskin", "Handa");
        List<Author> authors = new ArrayList<>();
        authors.add(author1);
        authors.add(author2);
        log.info("Creating tables");
        jdbcTemplate.execute("DROP TABLE author IF EXISTS");
        jdbcTemplate.execute("CREATE TABLE author(" + "id SERIAL,
        first_name varchar(255), last_name varchar(255))");
        authors.forEach(author -> jdbcTemplate.update("INSERT
        INTO author(first_name, last_name) VALUES (?,?)",
                author.getFirstName(), author.getLastName()));
        log.info("Records Saved");
        //retrieve saved records.
        log.info("Retrieving records");
        authors = jdbcTemplate.query("select * from author",
             (rs, rowNum) -> new Author(rs.getString("first_name"),
rs.getString("last_name")));
        authors.forEach(a -> log.info(a.getFirstName() + " " +
        a.getLastName()));

    }
}
```

The reason why **JdbcTemplate** gets autowired automatically is due to the inclusion of the **spring-data-jdbc** dependency in `pom.xml`.

To avoid SQL injection attacks, we have provided **?** to substitute our values provided in the **update()** method of **jdbcTemplate**. The following are the console logs after building the application and executing it:

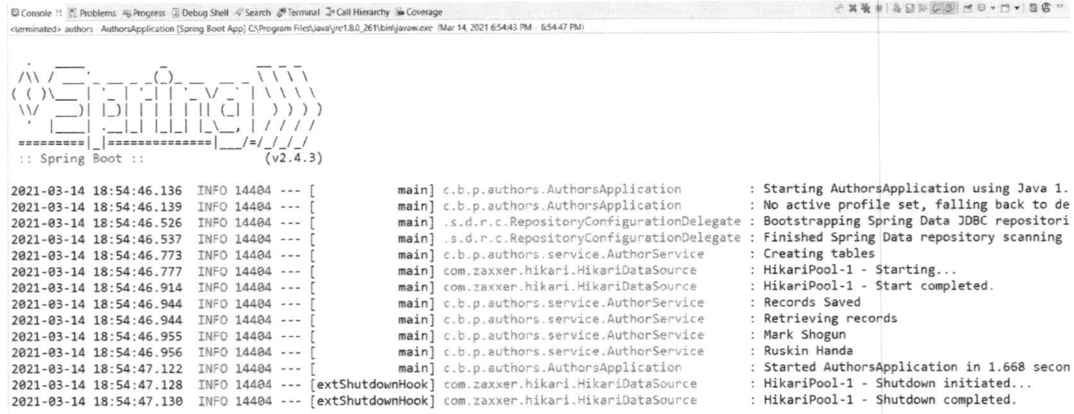

***Figure 5.3**: Console logs for Spring data JDBC*

Wow! Isn't it easy to create a simple JDBC Client application? Let us learn Spring data JPA in next section.

Accessing relational data using Spring data JPA with the in-memory database

We will use the same example as explained in the previous section where we used **JdbcTemplate** for saving and querying the data but now, we will use Spring Data JPA. Before we move towards another approach, let us discuss the basic fundamentals of JPA:

- JPA is **Java Persistence API** that is a specification related to saving or persisting Java objects which are required by businesses or applications to be saved. JPA is just a guideline which all **Object Relational Mapping** (**ORM**) models should follow like hibernate. Initially, JPA was limited to relational SQL, but now it has advanced to accommodate NoSQL operations as well.
- We will take the same example as discussed in the previous section, so that we can understand the differences while using **spring-data-jdbc** and **spring-data-jpa**.

  Replace the **spring-data-jdbc** dependency with **spring-data-jpa** in **pom.xml** as follows:

```
<dependency>
    <groupId>org.springframework.boot</groupId>
    <artifactId>spring-boot-starter-data-jpa</artifactId>
</dependency>
```

- Next, we modify the classes that we wish to persist or save in the database. For all those classes that are required to be saved are called entities and to let the framework know that this is the class we want to save, annotate the class with **`@Entity.`** This annotation comes as part of the **`javax.persistence`** API library which gets included while including the preceding dependency.

  The following code shows how we can define a simple entity class:

```
package com.bpb.publications.authors.model;

import java.io.Serializable;

import javax.persistence.Entity;
import javax.persistence.Id;
import javax.persistence.Table;

@Entity
@Table(name = "bpb_author")
public class Author implements Serializable {
    @Id
    private long id;
    private String firstName;
    private String lastName;

    public long getId() {
        return id;
    }

    public void setId(long id) {
        this.id = id;
    }
```

```
    public String getFirstName() {
        return firstName;
    }

    public void setFirstName(String firstName) {
        this.firstName = firstName;
    }

    public String getLastName() {
        return lastName;
    }

    public void setLastName(String lastName) {
        this.lastName = lastName;
    }

    public Author(String firstName, String lastName) {
        super();
        this.firstName = firstName;
        this.lastName = lastName;
    }

    @Override
    public String toString() {
        return "Author [id=" + id + ", firstName=" + firstName + ",
        lastName=" + lastName + "]";
    }

    public Author() {
        super();
    }

}
```

- `@Entity` annotation on a class denotes that it is a JPA entity. If `@Table` is not used, then the table is created with the same name as that of the `Entity` class. For overriding the database table name, you can provide a value to name the attribute of `@Table`.

  For JPA to know the ID, we annotate the attribute ID of the author class with the `@Id` annotation. We also need a default constructor as JPA uses it.

  We will now create an interface that extends `CrudRepository` to perform CRUD operations on the JPA entity. The following is the syntax:

```
package com.bpb.publications.authors.repository;

import org.springframework.data.repository.CrudRepository;

import com.bpb.publications.authors.model.Author;


public interface AuthorRepository extends CrudRepository<Author,
Long>{


}
```

- The `CrudRepository` interface takes the name of the entity and its primary key. Here, we have `Author` and `Long`, as the datatype of the ID attribute is long. `CrudRepository` has the following methods for helping the framework to perform the needed operations:
  - o `<S extends T> S save(S);`
  - o `<S extends T> java.lang.Iterable<S> saveAll(java.lang.Iterable<S>);`
  - o `java.util.Optional<T> findById(ID);`
  - o `boolean existsById(ID);`
  - o `java.lang.Iterable<T> findAll();`
  - o `java.lang.Iterable<T> findAllById(java.lang.Iterable<ID>);`
  - o `long count();`
  - o `void deleteById(ID);`
  - o `void delete(T);`
  - o `void deleteAll(java.lang.Iterable<? extends T>);`
  - o `void deleteAll();`

  The definitions of the preceding methods are already implemented within the framework. We just need to use the methods. *Isn't that simple?*

- Further, we will create a `service` class to access the database. The following snippet shows how to store the entity information and retrieve them using the **`AuthorRepository`** methods:

```
package com.bpb.publications.authors.service;

import javax.annotation.PostConstruct;

import org.slf4j.Logger;
import org.slf4j.LoggerFactory;
import org.springframework.beans.factory.annotation.Autowired;
import org.springframework.stereotype.Service;

import com.bpb.publications.authors.model.Author;
import com.bpb.publications.authors.repository.AuthorRepository;

@Service
public class AuthorService {

    private static final Logger log = LoggerFactory.
    getLogger(AuthorService.class);

    @Autowired
    AuthorRepository authorRepository;

    @PostConstruct
    public void postConstruct() {
        Author author = new Author();
        author.setId(1L);
        author.setFirstName("Mark");
        author.setLastName("Shogun");
        log.info("Performing saving data into database");
        authorRepository.save(author);
```

```
        log.info("Retrieve all records");
        log.info("Authors :" + authorRepository.findAll());
    }
}
```

- Let us now build the application using clean install from Maven build options and execute the application from STS. The following are the console logs after starting the application:

```
Console  Problems  Progress  Debug Shell  Search  Terminal  Call Hierarchy  Coverage
<terminated> authors - AuthorsApplication [Spring Boot App] C:\Program Files\Java\jre1.8.0_261\bin\javaw.exe (Mar 15, 2021 12:30:38 PM – 12:30:52 PM)

 ::                (v2.4.3)

:43.631  INFO 7552 --- [           main] c.b.p.authors.AuthorsApplication         : Starting AuthorsApplication using Java 1.8.0_261 on shagun
:43.635  INFO 7552 --- [           main] c.b.p.authors.AuthorsApplication         : No active profile set, falling back to default profiles: d
:44.551  INFO 7552 --- [           main] .s.d.r.c.RepositoryConfigurationDelegate : Bootstrapping Spring Data JPA repositories in DEFAULT mode
:44.749  INFO 7552 --- [           main] .s.d.r.c.RepositoryConfigurationDelegate : Finished Spring Data repository scanning in 162 ms. Found
:45.540  INFO 7552 --- [           main] com.zaxxer.hikari.HikariDataSource       : HikariPool-1 - Starting...
:46.832  INFO 7552 --- [           main] com.zaxxer.hikari.HikariDataSource       : HikariPool-1 - Start completed.
:46.975  INFO 7552 --- [           main] o.hibernate.jpa.internal.util.LogHelper  : HHH000204: Processing PersistenceUnitInfo [name: default]
:47.045  INFO 7552 --- [           main] org.hibernate.Version                    : HHH000412: Hibernate ORM core version 5.4.28.Final
:48.369  INFO 7552 --- [           main] o.hibernate.annotations.common.Version   : HCANN000001: Hibernate Commons Annotations {5.1.2.Final}
:48.631  INFO 7552 --- [           main] org.hibernate.dialect.Dialect            : HHH000400: Using dialect: org.hibernate.dialect.H2Dialect
:51.172  INFO 7552 --- [           main] o.h.e.t.j.p.i.JtaPlatformInitiator       : HHH000490: Using JtaPlatform implementation: [org.hibernat
:51.187  INFO 7552 --- [           main] j.LocalContainerEntityManagerFactoryBean : Initialized JPA EntityManagerFactory for persistence unit
:51.648  INFO 7552 --- [           main] c.b.p.authors.service.AuthorService      : Performing saving data into database
:51.777  INFO 7552 --- [           main] c.b.p.authors.service.AuthorService      : Retrieve all records
:51.905  INFO 7552 --- [           main] c.b.p.authors.service.AuthorService      : Authors :[Author [id=1, firstName=Mark, lastName=Shogun]]
:52.076  INFO 7552 --- [           main] c.b.p.authors.AuthorsApplication         : Started AuthorsApplication in 8.97 seconds (JVM running fo
:52.098  INFO 7552 --- [extShutdownHook] j.LocalContainerEntityManagerFactoryBean : Closing JPA EntityManagerFactory for persistence unit 'def
:52.099  INFO 7552 --- [extShutdownHook] .SchemaDropperImpl$DelayedDropActionImpl : HHH000477: Starting delayed evictData of schema as part of
:52.136  INFO 7552 --- [extShutdownHook] com.zaxxer.hikari.HikariDataSource       : HikariPool-1 - Shutdown initiated...
:52.154  INFO 7552 --- [extShutdownHook] com.zaxxer.hikari.HikariDataSource       : HikariPool-1 - Shutdown completed.
```

***Figure 5.4:** Console logs for Spring data JPA*

- The Spring framework scans for Spring data repositories and whenever it encounters an interface inheriting **`CrudRepository`** or any superset of **`JPARepository`**, it knows that there are repositories created within the project.
- It uses the default dialect: **`org.hibernate.dialect.H2Dialect`** as we have included the H2 database dependency. We will write more methods in **`AuthorRepository`** for more access to the database with different queries in the next section where we will use the MySQL database.

Just like how we have MySQL Workbench or MySQL CLI to view records, we also have the H2 console to view the H2 dashboard. The H2 console is disabled by default in Spring which can be enabled by putting `spring.h2.console.enabled=true` into properties and browsing `/h2-console` in the web-based application by having any of the web containers installed like Tomcat.

MySQL and its installation

MySQL is an open source relational DBMS system that uses **Structured Query Language (SQL)**. You can skip this section if you already have MySQL installed on your system.

The following procedure will allow you to install the MySQL server on your system:

1. Browse the following website:

   https://dev.mysql.com/downloads/windows/installer/8.0.html

   Select the MySQL version or alternatively browse the following website for downloading MySQL directly:

   https://dev.mysql.com/get/Downloads/MySQLInstaller/mysql-installer-community-8.0.21.0.msi

2. Click on the **`Download`** button as shown in the following screenshot:

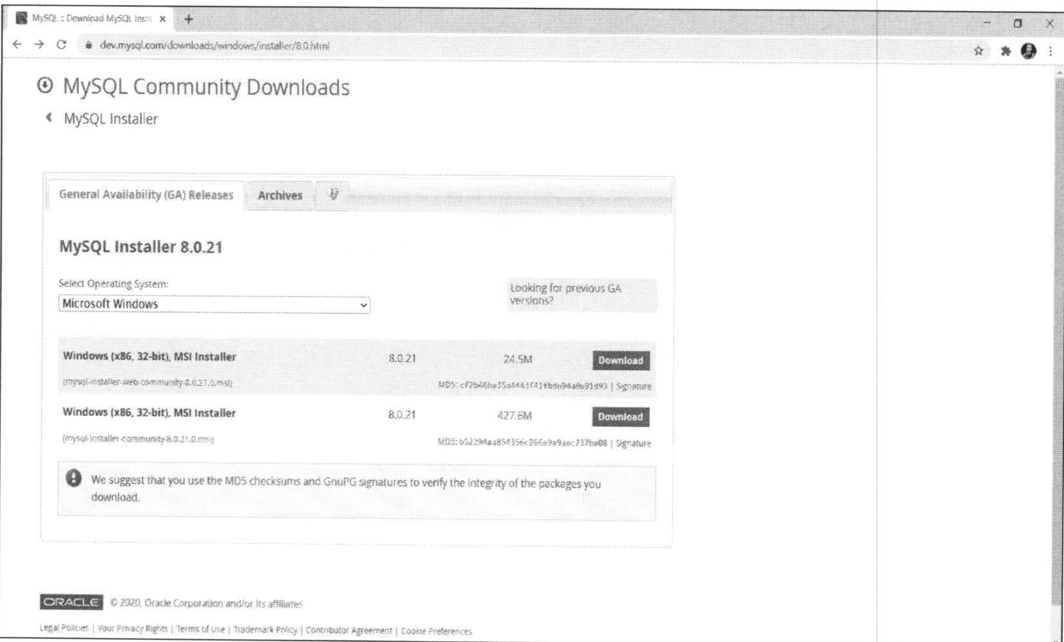

***Figure** 5.5: MySQL Download*

3. Open the installer file **`mysql-installer-community-8.0.21.0.msi`** and wait for the installer to appear on the screen:

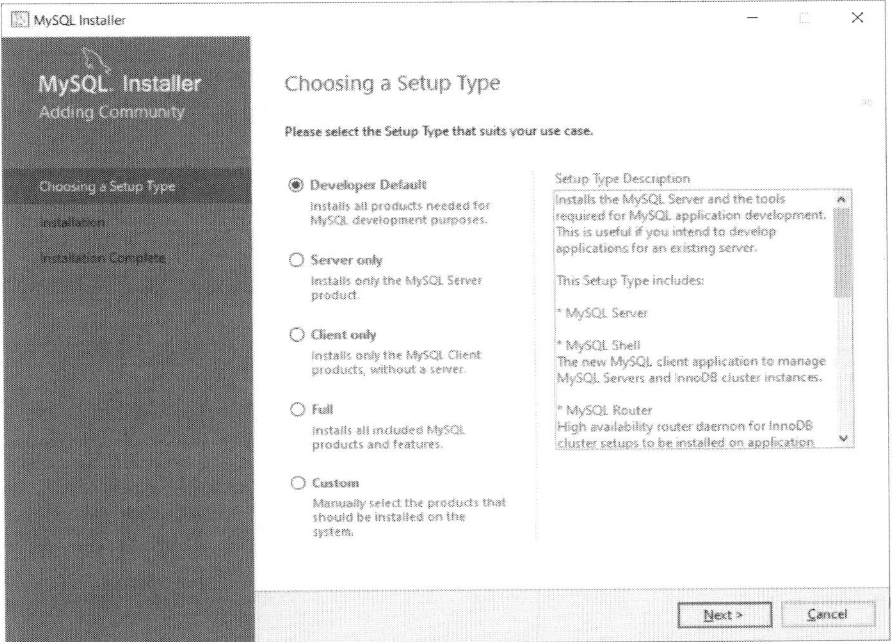

Figure 5.6: *MySQL setup type*

4. Click on **`Next`**.
5. You will see the following screen with the list of items that would be installed:

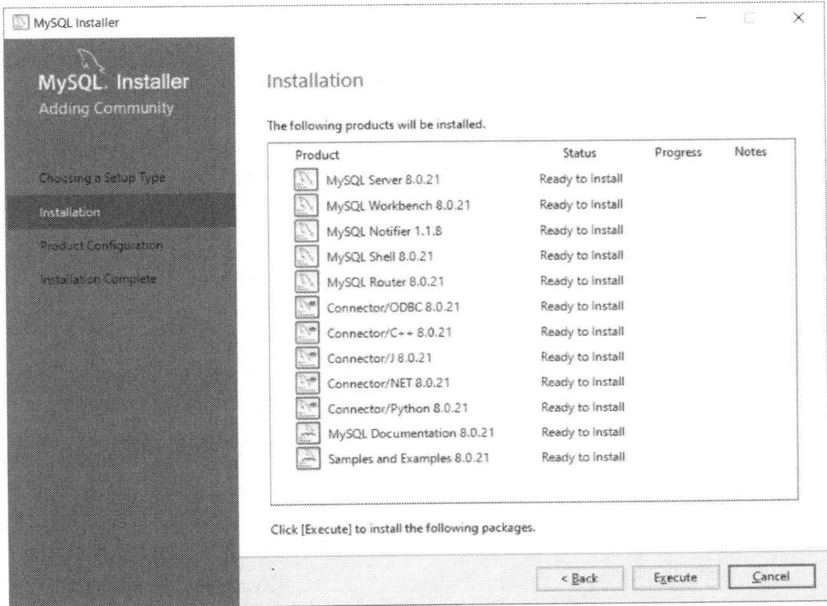

Figure 5.7: *MySQL tools installation*

6. Click on **Execute** and wait for the installation to complete.
7. Click on **Next** when the installation of tools is done.
8. For configuring the tools, click on **Next** when you see the following screen:

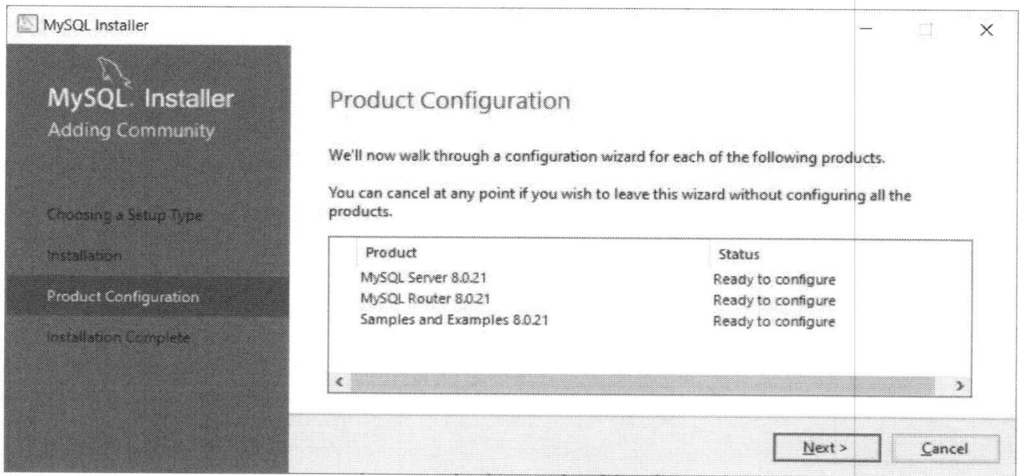

Figure 5.8*: MySQL configuration*

9. Select standalone MySQL server / Classic MySQL replication.
10. The server port can be modified at this step, and this port **3306** can be used later in our Spring Boot application:

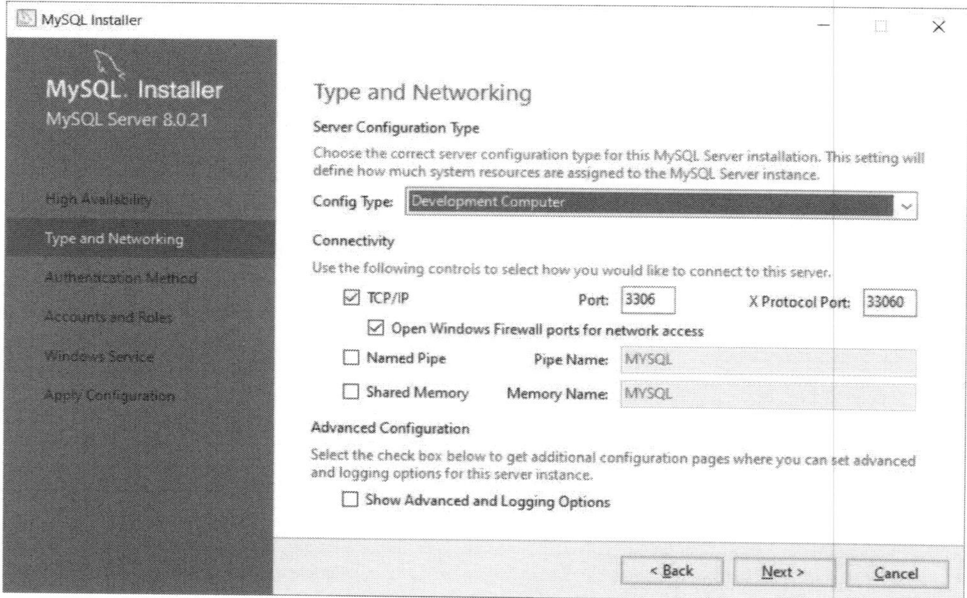

Figure 5.9*: Port configuration*

Now, provide a strong password of your choice and click on **Next** till you reach here:

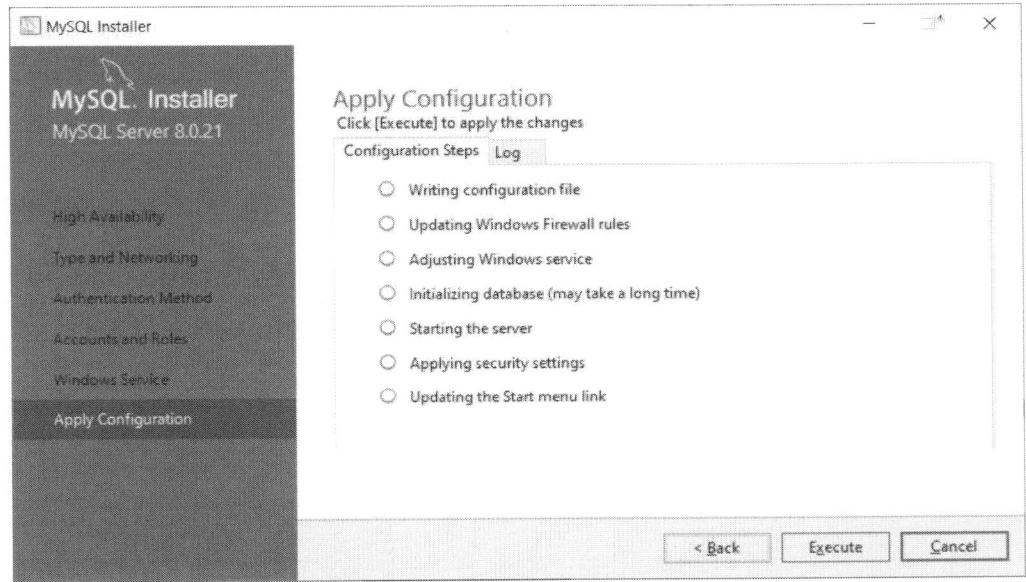

Figure 5.10: MySQL apply configuration

11. Click on **Execute**.
12. Finally, you will see the following installation screen:

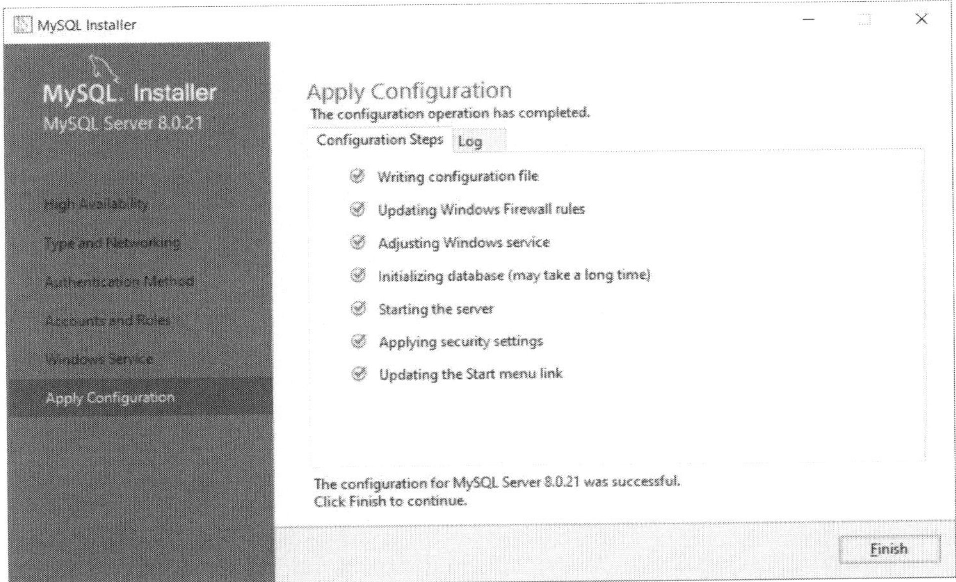

Figure 5.11: MySQL installation complete

13. Click on **Finish**.

We have now installed the MySQL server successfully.

To test the server setup correctly, wait for MySQL Workbench to launch after the installation is done and run the following SQL command:

```
select * from mysql.user
```

Now, let us connect our application with the MySQL database in the following section.

Accessing relational data using Spring data JPA with MySQL

In the earlier section, we have seen how to retrieve data using Spring data JPA and the H2 in-memory database. As the in-memory database has some limitations due to size and other factors, it's recommended that you have a dedicated database as it will persist data for a longer duration rather than evicting data on restart. Here, we will take MySQL as the underlying RDBMS and remove the H2 dependency. The following steps are followed for using MySQL instead of H2:

- Since we have included the following H2 dependency in preceding section, we will remove this:

  ```
  <dependency>
      <groupId>com.h2database</groupId>
      <artifactId>h2</artifactId>
      <scope>runtime</scope>
  </dependency>
  ```

  Add the following dependency for the MySQL connector Java:

  ```
  <dependency>
      <groupId>mysql</groupId>
      <artifactId>mysql-connector-java</artifactId>
      <scope>runtime</scope>
  </dependency>
  ```

- In *Chapter 3, Spring Boot Starter Dependencies and Auto-Configuration*, we faced an error - **Failed to determine a suitable driver class**. Now, we will learn how to resolve this error by including the following properties in the **application.yml** configuration file:

```
spring:
  jpa:
    hibernate:
      ddl-auto: update
    properties:
      hibernate:
        dialect: org.hibernate.dialect.MySQL8Dialect
  datasource:
    url: jdbc:mysql://localhost:3306/bpb
    username: root
    password: root
```

- Execute the following SQL command on MySQL Workbench to create the database:

  ```
  create database bpb;
  ```

- Now, build the application using the Maven command – **`mvn clean install`** and start the Spring Boot application. You will see the following logs in the console:

```
Console  Problems  Progress  Debug Shell  Search  Terminal  Call Hierarchy  Coverage
<terminated> authors - AuthorsApplication [Spring Boot App] C:\Program Files\Java\jre1.8.0_261\bin\javaw.exe (Mar 15, 2021 12:50:10 PM – 12:50:19 PM)

 (v2.4.3)

33  INFO 6108 --- [    main] c.b.p.authors.AuthorsApplication          : Starting AuthorsApplication using Java 1.8.0_261 on shagun-pc w
39  INFO 6108 --- [    main] c.b.p.authors.AuthorsApplication          : No active profile set, falling back to default profiles: defaul
56  INFO 6108 --- [    main] .s.d.r.c.RepositoryConfigurationDelegate : Bootstrapping Spring Data JPA repositories in DEFAULT mode.
71  INFO 6108 --- [    main] .s.d.r.c.RepositoryConfigurationDelegate : Finished Spring Data repository scanning in 94 ms. Found 1 JPA
46  INFO 6108 --- [    main] o.hibernate.jpa.internal.util.LogHelper  : HHH000204: Processing PersistenceUnitInfo [name: default]
89  INFO 6108 --- [    main] org.hibernate.Version                    : HHH000412: Hibernate ORM core version 5.4.28.Final
03  INFO 6108 --- [    main] o.hibernate.annotations.common.Version   : HCANN000001: Hibernate Commons Annotations {5.1.2.Final}
92  INFO 6108 --- [    main] com.zaxxer.hikari.HikariDataSource       : HikariPool-1 - Starting...
81  INFO 6108 --- [    main] com.zaxxer.hikari.HikariDataSource       : HikariPool-1 - Start completed.
95  INFO 6108 --- [    main] org.hibernate.dialect.Dialect            : HHH000400: Using dialect: org.hibernate.dialect.MySQL8Dialect
22  INFO 6108 --- [    main] o.h.e.t.j.p.i.JtaPlatformInitiator       : HHH000490: Using JtaPlatform implementation: [org.hibernate.eng
52  INFO 6108 --- [    main] j.LocalContainerEntityManagerFactoryBean : Initialized JPA EntityManagerFactory for persistence unit 'defa
05  INFO 6108 --- [    main] c.b.p.authors.AuthorsApplication          : Started AuthorsApplication in 4.962 seconds (JVM running for 7.
```

***Figure 5.12**: MySQL Spring Boot console logs*

- Here, we will use the hibernate dialect as **`org.hibernate.dialect.MySQL8Dialect`**. We had provided the following configuration:

```
spring:
  jpa:
    hibernate:
      ddl-auto: update
```

- The Spring Boot application will update the database with the entities defined in our application. If there exists no table named in entities or if there are entities existing in the application but not created in the database, the application will automatically create the tables with the required attributes.

  To know how exactly the JPA framework fires the query, you can turn on the SQL query logging by turning on the `show-sql` option from properties file as per the syntax: `spring.jpa.show-sql=true`.

- To verify the table creation, execute the following command in MySQL Workbench:

  ```
  desc bpb_author;
  ```

  The output of the preceding command is displayed in the following screenshot:

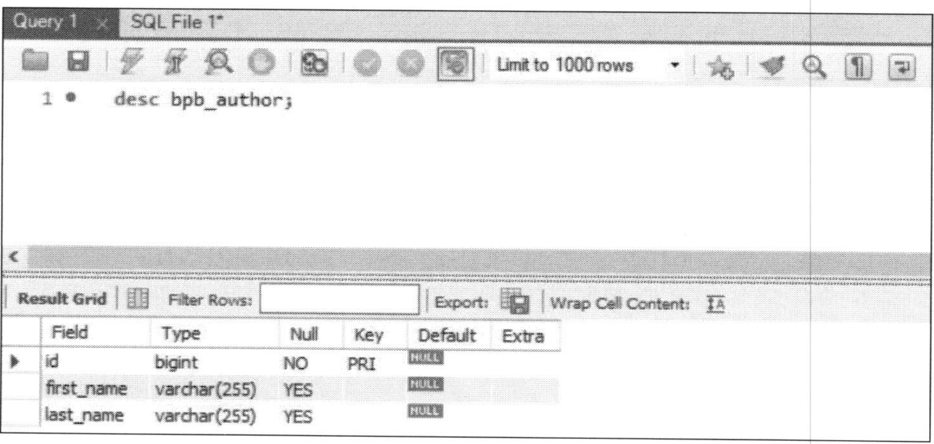

***Figure 5.13:** Verify table structure*

- To stop the database metadata or structure to update on each execution, you can change the **`ddl-auto`** to **`none`**. The following are the possible values of **`ddl-auto property:`** **`create`**, **`create-drop`**, **`none`**, **`update`**, and **`validate`**. The values are self- explanatory.
- Now you can restore the **`AuthorService`** code as follows:

  ```
  package com.bpb.publications.authors.service;
  import javax.annotation.PostConstruct;
  import org.slf4j.Logger;
  import org.slf4j.LoggerFactory;
  ```

```
import org.springframework.beans.factory.annotation.Autowired;
import org.springframework.stereotype.Service;
import com.bpb.publications.authors.model.Author;
import com.bpb.publications.authors.repository.AuthorRepository;

@Service
public class AuthorService {

    private static final Logger log = LoggerFactory.
    getLogger(AuthorService.class);

    @Autowired
    AuthorRepository authorRepository;

    @PostConstruct
    public void postConstruct() {
        Author author = new Author();
        author.setId(1L);
        author.setFirstName("Mark");
        author.setLastName("Shogun");
        log.info("Performing saving data into database");
        authorRepository.save(author);
        log.info("Retrieve all records");
        log.info("Authors :" + authorRepository.findAll());
    }
}
```

- There is no change in this file. We only changed the underlying database from in-memory H2 to MySQL RDBMS. By executing the application with the service class in place, the records will be inserted into the database and can be verified by executing the following command:

```
select * from bpb_author;
```

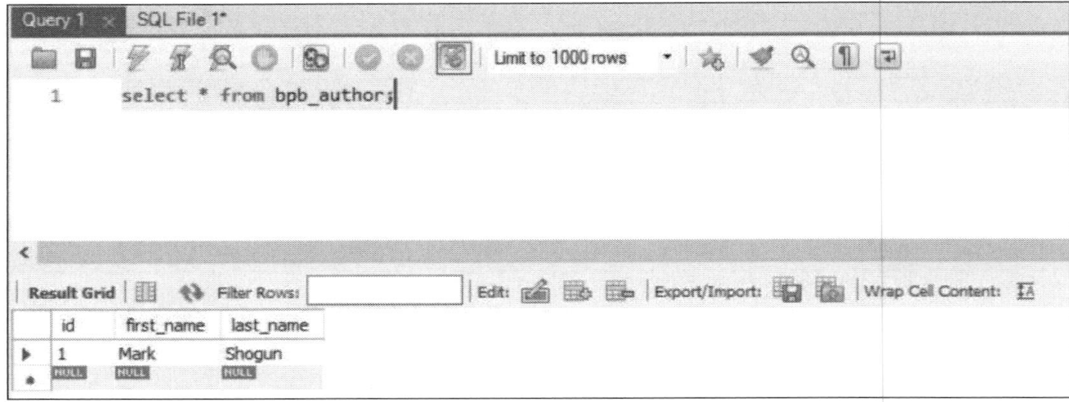

***Figure 5.14**: Verify table data*

- We have now understood how to include various dependencies and store them in the database. We have also seen that we need minimal configuration for the database while using Spring data JPA. In the next section, we will look at the different query methods that can be created for fetching data while using Spring data JPA.

Query methods in Spring data JPA

We can use the **findAll()** method of the **CrudRepository** interface to retrieve all records from the database for a given entity. There are certain methods that can be created having a defined naming convention for the method name to retrieve records as per the developers' choice like finding all records having the first name provided as per demand.

For example, we wish to retrieve all records where the user asks for the first name. Here, we need to declare the query method on the interface which extends **Repository** like **CrudRepository**. The following is the syntax:

```
package com.bpb.publications.authors.repository;
import java.util.List;
import org.springframework.data.repository.CrudRepository;
import com.bpb.publications.authors.model.Author;

public interface AuthorRepository extends CrudRepository<Author, Long> {

    List<Author> findByFirstName(String name);
}
```

Now, we can use the **findByFirstName()** method provided a **String** argument has the value of the first name so that the database can be queried by the first name. For instance:

```
List<Author> authors = authorRepository.findByFirstName("Mark");
```

The following are the use cases where we can have such methods on the interface:

- To retrieve all records having the first name and last name:

  ```
  List<Author> findByFirstNameAndLastName(String firstName, String lastName);
  ```

- To retrieve all records having either the first name or last name:

  ```
  List<Author> findByFirstNameOrLastName(String firstName, String lastName);
  ```

- Ordering the **resultSet** received:

  ```
  List<Author> findByLastNameOrderByFirstNameAsc(String lastName);
  ```

- Limiting the **resultSet** received:

  ```
  List<Author> findFirst10ByLastname (String lastName);
  ```

- Writing your own queries:

  ```
  @Query(value = "select * from bpb_author where first_name=?", nativeQuery = true)
  Author fetchByFirstName(String firstName);
  ```

- Search by property values.
- Let us modify the structure of entities. We will introduce a new entity **ZipCode** to store the Zip code for authors. The following are the code snippets:

  ZipCode.java

  ```
  package com.bpb.publications.authors.model;
  import java.io.Serializable;
  import javax.persistence.Entity;
  import javax.persistence.GeneratedValue;
  import javax.persistence.GenerationType;
  import javax.persistence.Id;


  @Entity
  public class ZipCode implements Serializable {
      @Id
  ```

```
    @GeneratedValue(strategy = GenerationType.AUTO)
    private long id;
    private String code;

    public ZipCode() {
        super();
        // TODO Auto-generated constructor stub
    }

    public String getCode() {
        return code;
    }

    public void setCode(String code) {
        this.code = code;
    }

    @Override
    public String toString() {
        return “ZipCode [id=” + id + “, code=” + code + “]”;
    }

}
```

ZipCodeRepository.java

```
package com.bpb.publications.authors.repository;
import org.springframework.data.repository.CrudRepository;
import com.bpb.publications.authors.model.ZipCode;

public interface ZipCodeRepository extends CrudRepository<ZipCode,
Long> {

}
```

Author.java

```
package com.bpb.publications.authors.model;

import java.io.Serializable;

import javax.persistence.Entity;
import javax.persistence.Id;
import javax.persistence.ManyToOne;
import javax.persistence.Table;

@Entity
@Table(name = "bpb_author")
public class Author implements Serializable {
    @Id
    private long id;
    private String firstName;
    private String lastName;
    @ManyToOne
    private ZipCode zipCode;

    public long getId() {
        return id;
    }

    public void setId(long id) {
        this.id = id;
    }

    public String getFirstName() {
        return firstName;
    }

    public void setFirstName(String firstName) {
        this.firstName = firstName;
```

```
    }

    public String getLastName() {
        return lastName;
    }

    public void setLastName(String lastName) {
        this.lastName = lastName;
    }

    public Author(String firstName, String lastName) {
        super();
        this.firstName = firstName;
        this.lastName = lastName;
    }

    public ZipCode getZipCode() {
        return zipCode;
    }

    public void setZipCode(ZipCode zipCode) {
        this.zipCode = zipCode;
    }

    public Author() {
        super();
    }

    @Override
    public String toString() {
        return "Author [id=" + id + ", firstName=" + firstName + ",
        lastName=" + lastName + ", zipCode=" + zipCode
                + "]";
    }
```

```
}
```

AuthorRepository.java

```
package com.bpb.publications.authors.repository;
import java.util.List;
import org.springframework.data.repository.CrudRepository;
import com.bpb.publications.authors.model.Author;

public interface AuthorRepository extends CrudRepository<Author,
Long> {

    List<Author> findByFirstName(String name);

    List<Author> findByZipCodeCode(String code);
}
```

AuthorService.java

```
package com.bpb.publications.authors.service;
import java.util.List;
import javax.annotation.PostConstruct;
import org.slf4j.Logger;
import org.slf4j.LoggerFactory;
import org.springframework.beans.factory.annotation.Autowired;
import org.springframework.stereotype.Service;
import com.bpb.publications.authors.model.Author;
import com.bpb.publications.authors.model.ZipCode;
import com.bpb.publications.authors.repository.AuthorRepository;
import com.bpb.publications.authors.repository.ZipCodeRepository;

@Service
public class AuthorService {

    private static final Logger log = LoggerFactory.
    getLogger(AuthorService.class);
```

```
    @Autowired
    AuthorRepository authorRepository;

    @Autowired
    ZipCodeRepository zipCodeRepository;

    @PostConstruct
    public void postConstruct() {

        Author author = new Author();
        author.setId(1L);
        author.setFirstName("Mark");
        author.setLastName("Shogun");
        ZipCode zipCode = new ZipCode();
        zipCode.setCode("400000");
        zipCodeRepository.save(zipCode);
        author.setZipCode(zipCode);
        log.info("Performing saving data into database");
        authorRepository.save(author);

        log.info("Retrieve all records");
        List<Author> authors = authorRepository.
        findByZipCodeCode("400000");
        log.info("Authors :" + authors);
    }
}
```

The following are the key differences from what we had earlier:

- Introduced the new entity **ZipCode** to store zip codes.
- Introduced the **@GeneratedValue** annotation to keep on generating auto generated incremented values for the identifier.
- Adding a new attribute **zipCode** having a mapping of **@ManyToOne** on the top of the variable. This says that **Author** is mapped to **ZipCode** entity in many-to-one relationship.

- The post construct method is modified to store the zip code in the database first and then linked to the variable with the author to have zip code references.

Now, when we look at the database structure, it looks like the following screenshot:

```
mysql> select * from zip_code;
+----+--------+
| id | code   |
+----+--------+
|  1 | 400000 |
+----+--------+
1 row in set (0.00 sec)

mysql> desc zip_code;
+-------+--------------+------+-----+---------+-------+
| Field | Type         | Null | Key | Default | Extra |
+-------+--------------+------+-----+---------+-------+
| id    | bigint       | NO   | PRI | NULL    |       |
| code  | varchar(255) | YES  |     | NULL    |       |
+-------+--------------+------+-----+---------+-------+
2 rows in set (0.00 sec)

mysql> select * from bpb_author;
+----+------------+-----------+-------------+
| id | first_name | last_name | zip_code_id |
+----+------------+-----------+-------------+
|  1 | Mark       | Shogun    |           1 |
+----+------------+-----------+-------------+
1 row in set (0.00 sec)

mysql> desc bpb_author;
+-------------+--------------+------+-----+---------+-------+
| Field       | Type         | Null | Key | Default | Extra |
+-------------+--------------+------+-----+---------+-------+
| id          | bigint       | NO   | PRI | NULL    |       |
| first_name  | varchar(255) | YES  |     | NULL    |       |
| last_name   | varchar(255) | YES  |     | NULL    |       |
| zip_code_id | bigint       | YES  | MUL | NULL    |       |
+-------------+--------------+------+-----+---------+-------+
4 rows in set (0.00 sec)
```

***Figure 5.15**: Table structure after adding zip code*

Now that we have understood different ways to access the database and query on them, we will now look into caching the commonly used data.

Caching

Caching the data is required when you know that there is frequent access to data models or the data static to the environment from where the values are being fetched. Here, we will take authors' info that will be inserted first into the database on the application startup and then we will call methods of the **CrudRepository** interface to retrieve data. We will also understand the usage of cache when we look into the response times of the data retrieved from the cache and from the database directly.

To simulate the database response time, we will delay the return type object by few seconds.

The following is the modified **AuthorService.java** file where we will call the **loadData()** method to retrieve records each time from the database whenever requested:

```
package com.bpb.publications.authors.service;
import java.util.ArrayList;
import java.util.List;
import org.slf4j.Logger;
import org.slf4j.LoggerFactory;
import org.springframework.beans.factory.annotation.Autowired;
import org.springframework.stereotype.Service;
import com.bpb.publications.authors.model.Author;
import com.bpb.publications.authors.repository.AuthorRepository;

@Service
public class AuthorService {

    private static final Logger log = LoggerFactory.getLogger(Author
    Service.class);

    @Autowired
    AuthorRepository authorRepository;

    public List<Author> loadData() throws InterruptedException {
        Thread.sleep(3000);
        List<Author> authors = new ArrayList<>();
```

```
        authorRepository.findAll().forEach(authors::add);
        return authors;
    }
}
```

We can now create a runner class that will call the **run()** method which in turn invokes the **loadData()** of **AuthorService**. The following is the snippet of the **ApplicationRunner.java** class:

```
package com.bpb.publications.authors;
import java.util.Date;
import org.slf4j.Logger;
import org.slf4j.LoggerFactory;
import org.springframework.beans.factory.annotation.Autowired;
import org.springframework.boot.CommandLineRunner;
import org.springframework.stereotype.Component;

import com.bpb.publications.authors.service.AuthorService;

@Component
public class ApplicationRunner implements CommandLineRunner {

    private static final Logger log = LoggerFactory.getLogger(Applica-
      tionRunner.class);

    @Autowired
    AuthorService service;

    @Override
    public void run(String... args) throws Exception {
        log.info("Loading Data at time :" + new Date());
        service.loadData();
        log.info("Loading Data at time :" + new Date());
        service.loadData();
        log.info("Loading Data at time :" + new Date());
```

```
        service.loadData();
        log.info("Loading Data at time :" + new Date());
        service.loadData();
        log.info("Loading Data at time :" + new Date());
        service.loadData();
    }

}
```

Here, we have called the **loadData()** several times. The following are the console logs showing the time logs:

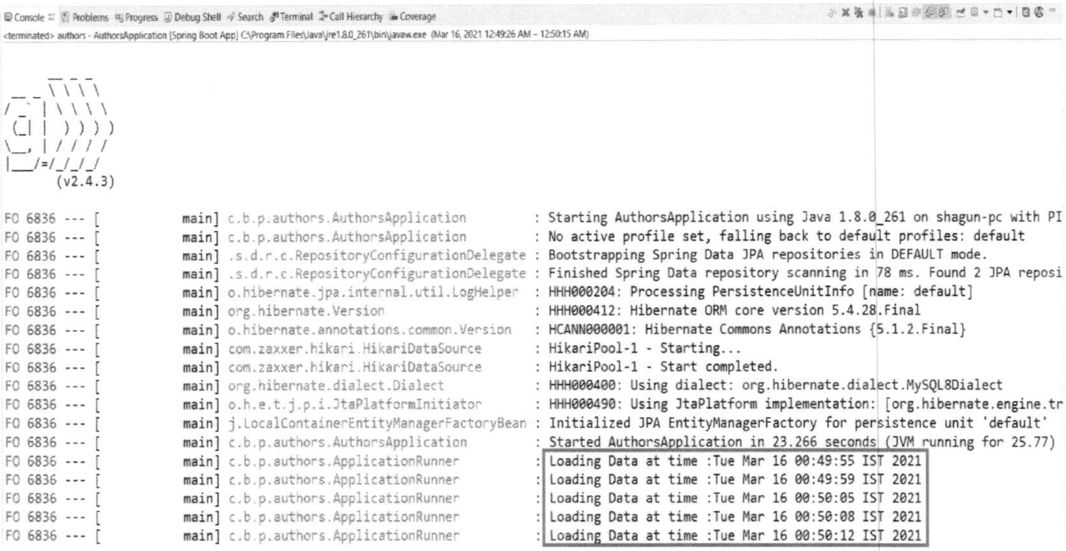

```
Console  Problems  Progress  Debug Shell  Search  Terminal  Call Hierarchy  Coverage
<terminated> authors - AuthorsApplication [Spring Boot App] C:\Program Files\Java\jre1.8.0_261\bin\javaw.exe (Mar 16, 2021 12:49:26 AM – 12:50:15 AM)

      ___
  __ _\ \ \ \
 / _` | \ \ \ \
 (_| |  ) ) ) )
 \__, | / / / /
 |___/=/_/_/_/
       (v2.4.3)

FO 6836 --- [           main] c.b.p.authors.AuthorsApplication         : Starting AuthorsApplication using Java 1.8.0_261 on shagun-pc with PI
FO 6836 --- [           main] c.b.p.authors.AuthorsApplication         : No active profile set, falling back to default profiles: default
FO 6836 --- [           main] .s.d.r.c.RepositoryConfigurationDelegate : Bootstrapping Spring Data JPA repositories in DEFAULT mode.
FO 6836 --- [           main] .s.d.r.c.RepositoryConfigurationDelegate : Finished Spring Data repository scanning in 78 ms. Found 2 JPA reposi
FO 6836 --- [           main] o.hibernate.jpa.internal.util.LogHelper  : HHH000204: Processing PersistenceUnitInfo [name: default]
FO 6836 --- [           main] org.hibernate.Version                    : HHH000412: Hibernate ORM core version 5.4.28.Final
FO 6836 --- [           main] o.hibernate.annotations.common.Version   : HCANN000001: Hibernate Commons Annotations {5.1.2.Final}
FO 6836 --- [           main] com.zaxxer.hikari.HikariDataSource       : HikariPool-1 - Starting...
FO 6836 --- [           main] com.zaxxer.hikari.HikariDataSource       : HikariPool-1 - Start completed.
FO 6836 --- [           main] org.hibernate.dialect.Dialect            : HHH000400: Using dialect: org.hibernate.dialect.MySQL8Dialect
FO 6836 --- [           main] o.h.e.t.j.p.i.JtaPlatformInitiator       : HHH000490: Using JtaPlatform implementation: [org.hibernate.engine.tr
FO 6836 --- [           main] j.LocalContainerEntityManagerFactoryBean : Initialized JPA EntityManagerFactory for persistence unit 'default'
FO 6836 --- [           main] c.b.p.authors.AuthorsApplication         : Started AuthorsApplication in 23.266 seconds (JVM running for 25.77)
FO 6836 --- [           main] c.b.p.authors.ApplicationRunner          : Loading Data at time :Tue Mar 16 00:49:55 IST 2021
FO 6836 --- [           main] c.b.p.authors.ApplicationRunner          : Loading Data at time :Tue Mar 16 00:49:59 IST 2021
FO 6836 --- [           main] c.b.p.authors.ApplicationRunner          : Loading Data at time :Tue Mar 16 00:50:05 IST 2021
FO 6836 --- [           main] c.b.p.authors.ApplicationRunner          : Loading Data at time :Tue Mar 16 00:50:08 IST 2021
FO 6836 --- [           main] c.b.p.authors.ApplicationRunner          : Loading Data at time :Tue Mar 16 00:50:12 IST 2021
```

***Figure 5.16**: Repetitive calls to database*

Here, you can see that there is a difference of **3** seconds due to hardcoded sleep time to produce a delay in sending the response. Usually, this response time depends on entities to the underlying databases and the number of records that a table stores verses the number of records that are being sent out using Java. Clearly, we see that each time the method is called it takes time to load the data and send it back. Thus, caching of the data is required now which will minimize the load time of records to a certain number where it feels like the data is loaded within no time.

To start with cache, import the following dependency into **`pom.xml`**:

```
<dependency>
  <groupId>org.springframework.boot</groupId>
  <artifactId>spring-boot-starter-cache</artifactId>
</dependency>
```

Now, we can enable cache on the method which actually retrieves the records by putting **`@Cacheable("authors")`** as shown in the following code:

```
@Cacheable("authors")
public List<Author> loadData() throws InterruptedException {
    Thread.sleep(3000);
    List<Author> authors = new ArrayList<>();
    authorRepository.findAll().forEach(authors::add);
    return authors;
}
```

The **@Cacheable** annotation says that the result of the method that is called can be cached.

To enable caching, we need to use **@EnableCaching** at the top of our Spring Boot application as shown in the following code:

```
@SpringBootApplication
@EnableCaching
public class AuthorsApplication {

    public static void main(String[] args) {
        SpringApplication.run(AuthorsApplication.class, args);
    }

}
```

Now, build the application and run it again. You will see the following logs where the time taken to retrieve the first record is **3** seconds and later on, there is no delay in retrieving records:

```
Console  Problems  Progress  Debug Shell  Search  Terminal  Call Hierarchy  Coverage
<terminated> authors - AuthorsApplication [Spring Boot App] C:\Program Files\Java\jre1.8.0_261\bin\javaw.exe (Mar 16, 2021 12:55:17 AM – 12:55:36 AM)

  .   ____          _            __ _ _
 /\\ / ___'_ __ _ _(_)_ __  __ _ \ \ \ \
( ( )\___ | '_ | '_| | '_ \/ _` | \ \ \ \
 \\/  ___)| |_)| | | | | || (_| |  ) ) ) )
  '  |____| .__|_| |_|_| |_\__, | / / / /
 =========|_|==============|___/=/_/_/_/
 :: Spring Boot ::                (v2.4.3)

..378  INFO 9976 --- [           main] c.b.p.authors.AuthorsApplication         : Starting AuthorsApplication using Java 1.8.0_261 on shagun-pc
..383  INFO 9976 --- [           main] c.b.p.authors.AuthorsApplication         : No active profile set, falling back to default profiles: defa
:.035  INFO 9976 --- [           main] .s.d.r.c.RepositoryConfigurationDelegate : Bootstrapping Spring Data JPA repositories in DEFAULT mode.
:.091  INFO 9976 --- [           main] .s.d.r.c.RepositoryConfigurationDelegate : Finished Spring Data repository scanning in 47 ms. Found 2 JP
:.882  INFO 9976 --- [           main] o.hibernate.jpa.internal.util.LogHelper  : HHH000204: Processing PersistenceUnitInfo [name: default]
:.988  INFO 9976 --- [           main] org.hibernate.Version                    : HHH000412: Hibernate ORM core version 5.4.28.Final
:.165  INFO 9976 --- [           main] o.hibernate.annotations.common.Version   : HCANN000001: Hibernate Commons Annotations {5.1.2.Final}
:.284  INFO 9976 --- [           main] com.zaxxer.hikari.HikariDataSource       : HikariPool-1 - Starting...
:.073  INFO 9976 --- [           main] com.zaxxer.hikari.HikariDataSource       : HikariPool-1 - Start completed.
:.103  INFO 9976 --- [           main] org.hibernate.dialect.Dialect            : HHH000400: Using dialect: org.hibernate.dialect.MySQL8Dialect
..833  INFO 9976 --- [           main] o.h.e.t.j.p.i.JtaPlatformInitiator       : HHH000490: Using JtaPlatform implementation: [org.hibernate.e
..865  INFO 9976 --- [           main] j.LocalContainerEntityManagerFactoryBean : Initialized JPA EntityManagerFactory for persistence unit 'de
:.647  INFO 9976 --- [           main] c.b.p.authors.AuthorsApplication         : Started AuthorsApplication in 11.943 seconds (JVM running for
:.649  INFO 9976 --- [           main] c.b.p.authors.ApplicationRunner          : Loading Data at time :Tue Mar 16 00:55:32 IST 2021
:.052  INFO 9976 --- [           main] c.b.p.authors.ApplicationRunner          : Loading Data at time :Tue Mar 16 00:55:36 IST 2021
:.052  INFO 9976 --- [           main] c.b.p.authors.ApplicationRunner          : Loading Data at time :Tue Mar 16 00:55:36 IST 2021
:.052  INFO 9976 --- [           main] c.b.p.authors.ApplicationRunner          : Loading Data at time :Tue Mar 16 00:55:36 IST 2021
:.053  INFO 9976 --- [           main] c.b.p.authors.ApplicationRunner          : Loading Data at time :Tue Mar 16 00:55:36 IST 2021
```

***Figure 5.17**: Cached data retrieval*

The following are few annotations related to the caching mechanism:

- **@Cacheable**: This is used to populate the cache based on the name passed to the annotation. For example: **@Cacheable("authors")**. This annotation when used stores the return value of the calling method.
- **@CacheEvict**: This annotation is used when we want to remove the unused data that is cached for a longer time to free out the memory used. Usage: **@CacheEvict(value = "authors", allEntries = true)**. This has the **allEntries** attribute which when is true will delete all entries in the cache.
- **@CachePut**: This annotation is used when we wish to update the cache without interfering with the execution of the method wherever called. This operation is useful when we want to update the database as well as the cache having the particular key. For example, **@CachePut(cacheNames="authors", key="#firstname")**.
- **@Caching**: This annotation can be used where we are having multiple caching annotations already in place. For example, **@Caching(evict = { @CacheEvict("authors"), @CacheEvict(cacheNames="authors", key="#p0") })**.
- **@CacheConfig**: This annotation is used at the top of the class to avoid specifying the name of cache again and again while using other caching annotations. For instance, the **AuthorService** class can be modified as follows:

```
@Service
```

```
@CacheConfig(cacheNames = "authors")
public class AuthorService {
   //some code
    @Cacheable
    public List<Author> loadData() throws InterruptedException {
      //some code
    }
}
```

Conclusion

In this chapter, we learned how to access the database and store data in the runtime database – **H2**, **persistent database MySQL**. We also learned how to install the MySQL database and do the Spring Boot configuration. Further, we looked into caching and viewed different annotations used in the caching mechanism.

In the next chapter, we will build a RESTFul microservice where we will create REST APIs and send data that is saved in the database as well as call external APIs.

Points to remember

- You can select any relational or NoSQL database to store the data. It is Spring Data JPA that will take care of the underlying queries that would be executed.
- If an application does not have a server like Tomcat, then that application with the database access shuts down after a minute.

Questions

1. How can you save data in the database?
2. How can you select all records from Spring data JPA?
3. How can you create custom query methods for filtering records?
4. How can you cache the data?
5. How can you auto-generate the value of a primary key using persistence API?
6. How do you mark an attribute primary key for the table?

CHAPTER 6
Building RESTFul Microservices

In the previous chapter, we used **Spring Data JPA** to interact with the database on startup. In real-world applications, there would be few use cases where the database queries are invoked at application startup and data is loaded into some Java collections, but *what if we want to extract data based on dynamic requests?* In this chapter, we will create a Spring Boot application where we will create RESTFul APIs to access databases and also interact with other microservices via APIs.

Structure

In this chapter, we will discuss the following topics:

- Creating RESTFul APIs
- Consuming RESTFul APIs
- Creating different profiles based on the environment
- Using Spring Boot actuators for getting telemetry data
- Custom health check indicators
- Exception handling using ControllerAdvice
- Service Discovery
- Using RestTemplate for calling APIs

- Routing a request via the API gateway with Spring Cloud Gateway
- Spring Cloud Gateway

Objectives

After studying this unit, you should be able to create and run a Spring Boot application in different profiling environments. You can get the application health using **actuator endpoints**. You will learn how to test RESTFul APIs using Postman and consume RESTFul APIs from other applications using RestTemplate.

Creating RESTful APIs

We will now create **Representational State Transfer** (**RESTful**) web APIs with Spring Boot. This REST style uses HTTP requests to access and use data. The request methods like **GET**, **POST**, **PUT**, and **DELETE** are most common types of requests that are created while accessing web applications. We will try to expose an API endpoint that accepts HTTP requests that returns required data in the form of JSON representation. Here, we will create several such endpoints which will create records in the database, read records, update records, and delete records. We will use different annotations which would be understood by the Spring web container for such operations by following steps:

1. Let's get started with creating **pom.xml**, models, repositories, services, and REST controllers. Our use case would be to create an application that gives data related to the book authored by **Author** that is published by **Publisher**.

   The following code is the skeleton for **pom.xml**:

```
<?xml version="1.0" encoding="UTF-8"?>
<project xmlns="http://maven.apache.org/POM/4.0.0"
    xmlns:xsi="http://www.w3.org/2001/XMLSchema-instance"
    xsi:schemaLocation="http://maven.apache.org/POM/4.0.0
    https://maven.apache.org/xsd/maven-4.0.0.xsd">
    <modelVersion>4.0.0</modelVersion>
    <parent>
        <groupId>org.springframework.boot</groupId>
        <artifactId>spring-boot-starter-parent</artifactId>
        <version>2.4.3</version>
        <relativePath /> <!-- lookup parent from repository -->
```

```
</parent>
<groupId>com.webservice</groupId>
<artifactId>Server</artifactId>
<version>0.0.1-SNAPSHOT</version>
<name>Web-Service</name>
<description>Server MVP</description>

<properties>
    <java.version>1.8</java.version>
</properties>

<dependencies>
    <dependency>
        <groupId>org.springframework.boot</groupId>
        <artifactId>spring-boot-starter-web</artifactId>
    </dependency>
    <dependency>
        <groupId>org.springframework.boot</groupId>
        <artifactId>spring-boot-starter-data-jpa</artifactId>
    </dependency>
    <dependency>
        <groupId>mysql</groupId>
        <artifactId>mysql-connector-java</artifactId>
        <scope>runtime</scope>
    </dependency>
</dependencies>

<build>
    <plugins>
        <plugin>
            <groupId>org.springframework.boot</groupId>
            <artifactId>spring-boot-maven-plugin</artifactId>
```

```
            </plugin>
        </plugins>
    </build>

</project>
```

2. We will include the following new dependencies for the given purposes:
   - **Lombok**: It is a Java component library that injects plugins to the editor and builds tools that don't require us to write methods like **`Getters`** and **`Setters`** for property variables specified in class and parameterized or no-argument constructors. Instead, we can use some annotations that take care of those methods. These help in removing the boilerplate code.

     The following is the dependency that can be used:

     ```
     <dependency>
         <groupId>org.projectlombok</groupId>
         <artifactId>lombok</artifactId>
         <scope>provided</scope>
     </dependency>
     ```
   - **Guava**: This is used to use features of the library built by Google. In this application, we will use the **`Lists`** class to generate the non-modified array list. The following is the dependency that can be used:

     ```
     <dependency>
         <groupId>com.google.guava</groupId>
         <artifactId>guava</artifactId>
         <version>30.0-jre</version>
     </dependency>
     ```
   - **Actuator**: This dependency enables production-ready features to help us monitor and manage applications like checking the application health and tracing HTTP requests. The following is the dependency that can be used:

     ```
     <dependency>
         <groupId>org.springframework.boot</groupId>
         <artifactId>spring-boot-starter-actuator</artifactId>
     </dependency>
     ```

- **Validation**: Starting from *Spring Boot 2.3.0.RELEASE*, Spring Boot Web and WebFlux Starters no longer depend on the **validation-api** dependency. So, we have to add the following dependency:

```
<dependency>
    <groupId>org.springframework.boot</groupId>
    <artifactId>spring-boot-starter-validation</artifactId>
</dependency>
```

3. Next, we will create the **SpringBootApplication** class called **WebServiceApplication.java**.

   The following is the code snippet for **WebServiceApplication.java**:

```
package com.bpb.publications.authors;
import org.springframework.boot.SpringApplication;
import org.springframework.boot.autoconfigure.
SpringBootApplication;

@SpringBootApplication
public class WebServiceApplication {

    public static void main(String[] args) {
        SpringApplication.run(WebServiceApplication.class, args);
    }

}
```

4. We will create **VO/Data Transfer Object** (**DTO**), entities, and repositories. In the previous chapter, we learned how to create entities and repositories. We will use the same knowledge here. **View Objects** (**VOs**) are the **Plain Old Java Object** (**POJO**) classes that are used for sending data to client applications and receiving data from client applications. Generally, these POJO classes have several attributes and their setters-getters. The following is the code snippet of the **Author Entity** class:

```
package com.bpb.publications.authors.entity;
import javax.persistence.Entity;
import javax.persistence.GeneratedValue;
import javax.persistence.GenerationType;
```

```
import javax.persistence.Id;
import javax.persistence.Table;
import javax.persistence.UniqueConstraint;

import lombok.Getter;
import lombok.Setter;

@Entity
@Table(name = "bpb_author", uniqueConstraints = @UniqueConstraint
(columnNames = { "name", "url" }))
@Getter
@Setter
public class Author {
    @Id
    @GeneratedValue(strategy = GenerationType.AUTO)
    private int id;

    private String url;
    private String name;
    private String bio;
}
```

We created the **author** entity with a unique constraint on the **name** and **url** attributes. Specifying details of uniqueness ensures that applications will handle the logic to save and handle exceptions on related data fields.

Another change you will see is the usage of **@Getter** and **@Setter** annotations. This helps us not to write getters and setters for the fields. *Isn't that a good feature?*

5. Now, let us create the **VO** class to manage the data from applications. The following is the snippet of the **AuthorVO** class:

```
package com.bpb.publications.authors.vo;
import javax.validation.constraints.NotEmpty;
import lombok.Getter;
import lombok.Setter;
```

```
@Getter
@Setter
public class AuthorVO {
    @NotEmpty
    private String url;
    @NotEmpty
    private String name;
    @NotEmpty
    private String bio;
}
```

We used the **@NotEmpty** annotation to check the emptiness of a data field. This helps us not to explicitly check for the length of the field. There are several other annotations provided in the **javax.validation** package of the **jakarta.validation-api** library such as **@NotNull**, **@Email**, **@Max**, **@Min**, **@ Negative**, **@Positive**, **@Size**, and many more.

Here, you will see DTO/VO objects when it interacts with client applications. The reason being for two separate classes, we need to segregate few data attributes which are not required to be sent to client applications. This provides more control to the data that is being sent out of the application. Here, the difference in the **Author** and **AuthorVO** class is the attribute **id**.

6. Next, we will create **AuthorRepository** to access the **Author** table. The following is the code snippet:

```
package com.bpb.publications.authors.repository;
import org.springframework.data.repository.CrudRepository;
import com.bpb.publications.authors.entity.Author;

public interface AuthorRepository extends CrudRepository<Author, Integer> {
    Optional<Author> findByNameAndUrl(String name, String url);
}
```

7. To use the **findByNameAndUrl()**method, we will create the following **AuthorService** class:

```
package com.bpb.publications.authors.service;
import java.util.ArrayList;
```

```
import java.util.List;
import java.util.Optional;
import org.springframework.beans.BeanUtils;
import org.springframework.beans.factory.annotation.Autowired;
import org.springframework.dao.DataAccessException;
import org.springframework.stereotype.Service;
import com.bpb.publications.authors.entity.Author;
import com.bpb.publications.authors.exception.NoRecordsException;
import com.bpb.publications.authors.repository.AuthorRepository;
import com.bpb.publications.authors.vo.AuthorVO;
import com.google.common.collect.Lists;

import lombok.extern.slf4j.Slf4j;

@Service
@Slf4j
public class AuthorService {

    @Autowired
    AuthorRepository authorRepository;

}
```

We will use **@Slf4j** for logging purpose. This is an alternative to have a logger variable inside the class. The class autowires **AuthorRepository** to perform save and search operations.

8. We will now add the following create and retrieve functionalities to **AvuthorService**:
   - **Create:** To map attributes of the **entity** class and the **VO** class, we used the **copyProperties** method of the **BeanUtils** class, which simply copies the values of the matching fields. Whenever there is an exception raised while performing database operations, the application throws the **DataAccessException** exception:

```
public boolean add(AuthorVO authorVO) {
    Author author = new Author();
```

```
    BeanUtils.copyProperties(authorVO, author);
    try {
        authorRepository.save(author);
    } catch (DataAccessException dae) {
        log.error("Error while saving into database :{}", dae.
        getMessage());
    }
    return true;
}
```

Wow! This is easy as we do not need to write different setters and getters for `VO` classes in our logic.

- **Retrieve**: While retrieving data from the repository, we will use the repositories method. Here, we created our own `findByNameAndUrl(name,url)` method to fetch data which matches the provided `name` and `url`. In general practices, we should be using `Optional` classes to avoid runtime exceptions, and to check whether any value is returned from the repository method, we will use `isPresent()` which returns `Boolean`:

```
public AuthorVO get(String name, String url) {
    Optional<Author> author = authorRepository.findByNameAndUrl
    (name, url);
    if (!author.isPresent()) {
        throw new NoRecordsException("No Records for Author " +
        name);
    }
    AuthorVO authorVO = new AuthorVO();
    BeanUtils.copyProperties(author.get(), authorVO);
    return authorVO;
}

public List<AuthorVO> getAll() {
    List<Author> authors = Lists.newArrayList(authorRepository.
    findAll());
    if (authors.isEmpty()) {
```

```
            throw new NoRecordsException("No Authors found");
        }
        List<AuthorVO> authorVOs = new ArrayList<>();
        authors.forEach(author -> {
            AuthorVO authorVO = new AuthorVO();
            BeanUtils.copyProperties(author, authorVO);
            authorVOs.add(authorVO);
        });
        return authorVOs;
    }

    public AuthorVO findById(int id) {
        Optional<Author> author = authorRepository.findById(id);
        if (!author.isPresent()) {
            throw new NoRecordsException("No Records for Author for
            ID " + id);
        }
        AuthorVO authorVO = new AuthorVO();
        BeanUtils.copyProperties(author.get(), authorVO);
        return authorVO;
    }
```

Further, we have the **Exception** class to handle database-related exceptions. There can be as many exception classes, as per demand. For instance, any errors we wish to raise can be done by having **BusinessException**. The following is the code snippet for **NoRecordsException**:

```
package com.bpb.publications.authors.exception;

public class NoRecordsException extends RuntimeException {

    public NoRecordsException(String message) {
        super(message);
    }

}
```

For these validations to work, we will have to add **`@Valid`** and **`@Validated`** annotations in the controller class. The main part for a web application is to have the REST endpoint API. We will understand the code basics from the following code snippet:

```
package com.bpb.publications.authors.controller;
import javax.validation.Valid;
import javax.validation.constraints.Positive;
import org.springframework.beans.factory.annotation.Autowired;
import org.springframework.http.HttpStatus;
import org.springframework.http.MediaType;
import org.springframework.http.ResponseEntity;
import org.springframework.validation.annotation.Validated;
import org.springframework.web.bind.annotation.GetMapping;
import org.springframework.web.bind.annotation.PathVariable;
import org.springframework.web.bind.annotation.PostMapping;
import org.springframework.web.bind.annotation.RequestBody;
import org.springframework.web.bind.annotation.RequestMapping;
import org.springframework.web.bind.annotation.RequestMethod;
import org.springframework.web.bind.annotation.RequestParam;
import org.springframework.web.bind.annotation.RestController;
import com.bpb.publications.authors.service.AuthorService;
import com.bpb.publications.authors.vo.AuthorVO;

@Validated
@RestController
@RequestMapping("/author")
public class AuthorController {

    @Autowired
    AuthorService authorService;

}
```

The following are few terminologies and annotations for a web application:

- **`@RestController`**: This annotation marks a class as the REST controller which has a combination of **`@Controller`** and **`@ResponseBody`** features. This annotation is used at the top of a class.
- **`@RequestMapping`**: This annotation is used for mapping HTTP web requests onto methods in classes that are annotated with **`@RestController`** or **`@ Controller.`** This annotation can be used on top of the class to have the same semantics to be followed for the methods inside the class. For instance, if you have multiple APIs **like `/product`, `/product/1`,** `and` **`/product/icecream`**, the prefix **`product`** repeats itself for all APIs. Thus, we can prefix all APIs with **`/product`** and can be placed at the top of the **`@RestController`** which will prefix the URL for all APIs under it. This annotation can be used at the method level as shown in the preceding snippet.

  The annotation has several attributes out of which it takes the **`Request`** method type in the **`method`** variable such as **`GET`, `HEAD`, `POST`, `PUT`, `PATCH`, `DELETE`, `OPTIONS`** `and` **`TRACE`**. The path mapping for an URL can be specified in the value attribute. By default, if we write **`@RequestMapping("/product")`**, the path value will be assigned to the value attribute. There can be multiple path mappings assigned to the single method.

  The method also takes information about the datatype which the API will consume and produce like **`JSON(APPLICATION_JSON_VALUE)`** and **`XML(APPLICATION_XML_VALUE)`**. All these HTTP specifications can be found in the **`org.springframework.http.MediaType`** class.
- **`@RequestParam:`** This annotation indicates that a method parameter should be bound to a web request parameter. For example, if you have some URL that accepts the name as the query string **`("/api?name=something"),`** then this annotation can be used to bind the query param **`name`** to a variable. The following is an example to retrieve the author by **`name`**:

  ```
  @RequestMapping(method = RequestMethod.GET, name = "Get Author By Name and URL", produces = MediaType.APPLICATION_JSON_VALUE)

  public ResponseEntity<?> getAuthor(@RequestParam(name = "name") String name, @RequestParam(name = "url") String url) {

    try {

         return new  ResponseEntity<>(authorService.get(name, url), HttpStatus.OK);

        } catch (Exception e) {

         returnnew ResponseEntity<>(newErrorMessage(e.getMessage()),
  ```

```
        HttpStatus.INTERNAL_SERVER_ERROR);
        }
}
```

- **@PathVariable:** This annotation indicates that a **method** parameter should be bound to a URI template variable. For example, in the API like **/api/1** where **1** is variable, we can use this annotation to bind with the Java variable to accommodate dynamic values. We have added the following code to search by the variable value:

```
@GetMapping(name = "Get Author By ID", value = "/{id}", produces =
MediaType.APPLICATION_JSON_VALUE)
    public ResponseEntity<?> getAuthorById(@PathVariable @
    Positive(message = "Invalid ID") int id) {
try {
    return new ResponseEntity<>(authorService.findById(id),
    HttpStatus.OK);
} catch (Exception e) {
    return new ResponseEntity<>(new ErrorMessage(e.getMessage()),
    HttpStatus.INTERNAL_SERVER_ERROR);
}
}
```

- **@PostMapping**: It is an alternative of **@RequestMapping(method = RequestMethod.POST)** used for updating resources in an application. It includes the following code to add **Author**:

```
@PostMapping(name = "Add Author", value = "/add", produces =
MediaType.APPLICATION_JSON_VALUE)
public ResponseEntity<?> addAuthor(@RequestBody @Valid AuthorVO
authorVO) {
try {
    return new ResponseEntity<>(authorService.add(authorVO),
    HttpStatus.OK);
} catch (Exception e) {
    return new ResponseEntity<>(new ErrorMessage(e.getMessage()),
    HttpStatus.INTERNAL_SERVER_ERROR);
}
}
```

- **@GetMapping:** It is an alternative of **@RequestMapping(method = RequestMethod.GET)** used for fetching resources from an application. For instance, the following code is used to fetch all **Authors**:

```
@GetMapping(name = "Get Authors", value = "/all", produces =
MediaType.APPLICATION_JSON_VALUE)
public ResponseEntity<?> getAuthors() {
  try {
  return new ResponseEntity<>(authorService.getAll(), HttpStatus.
  OK);
  } catch (Exception e) {
      return new ResponseEntity<>(new ErrorMessage(e.getMessage()),
      HttpStatus.INTERNAL_SERVER_ERROR);
  }
}
```

- **@RequestBody**: This annotation indicates a method parameter that should be bound to the body of the web request. The body of the request is passed through an **HttpMessageConverter** to resolve the **method** argument depending on the content type of the request.

There are several other mapping annotations like **@PutMapping**, **@DeleteMapping**, and **@PatchMapping** which are derived versions of **@RequestMapping**.

To handle any out-going exceptions in the custom format, we can have our own class which maps the error message. The following is the **ErrorMessage** class we created:

```
package com.bpb.publications.authors.exception;
import lombok.AllArgsConstructor;
import lombok.Getter;
import lombok.Setter;

@Getter
@Setter
@AllArgsConstructor
```

```
public class ErrorMessage {
    private String message;
}
```

This class uses **@AllArgsConstructor** to create a constructor using the field variable **message**.

To return the response from our application, we used an extension of **HTTPEntity ResponseEntity**, which also includes the HTTP status code. This class can be used over controllers and the RestTemplate.

At the end, we use the following properties in the **application.yml** file:

```
server:
  port: 8081
spring:
  jpa:
    show-sql: true
    hibernate:
      ddl-auto: create
    properties:
      hibernate:
        dialect: org.hibernate.dialect.MySQL8Dialect
  datasource:
    url: jdbc:mysql://localhost:3306/bpb
    username: root
    password: root
management:
  endpoints:
    web:
      exposure:
        include: '*'
```

Finally, we need to verify the package structure along with classes. The following screenshot is the snippet of Project Explorer:

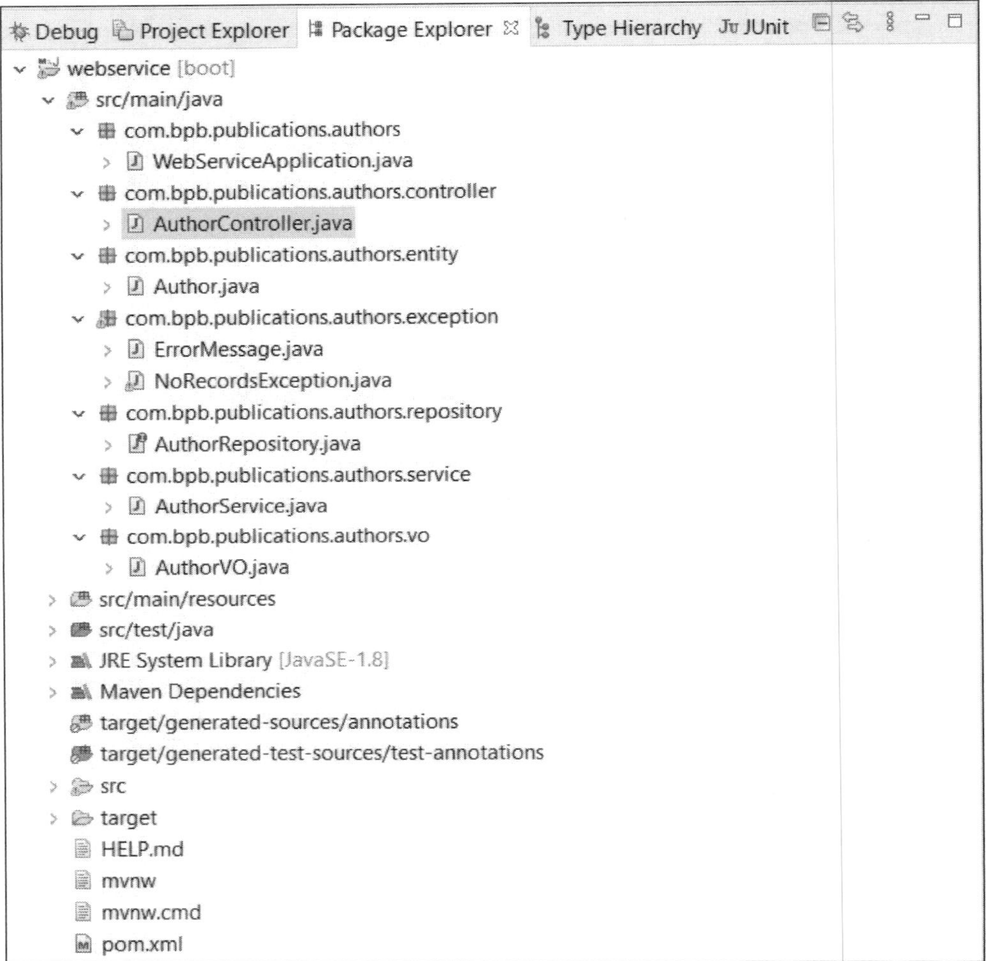

Figure 6.1: *Project Explorer*

Let us now execute the application. You will see the following logs after running **`WebServiceApplication`** as the Spring Boot application:

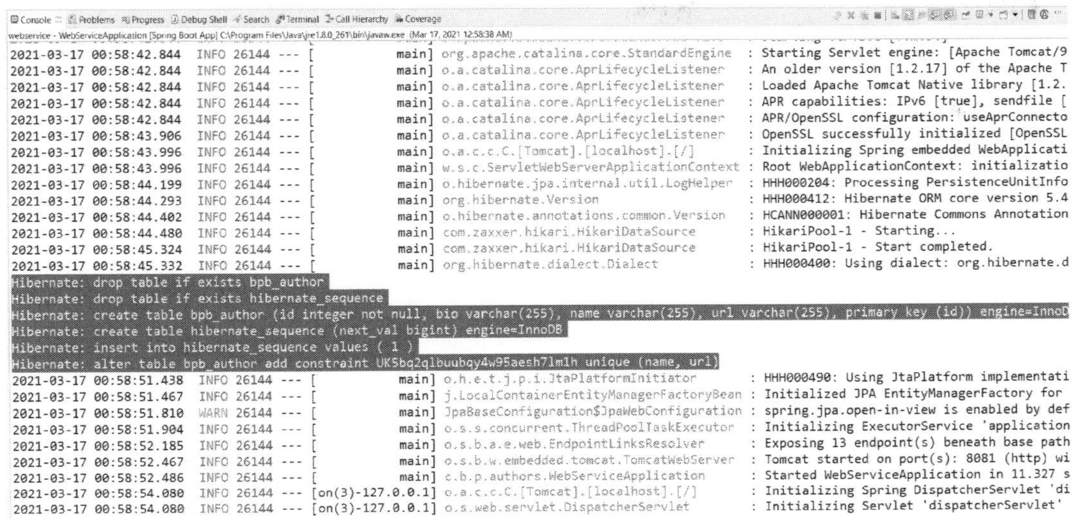

***Figure 6.2:** Console logs*

You will see few hibernate queries that are being executed for the first run. Once you see the preceding logs, update the **`ddl-auto`** to **`update`** or **`none`**.

Consuming RESTFul APIs

To check and test our APIs, we will consume the APIs from client applications like **Postman**, **JMeter**, and **Chrome**. Here, we will use Postman to consume the APIs and test.

To install Postman as an extension on Chrome, add the extension to Chrome by browsing the following link in Chrome:

https://chrome.google.com/webstore/detail/postman/fhbjgbiflinjbdggehcddcb-ncdddomop?hl=en

You can also download Postman as an application from the following link:

https://www.postman.com/downloads/

After Postman is installed, open the application and put the following details to test the endpoints:

- **Get all authors**: **`GET http://localhost:8081/author/all`**:

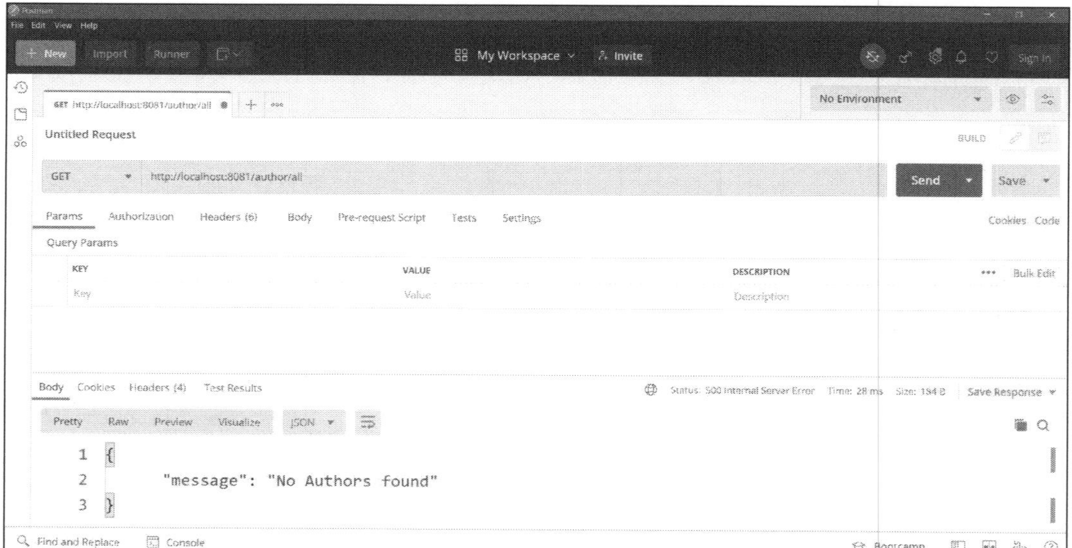

Figure 6.3: *Get all authors*

When you hit the preceding API, JPA fires the following query:

```
select author0_.id as id1_0_, author0_.bio as bio2_0_, author0_.name as name3_0_, author0_.url as url4_0_ from bpb_author author0_
```

- **Add author**: **`POST http://localhost:8081/author/add`**:

  Body : **{"url": "http://url1.com", "name": "name1", "bio": "bio1"}**

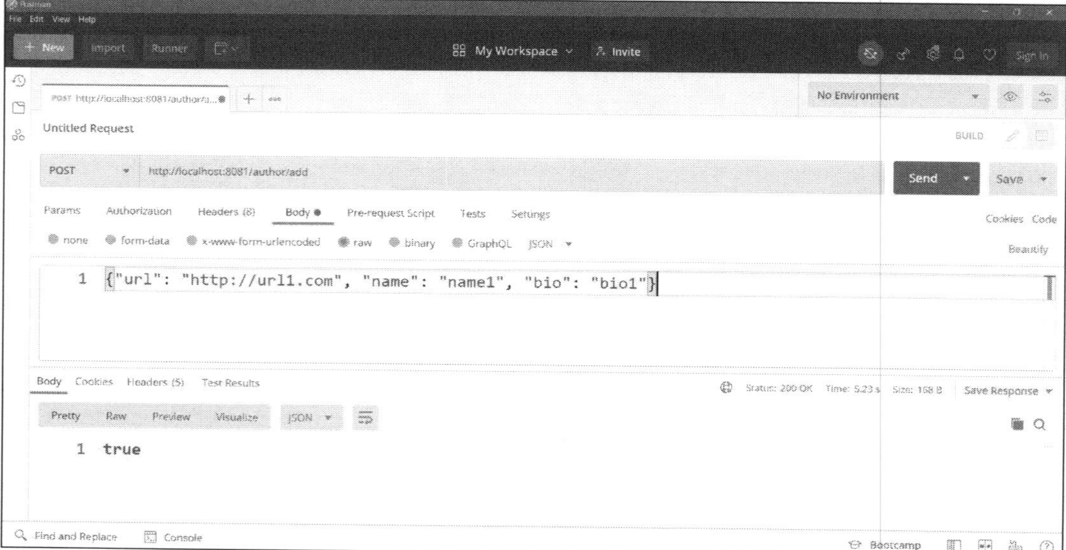

Figure 6.4: *Add author*

Queries that are being executed by JPA are listed as follows:

```
select next_val as id_val from hibernate_sequence for update
update hibernate_sequence set next_val= ? where next_val=?
insert into bpb_author (bio, name, url, id) values (?, ?, ?, ?)
```

- **Get author details by name and url**: **`GET http://localhost:8081/author?name=name1&url=http://url1.com`**.

  The following is the query executed for the preceding API:

  ```
  select author0_.id as id1_0_, author0_.bio as bio2_0_, author0_.
  name as name3_0_, author0_.url as url4_0_ from bpb_author author0_
  where author0_.name=? and author0_.url=?
  ```

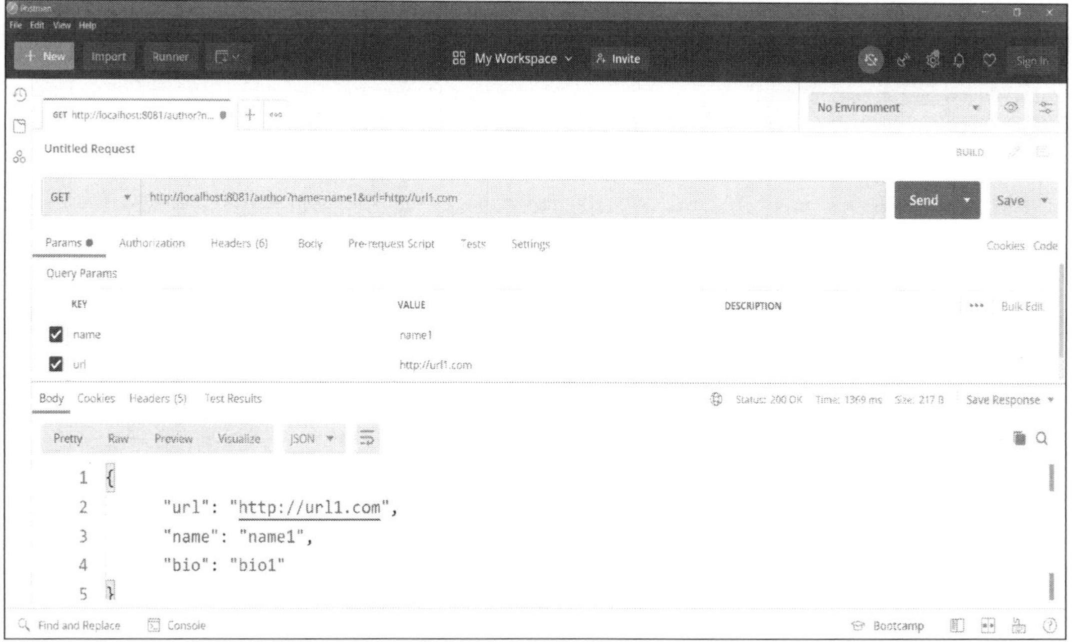

Figure 6.5: *Get author details by name and URL*

Now, when you again hit **`http://localhost:8081/author/all`** to fetch all authors' information, you will see the following response:

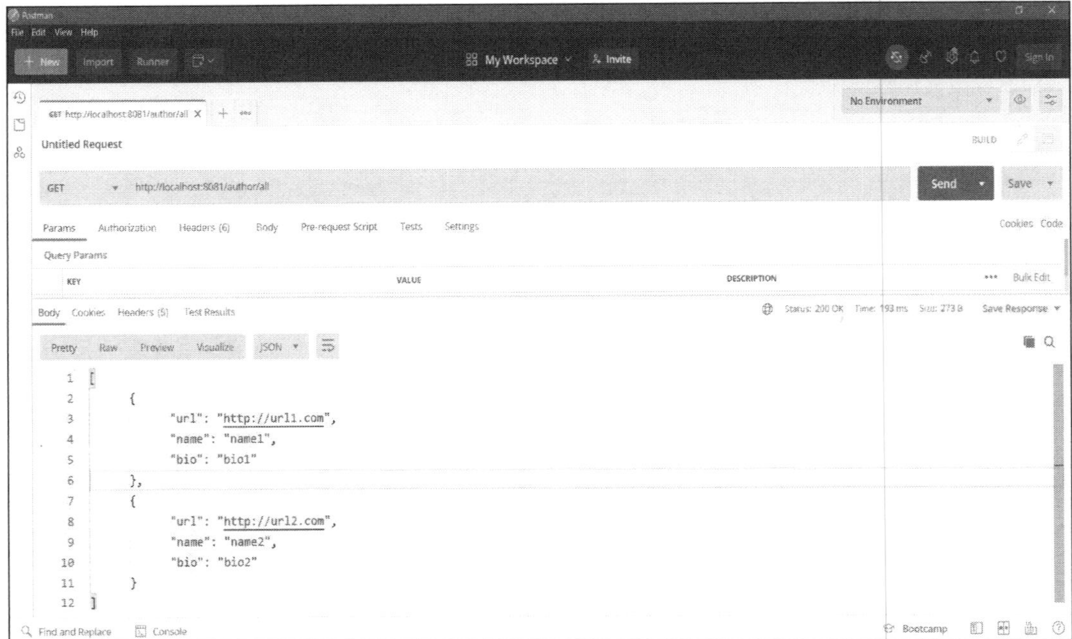

Figure 6.6: *Get all authors*

When you see the responses of an API from our application to a client application (that is, Postman), we can say that Postman has consumed our API.

Creating different profiles based on the environment

Assume that the current application we built is for development environment where we connect with the database that is set up on the local system. *What if you don't want to modify your application for selecting the database that is hosted on another server?*

There may be also a case where you wish to consume the external service having different URLs for different environments; in that case, you can't keep changing the configuration and deploying it again and again.

This can be resolved by selecting a proper profile before executing our Spring application. For this to accomplish, we need to rename **`application.yml`** to a different name based on the environment.

When there is no profile selected during the start of the application, you will see **`No active profile set, falling back to default profiles: default`** while booting up the application. In this way, you can verify the profile selected.

We have the following **application.yml** configuration in our previous sections:

```
server:
  port: 8081
spring:
  jpa:
    show-sql: true
    hibernate:
      ddl-auto: update
    properties:
      hibernate:
        dialect: org.hibernate.dialect.MySQL8Dialect
  datasource:
    url: jdbc:mysql://localhost:3306/bpb
    username: root
    password: root
management:
  endpoints:
    web:
      exposure:
        include: '*'
```

We can now tweak the configuration for prod using the same configuration details placed in a different file called **application-prod.yml**. Let us now create the production configuration for an application:

```
server:
  port: 8082
spring:
  jpa:
    show-sql: false
    hibernate:
      ddl-auto: none
    properties:
      hibernate:
```

```
      dialect: org.hibernate.dialect.MySQL8Dialect
  datasource:
    url: jdbc:mysql://somedomain.com:3306/bpb
    username: encryptedusername
    password: encryptedpassword
management:
  endpoints:
    web:
      exposure:
        include: '*'
```

Here, you will see that we changed few configurations for production. In real scenarios, this would be adopted when you promote your applications to higher regions. To start your application and to use this configuration, provide **`-Dspring.profiles.active=prod`** in VM arguments as shown in the following screenshot:

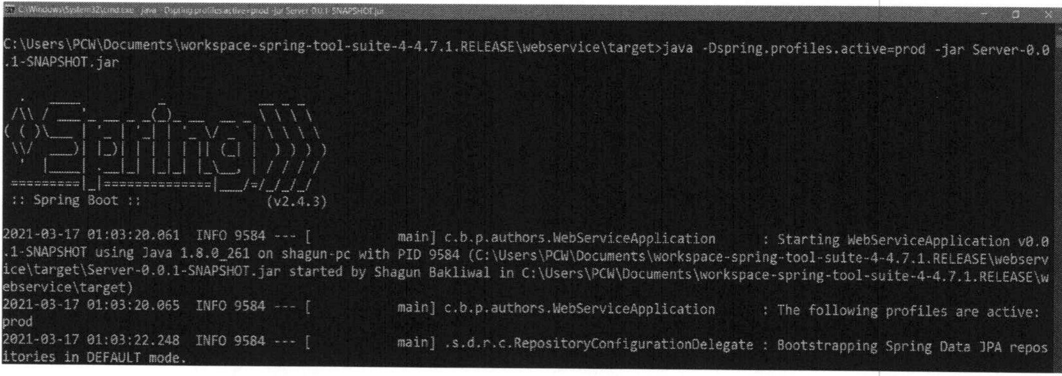

Figure 6.7: *Selecting prod profile in command line*

The command executed in the preceding screenshot: **`java -Dspring.profiles.active=prod -jar Server-0.0.1-SNAPSHOT.jar`**.

You can also modify the run configuration of STS by putting **`prod`** in **`Profile`** as shown in the following screenshot:

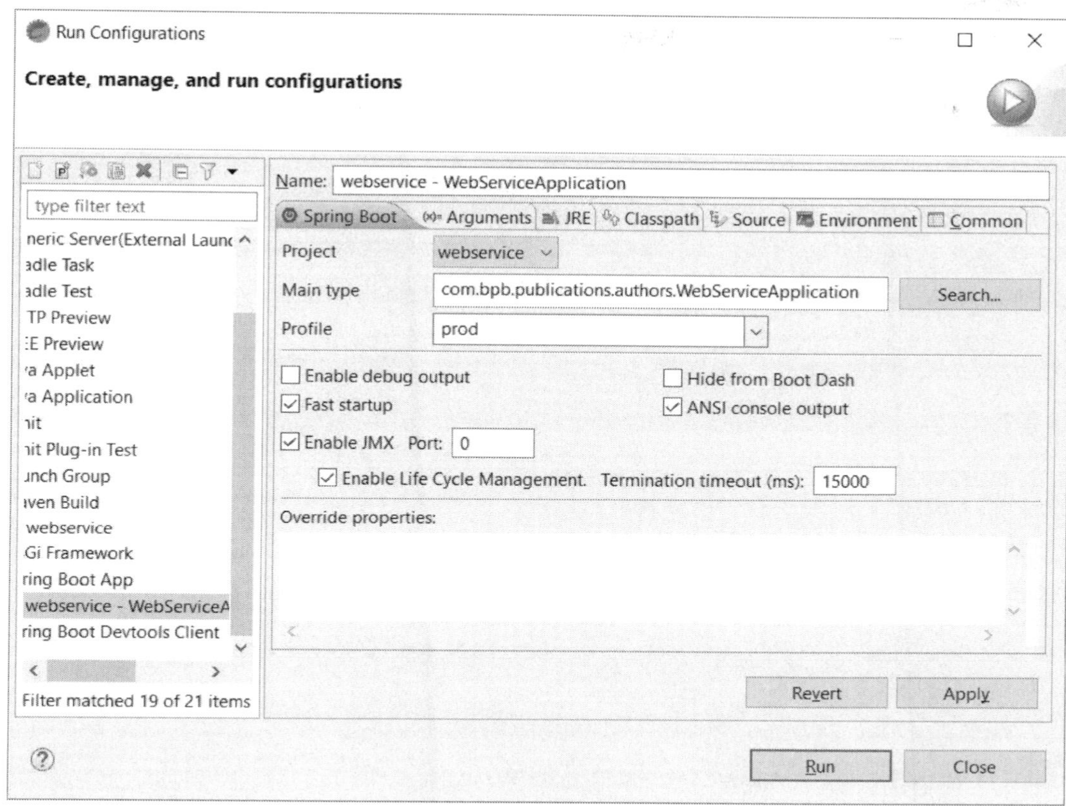

Figure 6.8: Selecting prod profile

When you run the application by selecting the preceding profile, you will see **`The following profiles are active: prod`** in console logs. This confirms the profile in which our application is running.

There is one more way to specify the active profiles in **`application.yml`**. The thought-process could be having a common configuration placed in **`application.yml`** and properties that differ can be placed in a different **`application-*.yml`**.

In the **`application.yml`** file, we can have the following configuration, so that at runtime you don't need to provide the profile:

```
server:
  port: 8081
spring:
  profiles:
    active: prod
```

Similarly, you can have different configuration files based on different environments like **dev**, **test**, **uat**, **prod**, **perf**, and so on.

If the properties specified are repeating within the application configuration, then the last configuration will be in action and override all previous configurations.

You can also create beans based on the profile in which the application is running. For this, we need to make use of the **@Profile** annotation on the top of the class where we want to create beans conditionally.

We will create one interface with common functionalities and two implementers for the same. The following is the interface that will be autowired later:

```
package com.bpb.publications.authors.service.interfaces;

public interface AppEnvironment {
    String name();
}
```

The following is the **DevEnvironment** class that implements the **AppEnvironment** interface:

```
package com.bpb.publications.authors.config;
import org.springframework.context.annotation.Profile;
import org.springframework.stereotype.Component;

import com.bpb.publications.authors.service.interfaces.AppEnvironment;

@Component
@Profile("dev")
//some code for changing properties related with the environment you running
public class DevEnvironment implements AppEnvironment {

    @Override
    public String name() {
        return "dev";
    }

}
```

The following is the **ProdEnvironment** class that implements the **AppEnvironment** interface:

```
package com.bpb.publications.authors.config;
import org.springframework.context.annotation.Profile;
import org.springframework.stereotype.Component;

import com.bpb.publications.authors.service.interfaces.AppEnvironment;

@Component
@Profile("prod")
//some code for changing properties related with the environment you running
public class ProdEnvironment implements AppEnvironment {

    @Override
    public String name() {
        return "prod";
    }

}
```

We will now autowire the interface in the **Component1HealthCheck** class and run the application with the **dev** profile. We will check the response in the next section.

Using Spring Boot actuators for getting telemetry data

We used **spring-boot-starter-actuator** to enable actuator endpoints to manage the application health and monitor the application condition. The first endpoint you should try is for checking the **/health** endpoint as follows:

```
C:\Users\PCW>curl localhost:8081/actuator/health
{"status":"UP"}
```

Spring Boot actuator endpoints are by default hosted on the default port specified for the application. Here, as we have the server running on port **8081**, the actuator endpoints are also opened to **8081** for checking the actuator endpoints.

To override the port, we can add the following configuration to change the port for all such management endpoints:

```
management:
  server:
    port: 9009
```

Changing the management port helps to secure at least these kinds of endpoints which expose the crucial information in terms of application. There are more built-in endpoints which are activated when the data is available.

You will see a log **`Exposing 13 endpoint(s) beneath base path '/actuator'`** when the application starts with the configuration **`management.endpoints.web.exposure.include=*`** **in application.yml**. The following are the few endpoints along with their details:

Name	URL	Detail
`self`	`/actuator`	Displays all actuator endpoints which are enabled.
`beans`	`/actuator/beans`	Displays the complete list of Spring Beans.
`caches-cache`	`/actuator/caches/{cache}`	Displays in-depth cache details.
`caches`	`/actuator/caches`	Displays available caches.
`health`	`/actuator/health`	Displays the application health information.
`health-path`	`/actuator/health/{*path}`	Displays the health of specific attributes coming as part of **`/health`**.
`info`	`/actuator/info`	Displays application-level info.
`conditions`	`/actuator/conditions`	Displays all **`@Conditional`** based configurations.
`configprops`	`/actuator/configprops`	Displays a list of all **`@ConfigurationProperties`**.
`env`	`/actuator/env`	Displays properties from Spring's **`ConfigurableEnvironment`**.
`heapdump`	`/actuator/heapdump`	It returns an **`hprof`** heap dump file.
`threaddump`	`/actuator/threaddump`	It performs the thread dump.
`metrics`	`/actuator/metrics`	Displays **`metrics`** information for the application.

Contd…

Name	URL	Detail
metrics-requiredMetricName	**/actuator/metrics/{requiredMetricName}**	Displays specific **metrics** information for the application.
scheduledtasks	**/actuator/scheduledtasks**	Displays the scheduled tasks.
mappings	**/actuator/mappings**	Displays a list of all **@RequestMapping** paths.

Table 6.1: *Actuator endpoints*

Custom health check indicators

Apart from the default information shown by health endpoints, we can customize the health check API by implementing some classes, so that we can have a thorough health check on the components used in the application. By default, the health endpoint gives the status of the application as **{"status":"UP"}** or **{"status":"DOWN"}**. We can have a detailed view of the health by having the following application configuration:

```
management:
  endpoint:
    health:
      show-details: always
```

Thus, by requesting **http://localhost:9009/actuator/health** now, we will see the following response:

```
C:\Users\PCW>curl http://localhost:9009/actuator/health
{"status":"UP","components":{"db":{"status":"UP","details":{"database":"MySQL","validationQuery":"isValid()"}},"diskSpace":{"status":"UP","details":{"total":209190907904,"free":105208123392,"threshold":10485760,"exists":true}},"ping":{"status":"UP"}}}
```

You can have your own custom health check by implementing **HealthIndicator** and overriding it's **health()** method. The following is the code snippet of our custom health check:

```
package com.bpb.publications.authors.actuator;
import org.springframework.beans.factory.annotation.Autowired;
import org.springframework.boot.actuate.health.Health;
```

```
import org.springframework.boot.actuate.health.HealthIndicator;
import org.springframework.stereotype.Component;
import com.bpb.publications.authors.service.interfaces.AppEnvironment;

@Component
public class Component1HealthCheck implements HealthIndicator {
    @Autowired
    AppEnvironment appEnvironment;

    @Override
    public Health health() {
       //some health check on any dependency which returns true or false.
        boolean running = true;
        if (running) {
            return Health.up().withDetail("component1", "value1").
            withDetail("env", checkEnv()).build();
        } else {
            return Health.down().withDetail("component1", "component1 is
            failing due to some error").withDetail("env", checkEnv()).
            build();
        }
    }



    public String checkEnv() {
        return appEnvironment.name();
    }
}
```

By having the preceding **HealthIndicator**, the response of the health endpoint is as follows:

```
C:\Users\PCW>curl http://localhost:9009/actuator/health
{"status":"UP","components":{"component1HealthCheck":{"sta-
tus":"UP","details":{"component1":"value1","env":"dev"}},"db":{"sta-
```

tus":"UP","details":{"database":"MySQL","validationQuery":"isValid()"}},"diskSpace":{"status":"UP","details":{"total":209190907904,"free":137937727488,"threshold":10485760,"exists":true}},"ping":{"status":"UP"}}}

In this way, you can have as many health checks for different dependencies or components used within the application. Also, you can configure the same type of configuration segregated for different environments.

When any of the components used within the application is not functioning properly, then turning down the health indicator for the same will turn down the health for the overall application.

Exception handling using ControllerAdvice

Our initial endpoint requests were more of valid data. But there would be many cases where the data which is being sent is not valid, not always available in the database, resources required to access that data are not responding well, or any malfunctioned input is being sent. It's better to handle all those exceptions around the controller as that is the starting point to make a call to services and related resources. Either of the validations involved check for the correctness of the input, the datatype, the value ranges, and so on. This can be accomplished by having conditional checks within the controller but that leads to a large number of lines for validation and at the end, the actual call is made to the service. Another disadvantage of this could be using the same set of rules again and again for different APIs and then maintaining all of the occurrences of such logic each time whenever the change is requested.

A possible solution could be to have a centralized place to handle all such exceptions and send the response from the application in an accurate manner. To start with this, let us check on the responses for invalid inputs. The following are few examples:

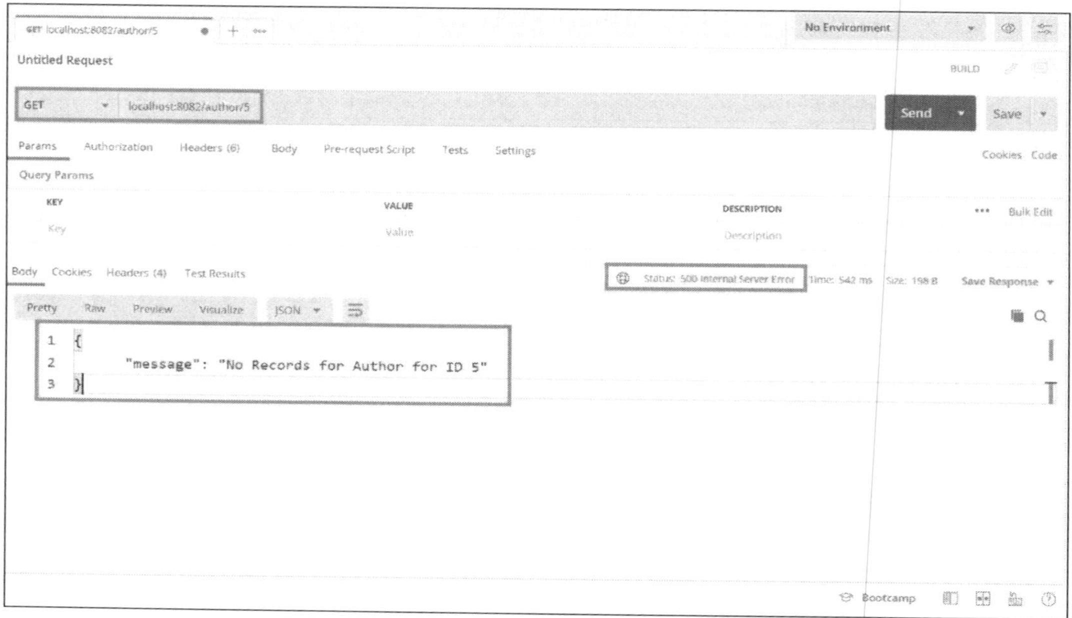

Figure 6.9: *No records error*

In the preceding screenshot, you can see HTTP **`500`** even though the message is for no records. Another example where you can provide the invalid parameters is shown in the following screenshot:

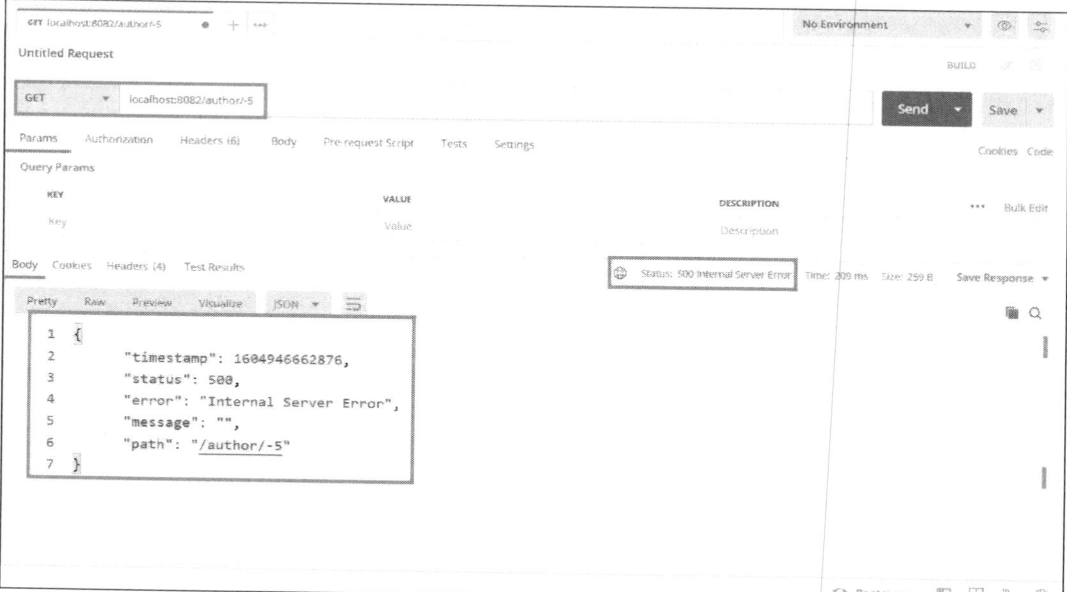

Figure 6.10*: Invalid inputs*

In the console logs, we can see logs for invalid values passed like **javax.validation.ConstraintViolationException: getAuthor.id: must be greater than 0**. Now, the question arises from *where is this error raised? Why are we getting the HTTP **500** error for No Records? Can we modify the HTTP status code based on our choices?*

All the preceding questions can be answered from putting the advice around the controller. Spring has an annotation **@ControllerAdvice** for carrying out such operations to handle errors easily and modify them accordingly. The following is the snippet for **AppControllerAdvice**:

```
package com.bpb.publications.authors.advice;
import java.util.Set;
import java.util.stream.Collectors;
import javax.validation.ConstraintViolation;
import javax.validation.ConstraintViolationException;
import org.springframework.http.HttpStatus;
import org.springframework.http.ResponseEntity;
import org.springframework.stereotype.Component;
import org.springframework.web.bind.annotation.ControllerAdvice;
import org.springframework.web.bind.annotation.ExceptionHandler;
import com.bpb.publications.authors.exception.ErrorMessage;
import com.bpb.publications.authors.exception.NoRecordsException;

@ControllerAdvice
@Component
public class AppControllerAdvice {

    @ExceptionHandler(ConstraintViolationException.class)
    public ResponseEntity<?> handleConstraintViolationExceptions
    (ConstraintViolationException ex) {
        Set<ConstraintViolation<?>> constraintViolations = ex.
        getConstraintViolations();
      return new ResponseEntity<>(new ErrorMessage(constraintViolations.
      stream()
                .map(constraintViolation -> constraintViolation.
                getMessage()).collect(Collectors.toList()).get(0)),
```

```
                HttpStatus.BAD_REQUEST);
    }

    @ExceptionHandler(NoRecordsException.class)
    public ResponseEntity<?> handleNoRecordsException(NoRecordsException
    ex) {
        return new ResponseEntity<>(new ErrorMessage(ex.getMessage()),
        HttpStatus.NOT_FOUND);
    }
}
```

Now, when we hit the **`/author/{id}`** API with invalid data like **`-5`** or some ID which doesn't exists, we should achieve the required error messages and HTTP status codes. The following is the screenshot for both cases:

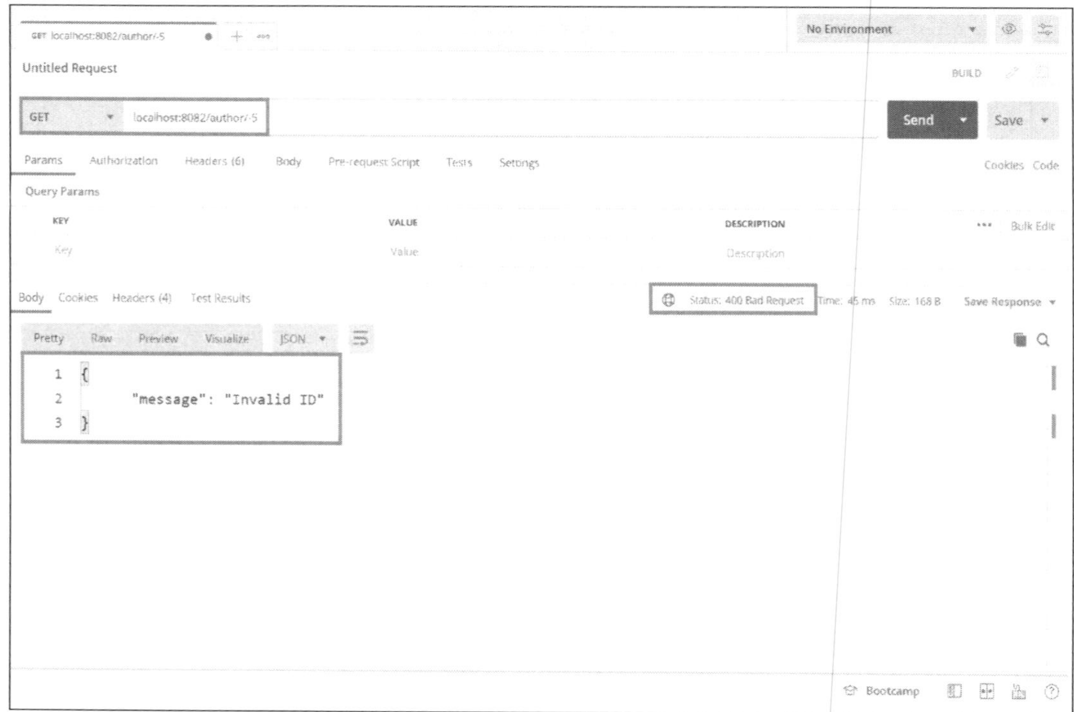

***Figure 6.11:** Customized error messages using controller advice*

Notice the HTTP status code when we provide the invalid ID. Next, we need to test for a record that doesn't exist. Before hitting the API, remove the catch block in the controller for the API which handles the exception. If the control reaches that block, then HTTP **404** via **ControllerAdvice** will not be sent. The following is the response of the same API with different inputs:

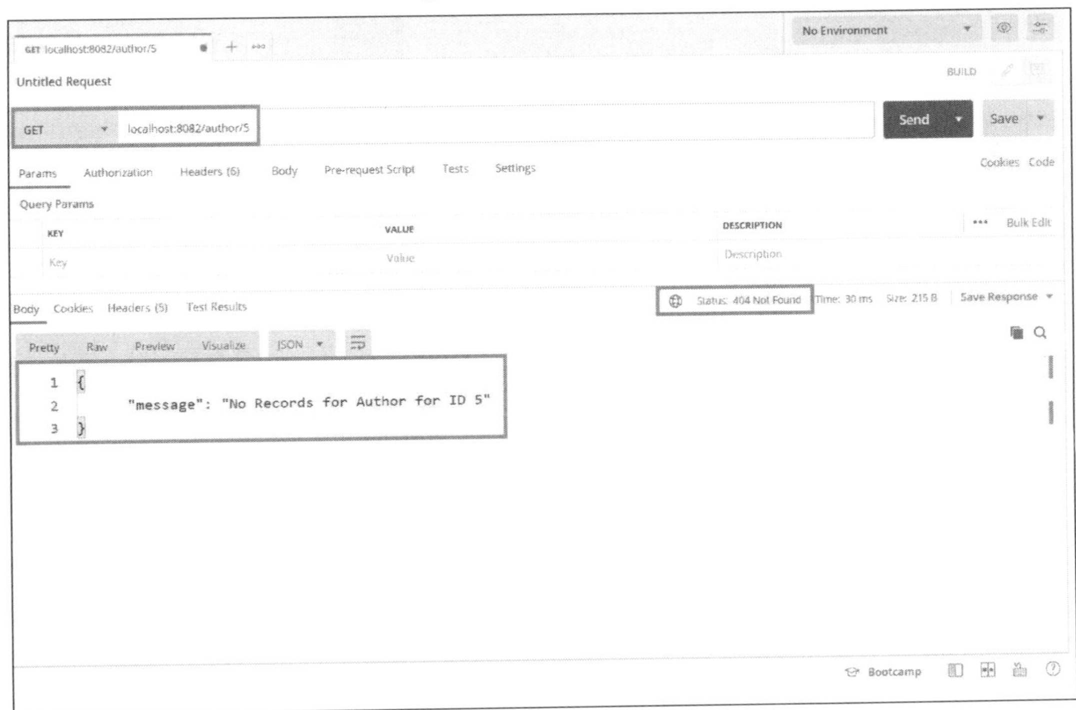

Figure 6.12: Customized error messages using controller advice for No Records

There may be cases when you receive the response in the XML format, but to stick to the JSON response on the exceptions handled by **ControllerAdvice**, you can modify the response sent by **ControllerAdvice** using the following snippet:

```
returnResponseEntity.status(HttpStatus.NOT_FOUND).contentType(MediaType.
APPLICATION_JSON).body(new ErrorMessage(ex.getMessage()));
```

where previously it was:

```
return new ResponseEntity<>(new ErrorMessage(ex.getMessage()), HttpStatus.
NOT_FOUND);
```

You must now have understood that you can handle all kinds of exceptions within the controller advice. Now, let us make a call to other APIs within our application using Eureka service discovery and service registry.

Service discovery

Spring Cloud Gateway provides a library for building the API Gateway on top of **Spring Webflu**x. This aims to provide a simple way to route to APIs. Using few annotations, you can quickly enable and configure the common patterns inside your application and build large distributed systems with Cloud components. The patterns provided include **service discovery (Eureka)**, **circuit breaker (Hystrix)**, **intelligent routing,** and **client-side load balancing (Ribbon)**. All these patterns will be understood in this chapter and the upcoming chapters. Let us create the Eureka server by following steps:

1. We will create a new project with the following **pom.xml**:

```
<?xml version="1.0" encoding="UTF-8"?>
<project  xmlns="http://maven.apache.org/POM/4.0.0"  xmlns:xsi="
http://www.w3.org/2001/XMLSchema-instance"
    xsi:schemaLocation="http://maven.apache.org/POM/4.0.0 https://
    maven.apache.org/xsd/maven-4.0.0.xsd">
    <modelVersion>4.0.0</modelVersion>
    <parent>
        <groupId>org.springframework.boot</groupId>
        <artifactId>spring-boot-starter-parent</artifactId>
        <version>2.4.3</version>
        <relativePath/> <!-- lookup parent from repository -->
    </parent>
    <groupId>com.webservice</groupId>
    <artifactId>WebServiceEurekaService</artifactId>
    <version>0.0.1-SNAPSHOT</version>
    <name>WebServiceEurekaService</name>
  <description>Spring Boot Project for Eureka Service</description>

    <properties>
        <java.version>1.8</java.version>
    </properties>

    <dependencies>
```

```
        <dependency>
            <groupId>org.springframework.cloud</groupId>
            <artifactId>spring-cloud-starter-netflix-eureka-
            server</artifactId>
        </dependency>
    </dependencies>
    <build>
        <plugins>
            <plugin>
                <groupId>org.springframework.boot</groupId>
                <artifactId>spring-boot-maven-plugin</artifactId>
            </plugin>
        </plugins>
    </build>
</project>
```

2. We have included **spring-cloud-starter-netflix-eureka-server** to use Eureka features. To allow Maven to download the dependency, we will add the following dependency management and repository to make the dependency available:

```
<dependencyManagement>
    <dependencies>
        <dependency>
            <groupId>org.springframework.cloud</groupId>
            <artifactId>spring-cloud-dependencies</artifactId>
            <version>2020.0.1</version>
            <type>pom</type>
            <scope>import</scope>
        </dependency>
    </dependencies>
</dependencyManagement>


<repositories>
```

```
        <repository>
            <id>spring-snapshots</id>
            <name>Spring Snapshots</name>
            <url>https://repo.spring.io/snapshot</url>
            <snapshots>
                <enabled>true</enabled>
            </snapshots>
        </repository>
        <repository>
            <id>spring-milestones</id>
            <name>Spring Milestones</name>
            <url>https://repo.spring.io/milestone</url>
        </repository>
    </repositories>
```

3. Then, create the following Java class having the **@EnableEurekaServer** annotation on top of **@SpringBootApplication**:

```
package com.bpb.publications.authors;
import org.springframework.boot.SpringApplication;
import org.springframework.boot.autoconfigure.
SpringBootApplication;
import org.springframework.cloud.netflix.eureka.server.
EnableEurekaServer;

@EnableEurekaServer
@SpringBootApplication
public class WebServiceEurekaServiceApplication {

    public static void main(String[] args) {
        SpringApplication.run(WebServiceEurekaServiceApplication.
        class, args);
    }

}
```

This is Eureka service registry. We used Spring Cloud's **`@EnableEurekaServer`** to create a registry with which other applications can communicate. The project is just like any other Spring Boot application but the difference is that the annotation **`@EnableEurekaServer`** enables the service registry.

4. You need to also specify the following configurations in the **`application.properties`** file:

```
server.port=7000
eureka.client.register-with-eureka=false
eureka.client.fetch-registry=false
```

This will help the Eureka server to establish different Eureka clients.

5. When you start the Eureka service application, you can browse **`http://localhost:7000/`** in Chrome, and you will see a dashboard as shown in the following screenshot:

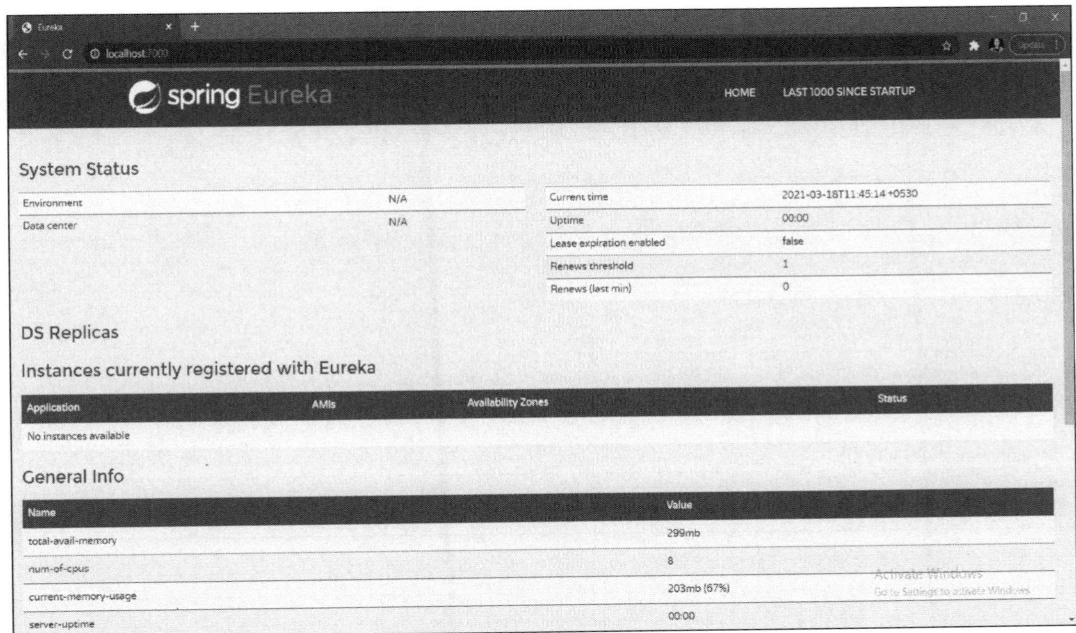

Figure 6.13: Eureka service

As we have not created any Eureka client, we will see that there are no instances available under heading **`Instances currently registered with Eureka`**.

6. Let us create the Eureka client for service discovery that registers itself with the service registry and use it to resolve its own host. The service registry is useful as it enables client-side load balancing and decouples the service

provider from consumers without the need of the actual DNS name for the API.

We will add the following dependencies to our existing client application where we created REST APIs:

```
<dependency>
    <groupId>org.springframework.cloud</groupId>
    <artifactId>spring-cloud-starter-netflix-eureka-client</
    artifactId>
</dependency>
<dependency>
    <groupId>org.springframework.cloud</groupId>
    <artifactId>spring-cloud-starter-netflix-eureka-server</
    artifactId>
</dependency>
<dependency>
    <groupId>com.sun.jersey.contribs</groupId>
    <artifactId>jersey-apache-client4</artifactId>
    <version>1.19.4</version>
</dependency>
```

7. We will also need **spring-cloud-dependencies**. The following is the code snippet:

```
<dependencyManagement>
    <dependencies>
        <dependency>
            <groupId>org.springframework.cloud</groupId>
            <artifactId>spring-cloud-dependencies</artifactId>
            <version>2020.0.1</version>
            <type>pom</type>
            <scope>import</scope>
        </dependency>
    </dependencies>
</dependencyManagement>
```

Further, we will add **`@EnableDiscoveryClient`** on top of the **`@SpringBootApplication`** class. It will activate the Netflix Eureka discovery client implementation.

8. Whenever our application starts, it looks for the application name specified in **`bootstrap.properties`** by convention, but it can be specified in the **`application.yml`** or **`application.properties`** file as follows:

```
spring:
  application:
    name: web-service
eureka:
  client:
    serviceUrl:
      defaultZone: http://localhost:7000/eureka/
```

9. When you start the client application, it will register the application to the Eureka server and its registry. You will also see the following logs which we picked up to specifically show logs related to the new code:

```
Console  Problems  Progress  Debug Shell  Search  Terminal  Call Hierarchy  Coverage
webservice - WebServiceApplication [Spring Boot App]
[            main] com.netflix.discovery.DiscoveryClient    : Initializing Eureka in region us-east-1
[            main] c.n.d.provider.DiscoveryJerseyProvider   : Using JSON encoding codec LegacyJacksonJson
[            main] c.n.d.provider.DiscoveryJerseyProvider   : Using JSON decoding codec LegacyJacksonJson
[            main] c.n.d.provider.DiscoveryJerseyProvider   : Using XML encoding codec XStreamXml
[            main] c.n.d.provider.DiscoveryJerseyProvider   : Using XML decoding codec XStreamXml
[            main] c.n.d.s.r.aws.ConfigClusterResolver      : Resolving eureka endpoints via configuration
[            main] com.netflix.discovery.DiscoveryClient    : Disable delta property : false
[            main] com.netflix.discovery.DiscoveryClient    : Single vip registry refresh property : null
[            main] com.netflix.discovery.DiscoveryClient    : Force full registry fetch : false
[            main] com.netflix.discovery.DiscoveryClient    : Application is null : false
[            main] com.netflix.discovery.DiscoveryClient    : Registered Applications size is zero : true
[            main] com.netflix.discovery.DiscoveryClient    : Application version is -1: true
[            main] com.netflix.discovery.DiscoveryClient    : Getting all instance registry info from the eureka server
[            main] com.netflix.discovery.DiscoveryClient    : The response status is 200
[            main] com.netflix.discovery.DiscoveryClient    : Starting heartbeat executor: renew interval is: 30
[            main] c.n.discovery.InstanceInfoReplicator     : InstanceInfoReplicator onDemand update allowed rate per min is 4
[            main] com.netflix.discovery.DiscoveryClient    : Discovery Client initialized at timestamp 1616046157727 with initial instances c
[            main] o.s.c.n.e.s.EurekaServiceRegistry        : Registering application WEB-SERVICE with eureka with status UP
[            main] com.netflix.discovery.DiscoveryClient    : Saw local status change event StatusChangeEvent [timestamp=1616046157735, curren
[nfoReplicator-0] com.netflix.discovery.DiscoveryClient    : DiscoveryClient_WEB-SERVICE/localhost:web-service:8081: registering service...
[            main] o.s.b.w.embedded.tomcat.TomcatWebServer  : Tomcat started on port(s): 8081 (http) with context path ''
[            main] .s.c.n.e.s.EurekaAutoServiceRegistration : Updating port to 8081
[nfoReplicator-0] com.netflix.discovery.DiscoveryClient    : DiscoveryClient_WEB-SERVICE/localhost:web-service:8081 - registration status: 20
[            main] o.s.cloud.commons.util.InetUtils         : Cannot determine local hostname
[            main] o.s.b.w.embedded.tomcat.TomcatWebServer  : Tomcat initialized with port(s): 9009 (http)
[            main] o.apache.catalina.core.StandardService   : Starting service [Tomcat]
[            main] org.apache.catalina.core.StandardEngine  : Starting Servlet engine: [Apache Tomcat/9.0.43]
[            main] o.a.c.c.C.[Tomcat-1].[localhost].[/]     : Initializing Spring embedded WebApplicationContext
[            main] w.s.c.ServletWebServerApplicationContext : Root WebApplicationContext: initialization completed in 171 ms
[            main] o.s.b.a.e.web.EndpointLinksResolver      : Exposing 16 endpoint(s) beneath base path '/actuator'
[            main] o.s.b.w.embedded.tomcat.TomcatWebServer  : Tomcat started on port(s): 9009 (http) with context path ''
```

***Figure 6.14**: Eureka client logs*

The highlighted part in the preceding screenshot shows the process of registering the web-service to the Eureka server. This name is the same that we provided in the application configuration.

In the same way, you will see the following logs in the Eureka server application:

```
2021-03-18 11:47:08.493 INFO 148 --- [nio-7000-exec-3] c.n.e.registry.
AbstractInstanceRegistry    : Registered instance WEB-SERVICE/
localhost:web-service:8081 with status UP (replication=false)
```

10. Now, when you load the dashboard again, you will see a new service registered as shown in the following screenshot:

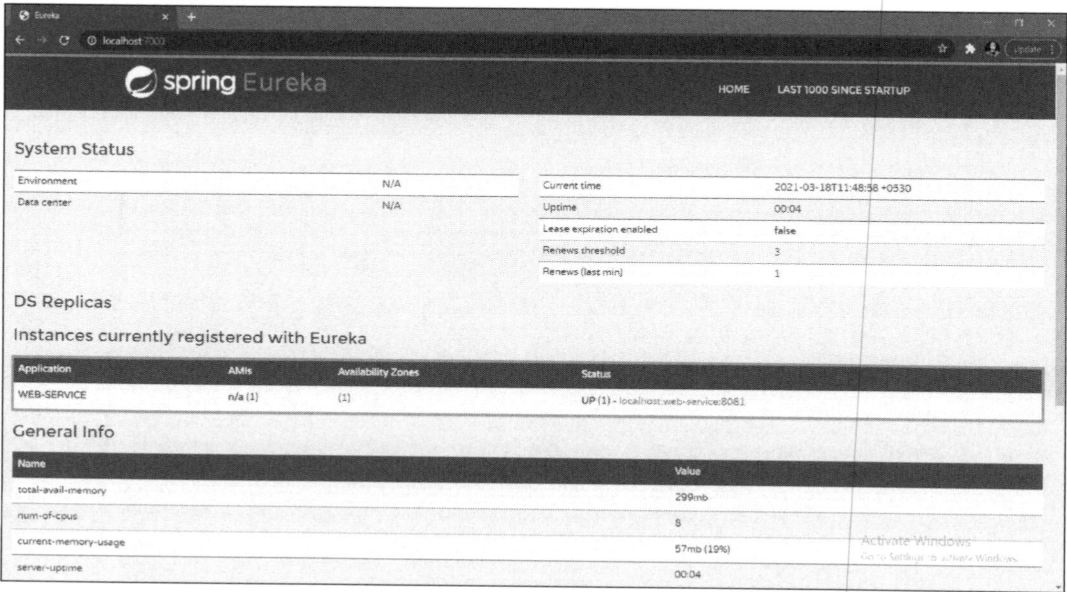

***Figure 6.15:** Eureka service new instance*

11. To check the details of the Eureka services running, we can create an endpoint like the following in the webservice project and request it from the browser:

```
@Autowired
private DiscoveryClient discoveryClient;

@GetMapping(name = "Get Eureka Service Instances", value = "/
service-instances", produces = MediaType.APPLICATION_JSON_VALUE)
public ResponseEntity<?> getEurekaServices() {
    System.out.println(discoveryClient.getInstances("web-
    service"));
    return new ResponseEntity<>(this.discoveryClient.
    getServices(), HttpStatus.OK);
}
```

This returns the response as **"["web-service"]"** when the API is requested. Also, a log is printed which shows the instance details as follows:

```
[[EurekaServiceInstance@2c86478e instance = InstanceInfo [instanceId = localhost:web-service:8081, appName = WEB-SERVICE, hostName = localhost, status = UP, ipAddr = 169.254.169.201, port = 8081, securePort = 443, dataCenterInfo = com.netflix.appinfo.MyDataCenterInfo@2640e5be]]
```

Now, we can do more stuff around it like calling an API of another application registered in the service registry by specifying the service URL pertaining to the Eureka server instance URL. This part of using the instance URL of the application registered in the service registry will be discussed in *Chapter 8, Building Resilient System*.

Let us now dive into creating our own API gateway to route the requests to a specific microservice.

Using RestTemplate for calling APIs

With Spring Boot, you can also call other APIs/URLs through the microservice. All you need is to create a bean of **RestTemplate** and autowire wherever necessary. To understand all functionalities of **RestTemplate**, we need to call methods of the **RestTemplate** class for numerous functions in a single API, but in a real-world application, it could be many API calls placed to fetch data from different systems from different parts of the application. Once we have the bean created of **RestTemplate** in our configuration class, we can autowire the **RestTemplate** object and use them.

The following is the snippet of a method whose request endpoint is **'/callAPI'**:

```
@Autowired
private RestTemplate restTemplate;


@GetMapping(name = "Call API using RestTemplate", value = "/callAPI", produces = MediaType.APPLICATION_JSON_VALUE)
public ResponseEntity<?> callAPIUsingRestTemplate() throws URISyntaxException {

    ResponseEntity<String> plainResponse = restTemplate
            .exchange(RequestEntity.get(new URI("http://localhost:8081/
```

```
        author/all")).build(), String.class);
log.info("Received Plain response from '/all' API :{}", plainResponse.
getBody());

AuthorVO authorVO = new AuthorVO();
authorVO.setUrl("url-called for PostForEntity /callAPI");
authorVO.setName("name-called for PostForEntity /callAPI");
authorVO.setBio("bio-called for PostForEntity /callAPI");
ResponseEntity<Boolean> booleanResponse = restTemplate
        .postForEntity(new  URI("http://localhost:8081/author/add"),
        authorVO, Boolean.class);
log.info("Received response from POST API '/add' (PostForEntity):{}",
booleanResponse.getBody());

AuthorVO authorVO1 = new AuthorVO();
authorVO1.setUrl("url-called for Exchange /callAPI");
authorVO1.setName("name-called for Exchange /callAPI");
authorVO1.setBio("bio-called for Exchange /callAPI");
HttpHeaders headers = new HttpHeaders();
headers.add("key1", "value1");
HttpEntity<AuthorVO> httpEntity = new HttpEntity<>(authorVO1,
headers);
ResponseEntity<Boolean> booleanResponse1 = restTemplate.exchange(new
URI("http://localhost:8081/author/add"),
        HttpMethod.POST, httpEntity, Boolean.class);
log.info("Received response from POST API '/add' (Exchange) :{}",
booleanResponse1.getBody());

ResponseEntity<List> pojoResponse = restTemplate
        .exchange(RequestEntity.get(new URI("http://localhost:8081/
        author/all")).build(), List.class);

log.info("Received POJO response from '/all' API :{}", pojoResponse.
getBody());
```

```
    return new ResponseEntity<>(null, HttpStatus.OK);
}
```

The following is the response:

```
2021-03-18 11:59:21.964  INFO 20420 --- [nio-8081-exec-4] c.b.p.a.controller.AuthorController      : Received Plain response from '/all' API :[{"url":"http://url1.com","name":"name1","bio":"bio1"},{"url":"http://url2.com","name":"name2","bio":"bio2"}]

2021-03-18 11:59:23.388  INFO 20420 --- [nio-8081-exec-4] c.b.p.a.controller.AuthorController      : Received response from POST API '/add' (PostForEntity):true

2021-03-18 11:59:23.716  INFO 20420 --- [nio-8081-exec-4] c.b.p.a.controller.AuthorController      : Received response from POST API '/add' (Exchange) :true

2021-03-18 11:59:23.761  INFO 20420 --- [nio-8081-exec-4] c.b.p.a.controller.AuthorController      : Received POJO response from '/all' API :[{url=http://url1.com, name=name1, bio=bio1}, {url=http://url2.com, name=name2, bio=bio2}, {url=url-called for PostForEntity /callAPI, name=name-called for PostForEntity /callAPI, bio=bio-called for PostForEntity /callAPI}, {url=url-called for Exchange /callAPI, name=name-called for Exchange /callAPI, bio=bio-called for Exchange /callAPI}]
```

We have used the following methods to use **`RestTemplate`**:

- **Use of Exchange method**: **`RequestEntity`** is the extension of **`HttpEntity`** along with the method type and the URI. Response type specifies the type of object that would be returned. The **`RequestEntity`** class has multiple methods for all types of HTTP methods like **`GET`**, **`POST`**, and so on. We have used **`RequestEntity.get()`** to get the **`HeadersBuilder`** object and create **`RequestEntity`** by using the **`build()`** method. We have also used the response type as **`List.class`** to typecast the response sent by an API to the **`List`** type. By default, the response type is of the **`String`** type. Following are the examples of using **exchange** method:

  a) Pass the request entity and response type: For example:

  ```
  ResponseEntity<List> plainResponse = restTemplate.exchange(RequestEntity.get(new  URI("http://localhost:8081/author/all")).build(), List.class);
  ```

  b) Pass the URI, HTTP method, **`HttpEntity,`** and response type: For example:

  ```
  HttpEntity<AuthorVO> httpEntity = new HttpEntity<>(authorVO1,
  ```

```
headers);
ResponseEntity<Boolean> booleanResponse1 = restTemplate.ex-
change(new URI("http://localhost:8081/author/add"),HttpMethod.
POST, httpEntity, Boolean.class);
```

- **Use of the PostForEntity method**: This method is an alternative to the **Exchange** method, where the **Http** method is **POST** by default when called. While calling the **POST** API, we can pass the request body or the payload in the **HttpEntity** class as follows:

```
AuthorVO authorVO = new AuthorVO();
authorVO.setUrl("url-called for PostForEntity /callAPI");
authorVO.setName("name-called for PostForEntity /callAPI");
authorVO.setBio("bio-called for PostForEntity /callAPI");
ResponseEntity<Boolean> booleanResponse = restTemplate
        .postForEntity(new URI("http://localhost:8081/author/
        add"), authorVO, Boolean.class);
```

  where **authorVO** is the actual payload created in Java.

  The Exchange method of **RestTemplate** is used most of the time. But we can also try specific methods too like **postForEntity**, **getForObject**, and so on.

The following are few methods of the **RestTemplate** class that can be used to call the API along with the method signature:

- Retrieve a representation by doing a **GET** on the specified URL, URI template and URL, respectively for all the three methods as follows:

```
public <T> T getForObject(String url, Class<T> responseType,
Object... uriVariables) throws RestClientException;
public <T> T getForObject(String url, Class<T> responseType, java.
util.Map<String, ?> uriVariables) throws  RestClientException;
public <T> T getForObject(java.net.URI url, Class<T> responseType)
throws RestClientException;
```

- Retrieve an entity by doing a **GET** on the specified URL, URI template and URL, respectively for all the three methods as follows:

```
public <T> ResponseEntity<T> getForEntity(String url, Class<T>
responseType, Object... uriVariables) throws RestClientException;
public <T> ResponseEntity<T> getForEntity(String url, Class<T>
responseType, java.util.Map<String, ?> uriVariables) throws
RestClientException;
```

```
public <T> ResponseEntity<T> getForEntity(java.net.URI url, Class<T> responseType) throws RestClientException;
```

- Retrieve all the headers of the resource specified by URL, URI template and URL, respectively for all the three methods as follows:

```
public HttpHeaders headForHeaders(String url, Object... uriVariables) throws RestClientException;
```

```
public HttpHeaders headForHeaders(String url, java.util.Map<String, ?> uriVariables) throws RestClientException;
```

```
public HttpHeaders headForHeaders(java.net.URI url) throws RestClientException;
```

- Create a new resource by POSTing the given object to the URL, URI template and URL, respectively for all the three methods as follows and return the value of the **`Location`** header:

```
public java.net.URI postForLocation(String url, Object request, Object... uriVariables) throws RestClientException;
```

```
public java.net.URI postForLocation(String url, Object request, java.util.Map<String, ?> uriVariables) throws RestClientException;
```

```
public java.net.URI postForLocation(java.net.URI url, Object request) throws RestClientException;
```

- Create a new resource by POSTing the given object to the URL, URI template and URL, respectively for all the three methods as follows and return the representation found in the response:

```
public <T> T postForObject(String url, Object request, Class<T> responseType, Object... uriVariables) throws RestClientException;
```

```
public <T> T postForObject(String url, Object request, Class<T> responseType, java.util.Map<String, ?> uriVariables) throws RestClientException;
```

```
public <T> T postForObject(java.net.URI url, Object request, Class<T> responseType) throws RestClientException;
```

- Create a new resource by POSTing the given object to the URL, URI template and URL, respectively for all the three methods as follows and return the response as **`ResponseEntity`**:

```
public <T> ResponseEntity<T> postForEntity(String url, Object request, Class<T> responseType, Object... uriVariables) throws RestClientException;
```

```
public <T> ResponseEntity<T> postForEntity(String url, Object request, Class<T> responseType, java.util.Map<String,?>uriVariables) throws RestClientException;

public <T> ResponseEntity<T> postForEntity(java.net.URI url, Object request, Class<T> responseType) throws RestClientException;
```

- Create or update a resource by PUTing the given object to the URL, URI template and URL, respectively for all the three methods as follows:

```
public void put(String url, Object request, Object... uriVariables) throws RestClientException;

public void put(String url, Object request, java.util.Map<String, ?> uriVariables) throws RestClientException;

public void put(java.net.URI, Object request) throws RestClientException;
```

- The following are the three methods to delete the resources at the specified URI:

```
public void delete(String url, Map<String,?> uriVariables) throws RestClientException;

public void delete(String url, java.util.Map<String, ?> uriVariables) throws RestClientException;

public void delete(java.net.URI url) throws RestClientException;
```

- The following are the two methods to execute the request specified in the given **RequestEntity** and return the response as **ResponseEntity**:

```
public <T> ResponseEntity<T> exchange(RequestEntity<?> entity, Class<T> responseType) throws RestClientException;

public <T> ResponseEntity<T> exchange(RequestEntity<?> entity, ParameterizedTypeReference<T> responseType) throws RestClientException;
```

- The following are the six methods to execute the HTTP method to the given URI template, write the given request entity to the request, and return the response as **ResponseEntity**:

```
public <T> ResponseEntity<T> exchange(String url, HttpMethod method, HttpEntity<?> requestEntity, Class<T> responseType, Object... uriVariables) throws RestClientException;

public <T> ResponseEntity<T> exchange(String url, HttpMethod method, HttpEntity<?> requestEntity, Class<T> responseType, java.util.Map<String, ?> uriVariables) throws RestClientException;
```

```
public <T> ResponseEntity<T> exchange(java.net.URI url, HttpMethod
method, HttpEntity<?> requestEntity, Class<T> responseType) throws
RestClientException;

public <T> ResponseEntity<T> exchange(String url, HttpMethod
method, HttpEntity<?> requestEntity, ParameterizedTypeReference<T>
responseType, Object... uriVariables) throws RestClientException;

public <T> ResponseEntity<T> exchange(String url, HttpMethod
method, HttpEntity<?> requestEntity, ParameterizedTypeReference<T>
responseType, java.util.Map<String, ?> uriVariables) throws
RestClientException;

public <T> ResponseEntity<T> exchange(java.net.URI url, HttpMethod
method, HttpEntity<?> requestEntity, ParameterizedTypeReference<T>
responseType) throws RestClientException;
```

Routing a request via the API gateway with Spring Cloud Gateway

Till now, we were requesting RESTFul APIs by the domain (**localhost:8081**) via Postman or any other HTTP client. But in general, you won't expose your domains for its usage to the outside world. That's where an API gateway comes into picture. You can hide your microservice REST APIs access behind an API Gateway such that direct access to those APIs is not possible. This will enhance the security of your application such that the actual URL of the application is not shared to consumers; instead the users can have an API gateway URL which is mapped to the REST API. Similarly, there can be multiple instances running for the same application and all those instances can be linked to the API gateway for proper load balancing across instances.

In addition to the preceding analogy, we were requesting APIs like **http://localhost:8081/author/5** which clearly shows that the application is hosted on the localhost domain. Let us now have a gateway that will call this API.

Spring Cloud Gateway

With the help of the Spring Cloud Gateway library, we can have the process of routing and filtering requests to a microservice application. We will now build a reverse proxy application that uses this library to forward requests to the microservice application.

We will create a new project – **routing-gateway** for all such routing mechanisms. The following is the skeleton of **pom.xml** for a web project:

```
<?xml version="1.0" encoding="UTF-8"?>
<project xmlns="http://maven.apache.org/POM/4.0.0" xmlns:xsi="http://www.w3.org/2001/XMLSchema-instance"
    xsi:schemaLocation="http://maven.apache.org/POM/4.0.0 https://maven.apache.org/xsd/maven-4.0.0.xsd">
    <modelVersion>4.0.0</modelVersion>
    <parent>
        <groupId>org.springframework.boot</groupId>
        <artifactId>spring-boot-starter-parent</artifactId>
        <version>2.4.3</version>
        <relativePath/> <!-- lookup parent from repository -->
    </parent>
    <groupId>com.bpb.publications</groupId>
    <artifactId>routing-gateway</artifactId>
    <version>0.0.1-SNAPSHOT</version>
    <name>routing-gateway</name>
    <description>Spring Boot Project for routing URLs</description>

    <properties>
        <java.version>1.8</java.version>
    </properties>

    <dependencies>
        <dependency>
            <groupId>org.springframework.cloud</groupId>
            <artifactId>spring-cloud-starter-gateway</artifactId>
        </dependency>
    </dependencies>

    <build>
        <plugins>
```

```
            <plugin>
                <groupId>org.springframework.boot</groupId>
                <artifactId>spring-boot-maven-plugin</artifactId>
            </plugin>
        </plugins>
    </build>

</project>
```

Here, we have included the following dependency of the Spring Cloud Starter Gateway to enable routing:

```
        <dependency>
            <groupId>org.springframework.cloud</groupId>
            <artifactId>spring-cloud-starter-gateway</artifactId>
        </dependency>
```

To download the related dependencies, we need to add the following dependency management:

```
<dependencyManagement>
    <dependencies>
        <dependency>
            <groupId>org.springframework.cloud</groupId>
            <artifactId>spring-cloud-dependencies</artifactId>
            <version>2020.0.1</version>
            <type>pom</type>
            <scope>import</scope>
        </dependency>
    </dependencies>
</dependencyManagement>
```

This can also be integrated with the Eureka server for service discovery. For now, we will keep it basic for a better understanding. To enable proxy, we need to create a bean of the type **RouteLocator**. The following is the code for the bean:

```
package com.bpb.publications.config;
import org.springframework.cloud.gateway.route.RouteLocator;
```

```
import org.springframework.cloud.gateway.route.builder.RouteLocator-
Builder;
import org.springframework.context.annotation.Bean;
import org.springframework.context.annotation.Configuration;

@Configuration
public class AppConfig {
    @Bean
    public RouteLocator myRoutes(RouteLocatorBuilder builder) {
        returnbuilder.routes().route(p->p.path("/author/**").uri("http://
        localhost:8081")).build();
    }

}
```

Next comes the configuration placed in **application.yml**. The following is the snippet of the **application.yml** file:

```
spring:
  application:
    name: routing-gateway

server:
  port: 8083
```

Here, we specified the host where the application is running on port **8081** on domain localhost, the path regular expression (**/author/**"**) for which all HTTP requests that matches this expression will route to the URL specified in **uri** method.

Now with the usual configuration of the application created in the previous section of this chapter for author application running on port **8081**, we were requesting APIs like **http://localhost:8081/author/5** which sends the request on the localhost domain. With the preceding configuration for the Spring Cloud Gateway application, we will now request **http://localhost:8083/author/5** as follows:

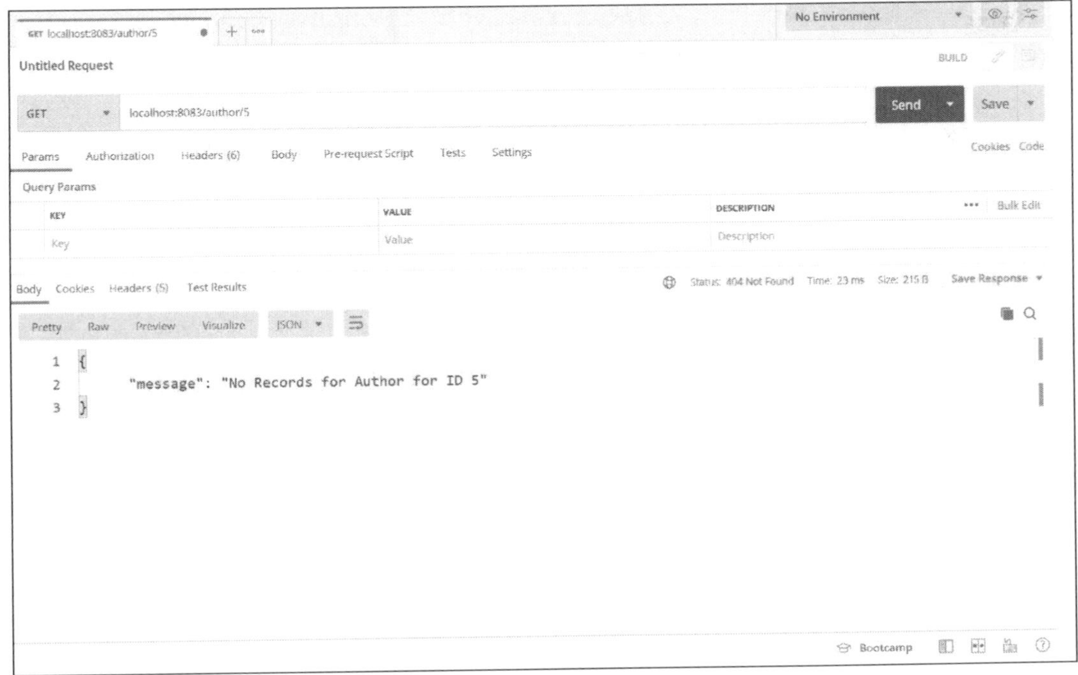

Figure 6.16: *Routing requests via API gateway*

Notice the domain is of the API gateway and not the application.

Conclusion

This chapter had set the expectations far enough for a developer to build up microservices stand-alone from scratch. In this chapter, we learned how to create microservices, consume them using the HTTP client like Postman, load different profiles and load their configurations, use of health checks, and handling exceptions using **`ControllerAdvice`**. We also looked into the Eureka service registry and routing the requests from our own API gateway to the microservice. In the next chapter, we will learn how to secure our web application with Spring filters.

Points to Remember

- Create a bean of **`RestTemplate`** with the timeouts set by using any **`ClientHttpRequestFactory`** before autowiring.
- Specify the **`spring.application.name`** property whenever you create a Spring Boot application.

- The Eureka service discovery discovers the application based on the application name.

Questions

1. What are different types of HTTP methods?
2. How to create GET RESTFul API?
3. How to consume POST API?
4. How to create the custom health check for the application?
5. How to handle dynamic query params?
6. How to hide an API behind the API gateway?
7. What is the use of `@ControllerAdvice`?
8. What is the other annotation used in conjunction with `@ControllerAdvice`?

CHAPTER 7
Securing a Web Application

In the previous chapter, we saw every information that is being sent out from the application is visible to any client who is accessing the application. In real life, the costliest aspect is the data and we just shared everything to the client who is accessing our APIs! In the previous chapter, we built a standalone microservice using the database, Eureka registry, RESTFul APIs, and what not. The thing that we missed is the security. *Who can access the APIs? Who can access the data? Which users are allowed to update the data? Who can be the admin to the application?* All these questions would be answered in this chapter.

Structure

In this chapter, we will discuss the following topics:

- Authentication and authorization concepts
- Spring security filters
- Enabling username and password security
- Disable security
- OAuth security
- Accessing REST secured APIs with the user role
- Uploading and downloading files from REST services

Objectives

After studying this unit, you should be able to understand the difference between **authentication** and **authorization**. You will be able to create a security layer around the application which decides who can access what and implement different types of security filters. You will create the *No-Auth* permit to access open APIs. You will learn how to log in to the application and access APIs via the username and password. This chapter also explains how to implement the **OAuth2 authentication and authorization** mechanism and use multiparts to upload files to the application server.

Authentication and authorization concepts

In the previous chapter, we had open access to all the APIs that were created we may not want that to be running in production. In general, the access is decided on the detailed retrieval of records or the kind of updates that may be performed on the resources. Sooner, the application which you build will require a security mechanism where certain users or a group of users have access to a particular part of the application. That's where we can use Spring security in our application with its features like authentication and authorization and avoid basic hacks to the application.

To start with Spring security, the following dependency is required to be included in **pom.xml**:

```
<dependency>
    <groupId>org.springframework.boot</groupId>
    <artifactId>spring-boot-starter-security</artifactId>
</dependency>
```

The moment you build your application after including the dependency and retrieve all authors, we can request the API **http://localhost:8081/author/all** from Postman. The following is the screenshot displaying an unauthorized error message with HTTP status code **401**:

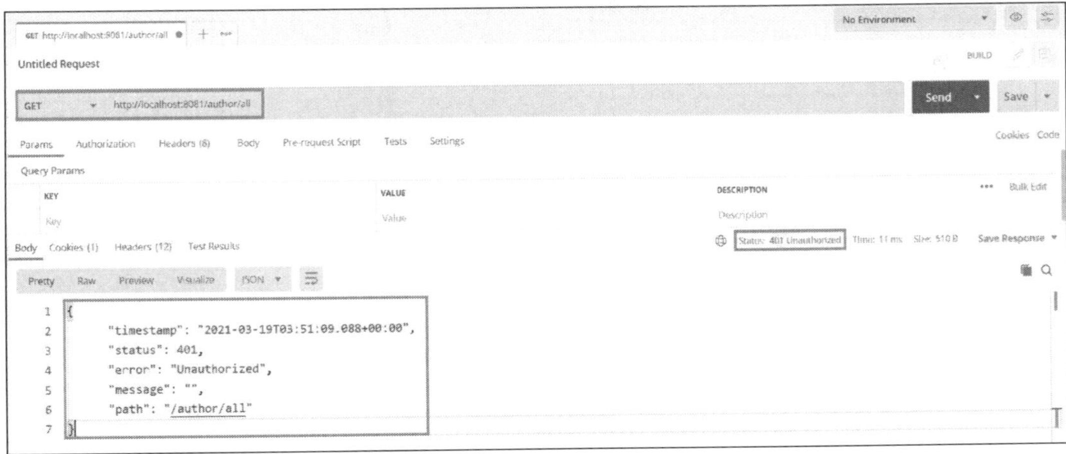

Figure 7.1: Unauthorized 401 error message

This means that the API is restricted to the users who logged into the application. In other words, this API is not open to every user.

If you try from Chrome, you will be redirected to the login screen which will ask you to feed in the username and password to access the API. The following screenshot displays the login screen:

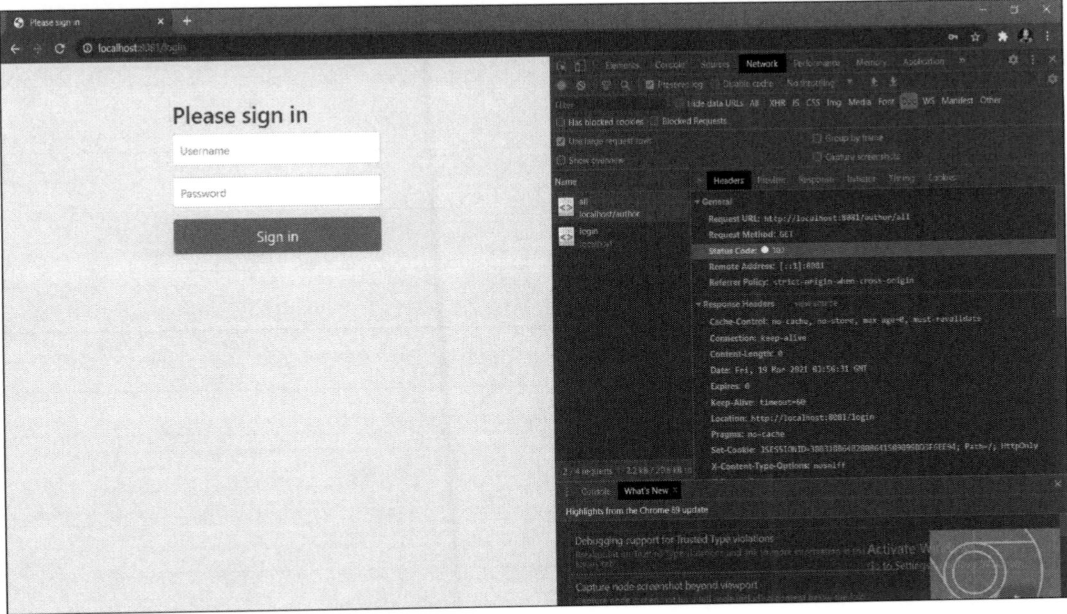

Figure 7.2: Redirects to login page

Now *how do we access this page?* Though it is our application and we own it, but we are now not able to access our APIs! That's due to the inclusion of Spring security!

Amazing! Now, our APIs are not open to all. But the question is still there about *how to access our APIs?*

Notice the console log when you started the application. The moment the application starts, you will see the following log which has the default password provided by Spring security:

```
2021-03-19 09:29:02.388 INFO 24140 --- [           main]
.s.s.UserDetailsServiceAutoConfiguration :


Using generated security password: 2e7e1774-e2b5-4e33-addb-9ef0fbb05be2
```

Now this is our password generated from a random UUID whose username is **`user`**. Provide the same to the login screen which we have in Chrome:

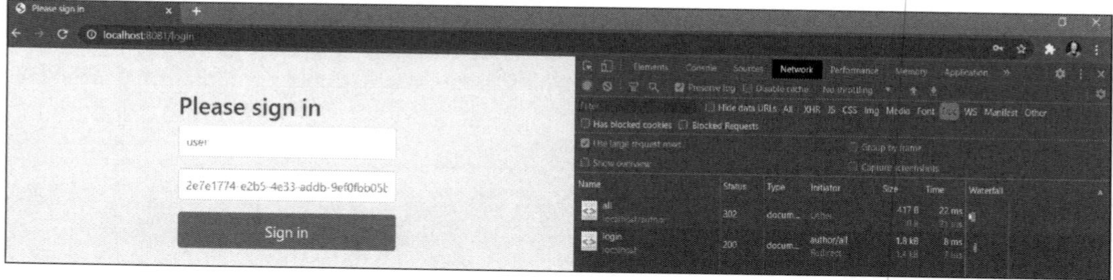

***Figure 7.3**: Feed credentials*

Now, hit on **`Sign in`**, and you will see the response which contains all your author details.

> **Try hitting all GET APIs after you feed in the credentials for the first time. Notice that all the APIs give responses as the session is maintained at the server side.**

Now, before understanding how we are able to see the authors, let us understand two concepts of security: **authentication** and **authorization**.

Authentication

Authentication is the first step of verification of the user who is accessing your web application. Usually, the authentication is done via the username and password in the same way when you log in to Google for accessing emails. Once the system verifies the validity of the password for the username, it allows access to the application. This is required to allow the user to know if he really has the access to perform the login operation or not. At the same time, the application needs to know if the accessing person is authenticated or not; if not, then any damage to the data is not rectified. Authentication allows the developer to know the logged in user has these many number of attributes which would be in-line to which the application persists. Once the user is authenticated, the application knows the **UserContext** and that can be used throughout the application to use the user's email, username, mobile number, and so on.

Authorization

Authorization is the second step performed after the user is authenticated. This step determines what kind of roles does the user have within the application. Whether he can visit certain pages, do some updates, delete some records, or even perform admin activities. Authorization can be customized to check after logging into the application; the roles can be mapped against a set of data where we can store roles for each user pertaining to a set of roles. Authorization can also be done via **OAuth** where OAuth doesn't tell anything about the user's email and other fields but tells the roles which he possesses. OAuth asks for token or the access code and when it is supplied to an API, the OAuth checks whether the token supplied has the same roles as the configured API.

So, considering the same concept, since we provided the username and password in the login screen, we are now able to access those APIs. Let us now deep dive into Spring security filters where we will understand different levels of processes involved once the user enters the password.

Spring security filters

The underlying technique in filters is all about how Spring manages **Java Servlet**. A servlet is created when you create any REST API. Rather would say, if we create a REST API via **`RequestMapping`**, Spring internally converts that into a servlet. When an API is requested to a Spring web application, **`DispatcherServlet`** redirects the HTTP request to our controllers. There is no security mechanism bounded for the routing, that is, it simply redirects the requests.

Ideally for the APIs which we want to restrict to our users, should have some kind of authentication/authorization headers before requests reach the controllers. That's where Spring filters come into picture and create an additional layer before redirecting the requests to controllers. When we create a Spring filter, it actually is placed ahead of servlets. Follow the steps below to implement security filter:

- Let us create following **HttpFilter** in the filters package:

```
package com.bpb.publications.authors.filters;
import java.io.IOException;
import javax.servlet.FilterChain;
import javax.servlet.ServletException;
import javax.servlet.http.HttpFilter;
import javax.servlet.http.HttpServletRequest;
import javax.servlet.http.HttpServletResponse;
import org.springframework.stereotype.Component;

@Component
public class SecurityFilter extends HttpFilter {

    @Override
    protected void doFilter(HttpServletRequest request,
HttpServletResponse response, FilterChain chain)
            throws IOException, ServletException {
        chain.doFilter(request, response);
    }

}
```

- Now, when you actually hit an API, it will be first routed to this filter and if the logic inside the filter says everything is okay, then the request reaches the controllers. The logic can be to validate headers, parameters, check username and password in the database, or check any kind of fraudulent activity. Once all are passed, **chain.doFilter(request, response)** allows the request to flow to the controller via Spring's **DispatcherServlet**. Failing to call the method will result in sending **200** HTTP status code with no response.
- A number of logic can be involved within **HttpFilter** – check for username and password authentication, check for authorization token validation, or check for roles that are in-line with the token, and setting back the response code by calling **response.setStatus(HttpServletResponse.SC_FORBIDDEN)** or **response.setStatus(HttpServletResponse.SC_UNAUTHORIZED)**.

- Here, the unauthorized error can be sent when either of the username and password is missing in the request or provides invalid credentials. Also, forbidden can be sent when there are some access issues where the user has access to the application, but is not allowed to access that particular API.

Enabling username and password security

Now that we have learned how to provide the default password that Spring created, it would never be the case where you actually want to dig out the password every time from logs to access the API. Instead, now we can have a username and password-based security to access the APIs. To have that logic to identify the correctness of hardcoded username and password, we need to inherit **`WebSecurityConfigurerAdapter`**. There are several methods in **`WebSecurityConfigurerAdapter`** which we can override with respect to our application security enhancements. However, let us start with username-password authentication.

The following snippet shows how to inherit **`WebSecurityConfigurerAdapter`**:

```
package com.bpb.publications.authors.security;

import org.springframework.context.annotation.Configuration;

import org.springframework.security.config.annotation.authentication.
builders.AuthenticationManagerBuilder;

import  org.springframework.security.config.annotation.web.configuration.
WebSecurityConfigurerAdapter;


@Configuration
public class SecurityConfigurationAdapter extends WebSecurityConfigurerAdapter
{

    @Override
    protected void configure(AuthenticationManagerBuilder auth) throws
    Exception {
        auth.inMemoryAuthentication().withUser("myuser").password("{noop}
        mypassword").roles("USER");
    }
}
```

The **inMemoryAuthentication** method of **AuthenticationManagerBuilder** allows in-memory authentication to **AuthenticationManagerBuilder** and returns a **InMemoryUserDetailsManagerConfigurer** to allow customization of the in-memory authentication. Now, if we access any API for the first time in a session with the username as **myuser** and password as **mypassword** in the login screen, we will be able to access our APIs. The placeholder **{noop}** in the password is required by Spring 5 which determines the password storage format. The role value **USER** provided to the roles method acts as a shortcut to assign the authority as **ROLE_USER**. The roles would be discussed in the latter part of this chapter.

To summarize, till now we have used the following two techniques:

- Accessing APIs via the default password generated via UUID with the username as **user**.
- Accessing APIs via the custom username and password placed within in-memory.

Disable security

Sometimes, there may be a case where even though you have included the Spring security starter pack, you wish to disable security. Such cases may lie under the developer's testing where the developer would be testing on the local machine which doesn't require any kind of authentication to access APIs. In such areas, a separate configuration can be approached within our **WebSecurityConfigurerAdapter**:

```
@Override
protected void configure(HttpSecurity http) throws Exception {
    http.authorizeRequests().antMatchers("*/**").permitAll();
}
```

The preceding snippet disables security for all the APIs. The **antMatchers** when used also support any wildcard in the request string. This looks perfect to disable security for example for API **/author/1**, **/author/all**. If we want to have dedicated authentication for certain APIs, then we need to run the following snippet which will disable security for few whereas enable for others:

```
@Override
protected void configure(HttpSecurity http) throws Exception {
    http.authorizeRequests().antMatchers("/author/all")
    .permitAll().anyRequest().authenticated();
}
```

The preceding snippet permits the access for the **`/author/all`** request or if requested, any other API returns the **`403 HTTP FORBIDDEN`** error.

OAuth security

OAuth is the standard for granting access to various resources across the Internet. For instance, when you wish to create an account on Stackoverflow, you can sign up using **`Sign up`** with a Google, GitHub, or Facebook account. When you click on any of those options, you will be redirected to the OAuth provider. Here, it can be Google, GitHub, or Facebook. Now, as you log in on **OAuth Provider Server**, you will be asked to allow the primary application, that is, Stackoverflow to *read* or *access* photos, account-related info, emails, and so on. Once you allow, you will be redirected back to Stackoverflow with a welcome page.

This is exactly a process OAuth authentication and authorization. Authentication is done when you provide your login details on the OAuth provider screen and authorization comes when you allow specific roles or access from the OAuth provider to your primary application.

The flow of OAuth security is shown in the following diagram:

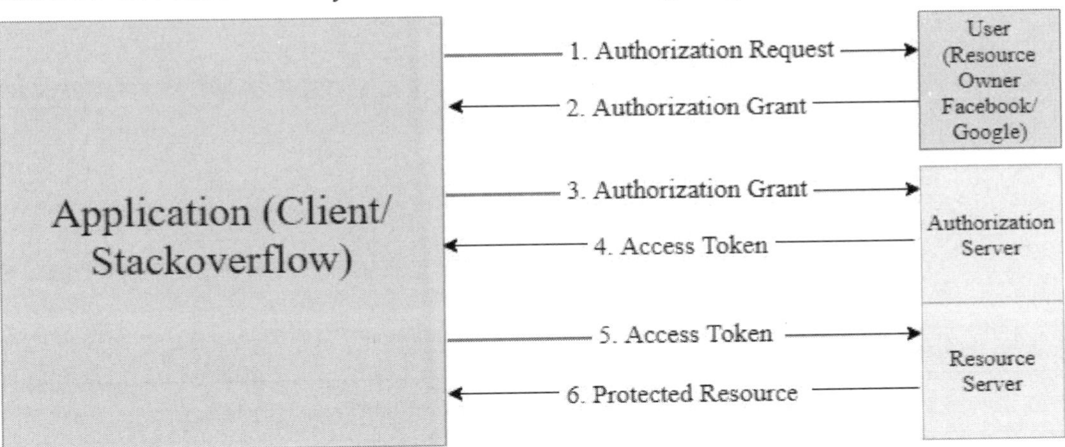

***Figure 7.4**: OAuth mechanism*

For our understanding, we will understand the latest OAuth – **OAuth2.0**. OAuth2 can be understood in two parts – **OAuth 2.0 Provider** and **OAuth 2.0 Client**. With respect to OAuth 2.0, a **resource server** is an application that protects protected resources via **OAuth Tokens**. The tokens are issued by an **authorization server** to the client application. The **client application** is the actual application where the resources are protected.

There is another authentication mechanism – **OpenID Connect** (**OIDC**) built on top of OAuth 2.0. The terminology changes for actors throughout the OIDC or OAuth 2.0 like:

Role	OAuth 2.0	OIDC
End user	Resource owner	End user
Application	Client	**Relying Party** (**RP**)
Identity provider	Authorization server	OpenID provider

***Table 7.1**: Actors and roles in OAuth 2.0 and OIDC*

OpenID is often used when a user signs in to the identity provider and then accesses other applications without logging in again or sharing login information.

We will now implement a custom solution where the client (user/postman) will access the protected resource (API) and it will be authenticated against an OAuth server (OAuth provider).

For implementing **OAuth2.0 features**, we can start by adding the following dependency to our project:

```
<dependency>
    <groupId>org.springframework.cloud</groupId>
    <artifactId>spring-cloud-starter-oauth2</artifactId>
    <version>2.2.4.RELEASE</version>
</dependency>
```

This dependency has everything related to validate APIs against an OAuth2 authorization server.

Further, we will need an **OAuth2 provider**. The OAuth2 provider exposes OAuth 2.0 protected resources which involves the configuration that allows you to create the OAuth 2.0 clients that can access its protected resources. The OAuth2.0 provider does this by managing and verifying the OAuth 2.0 tokens used to access the protected resources. These tokens are **Java Web Tokens** (**JWT**) which has the value of UUID, but if validated against a server, it will give you proper information about the user. The tokens can be understood as the encrypted information about the user and his roles.

The provider's role in OAuth2.0 is split into **authorization service** and **resource service** that can be placed within the same application or can be split across two applications. The resource service can also be incremented across different applications sharing the common authorization service. The requests which have the token are handled by MVC controller endpoints and their access are handled by Spring security filters. The following are two endpoints required in the Spring security filter in order to implement the OAuth2.0 authorization server:

- **AuthorizationEndpoint**: It is used to service requests for authorization. Default URL: **`/oauth/authorize`**.
- **TokenEndpoint**: It is used to service requests for access tokens. Default URL: **`/oauth/token`**.

We will have to permit access to all users for **TokenEndpoint** as that requires having open access to all users. Let us now dive deeper into writing authorization server configuration.

Whenever we create the authorization server, we need to consider which grant type should the client use to obtain the access token. The access token is a simple UUID. The grant types could be the authorization code, password, or refresh token. This server has the implementation for client details service as well as token services which enables or disables access to the endpoints.

Let us create an authorization server in the same project – webservice used in the previous chapter. The following is the code block for an authorization server:

```
package com.bpb.publications.authors.config;
import org.springframework.beans.factory.annotation.Autowired;
import org.springframework.context.annotation.Configuration;
importorg.springframework.security.authentication.AuthenticationManager;
import org.springframework.security.crypto.password.PasswordEncoder;
import  org.springframework.security.oauth2.config.annotation.configurers.
ClientDetailsServiceConfigurer;
import org.springframework.security.oauth2.config.annotation.web.
configuration.AuthorizationServerConfigurerAdapter;
import org.springframework.security.oauth2.config.annotation.web.
configuration.EnableAuthorizationServer;
import org.springframework.security.oauth2.config.annotation.web.
configurers.AuthorizationServerEndpointsConfigurer;
import org.springframework.security.oauth2.config.annotation.web.
configurers.AuthorizationServerSecurityConfigurer;

@Configuration
@EnableAuthorizationServer
```

```
public class AuthorizationServerConfig extends AuthorizationServerConfig-
urerAdapter {

    @Autowired
    private AuthenticationManager authenticationManager;

    @Autowired
    private PasswordEncoder passwordEncoder;
}
```

To enable the authorization server, we need to use **@EnableAuthorizationServer** on top of **@Configuration.** This is used to configure the OAuth 2.0 authorization server mechanism, with different methods overridden by inheriting **AuthorizationServerConfigurerAdapter** or **AuthorizationServerConfigurer.** The Adapter contains the following three methods, whose beans are injected by Spring:

- **ClientDetailsServiceConfigurer**: This defines the client details service. Important attributes of the client details are client ID, secret, scope, authorized grant types, and authorities. Here, we will use in-memory to store client details:

```
@Override
public void configure(ClientDetailsServiceConfigurer clients) throws
Exception {
    clients
    .inMemory()
    .withClient("my-client")
    .authorizedGrantTypes("client_credentials", "password")
    .authorities("ROLE_CLIENT", "ROLE_TRUSTED_CLIENT")
    .scopes("read", "write", "trust")
    .accessTokenValiditySeconds(86400)
    .secret(passwordEncoder.encode("secret"));

}
```

- **AuthorizationServerSecurityConfigurer**: It defines the security constraints on the token endpoint. Here, we will use the **isAuthenticated()** method to ensure everyone who reaches this token endpoint is authenticated. By default, the token access is set to **denyAll**. The method name inside the **checkTokenAccesss** method is a common built-in expression defined in Spring:

```
@Override
public void configure(AuthorizationServerSecurityConfigurer security)
throws Exception {
    security.checkTokenAccess("isAuthenticated()");
}
```

- **AuthorizationServerEndpointsConfigurer**: It defines the authorization and token endpoints and the token services. We will use the autowired **authenticationManager**:

```
@Override
public void configure(AuthorizationServerEndpointsConfigurer
endpoints) throws Exception {
    endpoints.authenticationManager(authenticationManager);
}
```

Next, we define the **Resource Server Config** within the same application. This serves resources that are protected in nature by the OAuth2 token. Spring provides this OAuth authentication mechanism which can be enabled by using **@EnableResourceServer** on top of **@Configuration** and inherit **ResourceServerConfigurerAdapter** or **ResourceServerConfigurer.** The **@EnableResourceServer** annotation adds a filter of type **OAuth2AuthenticationProcessingFilter** automatically to the Spring Security filter chain. The following is the snippet for **ResourceServerConfig**:

```
package com.bpb.publications.authors.config;
import org.springframework.context.annotation.Configuration;
import org.springframework.security.config.annotation.web.builders.
HttpSecurity;
import org.springframework.security.oauth2.config.annotation.web.
configuration.EnableResourceServer;
import org.springframework.security.oauth2.config.annotation.web.
configuration.ResourceServerConfigurerAdapter;

@Configuration
@EnableResourceServer
public class ResourceServerConfig extends ResourceServerConfigurerAdapter {
```

```
    @Override
    public void configure(HttpSecurity http) throws Exception {
        http
        .authorizeRequests()
        .antMatchers("/").permitAll()
        .antMatchers("/author/all").authenticated();
    }

}
```

Here, we can say that for all HTTP requests authorize all requests also requests that matches `/` in its URL, permits access to all users, but to the URL that matches `/author/all` that should be authenticated.

Now as we have autowired **`authenticationManager`**, all grant types are supported except the password, we need to make ensure that the **`UserDetailsService`** is the same as we provide.

Also, we need a table where we will store user details, for which we will create the **`User`** entity:

```
package com.bpb.publications.authors.entity;
import java.util.List;
import javax.persistence.Entity;
import javax.persistence.FetchType;
import javax.persistence.GeneratedValue;
import javax.persistence.Id;
import javax.persistence.OneToMany;

import lombok.Data;

@Entity
@Data
public class User {
    @Id
```

```
    @GeneratedValue
    private Long id;
    private String username;
    private String password;
    @OneToMany(fetch = FetchType.EAGER)
    private List<Role> roles;
    private boolean active;

}
```

For storing what all roles a user can have, we will need another table to store their roles. The following code is for **Roles.java**:

```
package com.bpb.publications.authors.entity;
import javax.persistence.Entity;
import javax.persistence.GeneratedValue;
import javax.persistence.Id;
import javax.persistence.Table;
import javax.persistence.UniqueConstraint;
import lombok.Data;

@Entity
@Data
@Table(uniqueConstraints = @UniqueConstraint(columnNames = { "name"}))
public class Role {
    @Id
    @GeneratedValue
    private Long id;
    private String name;
}
```

The preceding entities will store the user's details such as the username, password, his roles, and whether it's an active user or not. The **@OneToMany** annotation signifies that a single user can have multiple roles.

Further, in order to have our custom **User** table relate with **Authorities**, we will implement the class with **org.springframework.security.core.userdetails.UserDetails** where we can override methods as follows:

```
@Override
public Collection<? extends GrantedAuthority> getAuthorities() {
    List<SimpleGrantedAuthority> list = new ArrayList<>();
    roles.forEach(role -> list.add(new SimpleGrantedAuthority(role.
    getName())));
    return list;
}

@Override
public boolean isAccountNonExpired() {
    return active;
}

@Override
public boolean isAccountNonLocked() {
    return active;
}

@Override
public boolean isCredentialsNonExpired() {
    return active;
}

@Override
public boolean isEnabled() {
    return active;
}
```

Now, we will create a repository **UserRepository** from where we can look up the required user as follows:

```
package com.bpb.publications.authors.repository;
import java.util.Optional;
import org.springframework.data.repository.CrudRepository;
import com.bpb.publications.authors.entity.User;

public interface UserRepository extends CrudRepository<User,Long> {
    Optional<User> findByUsername(String username);
}
```

Also, the repository for roles for managing roles is as follows:

```
package com.bpb.publications.authors.repository;
import org.springframework.data.repository.CrudRepository;
import com.bpb.publications.authors.entity.Role;

public interface RoleRepository extends CrudRepository<Role, Long>{


}
```

We also need to modify the **SecurityConfigurationAdapter** class which we created earlier for enabling in-memory **AuthenticationManagerBuilder** for our custom hard-coded user. The following is the modified snippet for the **SecurityConfigurationAdapter** class:

```
package com.bpb.publications.authors.security;
import org.springframework.context.annotation.Bean;
import org.springframework.context.annotation.Configuration;
import org.springframework.security.authentication.AuthenticationManager;
import org.springframework.security.config.annotation.web.builders.
HttpSecurity;
import   org.springframework.security.config.annotation.web.configuration.
WebSecurityConfigurerAdapter;

@Configuration
public class SecurityConfigurationAdapter extends WebSecurityConfigurerAdapter
{
```

```
    @Override
    public void configure(HttpSecurity http) throws Exception {
        http.authorizeRequests().antMatchers("/oauth/token").
        permitAll().anyRequest().authenticated();
    }

    @Bean
    @Override
    public AuthenticationManager authenticationManagerBean() throws
    Exception {
        return super.authenticationManagerBean();
    }

}
```

Here, we have allowed access for **/oauth/token** to all users and enabled authentication for any other requests coming in. **/oauth/token** is the request URL against which the token mechanism works.

The last thing to do is to create a **UserDetailsService** as follows:

```
package com.bpb.publications.authors.service;
import java.util.Arrays;
import java.util.Optional;
import javax.annotation.PostConstruct;
import org.springframework.beans.factory.annotation.Autowired;
import org.springframework.security.core.userdetails.UserDetails;
import org.springframework.security.core.userdetails.UserDetailsService;
import org.springframework.security.core.userdetails.
UsernameNotFoundException;
import org.springframework.security.crypto.password.PasswordEncoder;
import org.springframework.stereotype.Service;
import com.bpb.publications.authors.entity.Role;
import com.bpb.publications.authors.entity.User;
import com.bpb.publications.authors.repository.RoleRepository;
import com.bpb.publications.authors.repository.UserRepository;
```

```
@Service
public class CustomUserDetailsService implements UserDetailsService {

    @Autowired
    private UserRepository userRepository;

    @Autowired
    private RoleRepository roleRepository;

    @Autowired
    PasswordEncoder passwordEncoder;
}
```

As we implement **UserDetailsService**, we need to implement its method. The following method is put into the same class:

```
    @Override
    public UserDetails loadUserByUsername(String username) throws
    UsernameNotFoundException {
        Optional<User> user = userRepository.findByUsername(username);
        if (user.isPresent()) {
            return user.get();
        } else {
            throw new UsernameNotFoundException("Invalid User :" +
            username);
        }
    }
```

This method checks whether the username provided exists in the database or not.

We can also have the custom code to insert a user into the database as the default user if it doesn't have any entry. The following snippet can be placed in the post construct of the bean:

```
    @PostConstruct
    public void postConstruct() {
```

```
        if (!userRepository.findByUsername("shagun").isPresent()) {
            Role role = new Role();
            role.setName("ROLE_USER");
            role = roleRepository.save(role);
            User user = new User();
            user.setUsername("shagun");
            user.setPassword(passwordEncoder.encode("sbakliwal"));
            user.setActive(true);
            user.setRoles(Arrays.asList(role));
            userRepository.save(user);
        }
    }
```

This class is loaded by Spring and called by **AuthenticationManager** to load the user by its username.

Now, we are ready to provide our **UserDetailsService** to **AuthenticationManager** as described earlier. For this, we need to autowire the following code in any of the configuration class:

```
@Autowired
public void authenticationManager(AuthenticationManagerBuilder builder, CustomUserDetailsService service) throws Exception {
    builder.userDetailsService(service);
}

@Bean
public PasswordEncoder getPasswordEncoder(){
    return new BCryptPasswordEncoder();
}
```

Now as we start the application, few tables will be created automatically if **ddl-auto** is set in configuration.

On using CURL command **http://localhost:8081/author/all** we would get following error:

{"error":"unauthorized","error_description":"Full authentication is required to access this resource"}.

This is due to the OAuth 2.0 resource server configuration. To make this work, that is, to access the preceding URL, we can use Postman or CURL command to generate the token for us.

Accessing REST secured APIs with the user role

Now to access the protected resource, the client needs a valid token which would be validated against the authorization server. To fetch the token, we can hit the CURL command or generate the token via Postman. We will see both ways to generate the token. The following are the examples:

- **CURL**: By using the **`curl`** command, we can access APIs like Postman. Here, we are requesting **`/oauth/token`** with grant type details as the password and providing credentials with authorization client details.

```
curl http://localhost:8081/oauth/token?grant_type=password -d
"username=shagun&password=sbakliwal" --user my-client:secret
```

- **Postman**: We can also hit the same API via Postman with the URL as **`http://localhost:8081/oauth/token?grant_type=password`** and the method type as **`POST`** with the username and password as **`shagun`** and **`sbakliwal`**, respectively as we configured in the **`PostConstruct`** method. We will also need to provide the authorization details as follows:

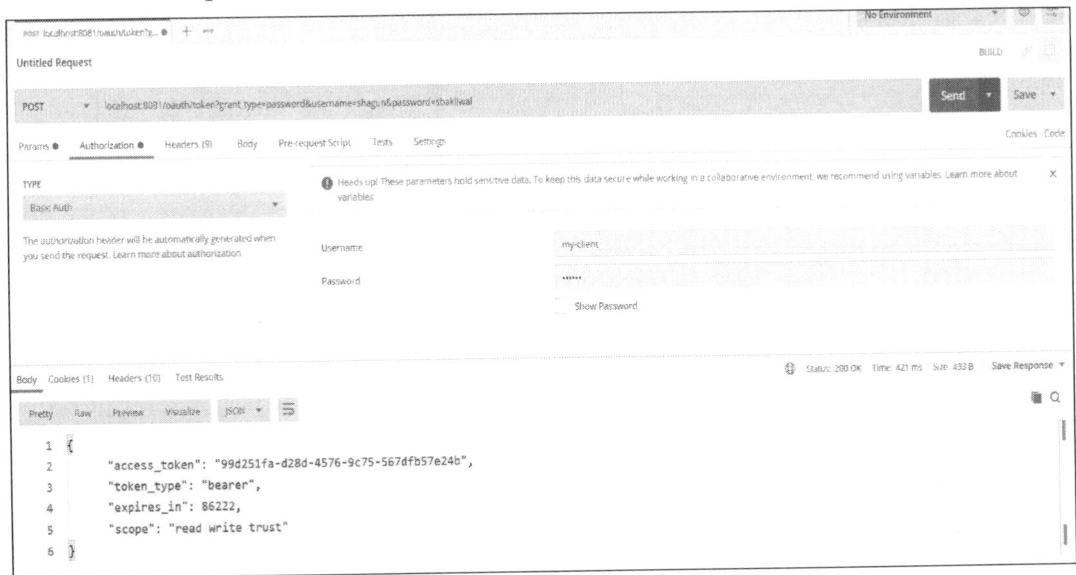

Figure 7.5: Generate token from Postman

In both the tools, we will get the same response: **{"access_token":"99d251fa-d28d-4576-9c75-567dfb57e24b","token_type":"bearer","expires_in":86222,"scope":"read write trust"}.** So, it can be drawn from the preceding response that a single user can have the same session throughout in the authorization server.

Wonder *how to use this access token to access the protected resource?*

It's simple. Provide the access token in the request as request params. For example,

http://localhost:8081/author/all?access_token=99d251fa-d28d-4576-9c75-567dfb57e24b will give you the correct response as it contains a valid token. This token will expire in **86400** seconds, that is, 24 hours as configured in the authorization server. In this way, a client can use this token throughout the day.

Uploading and downloading files from REST services

In this section, we will create different RESTful APIs that upload a file to the application server and another API downloads the file from the application server. To upload a file, the datatype of the file in REST API should be of the type **org.springframework.web.multipart.MultipartFile.** This datatype is the representation of the uploaded file in a multipart request. This object contains the data of the file, and it is the user who saves this file temporarily in the application server, to the desired location in the application server or to the database. We will take this file, and store this file in the desired location and then on request to download the API, we will fetch the same file and send it as the response. The following is the skeleton of the **DocumentController**:

```
package com.bpb.publications.authors.controller;
import java.io.IOException;
import java.nio.file.Files;
import java.nio.file.Path;
import java.nio.file.Paths;
import javax.annotation.PostConstruct;
import org.springframework.web.bind.annotation.RestController;

@RestController
public class DocumentController {
    private String uploadDirectory = "C:\\users\\PCW\\docstore";
```

```
    private Path docStore;

    @PostConstruct
    public void setUp() throws IOException {
      docStore = Paths.get(uploadDirectory).toAbsolutePath().normalize();
        Files.createDirectories(docStore);
    }
}
```

As soon as the bean of the **DocumentController** is created, the application will create directories if not present as set in the **uploadDirectory** variable. The following snippet creates a PUT endpoint for uploading a file:

```
@PutMapping("/upload")
public ResponseEntity<?> upload(@RequestParam("file") MultipartFile file) {
    try {
        Files.copy(file.getInputStream(), docStore.resolve(file.
        getOriginalFilename()),
                StandardCopyOption.REPLACE_EXISTING);
    } catch (IOException e) {
        e.printStackTrace();
        return ResponseEntity.status(HttpStatus.INTERNAL_SERVER_ERROR).
        body(e);
    }
    return ResponseEntity.ok("Successfully uploaded");
}
```

The preceding snippet copies the file with the same name to the application server and returns a successful response if the application is able to save the file. While copying the file, it will replace the existing file if present.

To download the file, we will create another endpoint which takes the file name and then the application looks for the file to download. The following snippet is used to download the file:

```
@GetMapping("/download")
public ResponseEntity<?> download(@RequestParam("filename") String file)
throws FileNotFoundException {
```

```
    InputStreamResource resource = new InputStreamResource(new
    FileInputStream(docStore.resolve(file).toFile()));
    return ResponseEntity.ok().contentType(MediaType.APPLICATION_OCTET_
    STREAM)
            .header(HttpHeaders.CONTENT_DISPOSITION, "attachment;
            filename=\"" + file + "\"").body(resource);
}
```

Let us now run the application and request for uploading and downloading the API via Postman. The following are the screenshots showing the RESTFul APIs:

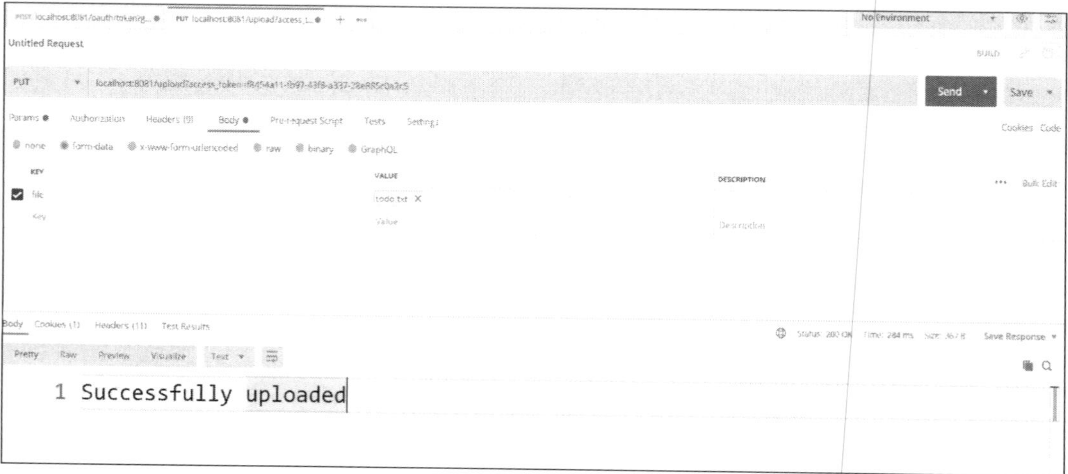

***Figure 7.6**: Upload file from Postman*

The following screenshot displays the downloaded file for the requested API:

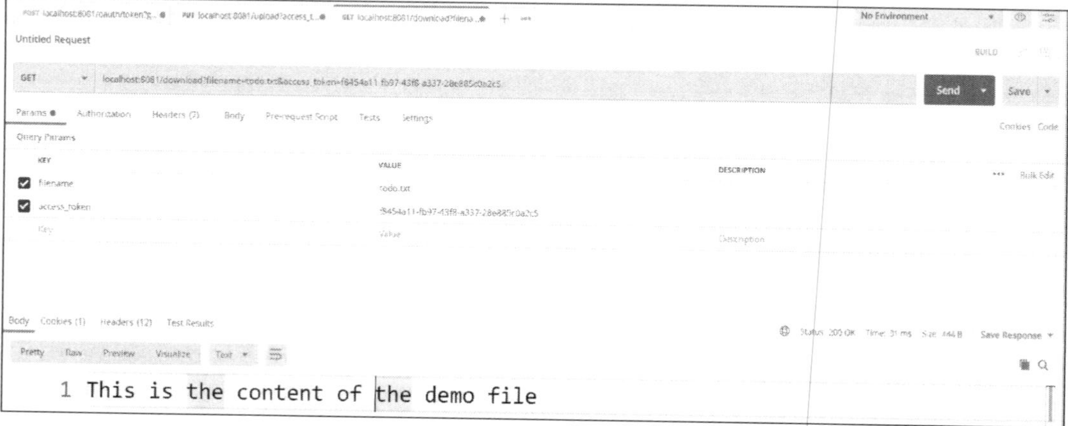

***Figure 7.7**: Download file from Postman*

If you browse the URL from a Chrome window, the file gets downloaded to the Downloads folder with the same name as you provided in the request.

Conclusion

This chapter helped us understand how to secure RESTful APIs via various methods of Spring security using the username and password. We learned how to implement OAuth 2.0 Authentication mechanism for authorizing different APIs for different users who have valid access tokens. We also learned how to upload and download the files to and from the application server. In the next chapter, we will learn how to build a resilient system so that the application is highly available to users and serves the request on demand.

Points to remember

- While developing a consumer of a secured API, the clients should be onboarded to access the authentication server.
- The authentication server and resource server configuration can be placed in different applications for better reusability.
- Always encrypt passwords while saving into the database.

Questions

1. How to enable basic security in a Spring Boot application?
2. Who decides the authorization roles for a trusted client?
3. What is OAuth 2.0 security and how does it work?
4. What are the two parts of OAuth 2.0 implementation?
5. How to disable security?
6. Explain security filters. How to apply different security filters?
7. What are multipart requests?

CHAPTER 8
Building Resilient System

With Spring security implemented in the previous chapter, we learned that the user of the application should have valid access tokens to access the APIs. In this chapter, we will learn how to handle many users requesting our APIs at the same time. We will learn how to sustain high traffic with different number of the same applications running on the same machine. If any part of the application continuously fails in serving the requests, then we will learn how to implement the **Circuit Breaker** to gracefully degrade the functionality so that the application continues to operate when a related service fails, preventing the failure from cascading and giving the failing service time to recover.

Structure

In this chapter, we will discuss the following topics:

- Client-side load balancing
- Circuit breaker
- Implementing Resilience4J

Objectives

After studying this unit, you should be able to:

- Understand how traffic is balanced across different application servers.
- Failing safe in case of any repeated errors in a time interval.
- Implementing different resilient patterns.

Client-side load balancing

Spring Boot has an interesting feature to support client-side load balancing that can be done easily with a simple configuration. This helps the client applications to connect to different servers based on the **Round Robin policy**. Load balancing offering is done using Netflix Ribbon for a microservice. Let us create a basic **`RestController`** that returns a random integer from a range of **`1`** to **`100`** by following steps:

- You will need to create a new Spring Boot project **`random-number-project`** with the following dependency to have REST features just as we learned in the previous chapters:

  ```
  <dependency>
      <groupId>org.springframework.boot</groupId>
      <artifactId>spring-boot-starter-web</artifactId>
  </dependency>
  ```

- Every time when we create a new Spring Boot project, we also get a simple class decorated with **`@SpringBootApplication`** having the **`main()`** method. Next, we will create a REST controller that returns a random integer. The following snippet can be added to your controller package:

  ```
  package com.bpb.publications.controller;
  import java.net.InetAddress;
  import java.net.UnknownHostException;
  import java.util.Random;
  import javax.servlet.http.HttpServletResponse;
  import org.springframework.beans.factory.annotation.Value;
  import org.springframework.web.bind.annotation.GetMapping;
  import org.springframework.web.bind.annotation.RestController;

  @RestController
  ```

```
public class RandomNumberController {

    @GetMapping("/generate")
    public int generateFrom1to100(@Value("${server.port}")
    Integer port, HttpServletResponse response)
            throws UnknownHostException {
        response.addHeader("origin", InetAddress.getLocalHost().
        getHostAddress() + ":" + port);
        return new Random().ints(1, 100).limit(1).findFirst().
        getAsInt();
    }
}
```

Here, we created a REST API **/generate** that takes the application server port and **HttpServletResponse** as parameters to the method. Note that even if we simply hit an endpoint, these params if included are automatically injected with each request that comes to the API. The port detail is captured using **server.port** which is specified in **application.yml.**

- To modify the response that will be sent out from this API can be modified by having **HttpServletResponse** as a parameter. We have used the object to add a header named as origin to store the application server's IP and the port on which the application is running. Now, whenever a user or client requests for this API, he will get the server IP and the port on which the application is running. You shouldn't expose these details in the production environment due to security concerns. Here, we have included it to understand the response is sent from which application server.

The following code is the content of **application.yml** where we will modify the port of the server:

```
spring:
  application:
    name: random-number-project


server:
  port: 7001
```

Till now we have created a REST controller that returns the random number and sets the server IP and port number in the **origin** header of the response.

To understand the real-world example, we will now run this application with different ports; say **7001**, **7002, 7003,** and so on as per the production requirement to support many users at the same time. This concludes that the application server is running with three different instances.

- To implement the client-side load balancing, we will now create a new Spring Boot application **my-client-application** which will act as the client running with one instance. The following snippet includes the required dependencies to adopt load balancing:

```
<dependencies>
    <dependency>
        <groupId>org.springframework.cloud</groupId>
        <artifactId>spring-cloud-starter-loadbalancer</artifactId>
    </dependency>
    <dependency>
        <groupId>org.springframework.boot</groupId>
        <artifactId>spring-boot-starter-web</artifactId>
    </dependency>
    <dependency>
        <groupId>org.projectlombok</groupId>
        <artifactId>lombok</artifactId>
        <scope>provided</scope>
    </dependency>
</dependencies>
```

You will notice a new dependency which has **groupId** as **org.springframework.cloud.** The artifact **spring-cloud-starter-loadbalancer** is the starter pack for the Spring cloud load balancer. The other dependencies are required to load REST-related features and the automated resource management such as to generate getters/setters and SLF4J to use the default logger.

- While we use the cloud dependency, we also need to add dependency management in order to use the correct repository which is supported by the parent of the project. The following is the snippet that we will place in **pom.xml**:

```
<dependencyManagement>
    <dependencies>
        <dependency>
```

```
                <groupId>org.springframework.cloud</groupId>
                <artifactId>spring-cloud-dependencies</artifactId>
                <version>2020.0.1</version>
                <type>pom</type>
                <scope>import</scope>
            </dependency>
        </dependencies>
    </dependencyManagement>
```

Since we are using *Spring Boot 2.4.3*, we can use the **2020.0.1** version of **spring-cloud-dependencies**.

- Next, we will now start configuring classes that are required for load balancing. The following is the configuration class we need to create a bean of **RestTemplate**:

```
package com.bpb.publications.configuration;
import org.springframework.cloud.client.loadbalancer.LoadBalanced;
import org.springframework.cloud.loadbalancer.annotation.
LoadBalancerClient;
import org.springframework.context.annotation.Bean;
import org.springframework.context.annotation.Configuration;
import org.springframework.web.client.RestTemplate;

@Configuration
@LoadBalancerClient(name = "random-number-project", configuration =
RandomNumberConfiguration.class)
public class RestTemplateConfig {

    @LoadBalanced
    @Bean
    RestTemplate restTemplate() {
        return new RestTemplate();
    }

}
```

We used two new annotations - **@LoadBalancerClient** and **@LoadBalanced.** The following is the definition of annotations:

- o **@LoadBalancerClient**: It is a declarative configuration for a load balancer client after which we can inject an instance of **LoadBalancerClientFactory** to access the client that is created. Here, we will specify the name of the load balancer client that uniquely identifies a set of client resources and configuration attributes to specify the configuration class that will help us to access different servers of other applications.
- o **@LoadBalanced**: This annotation is used to mark the **RestTemplate** bean to be configured to use **LoadBalancerClient**.

- Next, we will create a configuration class which we will specify in the **LoadBalancerClient** annotation – **RandomNumberConfiguration**. The following is the snippet:

```
package com.bpb.publications.configuration;
import java.util.Arrays;
import java.util.List;
import org.springframework.cloud.client.DefaultServiceInstance;
import org.springframework.cloud.client.ServiceInstance;
import org.springframework.cloud.loadbalancer.core.
ServiceInstanceListSupplier;
import org.springframework.context.annotation.Bean;
import org.springframework.context.annotation.Configuration;
import reactor.core.publisher.Flux;

@Configuration
public class RandomNumberConfiguration {

    @Bean
    ServiceInstanceListSupplier serviceInstanceListSupplier() {
        return new SimpleServiceInstanceListSupplier("random-
        number-project");
    }
}
```

- In this configuration class, we will create a bean of **ServiceInstanceList-Supplier** which will be used while connecting to clients. The **ServiceIn-stanceListSupplier** is just an interface which contains a list of **ServiceIn-stance** objects. The **ServiceInstance** represents an instance of a service in a discovery system.

  ServiceInstanceListSupplier is implemented by various classes, namely, **DiscoveryClientServiceInstanceListSupplier**, **NoopServiceIn-stanceListSupplier**, and **DelegatingServiceInstanceListSupplier**. Further as **DelegatingServiceInstanceListSupplier** is an abstract class, its implementers are **HealthCheckServiceInstanceListSupplier**, **CachingSer-viceInstanceListSupplier**, and **ZonePreferenceServiceInstanceList-Supplier**.

These different suppliers are used in different use cases. The following are the definitions of these suppliers:

- **DiscoveryClientServiceInstanceListSupplier:** It is a discovery-client-based **ServiceInstanceListSupplier** implementation. It uses **Reac-tiveDiscoveryClient** to get the instances.
- **NoopServiceInstanceListSupplier:** It is a no-op implementation of **Servi-ceInstanceListSupplier.** It doesn't contain any instances so it returns an empty list of **ServiceInstance.**
- **DelegatingServiceInstanceListSupplier:** It represents a **ServiceIn-stanceListSupplier** that implements **ServiceInstanceListSupplier** that can be used to create a delegate **ServiceInstanceListSupplier**.
- **CachingServiceInstanceListSupplier:** It is a **ServiceInstanceListSup-plier** implementation that tries to retrieve **ServiceInstance** objects from the **CachingServiceInstanceListSupplierCache** cache. If the cache is not available, then it retrieves instances using **DiscoveryClientServiceIn-stanceListSupplier**.
- **HealthCheckServiceInstanceListSupplier:** It is a **ServiceInstanceList-Supplier** implementation that verifies whether the instances are alive and only returns the healthy one, unless there are none. It uses **WebClient** to ping the **/actuator/health** endpoint of the instances to check the status of instances.
- **ZonePreferenceServiceInstanceListSupplier:** It is an implementation of **ServiceInstanceListSupplier** that filters instances retrieved by the delegate by zone. The zone is retrieved from the **spring.cloud.loadbalancer.zone** property. If the zone is not set or no instances are found for the requested zone, all instances retrieved by the delegate are returned.

However, we will create a custom **ServiceInstanceListSupplier** containing **DefaultServiceInstance** for different instances of the same application. The following is the code for **SimpleInstanceListSupplier**:

```
class SimpleServiceInstanceListSupplier implements ServiceInstanceList-
Supplier {

    private final String serviceId;

    SimpleServiceInstanceListSupplier(String serviceId) {
        this.serviceId = serviceId;
    }

    @Override
    public String getServiceId() {
        return serviceId;
    }

    @Override
    public Flux<List<ServiceInstance>> get() {
        return Flux.just(Arrays.asList(new
        DefaultServiceInstance(serviceId + "1", serviceId, "localhost",
        7001, false),
                new DefaultServiceInstance(serviceId + "2", serviceId,
                "localhost", 7002, false),
                new DefaultServiceInstance(serviceId + "3", serviceId,
                "localhost", 7003, false)));
    }
}
```

As we started with creating an application server with REST Controller to generate random numbers running on port **7001** on the localhost server, we provided those details containing instances of all applications running on different machines with different ports like **7002** and **7003** to this supplier on the localhost machine. The **get()** method returns a flux of list of all **ServiceInstance** which are running on different systems. A **flux** object represents a reactive sequence of *0..N* items, while a **mono** object represents a single-value-or-empty *(0..1)* result.

Lastly, we will create a controller that invokes an API of theapplication server with the load balancer client name. The following is the code for **MyServiceController**:

```
package com.bpb.publications.controller;
import org.springframework.beans.factory.annotation.Autowired;
import org.springframework.http.ResponseEntity;
import org.springframework.web.bind.annotation.RequestMapping;
import org.springframework.web.bind.annotation.RestController;
import org.springframework.web.client.RestTemplate;
import lombok.extern.slf4j.Slf4j;

@RestController
@Slf4j
public class MyServiceController {
    @Autowired
    RestTemplate restTemplate;

    @RequestMapping("/loadbalancedAPI")
    public Integer loadbalancedAPI() {
        ResponseEntity<Integer> response = restTemplate.
        getForEntity("http://random-number-project/generate", int.
        class);
        log.info("Responding Server Origin: " + response.getHeaders().
        getOrigin());
        return response.getBody();
    }

}
```

The API **/loadbalancedAPI** makes a REST Call to the application server with the host name as **random-number-project.** Note this name was configured in **RestTemplateConfig**. Since our API returned an integer value, we made the response type as **`int.class`**. On hitting this API, it will start logging the application server (random-number-project) origin which is a combination of the host and port.

Now we will start the **`random-number-project`** on three different ports using the command: **`java -Dserver.port=<port> -jar random-number-project-0.0.1-SNAPSHOT.jar`** with the port number as **`7001`**, **`7002`** and **`7003`** and start **`my-client-application`** using the command: **`java -jar my-client-application-0.0.1-SNAPSHOT.jar`** running on port **`8888`**.

When you browse the URL **`http://localhost:8888/loadbalancedAPI`** on Chrome and refresh it multiple times, then you will notice the following logs in the console showing the response from three different servers:

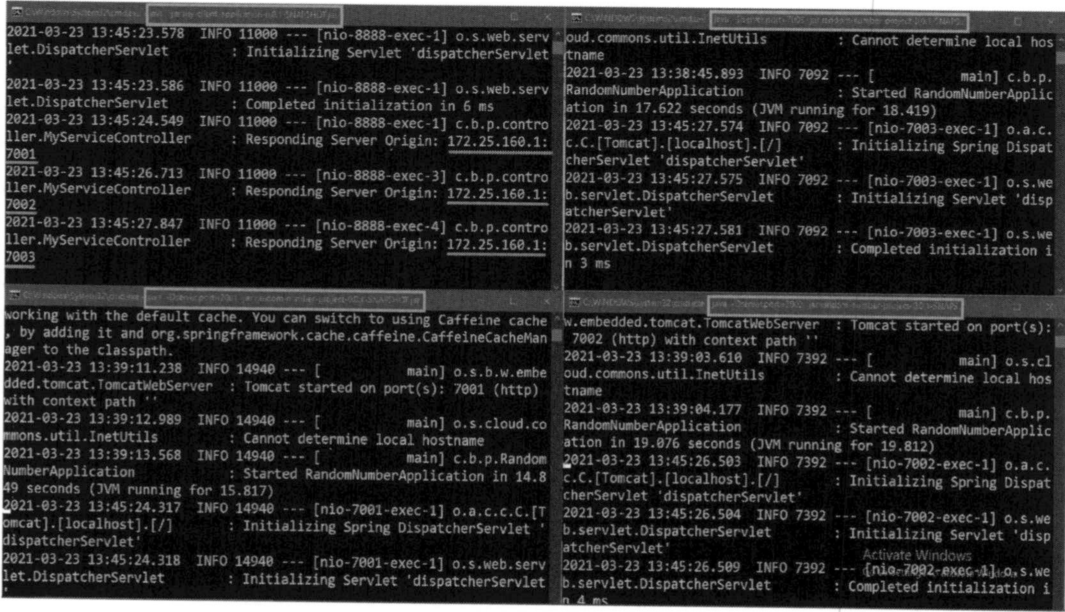

Figure 8.1: *Console logs*

The green line highlighted in the screenshot of the first console depicts which server responds back. We have now implemented a simple client-side load balancing using **`ServiceInstanceListSupplier`**.

Circuit breaker

It is usual for a microservice or a simple web application to make multiple remote calls to other services spread across different machines or Internet for performing some operations. For making a call to remote services, it might happen that the service may fail to give responses within a proper interval of time. In such cases, there should be some timeout set so that the application doesn't hang forever to fetch the response. To overcome these unlimited failure calls, we can implement the function call to be inside the circuit breaker object that makes a remote service call. Once the failure threshold count is crossed, the circuit breaker gets activated and avoids further calls to failure services, so that the actual service is not hit continuously.

While implementing the circuit breaker, the underlying technique of pausing the further call depends on the three stages of state of making that external call. Those three stages of circuit breaker are as follows:

- **Open circuit:** This becomes active when the external call failure crosses the threshold of the failure count. If the circuit is in the open state, then no further calls to the external service are placed and the application returns an error message.
- **Closed circuit:** This is the primary state of circuit that allows you to make external calls which always returns a success value from the external service.
- **Half open circuit**: It is used to check whether the service responds well or not, after waiting for the specified configuration of the circuit breaker. When the circuit is in the half open state, then the real call to the external service is made once as a trial call and on failure to the call, it changes the state back to the open state to avoid further calls.

All these states of the circuit breaker maintain the count of failed calls so that it gets reset whenever there is a successful response. We will use this feature in our microservices to degrade the functionality of the service gracefully when the external service fails to respond to allow the application serve requests continuously preventing cascade failures. We will now look into implementing the circuit breaker using **Resilience4J**. Let us implement the circuit breaker in the next section.

Implementing Resilience4J

The **Resilience4J** framework is a light-weight easy-to-use fault tolerant library that is built on top of **Hystrix**. Hystrix is now in the maintenance mode after *Spring Boot 2.4.0*. Resilience4J is one of the libraries which helps us to make the system fault tolerant to avoid cascading failures of the components that we build within a microservice. It just sits before the external call and monitors the responses. If the response time crosses the threshold or if there are errors while calling the external service, the application tends to react with the fallback methods we define. It is majorly used within a distributed system. We will use the same **`my-client-application`** which was running on port **`8888`** for implementing the circuit breaker. Resilience4J came into picture when the support and enhancements for Hystrix went into the divest state. Resilience4J is the new library with more features than Hystrix and so it is recommended that you use Resilience4J to build a fault tolerant system.

To include Resilience4J features, we need to include the following dependencies:

```
<dependency>
    <groupId>io.github.resilience4j</groupId>
    <artifactId>resilience4j-spring-boot2</artifactId>
</dependency>
<dependency>
    <groupId>io.github.resilience4j</groupId>
    <artifactId>resilience4j-micrometer</artifactId>
</dependency>
<dependency>
    <groupId>io.github.resilience4j</groupId>
    <artifactId>resilience4j-circuitbreaker</artifactId>
</dependency>
<dependency>
    <groupId>org.springframework.boot</groupId>
    <artifactId>spring-boot-starter-actuator</artifactId>
</dependency>
<dependency>
    <groupId>org.springframework.boot</groupId>
    <artifactId>spring-boot-starter-aop</artifactId>
</dependency>
```

After including these dependencies, it is all about how we set up the configurations which contain different patterns on what to do in case of service failure, how much time the application will have wait for to change the state of the circuit breaker, the threshold count on which the circuit should get open, and allow different exceptions to allow bypassing the circuit breaker. By default, if any kind of exception is raised by the remote service, the counter which the circuit breaker maintains gets increased and if we whitelist those exceptions, then the counter remains the same as those exceptions are treated as business exceptions.

The following are the resiliency patterns which are handled gracefully by the Resilience4J library:

- **`Timeout:`** This is the foremost feature required whenever the application makes the call to other services via **`RestTemplate`**. We specify the time duration for which the **`RestTemplate`** should be allowed to connect to the external service within a time duration and wait for it to read the response. If this timeout is crossed, then the related exception is raised stating that the request is being timed out. This ensures that the application no longer waits indefinitely to get the response. To implement this timeout, we can have the following snippet in place while creating a **`RestTemplate`**:

```
@Bean
RestTemplate restTemplate() {
    return new RestTemplateBuilder()
            .setConnectTimeout(Duration.ofMinutes(2))
            .setReadTimeout(Duration.ofMinutes(2))
            .build();
}
```

- **`retry:`** This mechanism deals with retrying the **`RestTemplate`** call again to the remote service whenever there is some network issue that is other than business exceptions being raised to ensure if there is any latency in the network, the request can be retried. For this, we can always have a custom solution to retry, but Resilience4J already has this feature implemented. As a part of retry, we can specify for how many times the service should be invoked and the time interval between each retry. Further, if we have a set of exceptions for which if raised, there should be no retry. The following configuration needs to be placed in **`application.yml`**:

```
resilience4j:
  retry:
    instances:
      random-number-generator-circuit-breaker:
        max-attempts: 4
        wait-duration: 1s
        retry-exceptions:
          - org.springframework.web.client.ResourceAccessException
          - java.net.ConnectException
```

In these properties, we specified that in case of failure in receiving responses from the external service for the list of exceptions present in **`retry-`**

`exceptions`, we need to retry for maximum **`4`** times to receive the response with the delay of `1` second in each call.

To activate the retry mechanism, we need to place the **`@Retry`** annotation on the top of the method which tends to raise an exception like the external service failure. The following is the snippet:

```
@Retry(name = "random-number-generator-circuit-breaker")
    public Integer callRandomNumberService() {
        ResponseEntity<Integer> response = restTemplate.
        getForEntity("http://random-number-project/generate",
                int.class);
        return response.getBody();
    }
```

For testing, we can turn off the remote service and try hitting the external service. We will see the following logs when we enable the debug logging output which shows that there were four retries made to the external service by **`RestTemplate`**:

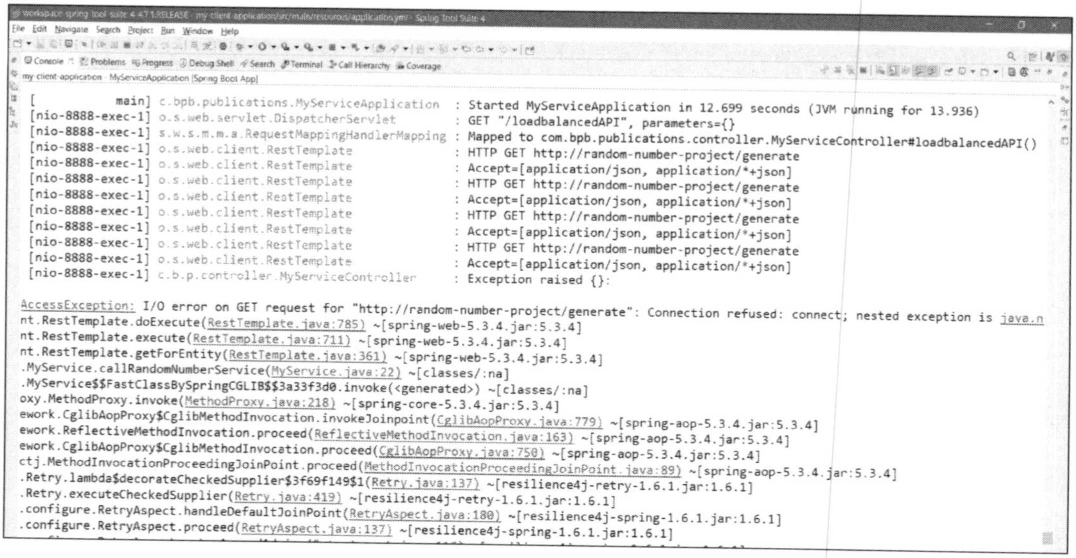

```
[           main] c.bpb.publications.MyServiceApplication  : Started MyServiceApplication in 12.699 seconds (JVM running for 13.936)
[nio-8888-exec-1] o.s.web.servlet.DispatcherServlet        : GET "/loadbalancedAPI", parameters={}
[nio-8888-exec-1] s.w.s.m.m.a.RequestMappingHandlerMapping : Mapped to com.bpb.publications.controller.MyServiceController#loadbalancedAPI()
[nio-8888-exec-1] o.s.web.client.RestTemplate              : HTTP GET http://random-number-project/generate
[nio-8888-exec-1] o.s.web.client.RestTemplate              : Accept=[application/json, application/*+json]
[nio-8888-exec-1] o.s.web.client.RestTemplate              : HTTP GET http://random-number-project/generate
[nio-8888-exec-1] o.s.web.client.RestTemplate              : Accept=[application/json, application/*+json]
[nio-8888-exec-1] o.s.web.client.RestTemplate              : HTTP GET http://random-number-project/generate
[nio-8888-exec-1] o.s.web.client.RestTemplate              : Accept=[application/json, application/*+json]
[nio-8888-exec-1] o.s.web.client.RestTemplate              : HTTP GET http://random-number-project/generate
[nio-8888-exec-1] o.s.web.client.RestTemplate              : Accept=[application/json, application/*+json]
[nio-8888-exec-1] c.b.p.controller.MyServiceController     : Exception raised {}:

AccessException: I/O error on GET request for "http://random-number-project/generate": Connection refused: connect; nested exception is java.n
nt.RestTemplate.doExecute(RestTemplate.java:785) ~[spring-web-5.3.4.jar:5.3.4]
nt.RestTemplate.execute(RestTemplate.java:711) ~[spring-web-5.3.4.jar:5.3.4]
nt.RestTemplate.getForEntity(RestTemplate.java:361) ~[spring-web-5.3.4.jar:5.3.4]
.MyService.callRandomNumberService(MyService.java:22) ~[classes/:na]
.MyService$$FastClassBySpringCGLIB$$3a33f3d0.invoke(<generated>) ~[classes/:na]
oxy.MethodProxy.invoke(MethodProxy.java:218) ~[spring-core-5.3.4.jar:5.3.4]
ework.CglibAopProxy$CglibMethodInvocation.invokeJoinpoint(CglibAopProxy.java:779) ~[spring-aop-5.3.4.jar:5.3.4]
ework.ReflectiveMethodInvocation.proceed(ReflectiveMethodInvocation.java:163) ~[spring-aop-5.3.4.jar:5.3.4]
ework.CglibAopProxy$CglibMethodInvocation.proceed(CglibAopProxy.java:750) ~[spring-aop-5.3.4.jar:5.3.4]
ctj.MethodInvocationProceedingJoinPoint.proceed(MethodInvocationProceedingJoinPoint.java:89) ~[spring-aop-5.3.4.jar:5.3.4]
.Retry.lambda$decorateCheckedSupplier$3f69f149$1(Retry.java:137) ~[resilience4j-retry-1.6.1.jar:1.6.1]
.Retry.executeCheckedSupplier(Retry.java:419) ~[resilience4j-retry-1.6.1.jar:1.6.1]
.configure.RetryAspect.handleDefaultJoinPoint(RetryAspect.java:180) ~[resilience4j-spring-1.6.1.jar:1.6.1]
.configure.RetryAspect.proceed(RetryAspect.java:137) ~[resilience4j-spring-1.6.1.jar:1.6.1]
```

***Figure 8.2**: Console logs for retry debug enabled*

To check metrics for the retry, put the following properties in config:

```
management:
  server:
    port: 9999
```

```
  endpoint:
    metrics:
      enabled: true
  endpoints:
    web:
      exposure:
        include: '*'
```

We will request **http://localhost:9999/actuator/retryevents** to see the time of retries made which failed due to some reasons.

- **CircuitBreaker:** This mechanism places a circuit breaker in between the process that may take a longer time to process. This library will change the state of the circuit breaker to **OPEN**, **HALF_OPEN,** and **CLOSED** depending on the behavior of the external service. These states of the circuit breaker are discussed briefly in the previous section. To enable the circuit breaker using Resilience4J, we don't need to use **@EnableCircuitBreaker** as we used for **Hystrix** circuit breaker. The method should be annotated with the **@CircuitBreaker** with the name of the circuit breaker as given in the following code:

```
@CircuitBreaker(name = "random-number-generator-circuit-breaker")
public Integer callRandomNumberService() {
    ResponseEntity<Integer> response = restTemplate.
    getForEntity("http://random-number-project/generate",
            int.class);
    return response.getBody();
}
```

After placing this annotation, we need to configure the circuit breaker in **application.yml** as follows:

```
resilience4j:
  circuitbreaker:
    instances:
      random-number-generator-circuit-breaker:
        wait-duration-in-open-state: 5s
        failure-rate-threshold: 50
        sliding-window-size: 20
```

```
        sliding-window-type: count-based
        minimum-number-of-calls: 5
        permitted-number-of-calls-in-half-open-state: 1
        automatic-transition-from-open-to-half-open-enabled: true
        register-health-indicator: true
        slow-call-duration-threshold: 7000
        slow-call-rate-threshold: 50
```

This configuration says that for **random-number-generator-circuit-breaker,** change the status of circuit to **OPEN** if minimum of **5** calls are failed to external service and stay in **OPEN** state for **5** seconds so that the future calls to failing external service are not made. After **5** seconds, we need to change the circuit state to **HALF OPEN** permitting **1** call to that external service. The automatic transition from the **OPEN** state to **HALF OPEN** is managed by a Boolean value. This configuration also handles the state if the external service doesn't respond in **7000** ms. This configuration is **count-based**, which means if **5** calls fail, then we need to **OPEN** the circuit. This configuration can also be **time-based** by changing **sliding-window-type**. The failure threshold is configured to **50%** for instance if out of all the external requests if **50%** requests are failing then change the circuit breaker status. By default, the state of the circuit breaker is **CLOSED**, which means the application can make the call to the external service. Once the state is changed to **OPEN**, no more calls can be placed to the external service.

To track every metric of the circuit breaker, we can enable the metrics and health for the circuit breaker by putting the following configuration:

```
management:
  server:
    port: 9999
  endpoint:
    metrics:
      enabled: true
    health:
      enabled: true
      show-details: always
    circuitbreakers:
      enabled: true
```

```
endpoints:
  web:
    exposure:
      include: '*'
health:
  circuitbreakers:
    enabled: true
metrics:
  enable:
    resilience4j:
      circuitbreaker:
          calls: true
  distribution:
    percentiles-histogram:
      http:
        server:
          requests: true
      resilience4j:
        circuitbreaker:
          calls: true
```

After having these configurations, try hitting **http://localhost:9999/actuator/health** to check the health of the application. This will return a similar response as follows:

```
{
   "status":"UP",
   "components":{
      "circuitBreakers":{
         "status":"UP",
         "details":{
            "random-number-generator-circuit-breaker":{
               "status":"UP",
```

```
                    "details":{
                        "failureRate":"-1.0%",
                        "failureRateThreshold":"50.0%",
                        "slowCallRate":"-1.0%",
                        "slowCallRateThreshold":"50.0%",
                        "bufferedCalls":0,
                        "slowCalls":0,
                        "slowFailedCalls":0,
                        "failedCalls":0,
                        "notPermittedCalls":0,
                        "state":"CLOSED"
                    }
                }
            }
        }
    }
}
```

The circuit breaker will change the status when there is a change in the state from **CLOSED** to **OPEN** or **HALF OPEN**. The failure rate when turned to 100% will **OPEN** the circuit. **bufferedCalls** stores the count in the current ring buffer. This count is increased for each failure and once the count reaches the threshold, the circuit is **OPEN**. As the **bufferedCalls** is increased, the **failedCalls** count also increases. After the circuit is in the **OPEN** state, if there are further calls to the external service, the **notPermittedCalls** counter is increased. All counters are reset when the circuit is in the **HALF OPEN** state.

When the circuit is in the **OPEN** state, further calls to the external service is not placed and before that, the circuit breaker throws an **io.github.resilience4j.circuitbreaker.CallNotPermittedException** for the clients to understand that there is a failure in the external service.

You can have as many circuit breakers as you want for each external call to make the system resilient enough.

- **fallback:** This mechanism deals with handling the response in case of any failure in the external service call. Whenever the external call fails, we can send our own message or own data instead of throwing an exception. This

fallback doesn't change the circuit breaker state. To configure a **fallback**, the annotations are required to be modified as follows:

```
@CircuitBreaker(name = "random-number-generator-circuit-breaker",
fallbackMethod = "fallbackMethodForRandomNumberProject")
public Integer callRandomNumberService() {
    ResponseEntity<Integer> response = restTemplate.
    getForEntity("http://random-number-project/generate",
            int.class);
    return response.getBody();
}

public Integer fallbackMethodForRandomNumberProject(Throwable e) {
    return 101;
}
```

We modified the annotation to accept the name of the **fallback** method. This **fallback** method hence created has the same signature as that of the original method plus a placeholder for **Throwable** datatype to handle the exception raised when the actual call was placed. The same **fallback** mechanism is also available in case of **retry**. The **101** in the return value makes us understand that it is the incorrect response as the external service has to return a number between **1** to **100**.

- **bulkhead**: This mechanism deals with the availability of the service to stay available all time even if one of the application services fail. This allows the application to not go down due to any of its service failure. This ensures that the burden to the service is reduced to serve the concurrent requests. There are two implementations of the **bulkhead** patterns:
    - **Semaphore:** This limits the number of concurrent requests and rejects if the counter reaches the threshold.
    - **FixedThreadPoolBulkhead:** This isolates a particular thread from the thread pool to serve requests only for the given service. There is a waiting queue also that maintains which will raise **io.github.resilience4j.bulkhead.BulkheadFullException** for any requests coming in if the thread pool and queue are full.

    The following is the configuration to enable **bulkhead**:

```
resilience4j:
  bulkhead:
```

```
      instances:
        random-number-generator-circuit-breaker:
          max-wait-duration: 2000ms
          max-concurrent-calls: 2
    thread-pool-bulkhead:
      instances:
        random-number-generator-circuit-breaker:
          max-thread-pool-size: 1
          core-thread-pool-size: 1
          queue-capacity: 1
```

The **max-concurrent-calls** maintains the count of parallel execution and **max-wait-duration** maintains the time count for which the next thread has to wait to maintain the concurrent call.

In the method, where we wish to maintain the bulkhead, place **@Bulkhead** at the top of the method, and you can also have a **fallback** method configured as follows:

```
@Bulkhead(name = "random-number-generator-circuit-breaker",
fallbackMethod = "fallbackMethodForRandomNumberProject")
public Integer callRandomNumberService() {
    ResponseEntity<Integer> response = restTemplate.
    getForEntity("http://random-number-project/generate",
            int.class);
    return response.getBody();
}


public Integer fallbackMethodForRandomNumberProject(Throwable e) {
    return 101;
}
```

Congratulations! We have implemented the Resilience4J circuit breaker in the Spring application to protect against cascading failures and to provide fallback behavior for potentially failing calls.

Conclusion

We learned how to make the system resilient enough to serve the clients at all times without degrading the overall performance of the application. We learned how to set different timeouts by configuring **`RestTemplate`** and resiliency patterns such as circuit breaker, bulkheads, and retry. Further, we have also looked into client-side load balancing along with Resilience4J.

In the next chapter, we will learn about logging patterns and different tools to analyze the logs.

Points to remember

- Handling the **`CallNotPermittedException`** `is` outside the scope of the method where an external call is made.
- If fallbacks are configured, then the counters shown in the health of the circuit breaker remains unchanged.
- Always have a custom code to pick up the configuration for different servers to create a **`ServiceInstanceListSupplier`**.

Questions

1. How do you enable client-side load balancing?
2. What are Hystrix and Resilience4J?
3. How do you configure the connect timeout for **`RestTemplate`**?
4. What is the need of a load balancer client?
5. How can we create different service instances to pass on requests to each server?
6. What is a circuit breaker and its three states?
7. What are the resiliency patterns offered by Resilience4J?
8. Explain the transition of states in the circuit breaker.

CHAPTER 9
Logging

We learned how to make a system resilient by using resiliency patterns in the previous chapter *Building Resilient System* which focuses on the **Non-Functional Requirement** (**NFR**) in any application. Another aspect of NFR is logging. The way we log the information is equally important as the quality of code we develop. In this chapter, we will learn how to log the information and analyze it using some pretty good tools.

Structure

In this chapter, we will discuss the following topics:

- Different ways of logging data
- Logback
- Understanding Spring Cloud Sleuth and Zipkin log aggregation
- Using **ELK** for analyzing events

Objective

After studying this unit, you should be able to understand different ways of logging data and the flow of requests from one application to another. We will analyze events in Kibana.

Different ways of logging data

Till now, we learned how to save and fetch data from database, call external services, prepare the system to be resilient enough to handle traffic to fallback to different method, but all of these features are implemented to have fail-safe self-resilient application so that it can handle any infrastructure error. If any error occurred then the logs can help to analyze error. Yes, **logs** play an important role while debugging any application for any functionality. The simplest way of logging is to use `System.out.print()` which will post the logs to the console. When you turn on logs in the debug mode by setting **`debug=true`** in **`application.yml,`** you will see all logs which were never seen earlier as shown in the following screenshot:

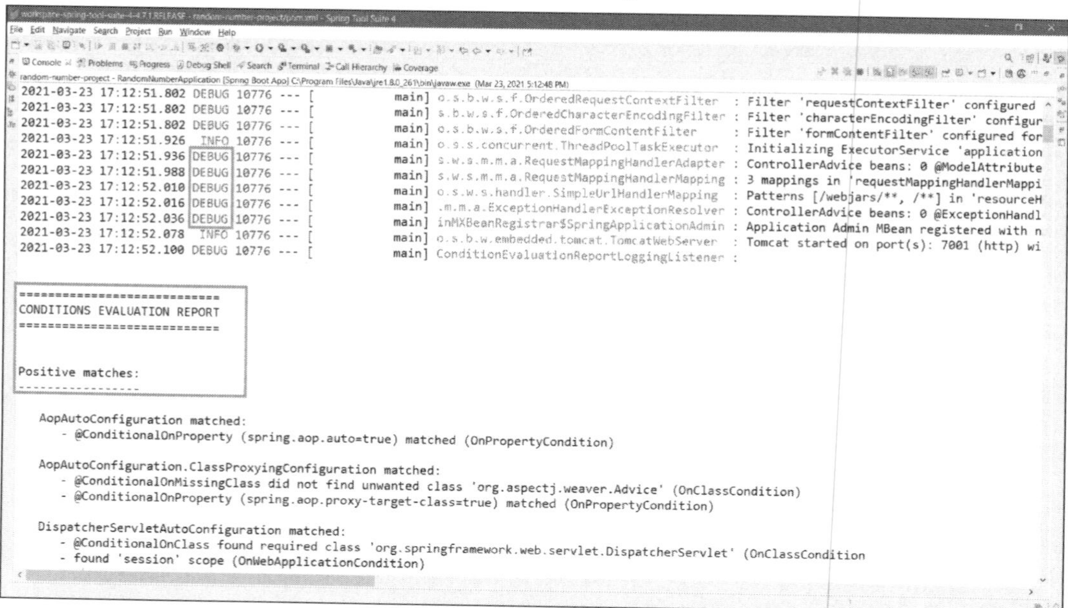

Figure 9.1: Debug enabled console logs

It displays all the logs which use the level **`DEBUG`**. These levels of logs will be discussed in the next section. You will also see that there is one **Conditions Evaluation Report** coming up. This report shows all the auto-configuration that runs behind the startup and creation of beans. This report is very useful when you are deep into auto configuration via multiple beans of the same type.

Let's take a look at the different logging patterns offered by logback.

Logback

Logback is one of the fundamental ways and the default mechanism of the logging framework used for logging. This framework is a superset of the older framework **Log4J** providing less ways of configuration and flexibility. Logback comprises three components – **Logger**, **Appenders,** and **Layouts**:

- **Logger: This** contains the data or information that we log. This is the class that applications use while logging.
- **Appenders: This** places the log messages to the final destinations like the console or file. A logger can have multiple appenders.
- **Layout: This** shows the format in which we should see the logs.

Follow the below steps for using logback features:

- We need to include the following dependency which is also included in **`spring-boot-starter-logging`** which is also a part of **`spring-boot-starter`**:

```
<dependency>
    <groupId>ch.qos.logback</groupId>
    <artifactId>logback-classic</artifactId>
    <version>${logback.version}</version>
</dependency>
<dependency>
    <groupId>org.apache.logging.log4j</groupId>
    <artifactId>log4j-to-slf4j</artifactId>
    <version>2.13.3</version>
</dependency>
<dependency>
    <groupId>org.slf4j</groupId>
    <artifactId>jul-to-slf4j</artifactId>
    <version>${slf4j.version}</version>
</dependency>
```

- In *Spring Boot 2.4.3*, the versions of **Logback** and **Slf4J** are *1.2.3* and *1.7.30,* respectively. To use the logback, we can create a **logback.xml** in **resources** folder as follows:

```
<configuration>
  <appender name="STDOUT" class="ch.qos.logback.core.
  ConsoleAppender">
    <encoder>
      <pattern>%d{HH:mm:ss.SSS} [%thread] %-5level %logger{36} -
      %msg%n</pattern>
    </encoder>
  </appender>
  <root level="debug">
    <appender-ref ref="STDOUT" />
  </root>
</configuration>
```

  It's not mandatory to have this file, but if we want to change the way logs will be processed, then we can add this file. We provide the appender's name as **STDOUT** which is referenced in **appender-ref** inside the **root** tag. The **appender** requires the qualified name of the class of the **Appender**. Here, as we wish to put logs in the console, we use **ch.qos.logback.core.ConsoleAppender**. You can also use **ch.qos.logback.core.FileAppender** if we want all logs to go to the file. The **appender** requires a pattern in which we can log. The preceding pattern takes the timestamp, the thread name, the logging level, and the message. Finally, we need to specify that we want to use the **debug** level logging at the root level which will use the **STDOUT** appender.

- When we build with the preceding XML and put the log using the logger, you will see the following logs with the pattern:

```
10:05:01.733 [main] ERROR c.b.p.RandomNumberApplication - Error
log from RandomNumberApplication for logging level ERROR
```

- You can also attach a pattern layout to this to have colorful logging by placing the layout inside the **appender** as follows:

```
<appender name="STDOUT" class="ch.qos.logback.core.
ConsoleAppender">
```

```
    <layout class="ch.qos.logback.classic.PatternLayout">
        <Pattern>%black(%d{ISO8601}) %highlight(%-5level)
        [%blue(%t)] %yellow(%C{1.}): %msg%n%throwable</Pattern>
    </layout>
</appender>
```

- Let us use the logger inside our **main** method as seen in the following code snippet:

```
package com.bpb.publications;
import org.slf4j.Logger;
import org.slf4j.LoggerFactory;
import org.springframework.boot.SpringApplication;
import org.springframework.boot.autoconfigure.
SpringBootApplication;

@SpringBootApplication
public class RandomNumberApplication {

    private static final Logger logger = LoggerFactory.
    getLogger(RandomNumberApplication.class);

    public static void main(String[] args) {
        logger.error("Error log from {} for logging level {}",
        RandomNumberApplication.class.getSimpleName(), "ERROR");
       SpringApplication.run(RandomNumberApplication.class, args);

    }

}
```

This will log in the colorful format in the console as follows:

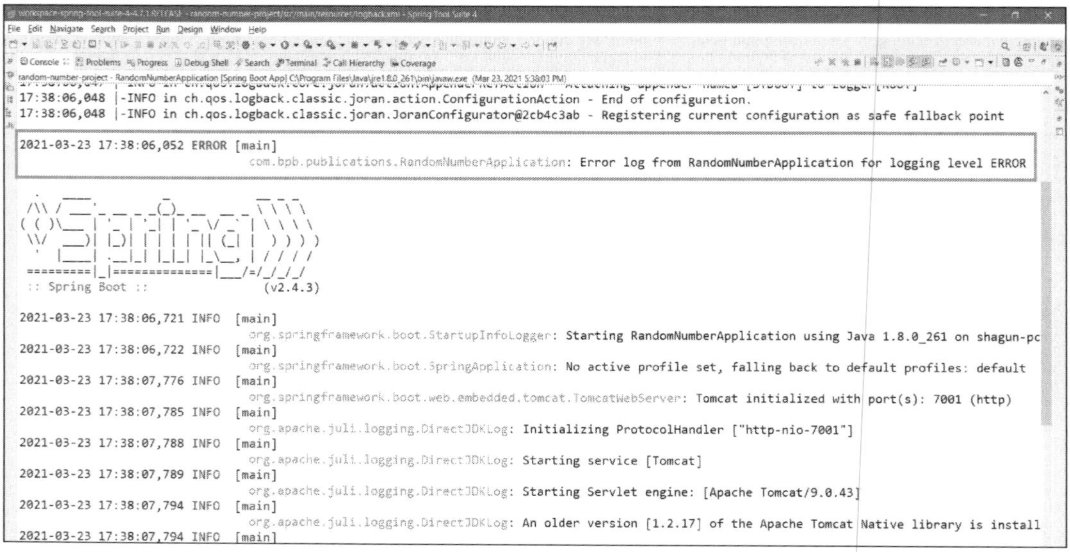

Figure 9.2: *Pattern layout in logback*

The **{}** specified will pick up the placeholder value just placed after the comma (**,**) after the message in double quotes. This is called **parameterized log**. You can place as many **{}** as many variables are there in your log separated by commas at the end. For instance, place the following log in the Java class.

For logging into the file, we can use **file** appender in **logback.xml** as follows:

```
<configuration>
   <appender name=”FILE” class=”ch.qos.logback.core.FileAppender”>
       <file>myfile.log</file>
       <append>true</append>
       <encoder>
           <pattern>%-4relative %d{yyyy-MM-dd HH:mm:ss.SSS}
           [%thread] %-5level %logger{35} - %msg%n</pattern>
       </encoder>
   </appender>
   <root level=”info”>
       <appender-ref ref=”FILE” />
   </root>
```

```
</configuration>
```

This configuration will take all the logs and append in the file called as **myfile.log**. We can remove the **append** tag if we don't want to append logs to the same file.

- You can also set specific logs to go to the console or to the file. But before that, let us take a look at the logging levels. There are five logging levels listed as follows in hierarchy:
  - o **ERROR:** To display all error logs.
  - o **WARN:** To display all warning logs.
  - o **INFO:** To display all informational logs. This is the general logging level which we will use.
  - o **DEBUG:** To display all debug level logs for the purpose of what's happening under the hood. It is optional to show all debug logs.
- **TRACE:** To display the tracing of what's going on in and out of the functionality.

> **To change the logging level at runtime without making any changes in the configuration, run the jar file with the option for the logging level. For example, `java -jar <jar> --debug`.**

- It is up to the developer to use different logging levels at different places. We can also decide a selective way of logging for a particular package or class file by providing the following configuration in Logback:

```
<logger name="com.bpb.publications" level="debug" />
   <root level="info">
    <appender-ref ref="STDOUT" />
</root>
```

This configuration says that for all classes in the **com.bpb.publications** package, we should use debug level logging. By having this level of logging, we can see **error, info, warn,** and **debug** level logs. By default, if we use the logging level as **info**, it will not print the debug logs.

- You can also attach a **rolling** policy to the appenders where the logs will be created based on a pattern like time-based and size-based as follows:

```
<configuration>
    <appender name="FILE_ROLLING"
        class="ch.qos.logback.core.rolling.RollingFileAppender">
        <file>myfile.log</file>
```

```
        <encoder
            class="ch.qos.logback.classic.encoder.
            PatternLayoutEncoder">
            <Pattern>%-4relative   %d{yyyy-MM-dd   HH:mm:ss.SSS}
            [%thread] %-5level
                %logger{35} - %msg%n</Pattern>
        </encoder>
        <rollingPolicy
            class="ch.qos.logback.core.rolling.
            TimeBasedRollingPolicy">
            <fileNamePattern>archived/myfile-%d{yyyy-MM-dd}.%i.log
            </fileNamePattern>
            <timeBasedFileNamingAndTriggeringPolicy
                class="ch.qos.logback.core.rolling.
                SizeAndTimeBasedFNATP">
                <maxFileSize>1KB</maxFileSize>
            </timeBasedFileNamingAndTriggeringPolicy>
        </rollingPolicy>
    </appender>

    <root level="info">
        <appender-ref ref="FILE_ROLLING" />
    </root>
</configuration>
```

- This configuration when placed rolls the logging file based on the file size and time. If the day is changed or the file size has crossed the maximum file size, here **1 KB**, the related log files will be moved to the archived folder where logs files are indexed with the number as suffix. This will ensure that the file placed at root, that is, **`myfile.log`** will contain the latest logs and other log files placed in the archived folder will be subsequently contain older logs. You will notice the following structure of project explorer when there are multiple logs files created:

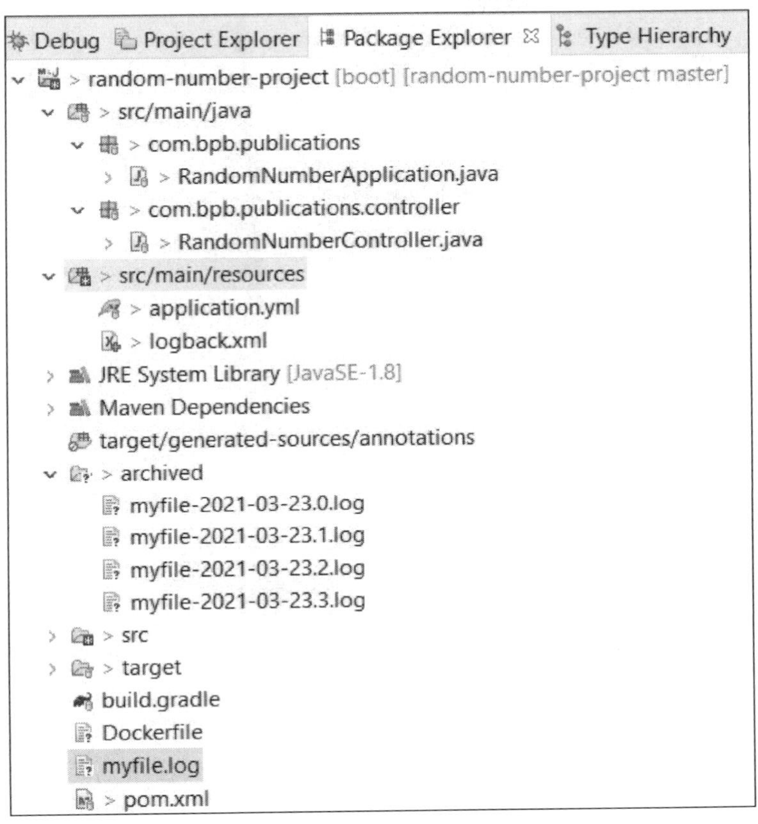

***Figure 9.3**: Project explorer after rolling policy for Logback*

Till now, we have only created **`logback.xml`** which contains the configuration of logging. Spring also supports the configuration file named after **`logback-spring.xml`**. The convention is to use the **`-spring`** variant whenever possible.

In our previous chapters, we also used the **Lombok** dependency and the annotation **`@Slf4J`** at the top of the classes. This is another way to not declare the logger variable from **`LoggerFactory`** and log our data in the console or file. This boilerplate code is removed as an advantage of using the annotation **`@Slf4J`**. Let us now deep dive into distributed tracing solution – **Spring Cloud Sleuth**.

Understanding Spring Cloud Sleuth and Zipkin log aggregation

Spring Cloud Sleuth is a feature or dependency that is provided by Spring Cloud to trace the external calls made from the microservice. This external call could be made directly by using **RestTemplate** or going via **Zuul's API Gateway** or even using **Kafka** or **RabbitMQ** which are the common messaging systems. To visualize the traces, **Zipkin** helps us. Zipkin is another Java application that can be downloaded from the following website:

https://search.maven.org/remote_content?g=io.zipkin&a=zipkin-server&v=LATEST&c=exec

We need such tools or mechanisms for tracking the requests that pass through multiple microservices or applications. It is actually easy to determine the performance of the application in a way such that if any component fails within the flow, it can be identified by simply looking into the **Zipkin dashboard**.

The preceding link when downloaded sets up the Zipkin server and the Zipkin dashboard for us which can be browsed by running the command: **`java -jar zipkin-server-2.23.2-exec.jar`** or the latest version of the Zipkin can be provided. Once the application is up, you can browse **`http://localhost:9411`** on Chrome to load the Zipkin dashboard. This dashboard will be explored in detail once we have some data around it by reusing the microservices which we had in the previous chapter – **`random-number-project`** and **`my-client-application`**.

To revise, **`random-number-project`** is a simple REST application having a controller that generates a random number and **`my-client-application`** deals with load balancing strategies to connect with the **`random-number-project`** via **`spring-cloud-loadbalancer`** and the **`RestTemplate`**.

We can put the following dependency in **`random-number-project`** and **`my-client-application`** for loading sleuth and Zipkin features:

```
<dependency>
    <groupId>org.springframework.cloud</groupId>
    <artifactId>spring-cloud-starter-sleuth</artifactId>
</dependency>
<dependency>
    <groupId>org.springframework.cloud</groupId>
```

```
    <artifactId>spring-cloud-sleuth-zipkin</artifactId>
</dependency>
```

This dependency contains all the required dependencies to load Sleuth and Zipkin. Since it's a dependency offered in **org.springframework.cloud**, we need to add the following dependency management to allow Spring to download the correct dependencies:

```
<dependencyManagement>
    <dependencies>
        <dependency>
            <groupId>org.springframework.cloud</groupId>
            <artifactId>spring-cloud-dependencies</artifactId>
            <version>2020.0.1</version>
            <type>pom</type>
            <scope>import</scope>
        </dependency>
    </dependencies>
</dependencyManagement>
```

After adding the preceding snippet in **pom.xml,** let us add a logger in the API to see some new fields that will come up when the API is actually invoked. For simplicity, we can modify the class in **random-number-project** as follows to have the logger while throwing an exception and while returning a valid response:

```
@RestController
public class RandomNumberController {


    private static final Logger log = LoggerFactory.
    getLogger(RandomNumberController.class);


    @GetMapping("/generate")
    public int generateFrom1to100(@Value("${server.port}") Integer port,
    HttpServletResponse response)
            throws UnknownHostException {
        response.addHeader("origin", InetAddress.getLocalHost().
        getHostAddress() + ":" + port);
```

```
        int a = new Random().ints(1, 100).limit(1).findFirst().getAsInt();
        if (a > 50) {
            log.error("Throwing exception as number is greater than
            50");// any business exception for testing
            throw new NumberFormatException("number between 50 and
            100");
        }
        log.info("Returning response as {}", a);
        return a;
    }
}
```

The following screenshot displays the **Sleuth Console** log when you start the application:

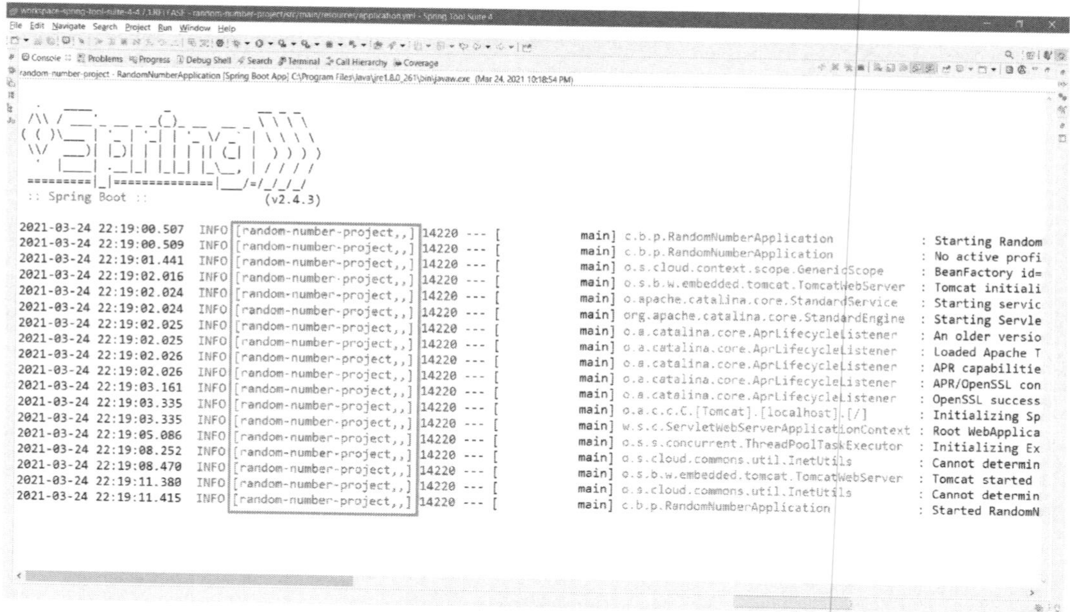

Figure 9.4: *Sleuth console*

Notice that the application name has started coming up after the logging level as we specified **spring.application.name=random-number-project** in **application.yml**. Moreover, there are three commas. Wonder *what are they? Why are they empty?*

They are the placeholders for storing **TraceId**, **SpanId**, **Zipkin-Export**. **TraceId** or **ParentId** is used to track the complete end-to-end flow for the API that is being requested. You can think that there is one API created which calls **`service1`** within the same project and it invokes **`service2`** which is outside the application. Then, **`TraceId`** will help you to uniquely identify that the user who requested the API is tracing through **`service1`** and **`service2`** which actually means that we can track the request for that particular user. This helps in tracking as per the user hits.

`SpanId` is clubbed along-with the **`TraceId`**. This **`SpanId`** is different for every request and response that is in the workflow. Considering the same example, **`service1`** and **`service2`** which is invoked by the user will have different **`SpanId`**, but the same **`TraceId`**.

The third placeholder is the **`Zipkin-export`**. The value of this placeholder is set to false by default, but if set true then all our logs will be exported to **Zipkin Server** for traceability.

Now, let us start the **`random-number-project`** on three different ports as we did in the previous chapter along with the **`Zipkin server`** and **`my-client-application`** as follows:

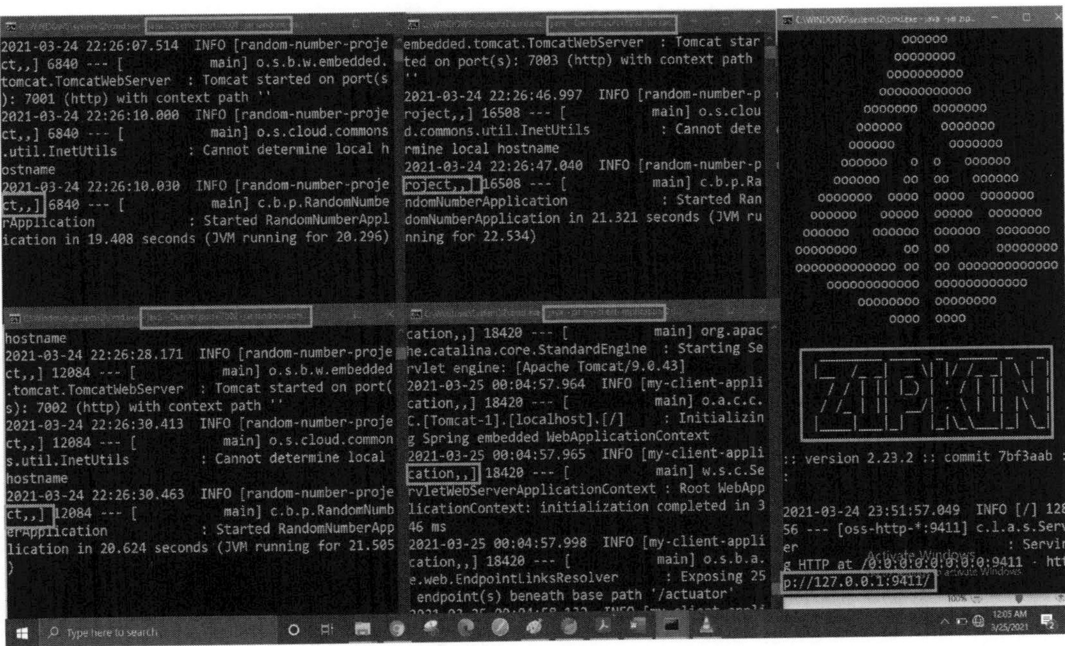

Figure 9.5: Console logs for startup of Sleuth apps and Zipkin servers

Here are the commands used for starting all servers as shown in the preceding screenshot:

```
java -Dserver.port=7001 -jar random-number-project-0.0.1-SNAPSHOT.jar
java -Dserver.port=7002 -jar random-number-project-0.0.1-SNAPSHOT.jar
java -Dserver.port=7003 -jar random-number-project-0.0.1-SNAPSHOT.jar
java -jar my-client-application-0.0.1-SNAPSHOT.jar
java -jar zipkin-server-2.23.2-exec.jar
```

The *highlighted* sections show that servers start on different ports and have sleuth enabled as it has three placeholders for placing **`TraceId`**, **`SpanId`,** and **`zipkin-export`**.

Now, let us request the API with the following command:

```
curl http://localhost:8888/loadbalancedAPI
```

The output of the preceding request is shown in the following screenshot :

```
C:\WINDOWS\system32\cmd.exe
Microsoft Windows [Version 10.0.19041.867]
(c) 2020 Microsoft Corporation. All rights reserved.

C:\Users\PCW>curl http://localhost:8888/loadbalancedAPI
70
```

Figure 9.6: *Curl my-client-application API*

As we see the response is *70* that has come from our **`my-client-application`** that made a call to **`random-number-project`** via **`RestTemplate`**. Notice the logs of both the applications as shown in the following screenshot:

```
2021-03-25 01:21:52.963  INFO [my-client-application,,] 14228 --- [           main] o.s.b.w.embedded.tomcat.TomcatWebServer  : Tomcat s
tarted on port(s): 9999 (http) with context path ''
2021-03-25 01:21:54.316  INFO [my-client-application,,] 14228 --- [nio-8888-exec-1] o.a.c.c.C.[Tomcat].[localhost].[/]       : Initiali
zing Spring DispatcherServlet 'dispatcherServlet'
2021-03-25 01:21:54.316  INFO [my-client-application,,] 14228 --- [nio-8888-exec-1] o.s.web.servlet.DispatcherServlet        : Initiali
zing Servlet 'dispatcherServlet'
2021-03-25 01:21:54.322  INFO [my-client-application,,] 14228 --- [nio-8888-exec-1] o.s.web.servlet.DispatcherServlet        : Complete
d initialization in 3 ms
2021-03-25 01:21:54.832  INFO [my-client-application,,] 14228 --- [           main] o.s.cloud.commons.util.InetUtils         : Cannot d
etermine local hostname
2021-03-25 01:21:54.880  INFO [my-client-application,,] 14228 --- [           main] c.bpb.publications.MyServiceApplication  : Started
MyServiceApplication in 24.58 seconds (JVM running for 25.338)
2021-03-25 01:21:57.952  INFO [my-client-application,d56cf3675ecc026e,d56cf3675ecc026e] 14228 --- [nio-8888-exec-1] com.bpb.publication
s.service.MyService    : Received response as 70 from [172.25.160.1:7001]

2021-03-25 01:21:57.781  INFO [random-number-project,,] 15212 --- [nio-7001-exec-4] o.a.c.c.C.[Tomcat].[localhost].[/]       : Initiali
zing Spring DispatcherServlet 'dispatcherServlet'
2021-03-25 01:21:57.781  INFO [random-number-project,,] 15212 --- [nio-7001-exec-4] o.s.web.servlet.DispatcherServlet        : Initiali
zing Servlet 'dispatcherServlet'
2021-03-25 01:21:57.786  INFO [random-number-project,,] 15212 --- [nio-7001-exec-4] o.s.web.servlet.DispatcherServlet        : Complete
d initialization in 2 ms
2021-03-25 01:21:57.866  INFO [random-number-project,d56cf3675ecc026e,94f28f6a793fbd08] 15212 --- [nio-7001-exec-4] c.b.p.controller.Ra
ndomNumberController   : Returning response as 70
```

Figure 9.7: *Illustration of TraceId and SpanId*

The *green* color shows the **`TraceId`** and the *yellow* color shows the **`SpanId`**. Notice that the **`TraceId`** and **`SpanId`** on the first console, that is, **`my-client-application`** has the same value. This is because that is the origination point for the API that is logged in Sleuth. Now as the flow reaches to the second application, that is, **`random-number-project`** the **`SpanId`** of **`my-client-application`** is copied to **`TraceId`** of **`random-number-project`** and the new **`SpanId`** is generated for **`random-number-project`**.

Now we can understand these different **`TraceId`** and **`SpanId`** on the Zipkin dashboard as we browse **`http://localhost:9411`** as shown in the following screenshot:

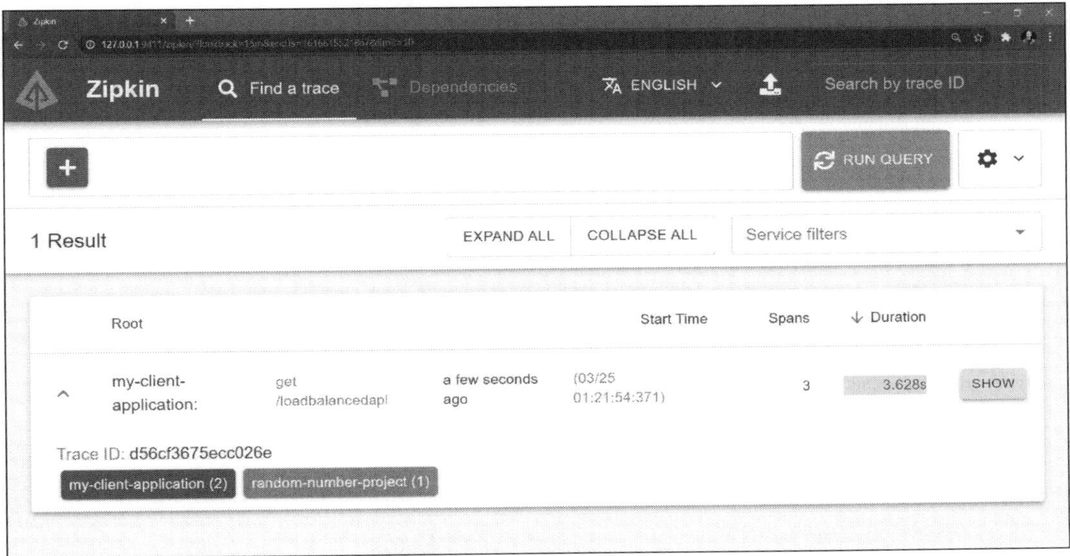

***Figure 9.8:** Illustration of Zipkin dashboard*

Click on the **`RUN QUERY`** button that will give out all the traces that were done within the last *30* minutes as configured with results limited to *10*. As we requested the API, the requests went to two different apps with a common trace ID. This dashboard also shows up the time taken for each microservice to serve the response. To check the detailed relative timelines that each microservice – **client** and **server** took the request and sent the response, click on the **`SHOW`** button after duration. You will land up on the following page:

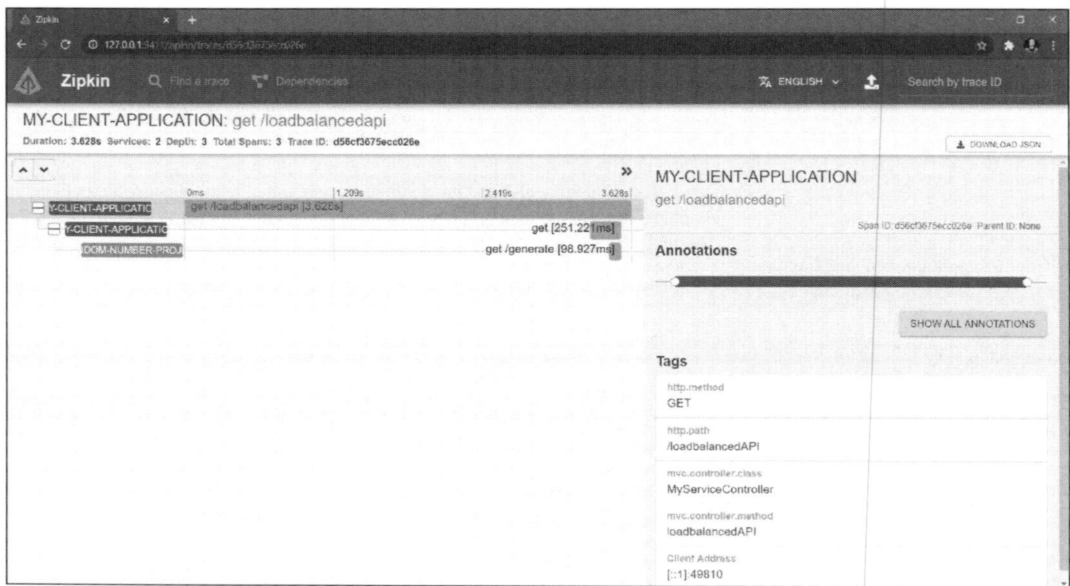

Figure 9.9: *Detailed listing of Zipkin*

The preceding screenshot shows the span ID and trace ID that were involved to serve the workflow. It also shows to which method of controller the request has reached. The color on the hierarchy changes when the request fails with any error. The error message hence generated is shown in tags. For instance, when we request for multiple times, it goes into our custom logic that throws the exception. The dashboard in that case looks like the following screenshot:

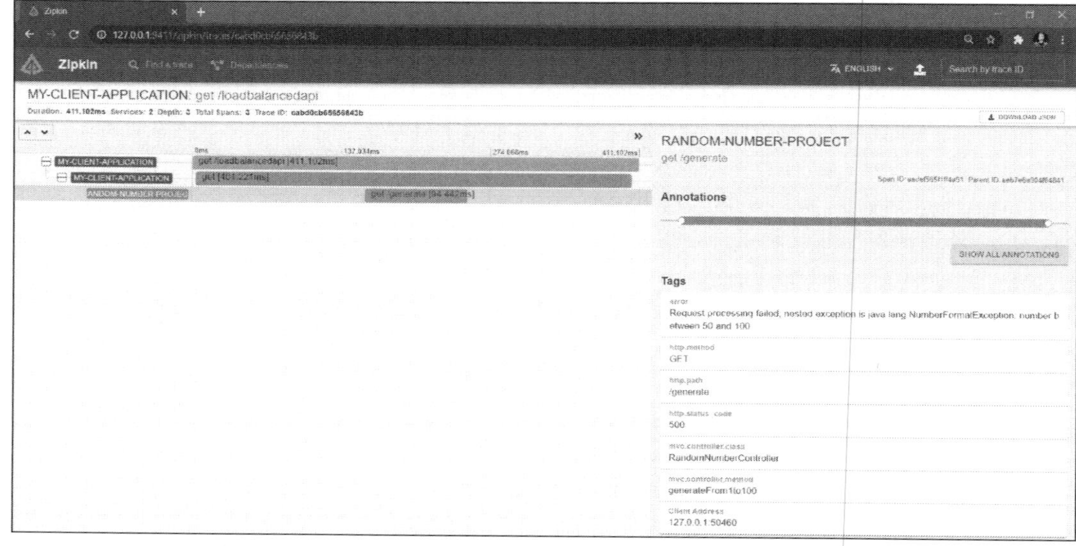

Figure 9.10: *Failed calls*

This is how we can trace the individual calls within a microservice when we use Sleuth and Zipkin. Let's take a look at some tools which can visualize our data more effectively.

Using ELK for analyzing events

ELK is the acronym for open-source projects- **Elasticsearch, Logstash, and Kibana**. These are the tools offered by Elastic Cloud commonly known as **ELK Stack**. Elasticsearch is a search and analytics engine which takes care of storage. Logstash is a server-side data processing pipeline that ingests data from multiple sources simultaneously, filters it, transforms it, and then sends data to Elasticsearch. Kibana allows users to visualize data with charts and graphs. These three different tools can be downloaded from the following websites:

- **https://www.elastic.co/downloads/elasticsearch**
- **https://www.elastic.co/downloads/logstash**
- **https://www.elastic.co/downloads/kibana**

We will use *v7.10.2* out of the three tools as these were the latest at the time. After extracting or installing the setup for the preceding tools, all we need to do is start batch executables for all the three. The next thing to do is to configure the Logback to send all the logs of the application to the log file. We will discover a different way of logging all events to a file by tailing logs with the help of a terminal. To tail the logs into the file, run the following command that will start writing all the logs to a specific location into a specific file:

```
java -jar random-number-project-0.0.1-SNAPSHOT.jar > F:\elk\logs\data.
log
```

Before running the preceding command, we have to configure the logstash to pick up the log events from the file we specify. This can be done by writing **`logstash.conf`** inside the folder **`F:\elk\logstash-7.10.2\config`** as we did while installing all tools inside **`F:\elk`**. The following is the configuration that we need to specify:

```
input {
    file {
        path => "F:/elk/logs/*.log"
        codec => "plain"
        type => "logback"
    }
```

```
}

output {
    stdout { }
    elasticsearch {
        hosts => ["localhost:9200"]
        index => "random-number-project-index-%{+YYYY.MM.dd}"
    }
}
```

The preceding configuration is provided to logstash to make it understand that the path from where it should pick up the log file is **`F:/elk/logs/*.log`**. The asterisks say that it can take any file which has **`.log`** as extension. Further, we specify that the file should be read as is, that is, in plain format. Here, we can also specify the log format. Thus, the input is taken from this file and indexed at index **`random-number-project-index-%{+YYYY.MM.dd}`**. This index will be evaluated against a date when the logs are generated. This index is created inside the elastic search.

This is the only configuration that is required to send the logs to ELK. *Pretty easy!*

Next, we need to start the three tools by executing the following batch files in order:

- **Elasticsearch:** **`F:\elk\elasticsearch-7.10.2\bin\elasticsearch.bat`**. This application is hosted on port **`9200`**.
- **Kibana:** **`F:\elk\kibana-7.10.2\bin\kibana.bat`**. This is hosted on the default port **`5601`**.
- **Logstash:** **`F:\elk\logstash-7.10.2\bin\logstash.bat -f ..\config\logstash.conf`**. **`-f`** option denotes to take the configuration file from the **`config`** folder.

Once the ELK is up and running, we need to start our application **`-random-number-project`**. You will see the following console of logstash that displays the JSON format structure of the event:

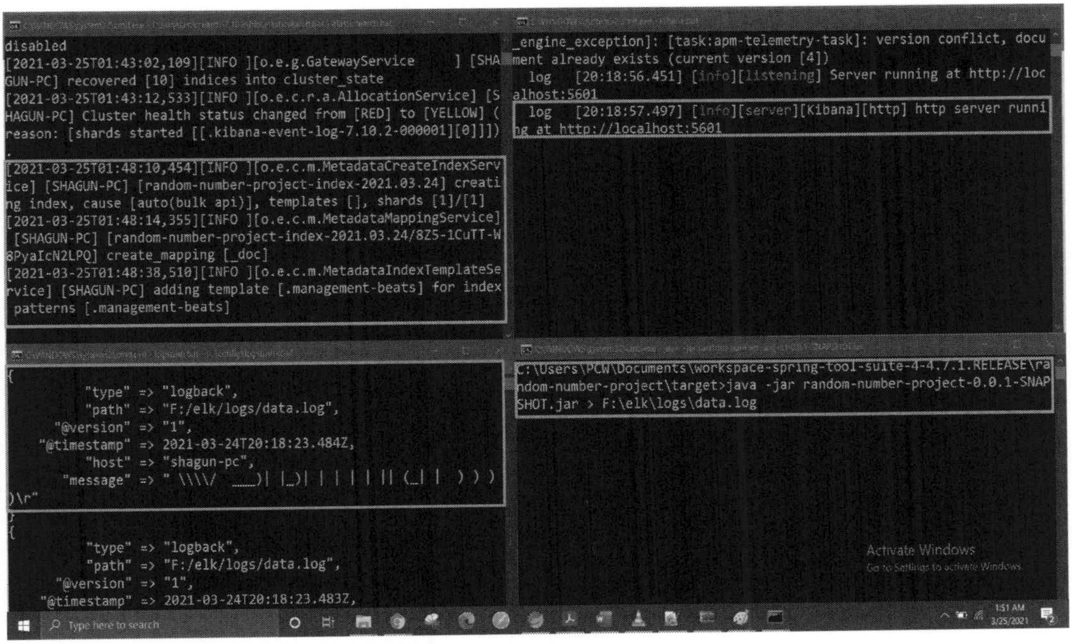

Figure 9.11: Logstash console showing logs picked up

The events containing the timestamp, path of the file, file type, actual event in the form of message, the version, and host is published to logstash.

Now we got our logs streamed to the ELK. To view them, we need to create an index in Kibana that will link the Elasticsearch index to Kibana. The steps are as follows:

1. Browse **`http://localhost:5601`** to open the Kibana dashboard.
2. Navigate to **`Stack Management`** under the **`Management`** tab as shown in the *hamburger* menu.
3. Click on **`Index Patterns`** under **`Kibana.`** Alternatively, you can browse **`http://localhost:5601/app/management/kibana/indexPatterns`** directly to create the index pattern.
4. Type the pattern as **`random-number-project-index-*`** as shown in the following screenshot:

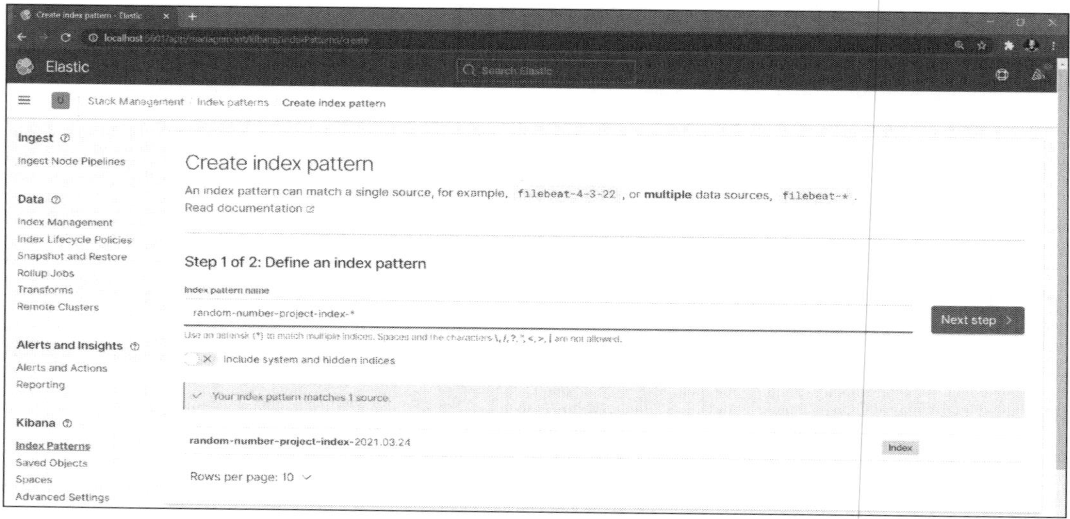

Figure 9.12: Creating index pattern

5. Click on **`Next step`** and click on **`I don't want to use the time filter in configuration setting for time field`**.
6. Click on **`Create Index Pattern`** to finish.

Once the pattern is created, you will see few fields like **`@timestamp`**, **`@version,`** and so on depending on the contents you have in the log file. Now to view the logs, go back to **`Discover`** under **`Kibana`** from the *hamburger* menu. Wait for the page to load and then you will be able to see all your application logs as shown in the following screenshot:

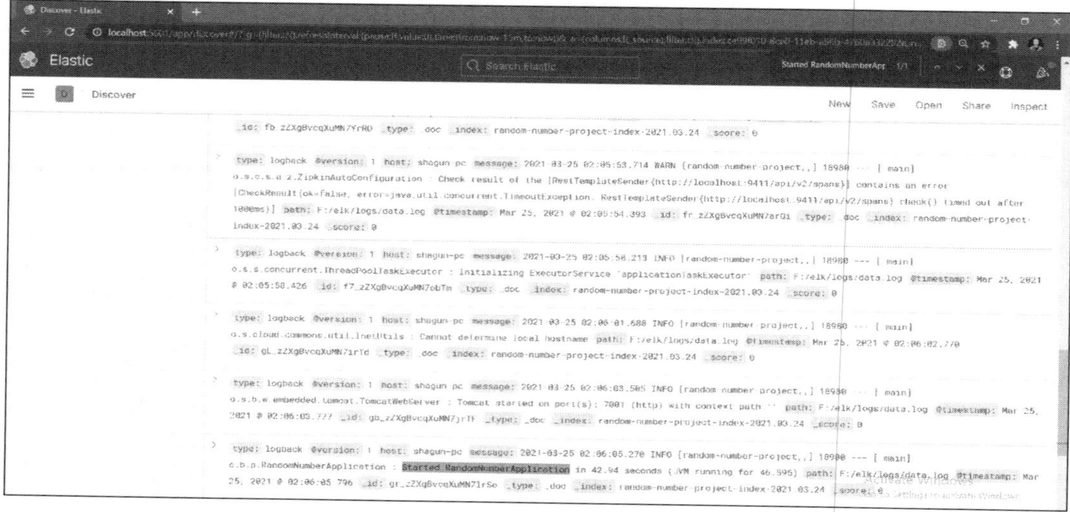

Figure 9.13: Discover logs in Kibana

Congratulations! You have just completed seeing logs inside Kibana. Kibana takes the query parameters in the form of **Kibana Query Language** (**KQL**). Query could be as simple as **"field": "<search value>"** or simply the value you are looking for. For instance, the following screenshot will help you to look for a particular keyword in logs:

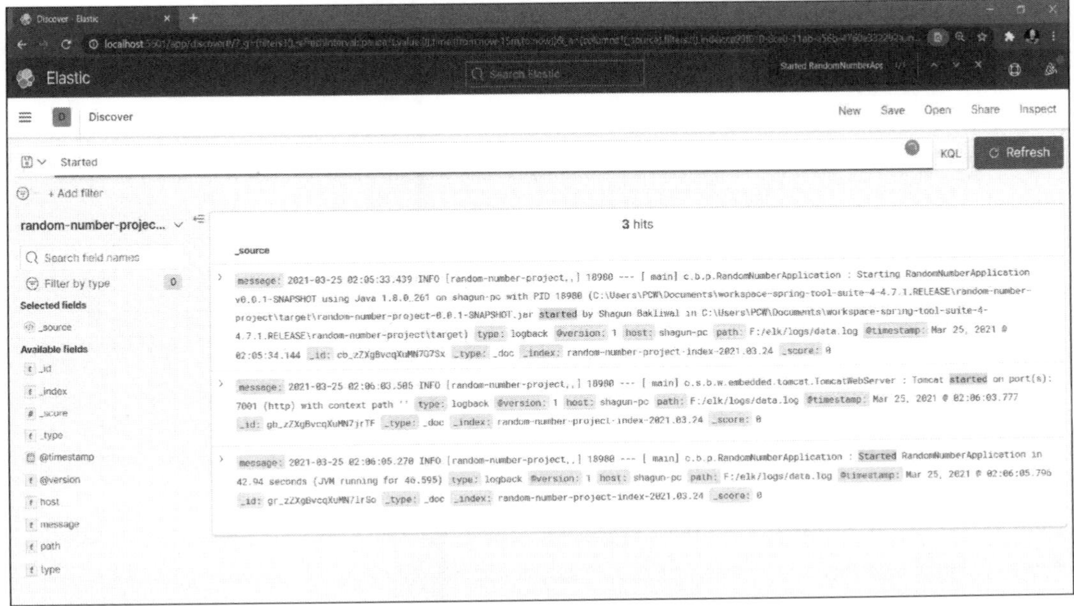

Figure 9.14: *Writing KQL*

Conclusion

This chapter has set the expectations so far in terms of running the application and saving logs to the file or console using Logback. We also learned about different appenders that can be included inside Logback to customize the pattern in the way the logs should be saved. With the help of Sleuth and Zipkin, we were able to understand how to trace the request comes to the server and sends back the response, the timelines, and the errors if any. We also learned how to set up **Elasticsearch, Logstash, and Kibana** (**ELK**) to analyze the events that come in the logs.

In the next chapter, we will learn how to document REST endpoints for the consumer to help them consume REST services and prepare Swagger contracts and allow Spring to produce POJO models for **Data Transfer Objects**.

Points to Remember

- Have proper regular expressions in the Logback file for pattern matching.
- Parent Id in sleuth will be none for the very first request that comes into the workflow.
- Always start the ELK in order *Elasticsearch > Kibana > Logstash* to avoid any loss of data or incurring any error.

Questions

1. How do you configure Logback?
2. What are appender, logger, and layout in Logback?
3. How do you start the debug logging?
4. How can we have logs in different log files once the day has ended?
5. What are different logging levels?
6. How do you set up Zipkin and Sleuth?
7. What are **`TraceId`**, **`ParentId,`** and **`SpanId`**?
8. What is ELK? Describe each component.
9. How do you send your application logs to Kibana?

Chapter 10
Working with the Swagger API Management Tool

In the previous chapter, we learned how to prepare log files using **Logback** and send them to **Kibana** for analyzing events. This chapter is more about following good practices such as **documentation**. In this chapter, we will learn how to prepare Swagger documents so that the consumer of the application knows what the API expects and the format on how the application will send the response. We will also see how to generate the data transfer objects when the application is the consumer.

Structure

In this chapter, we will discuss the following topics:

- API documentation
- Implementing Swagger
- Swagger UI
- Annotations used in the Swagger documentation
- Creating models using Swagger Codegen

Objectives

After studying this unit, you should be able to understand how to write the documentation for REST API. Hit the API just like Postman or any other REST client. You can create data transfer objects using **`swagger.yml`**.

API documentation

Documenting API is as important as writing good quality code. Generally, if you are developing a scalable product, then you must be developing different back-end and front-end systems. In such cases, the frontend team has to wait for the service preparation at the backend. They may also choose an option to start the development of the frontend in a mindset that they can integrate well with the services when they are done. At those times, it may be difficult enough if the design or the approach to integrate doesn't align well. Alternatively, you then have to expose the APIs with a dummy JSON request and response. That is also a possible solution but not feasible as the backend team has to continuously keep a track of the signature that is shared with its consumer application. In such scenarios, it is essential to have an API specification which will act as a common standard for all of its consumers for REST services. Also, there should be detailed information about the fields that would be shared with consumers and actors. Information like what could be possible values for an attribute, the datatype it consumes, and so on.

Keeping this in mind, the document should also describe any change that is made to the API since inception. Doing this as a manual ask is tiring, but there is a tool that can solve this problem. We will now look into the solution called Swagger.

Swagger is an open-source API specification tool that is well-versed with the request and response attributes along with showing all those attributes in the proper format in its UI. It is built by *SmartBear Software*. SmartBear is behind some of the biggest names in the software space, including **Swagger**, **SoapUI**, and **QAComplete**. We will look into Swagger 2 for web applications that will internally use the **Springfox** implementation of Swagger. For this, we will use our existing application – webservice as it is a web application which we created in *Chapter 6, Building RESTFul Microservices* with few REST endpoints. We will also add an API to understand POST APIs with Swagger.

Implementing Swagger

Follow the below steps to start using Swagger:

- We will need to add the following dependency in **pom.xml**:

```
<dependency>
    <groupId>io.springfox</groupId>
    <artifactId>springfox-boot-starter</artifactId>
    <version>3.0.0</version>
</dependency>
```

- After including the preceding starter pack, it will load the following dependencies:

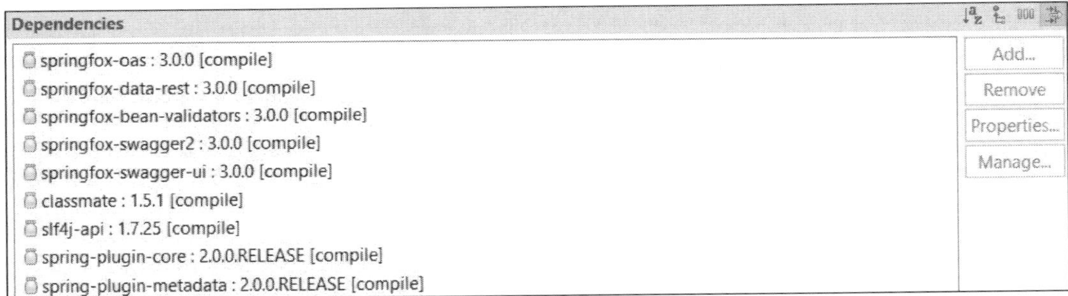

***Figure 10.1:** Dependencies for springfox-boot-starter*

- Out of the preceding dependencies, earlier versions of Springfox only required dependencies such as **springfox-swagger2** and **springfox-swagger-ui**. The former one is used to create the Swagger documentation and the latter uses that documentation and creates a REST client around it which provides data to hit the API. We will see the UI in the latter section of this chapter.

  Further, we need to create the bean of the **Docket** class to configure Swagger. The **Docket** is a builder that creates a primary interface in the Springfox framework. We can create the bean as follows:

```
package com.bpb.publications.authors.config;
import org.springframework.context.annotation.Bean;
import org.springframework.context.annotation.Configuration;
import springfox.documentation.builders.PathSelectors;
import springfox.documentation.builders.RequestHandlerSelectors;
import springfox.documentation.spi.DocumentationType;
import springfox.documentation.spring.web.plugins.Docket;
```

```
@Configuration
public class SwaggerConfiguration {

    @Bean
    public Docket api() {
        return new Docket(DocumentationType.SWAGGER_2)
                .select()
                .apis(RequestHandlerSelectors.any())
                .paths(PathSelectors.any())
                .build();
    }

}
```

- This bean is configured to use **DocumentationType** as **SWAGGER_2** that uses the 2.0 specification of Swagger. Other **DocumentationType** are **SWAGGER_12** and OAS_30. The **select()** method of **Docket** creates a builder for the API selection. Next, we will define the predicate of **RequestHandler** that can satisfy any **RequestHandler**. We will also specify the predicate which accepts any **Path** string. Finally, we will build the whole configuration and create a **Docket** that will be used to configure Swagger.

  The preceding bean of **Docket** considers all the controllers created in any package. To configure Swagger to only consider the base package, the bean can be modified as follows:

```
@Bean
public Docket api() {
    return new Docket(DocumentationType.SWAGGER_2)
            .select()
            .apis(RequestHandlerSelectors.basePackage("com.bpb.
            publications.authors"))
            .build();
}
```

Further, we can also provide API-specific information by creating the **ApiInfo** object and passing it to **Docket** as follows:

```
@Bean
public Docket api() {
    return new Docket(DocumentationType.SWAGGER_2)
            .select()
            .apis(RequestHandlerSelectors.any())
            .paths(PathSelectors.any())
            .build()
            .apiInfo(apiInfo());
}

private ApiInfo apiInfo() {
    return new ApiInfo(
            "Web Service for Authors",
            "The project contains APIs for managing Authors
            Information",
            "API v1",
            "These are my terms of service",
            new Contact("Developer", "www.webaddress.com",
            "abcd@emailprovider.com"),
            "This is the license of API",
            "www.mylicencekey.com",
            Collections.emptyList());
}
```

ApiInfo is created by passing *title, description, version, terms of service URL, contact, license, license URL,* and *list of vendor extensions* to its constructor.

Swagger UI

Once the Swagger configuration is set up, we can build the project and run the Spring Boot class. Browse **http://localhost:8082/swagger-ui/** and you will see the following screen as shown in the following screenshot:

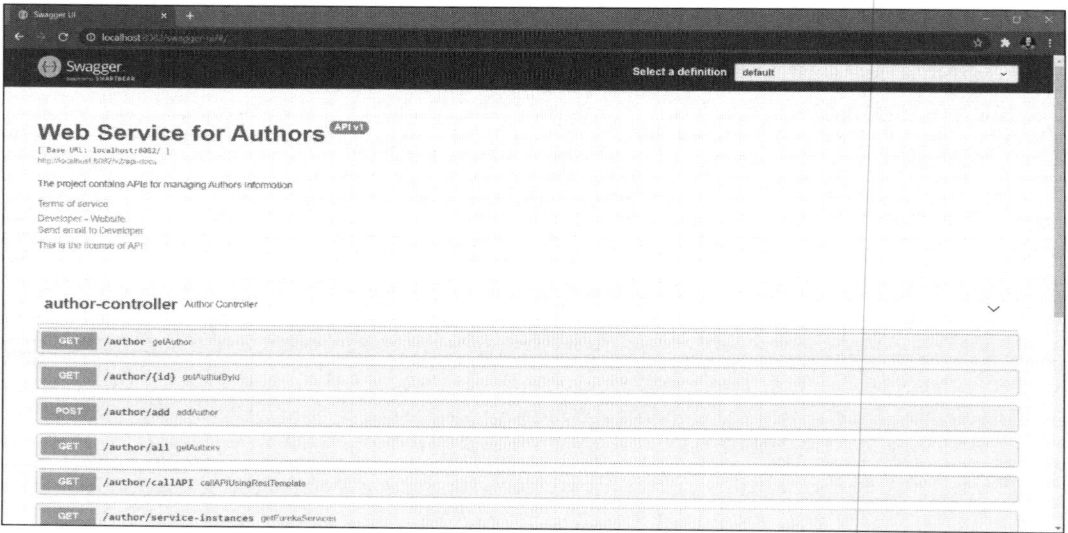

***Figure 10.2**: Swagger UI*

This page will show all the controllers which contain all valid HTTP methods endpoints. If you have different controllers, then different collapsible dropdowns will be there containing the endpoints created under that controller. This data is populated from **`http://localhost:8082/v2/api-docs`** which returns a JSON dump that Swagger 2 generates for the REST endpoints. Exploring any of them in the Swagger UI will guide you to understand the input parameters required to call the API and the different HTTP response codes as shown in the following screenshot:

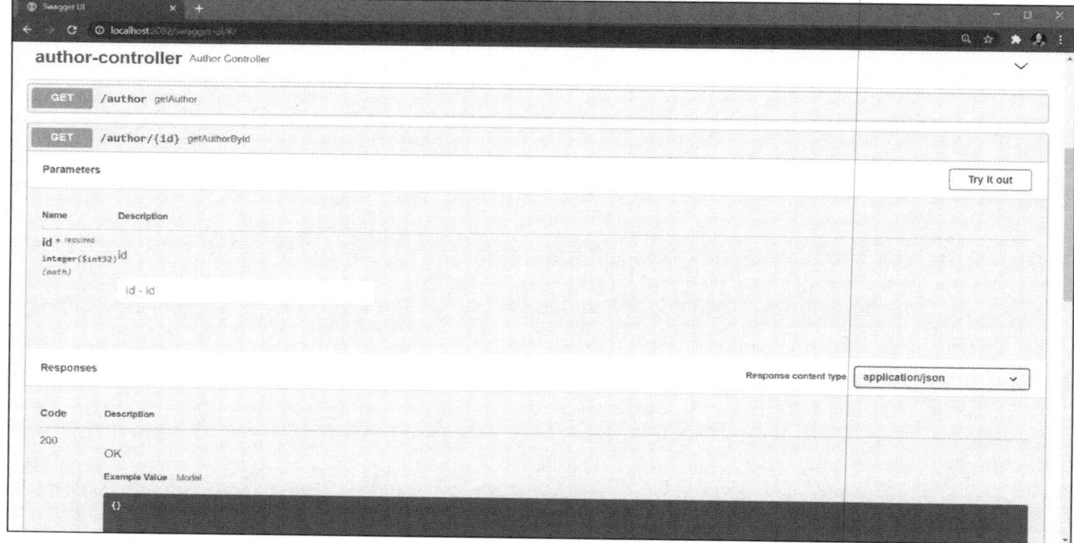

***Figure 10.3:** Swagger for getAuthorById*

The preceding API takes an integer specifically **`int32`** and places the input value in the **`id`** parameter. For sending request to API, click on the **`Try it out`** button and provide the specific value in the input label and then click on **`Execute`**. The output will be as shown in the following screenshot:

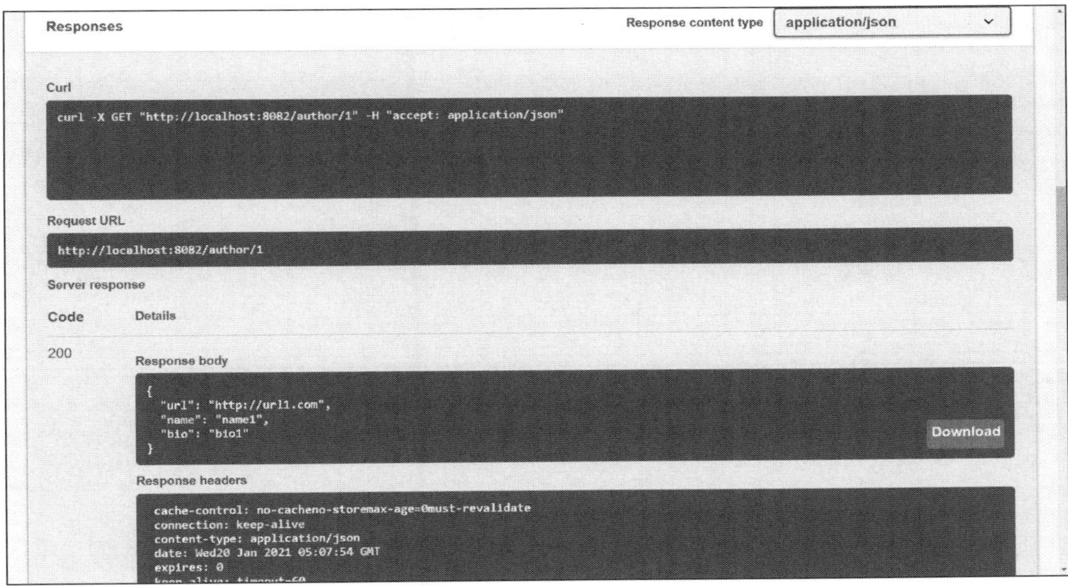

Figure 10.4: *Requesting GET API from Swagger*

It shows the response body linked with the HTTP code **`200`** if the response is successful. It also shows the response headers as seen from Postman. On a successful hit, you can download the response into a file. Similarly, you can request for POST API such as **`/author/add`** which takes the request body which takes the **`authorVO`** with the value:

```
{
  "bio": "this is my bio",
  "name": "John Mark",
  "url": "www.johnmark.com"
}
```

The response will be as shown in the following screenshot:

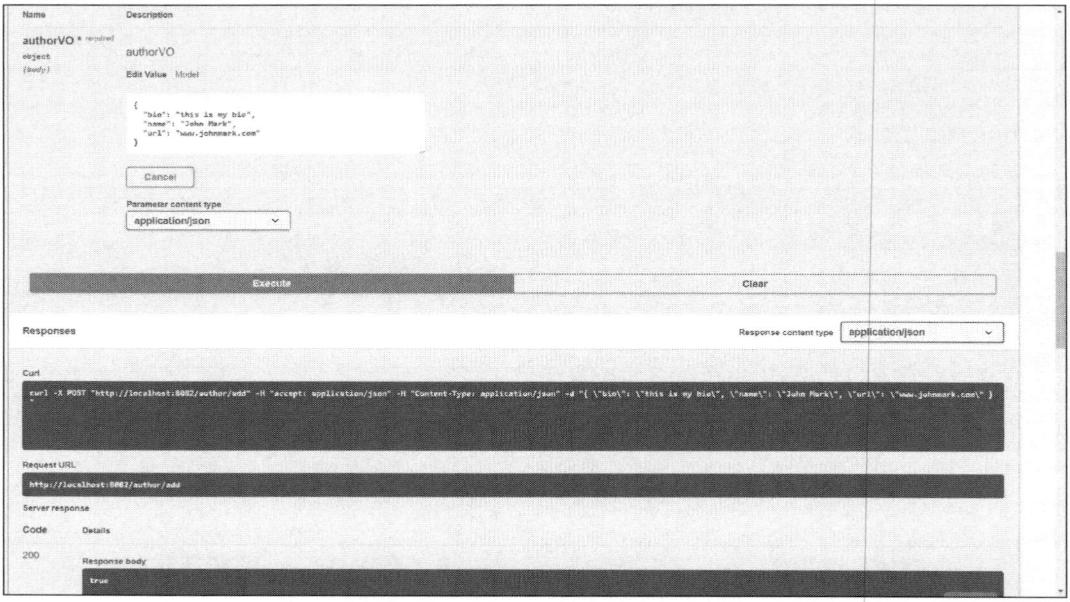

***Figure 10.5**: Requesting POST API from Swagger*

Annotations used in the Swagger documentation

Swagger provides few annotations that help you in the documentation for the attributes that are being sent to the server as requests, providing the description of each field and letting the consumer know what values those attributes accept. It also gives out information on which attributes will be sent in response along with the HTTP status code. The list of annotations along with their usage is described as follows:

- **`@Api:`** This annotation is used at the top of the class to mark it as a Swagger resource. This annotation has many attributes, but the common ones can be for example with usage:

  ```
  @Api(value = "manage authors", description = "This controller contains all the endpoints that can manage author information", tags = "Author Info, Manage author")
  ```

  `value` is ignored as of *Swagger 1.5.x* if the tags are not provided. The **`description`** gives a highlight for the controller class about the endpoints it contains. **`tags`** accept comma separate strings which can replace the name of the controller with these tags. After using this annotation, the Swagger UI looks like this:

Author Info, Manage author This controller contains all the endpoints that can manage author information

GET /author Get Author Details by Name and URL

GET /author/{id} getAuthorById

POST /author/add addAuthor

GET /author/all getAuthors

GET /author/callAPI callAPIUsingRestTemplate

GET /author/service-instances getEurekaServices

Figure 10.6: Api annotation usage

- **`@ApiOperation:`** This annotation is used on top of the **`@RequestMapping`** method or relative mapping annotation and for each of our REST endpoints, we can specify what operation will it perform and what type of response it returns if requested by using this annotation. The usage of the annotation can be as follows:

  ```
  @ApiOperation(value = "Get Author Details by Name and URL", response = ResponseEntity.class, notes = "This is the notes section to describe detailed information", tags = "Fetch details of author using Name and URL", nickname = "/author")
  ```

  `value` gives out the operation details. **`notes`** can describe what that API is supposed to do in detail. If you provide the tags in **`@ApiOperation,`** then a new item would be added in the Swagger UI pertaining to the same operation. So, *don't get confused!* After using this annotation, the Swagger UI will look like this:

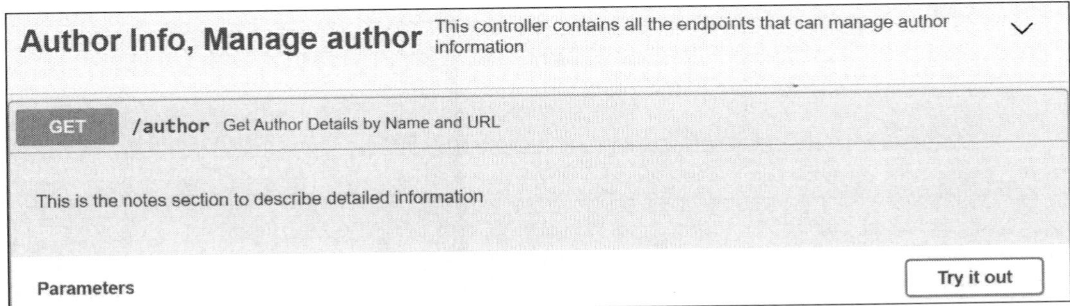

Figure 10.7: ApiOperation annotation usage

- **`@ApiResponse` and `@ApiResponses`:** This annotation is used on top of **`@RequestMapping`** or relative mapping annotation which customizes the message that would be shown in terms of the response HTTP status code. A list of **`@ApiResponse`** can be used inside **`@ApiResponses`** to accumulate all customized messages in one place. For example:

```
@ApiResponses(value = { @ApiResponse(code = 200, message = "Successfully retrieved"),
        @ApiResponse(code = 401, message = "You are not authorized to access the API"),
        @ApiResponse(code = 403, message = "You don›t have proper roles to access the API"),
        @ApiResponse(code = 404, message = "No records") })
```

The annotation takes the value of the HTTP status code in the code attribute and the customized message in the message attribute. After using this annotation, the Swagger UI looks like this:

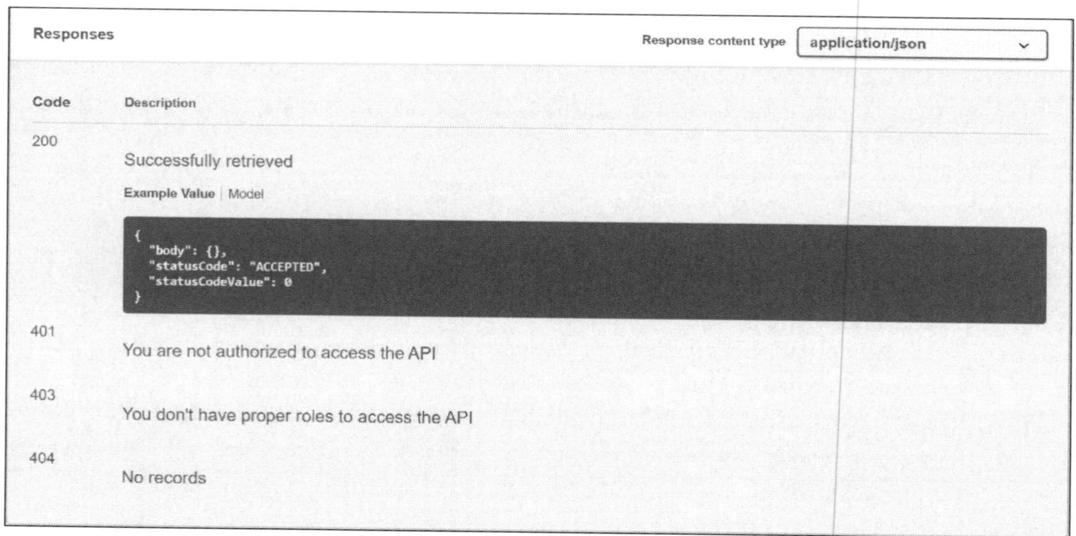

***Figure 10.8**: ApiResponses annotation usage*

To sum up all these configurations, the following snippet helps you to understand the placeholders for these annotations:

```
@Api(value = "manage authors", description = "This controller contains all the endpoints that can manage author information", tags = "Author Info, Manage author")
```

```
public class AuthorController {

    @ApiOperation(value = "Get Author Details by Name and URL",
    response = ResponseEntity.class, httpMethod = "GET", notes =
    "This is the notes section to describe detailed information",
    tags = "Fetch details of author using Name and URL", nickname
    = "/author")
    @ApiResponses(value = { @ApiResponse(code = 200, message =
    "Successfully retrieved"),
            @ApiResponse(code = 401, message = "You are not
            authorized to access the API"),
            @ApiResponse(code = 403, message = "You don›t have
            proper roles to access the API"),
            @ApiResponse(code = 404, message = "No records") })
    @RequestMapping(method = RequestMethod.GET, name = "Get Author
By Name and URL", produces = MediaType.APPLICATION_JSON_VALUE)
   public ResponseEntity<?> getAuthor(@RequestParam(name = "name")
String name,
            @RequestParam(name = "url") String url) {
        return new ResponseEntity<>(authorService.get(name, url),
        HttpStatus.OK);
    }
}
```

Is there anything for the request body that reaches the controller?

Those are called the models which are like simple POJOs. Here, in this example, in the API, we expect the object of type **AuthorVO**. So, the same is listed under the **Models** section at the end of the Swagger UI as shown in the following screenshot:

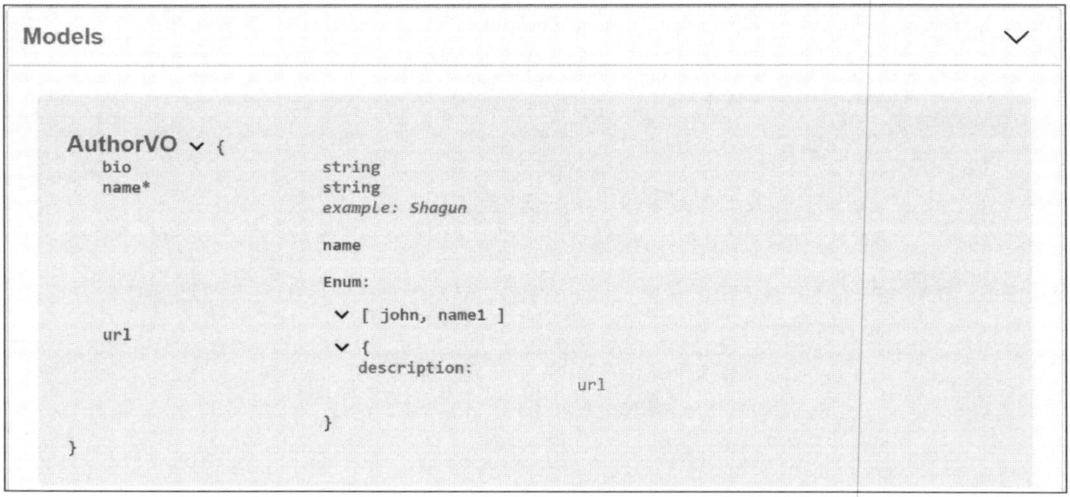

```
Models

AuthorVO {
    bio          string
    name*        string
                 example: Shagun

                 name

                 Enum:
                   [ john, name1 ]
    url            {
                     description:
                                      url
                 }
}
```

***Figure 10.9**: Models shown in Swagger UI*

Even this can be customized by using one more annotation which is commonly used at the field level for all the objects that are present in the request body. This annotation is **`@ApiModelProperty`**. For example:

```
public class AuthorVO implements Serializable {
    @ApiModelProperty(example = "www.example.com", notes = "This is
    the name of the author", value = "url", dataType = "string")
    private String url;
    @ApiModelProperty(allowableValues = "john, name1", example =
    "Shagun", notes = "This is the name of the author", value =
    "name" , required = true)
    private String name;
    private String bio;
}
```

This annotation takes values that are allowed for the variable in **`allowableValues`**. We can also specify a sample input in the **`example.`** It also allows us to mark the variable as mandatory or not by flipping the **`required`** variable. By putting the preceding annotation, the object **`AuthorVO`** is shown under **`Models`** which is a collapsible item at the end of the Swagger UI. You will see the following structure:

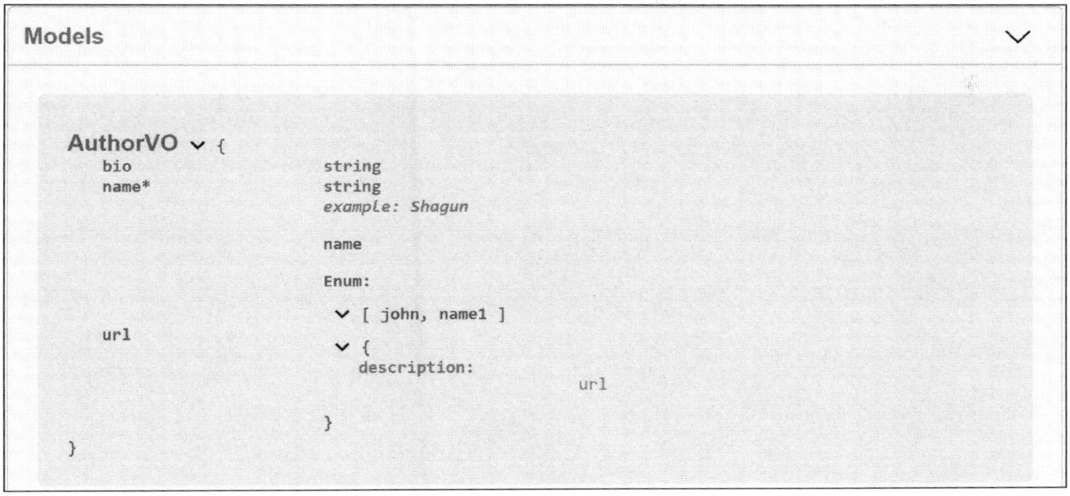

```
Models

AuthorVO ∨ {
    bio                 string
    name*               string
                        example: Shagun

                        name

                        Enum:
                          ∨ [ john, name1 ]
    url
                          ∨ {
                            description:
                                                url

                        }
}
```

Figure 10.10: Models used in RestController

There may be cases where we may use the same datatype as an input and output for the API, but we want to suppress the variable from the input so that it doesn't have any value coming in from the request. The variable can be marked as **readOnly** using the following property on top of the variable:

```
@ApiModelProperty(allowableValues = "a,b,c", example = "a", notes =
"This is the ready only field", value = "fieldNotShownInSwaggerForWriting"
, readOnly = true)
private String fieldNotShownInSwaggerForWriting;
```

Creating models using Swagger Codegen

Till now, we have used Swagger annotations on the classes that we created. We can also create classes with the help of the **.yml** file.

This **.yml** file called **Swagger Spec** contains a proper structure of the attributes along-with its datatype and other rules. The custom model class which we created looks like the following screenshot:

```java
package com.bpb.publications.authors.vo;

import javax.validation.constraints.NotEmpty;

import lombok.Getter;
import lombok.Setter;

@Getter
@Setter
public class AuthorVO {
    @NotEmpty
    private String url;
    @NotEmpty
    private String name;
    @NotEmpty
    private String bio;
}
```

***Figure 10.11**: Custom model class*

Though initially, we mentioned that the string value should not be empty but we also didn't mention how much minimum or maximum size that string can contain. Such kind of information can be enhanced and auto-generated by using **Swagger Codegen**.

We can create these classes or models by using Swagger Codegen. Swagger Codgen can take YML or JSON as input, but here, we will use YML files to generate the models for us. As we know, Swagger renders the APIs and its Model details from **`http://localhost:8082/v2/api-docs`**, so we can also refer to the same to create the YML definition. This API returns a JSON response which can be converted to YML from any tool. Once the YML is created, we can place the YML file in **`swagger-codegen-maven-plugin`** inside its configuration. For example, we can place the contents of the YML file in the **`webservice-swagger-contract.yml`** file as follows:

```yaml
---
swagger: '2.0'
info:
  description: The project contains APIs for managing Authors Information
  version: API v1
  title: Web Service for Authors
  termsOfService: These are my terms of service
  contact:
```

```
    name: Developer
    url: www.webaddress.com
    email: abcd@emailprovider.com
  license:
    name: This is the license of API
    url: www.mylicencekey.com
host: localhost:8082
basePath: "/"
tags:
- name: Author Info, Manage author
  description: This controller contains all the endpoints that can manage
author information
```

This is the basic Swagger spec which takes the version of Swagger that we are using and its information is taken from the **ApiInfo** that we created in the **com.bpb.publications.authors.config.SwaggerConfiguration** class. Further, we can specify where our API will be hosted in the host tag with **basePath** '/'. This **basePath** is set to **'/'** and further, as we included **'/author'** at the top of our controller, we can prefix all our APIs in this YML with the same name as we go forward. As we defined tags at the top of the controller, the same can be explicitly defined over here.

Now, to create different models or POJO classes for sending information from or to the application, we need to provide **definitions** as follows:

```
definitions:
  AuthorVO:
    type: object
    required:
    - name
    properties:
      bio:
        type: string
        description: This is the bio of the author
        minLength: 0
        maxLength: 500
      name:
```

```
        type: string
        example: Shagun
        description: This is the name of the author
        minLength: 0
        maxLength: 20
      url:
        type: string
        example: www.example.com
        description: This is the url of the author
        minLength: 0
        maxLength: 50
    title: AuthorVO
```

It takes the name of the **`AuthorVO`** class which is of type `object`. Whenever we use this model, we say that we require the field name to be populated always which is turned on by flagging `required` to true. Then, we can specify any number of attributes that are required in this class under the **`properties`** tag which tags the name of the attribute, its datatype in **`type`**, **`description`,** and other optional fields like **`length`, `example`**, and so on. Finally, we can give the `title` the same name as that of the class. Other specifications can be learned from the following website which Swagger supports:

https://swagger.io/specification After placing the preceding configuration, save the file and put the following configuration in **`pom.xml`** inside the **`build`** tag:

```
<plugin>
    <groupId>io.swagger</groupId>
    <artifactId>swagger-codegen-maven-plugin</artifactId>
    <version>2.4.7</version>
    <executions>
        <execution>
            <goals>
                <goal>generate</goal>
            </goals>
            <configuration>
                <inputSpec>${yaml.file}</inputSpec>
```

```
            </configuration>
        </execution>
    </executions>
</plugin>
```

This plugin helps us to generate the files which is compatible with Maven. You can also use the Gradle plugin if your project uses Gradle. We can specify the input YML in **inputSpec** of the **configuration** tag. Then, place the following configurations inside the **configuration** tag:

```
<configuration>
    <inputSpec>${yaml.file}</inputSpec>
    <output>${project.basedir}/src/main/java</output>
    <language>spring</language>
    <invokerPackage>${project.groupId}.swagger.invoker</invokerPackage>
    <generateApis>false</generateApis>
    <generateSupportingFiles>false</generateSupportingFiles>
    <modelPackage>com.bpb.publications.authors.vo</modelPackage>
    <configOptions>
        <sourceFolder>/</sourceFolder>
        <library>spring-boot</library>
        <interfaceOnly>true</interfaceOnly>
        <useBeanValidation>true</useBeanValidation>
        <dateLibrary>java8</dateLibrary>
        <java8>true</java8>
    </configOptions>
</configuration>
```

The following are the general configuration parameters:

- **inputSpec**: This takes the input specification YML file path.
- **language**: This specifies in which language we want to generate the class.
- **output**: This is the target output path. If it is not specified, then all files are created in **${project.build.directory}/generated-sources/swagger.**
- **invokerPackage**: This is the package to use for the generated invoker objects.

- **generateApis**: This generates the APIs for the spec present in YML. We set this to false as we don't want APIs to be generated. You can also create APIs using Swagger Codegen.
- **generateSupportingFiles**: This generates the supporting files. We set it to **false** as we don't need other files except the POJO class.
- **modelPackage**: This specifies the package to use for generated model objects / classes.
- **configOptions**: This takes a set of key value pairs in XML which are linked with the language we provided. Here, we specify that to create files in the '/' folder by using the **spring-boot** library.
- **generateModels**: This is true by default to generate the models.

Lastly, we need to provide the following properties in **pom.xml**:

```
<properties>
    <yaml.file>${project.basedir}/src/main/resources/webservice-swagger-contract.yml</yaml.file>
    <generated-sources-path>${project.build.directory}/generated-sources</generated-sources-path>
    <generated-sources-java-path>main/java</generated-sources-java-path>
</properties>
```

These properties define the Swagger conventions for generated sources. Now, build the project using **mvn clean install**, and you will see the following logs:

```
[INFO] --- swagger-codegen-maven-plugin:2.4.7:generate (default) @ Server ---
[INFO] reading from C:/Users/PCW/Documents/workspace-spring-tool-suite-4-4.7.1.RELEASE/webservice/src/main/resources/webservice-swagger-contract.yml
[INFO] Set base package to invoker package (com.webservice.swagger.invoker)
[INFO] writing file C:\Users\PCW\Documents\workspace-spring-tool-suite-4-4.7.1.RELEASE\webservice\src\main\java\\com\bpb\publications\authors\vo\AuthorVO.java
```

When you take a look at the preceding logs, you will see that the files are generated inside the **com\bpb\publications\authors\vo** folder. This class has all the details and rules set up according to the spec we provided. It uses validation annotations if we specify the rule on the value of the attributes. The following is the code snippet from an auto generated file:

```java
package com.bpb.publications.authors.vo;

import java.util.Objects;
import javax.validation.constraints.NotNull;
import javax.validation.constraints.Size;
import org.springframework.validation.annotation.Validated;
import com.fasterxml.jackson.annotation.JsonProperty;
import io.swagger.annotations.ApiModelProperty;

/**
 * AuthorVO
 */
@Validated
@javax.annotation.Generated(value = "io.swagger.codegen.languages.SpringCodegen", date = "2021-01-24T12:32:55.918+05:30")

public class AuthorVO  {
  @JsonProperty("bio")
  private String bio = null;

  @JsonProperty("name")
  private String name = null;

  @JsonProperty("url")
  private String url = null;

  public AuthorVO bio(String bio) {
    this.bio = bio;
    return this;
  }

  /**
   * This is the bio of the author
   * @return bio
  **/
  @ApiModelProperty(value = "This is the bio of the author")

@Size(min=0,max=500)
  public String getBio() {
    return bio;
  }
```

Figure 10.12: *Auto generated models class*

Now, as we start the application and open the Swagger UI, you will notice the models incorporating these values:

```
Models

AuthorVO ⌄ {
   bio                 string
                       minLength: 0
                       maxLength: 500

                       This is the bio of the author

   name*               string
                       example: Shagun
                       minLength: 0
                       maxLength: 20

                       This is the name of the author

   url                 string
                       example: www.example.com
                       minLength: 0
                       maxLength: 50

                       This is the url of the author

}
```

Figure 10.13: *Auto generated models*

The asterisks symbol * in variable name is coming due to the required field set true in specification.We can now use this model in our source code by simply importing this class. Also note, making any change to this class file will revert the changes as soon as you build the module as this class is generated every time you build it.

In this way, you can have multiple POJO classes created through the Codegen plugin and eliminate and manage them in the custom class. As the producer or the consumer requires change in the format of request or response, we need to only modify this contract and make relative changes in our service class to serve the purpose.

Conclusion

This chapter helped us in understanding how much documentation is important for the producers and consumers and maintaining them inside the project itself through Swagger. We also learned how to create API specification using the Swagger Codegen plugin and generate models used within the application that are placed in the application layer for requests and responses. In the next chapter, we will take a look at how to write unit and integration testing.

Points to remember

- We can maintain the contract of our APIs using YML or JSON configurations, thus moving away from the custom class creation for sending responses.
- The Swagger UI has no security implemented by default. We need to have explicit role mapping for maintaining proper access.

Questions

1. What is Swagger?
2. How do you see your APIs in the Swagger UI?
3. How to provide the metadata information of the application in the Swagger UI?
4. What dependencies and plugins you need to generate the models?

CHAPTER 11

Testing a Spring Boot Application

In the previous chapter, we learned how to document our APIs so that the consumers can be developed parallelly even when producers of API are in the development phase. It also helped both the applications to be in sync with requests and responses for an API. This chapter will help you to understand how to write unit test cases in a Spring Boot application.

Structure

In this chapter, we will discuss the following topics:

- Unit testing and integration testing
- Writing a unit test using the JUnit framework
- Writing a unit test using the Mockito framework
- Checking code coverage
- Testing RESTFul web services
- Cucumber automation testing

Objective

After studying this unit, you should be able to write test cases for all functionalities. You will understand how to write the integration test. You can write test cases using the **Cucumber** framework and check the code covered while executing test cases.

Unit testing and integration testing

So far, we have written good codes, but *how do we assure they will work as expected all the time?* Assume a scenario where we are increasing the functionality of our application incrementally that is already working in production. One new change can have a large impact until it is thoroughly tested. This thorough testing is always required for the code that is being developed. But *when do we test those in our dev environments? UAT? Production? No!* That code can be tested locally as well. Yes, by writing proper unit test cases and integration test cases, a developer can get the testing done locally so that he can be sure that the application will not break through in cloud environments where applications would be deployed.

Writing unit test cases will also ensure that the developer or the QA tester checks whether all the functionalities or rules are covered while writing the code. There are two frameworks for writing the test cases – **JUnit** and **Mockito**:

- JUnit helps to write the basic test cases like the basic input to the method which does some calculations and outputs the data. This output is tested against the expected value of the returning data from the method. If this assertion is passed, then we say that the code is tested correctly. The assertion may fail if the expected value doesn't match with the actual value. Mockito comes into picture when we don't want to hit the actual resources like database, controllers, or any other REST client. We can mock these resources as if they are returning the custom responses as we expect. Hence, when we have the custom response which is expected, it is easy to write the unit test for our module. In the Mockito framework, there are such dependencies of resources; hence, this testing is called **Integration Testing** as we collectively test from end-to-end. This end-to-end comprises the flow that comes from controllers to service to repositories like database and other REST clients if used.

Writing a unit test using the JUnit framework

For writing JUnit test cases, follow below procedure:

1. We will include the following dependency which also comes by default while creating the Spring Boot project from Spring Initializr:

```
<dependency>
    <groupId>org.springframework.boot</groupId>
    <artifactId>spring-boot-starter-test</artifactId>
    <scope>test</scope>
</dependency>
```

   This dependency contains a lot of dependencies like **spring-boot-starter**, **spring-boot-test**, **spring-boot-test-autoconfigure**, **junit-jupiter**, **mockito-core**, **mockito-junit-jupiter**, **spring-test**, and so on. All are required for writing test cases in a Spring Boot application. Next, we can start with writing the first unit test. As we developed the webservice in the previous few chapters, we will use the same to understand the different types of test cases that can be developed. The following are the test cases that are written in the **src\test\java\com\bpb\publications\authors\service** folder:

```
package com.bpb.publications.authors.service;
import static org.junit.jupiter.api.Assertions.*;
import org.junit.jupiter.api.BeforeEach;
import org.junit.jupiter.api.Test;

class AuthorServiceTest {

    @BeforeEach
    void setUp() throws Exception {
    }

    @Test
    void test() {
        fail("Not yet implemented");
```

```
    }

}
```

The method annotated with **@BeforeEach** will execute for all the methods that are annotated with the **@Test**. **@Test** methods are the actual methods that have the code written to test the functionality. If you start creating a JUnit test case, it will create the preceding code by default. The **fail()** method of the **Assertions** packages tells the framework that the test has failed.

2. Now, if there is no dependency on any objects, any Spring Beans, no context, and there are only static calculations or mapping that doesn't require any resources, then the JUnit test case for a simple add method to sum up to numbers would be as follows:

```
package com.bpb.publications.authors.service;
import org.junit.jupiter.api.Assertions;
import org.junit.jupiter.api.BeforeEach;
import org.junit.jupiter.api.Test;

class AuthorServiceTest {

    AuthorService authorService;
    @BeforeEach
    void setUp() throws Exception {
        authorService = new AuthorService();
    }

    @Test
    void test() {
        Assertions.assertEquals(3, authorService.sum(1, 2));
    }

}
```

Note that we have created a new instance of the **AuthorService** in **setUp()** method. The check on any test that we wish to check can be done using

Assertions. The **Assertions** class has many methods that can check equality of the expected value and the actual value returned or evaluates the actual value against few collections. Here, we will use the **assertEquals** method to check the value returned by some method called sum which should match with the expected value as **3**.

3. Once you write this test case, right click on the method and click on **Run as** -> **JUnit test**, you will see the following execution:

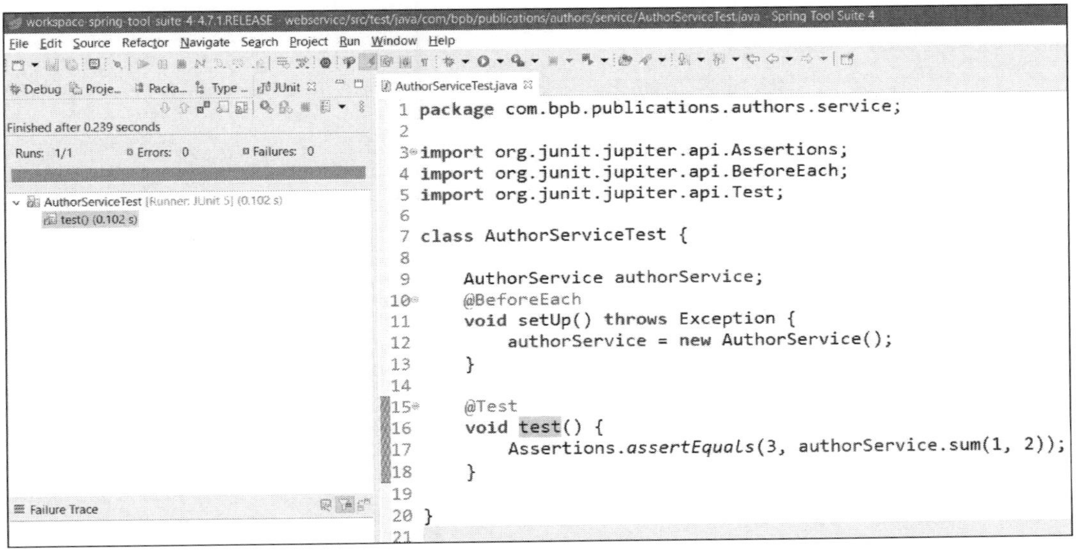

Figure 11.1: *First JUnit test*

On the left-hand side, you will see the class name for which the test is executed and the methods which are executed as part of the test. The green color is the progress bar which shows that all test cases were successfully executed and met the assertions. Any failure in the test case will change the color to red and the failure count will increase.

Till now, the preceding test case didn't use any Spring-related objects. We will now modify the test case to find the author by **Id** by writing the following test:

```
@Test
void findByIdTest() {
    Assertions.assertEquals(3, authorService.findById(1));
}
```

4. Then, after running the preceding test, it will fail with the stack trace as shown in the following screenshot:

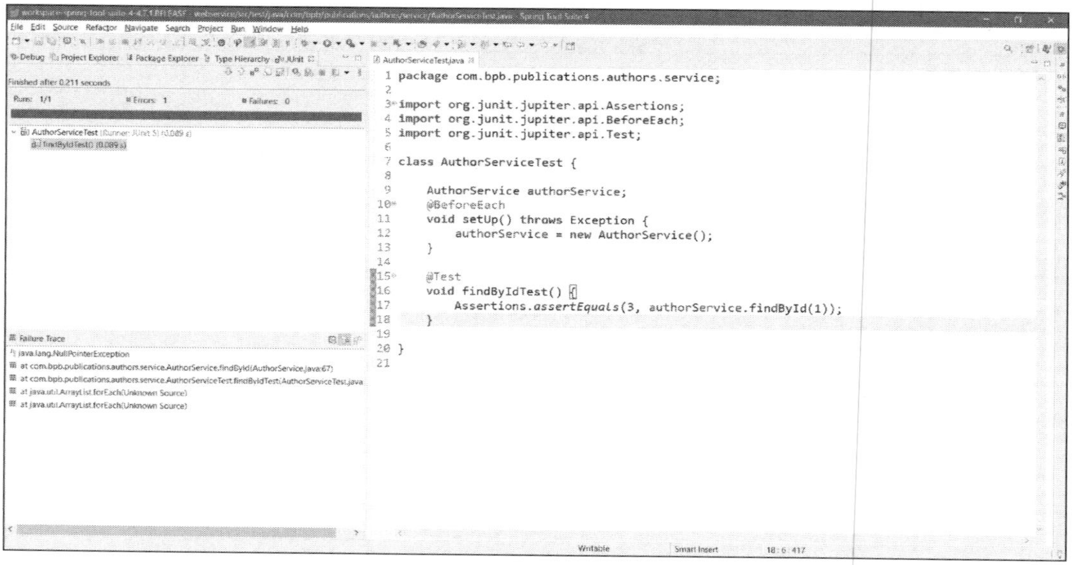

Figure 11.2: findById test

The error is about the **NullPointerException** which is raised at line *67* of the **AuthorService** class. This line contains the repository call **authorRepository.findById(id);** The reason for this error is due to no reference for **AuthorRepository** was found and hence, it was set to null during the test. The reason for not getting the reference is due to the instantiation of the **AuthorService** class using a **new** keyword.

JUnit test case helps in writing the unit test cases, but it lacks the functionality to use object references that lie within the Spring context. For instance, we saw **NullPointerException** thrown while using **AuthorRepository**. *How do we resolve this? How do we pass the value of **AuthorRepository** into **AuthorService** while running our test?* This can be answered in the next section by using the Mockito framework.

Writing a unit test using the Mockito framework

For writing Mockito test cases, follow below procedure:

1. As the **Mockito** dependency is included within **spring-boot-starter-test,** we don't need to add the dependency explicitly. We can tweak the same code as discussed in the previous section as follows:

```
package com.bpb.publications.authors.service;

import java.util.Optional;

import org.junit.jupiter.api.Assertions;
import org.junit.jupiter.api.BeforeEach;
import org.junit.jupiter.api.Test;
import org.mockito.Mockito;

import com.bpb.publications.authors.entity.Author;
import com.bpb.publications.authors.repository.AuthorRepository;

class AuthorServiceTest {

    AuthorService authorService;
    Author author;

    @BeforeEach
    void setUp() throws Exception {
        authorService = new AuthorService();
        author = new Author();
        author.setId(1);
        author.setName("Shagun");
    }
}
```

Here, we added a global variable for **Author** to store author details against which we are setting the actual data. This variable is initialized in the **setUp()** method.

2. Now, we can add the test method to test the **findById** method of **AuthorService as follows**:

```
@Test
void findByIdTest() {
```

```
        authorService.authorRepository = Mockito.mock(AuthorRepos-
        itory.class);
        Mockito.when(authorService.authorRepository.findById(Mocki-
        to.any())).thenReturn(Optional.of(author));
        Assertions.assertEquals("Shagun", authorService.findById(1).
        getName());
    }
```

3. As we are in the same package of the test class where we also have the original code, we are able to access the repository directly. Well, that's fine. This can be correctly by using a repository without using an **AuthorService** reference. But for now, let us see how to mock the external references. Here, we will create the mock object of type **AuthorRepository.class** by writing **Mockito.mock(AuthorRepository.class)** which returns the same datatype as we pass.
4. Now, wherever we use the repository in the actual code, if any method is invoked from the repository, then it returns the actual data. We will create an object of the **Author** and provide its ID and name. This repository when called can return the actual data or add the functionality to the mock object by calling the **when()** method of Mockito which accepts the mock object like **authorRepository** and calls the method for which we need a mock object as the response whenever the **authorRepository.findById()** is called **return author's reference**. The **findById()** method is called in the **when()** method, so if any value is provided to the **findById()** method by putting **Mockito.any(),** then it returns our custom reference of the type **Author.**
5. Lastly, call the actual method from the service class which will use our mocked repository and compare the value equality, that is, the expected value and actual value by calling the **assertEquals()** method. Mockito also ensures whether the **mock** method is being called or not with the required arguments by calling the **verify()** method as follows:

```
@Test
void findByIdTest() {
    authorService.authorRepository = Mockito.mock(AuthorReposito-
    ry.class);
    Mockito.when(authorService.authorRepository.findById(Mockito.
    any())).thenReturn(Optional.of(author));
    Assertions.assertEquals("Shagun",   authorService.findById(1).
    getName());
```

```
        Mockito.verify(authorService.authorRepository).findById(1);
    }
```

If we change the verification to the following code, then it will throw an error for different arguments passed:

```
Mockito.verify(authorService.authorRepository).findById(2);
```

You can also verify how many times the method is called for the mocked object. For instance, here we mocked **authorRepository**, and to verify that the **findById(1)** is called once, we can call the verify method with the **VerificationMode** object. This **VerificationMode** can be referenced by the static method of Mockito – **times()**. The following snippet verifies the number of times the method has been called:

```
Mockito.verify(authorService.authorRepository, Mockito.times(1)).
findById(1);
```

If the number of times value doesn't match with the call placed, then **org.mockito.exceptions.verification.TooFewActualInvocations** is thrown.

This is one of the ways to use the **mock** object. Now, let us look at another way using **annotation**. Yes, there are few annotations for mocking objects and injecting mocks. Before going ahead, the following are few annotations that we need to understand:

- **@RunWith**: It is used to integrate the test context with test frameworks or to change the overall execution flow in the test cases in JUnit version 4 also called as **JUnit 4** or **Cucumber Automation Test**. This annotation is placed at the top of the test class.
- **@ExtendWith**: This annotation provides a similar functionality as **@RunWith.** It takes the class of type **Extension** that is used for the annotated test class or test method. We will use this annotation since we will use the latest JUnit 5.
- **@Mock**: This annotation is used to inject a mock for an instance variable that is used anywhere in the class for which the test cases are to be written and it can be used anywhere in the test class.
- **@Spy**: This annotation is used to create a spy on real objects. When we annotate on the variable, the Mockito calls the actual method of the real object for which we declare the variable.
- **@InjectMocks**: This annotation is also used to inject a mock for the test class instance through which we call the methods of the class which are in the test. **@InjectMocks** will only inject mocks/spies created using the **@Spy** or **@Mock** annotation.

Let us use few of them to redefine the **AuthorServiceTest** class by following below steps:

1. Modify the **AuthorServiceTest** class as follows:

```
package com.bpb.publications.authors.service;
import org.junit.jupiter.api.extension.ExtendWith;
import org.mockito.InjectMocks;
import org.mockito.Mock;
import org.mockito.junit.jupiter.MockitoExtension;

import com.bpb.publications.authors.entity.Author;
import com.bpb.publications.authors.repository.AuthorRepository;

@ExtendWith(MockitoExtension.class)
class AuthorServiceTest {
    @InjectMocks
    AuthorService authorService;

    Author author;

    @Mock
    AuthorRepository authorRepository;
}
```

2. Now, we can add the **setUp()** method and the test method as follows:

```
@BeforeEach
void setUp() throws Exception {
    MockitoAnnotations.initMocks(this);
    author = new Author();
    author.setId(1);
    author.setName("Shagun");
}
```

3. As we use **`@InjectMocks`** and **`@Mock`**, to initialize those objects, we need to use **`MockitoAnnotations.initMocks(this)`** and the test method looks as follows:

```
@Test
void findByIdTest() {
    Mockito.when(authorRepository.findById(Mockito.any())).then-
    Return(Optional.of(author));
    Assertions.assertEquals("Shagun",authorService.findById(1).
    getName());
    Mockito.verify(authorRepository).findById(1);
    Mockito.verify(authorRepository, Mockito.times(1)).findBy-
    Id(1);
}
```

Checking code coverage

Now, why do we write test cases? To measure if all parts of the code are tested, there is a software metric called **code coverage** that can be plugged in while we run test cases. This metric can be measured by the **JaCoCo** plugin which measures how many lines of code are executed during the test, and at the end of the build process, it generates an HTML report depicting how much code is covered. For example, take the preceding test class containing the **`findById`** test, we can include the following plugin into **`pom.xml`**:

```
<plugin>
    <groupId>org.jacoco</groupId>
    <artifactId>jacoco-maven-plugin</artifactId>
    <executions>
        <execution>
            <goals>
                <goal>prepare-agent</goal>
            </goals>
        </execution>
        <execution>
            <id>report</id>
            <phase>prepare-package</phase>
```

```
            <goals>
                <goal>report</goal>
            </goals>
        </execution>
    </executions>
</plugin>
```

Thus, after building the project using **`mvn clean install`,** the reports are generated inside **`target/site/jacoco/index.html`.** Browsing **`index.html`** will show you code coverage for the preceding test method as shown in the following screenshot:

Web-Service

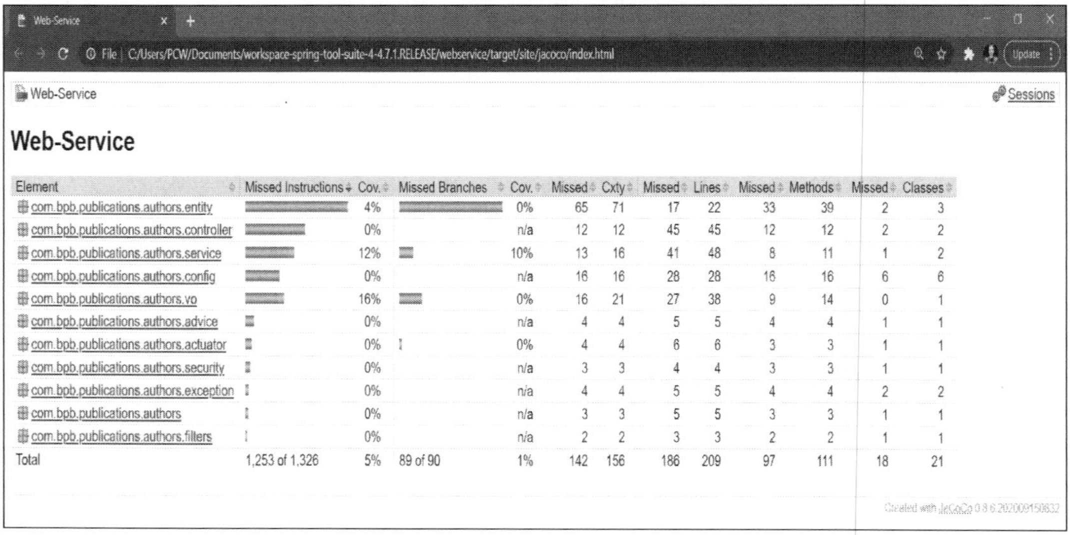

Element	Missed Instructions	Cov.	Missed Branches	Cov.	Missed	Cxty	Missed	Lines	Missed	Methods	Missed	Classes
com.bpb.publications.authors.entity		4%		0%	65	71	17	22	33	39	2	3
com.bpb.publications.authors.controller		0%		n/a	12	12	45	45	12	12	2	2
com.bpb.publications.authors.service		12%		10%	13	16	41	48	8	11	1	2
com.bpb.publications.authors.config		0%		n/a	16	16	28	28	16	16	6	6
com.bpb.publications.authors.vo		16%		0%	16	21	27	38	9	14	0	1
com.bpb.publications.authors.advice		0%		n/a	4	4	5	5	4	4	1	1
com.bpb.publications.authors.actuator		0%		0%	4	4	6	6	3	3	1	1
com.bpb.publications.authors.security		0%		n/a	3	3	4	4	3	3	1	1
com.bpb.publications.authors.exception		0%		n/a	4	4	5	5	4	4	2	2
com.bpb.publications.authors		0%		n/a	3	3	5	5	3	3	1	1
com.bpb.publications.authors.filters		0%		n/a	2	2	3	3	2	2	1	1
Total	1,253 of 1,326	5%	89 of 90	1%	142	156	186	209	97	111	18	21

Figure 11.3: *JaCoCo code coverage report*

The *red* color in the report shows you the status of the uncovered lines and *green* shows the covered lines while in the test mode. This report shows you how many numbers of lines are coded, how many are covered, missed, and an overview of the method and classes inside the package. Browsing to the package **`com.bpb.publications.authors.service`** for which we had written the test method will show you a coverage report as shown in the following screenshot:

```
        BeanUtils.copyProperties(author.get(), authorVO);
        return authorVO;
    }

    public List<AuthorVO> getAll() {
        List<Author> authors = Lists.newArrayList(authorRepository.findAll());
        if (authors.isEmpty()) {
            throw new NoRecordsException("No Authors found");
        }
        List<AuthorVO> authorVOs = new ArrayList<>();
        authors.forEach(author -> {
            AuthorVO authorVO = new AuthorVO();
            BeanUtils.copyProperties(author, authorVO);
            authorVOs.add(authorVO);
        });
        return authorVOs;
    }

    public AuthorVO findById(int id) {
        Optional<Author> author = authorRepository.findById(id);
        if (!author.isPresent()) {
            throw new NoRecordsException("No Records for Author for ID " + id);
        }
        AuthorVO authorVO = new AuthorVO();
        BeanUtils.copyProperties(author.get(), authorVO);
        return authorVO;
    }


}
```

Figure 11.4: Detailed coverage of lines

Here, again the *red* color shows the uncovered lines of code in the test, and the *green* color shows the lines covered in the test. The *yellow* color line has a diamond sign which says that one of the branches as this is an `if()` conditional construct is missed while writing the test cases. To cover all lines of code, you need to cover all kinds of conditions which are there in the functionality in test classes. Ideally, 100% code coverage says that your code is tested fully. But if that's not the case, then either the code written is a dead code or requires to be tweaked while writing the test cases.

The code coverage can also be checked by installing **`EclEmma Java Code Coverage`** from **`Eclipse Marketplace`** as shown in the following screenshot:

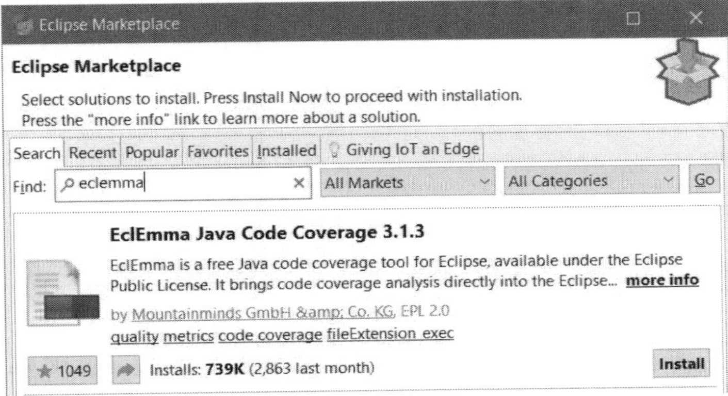

Figure 11.5: Searching solutions in Eclipse Marketplace

And the same coverage can be seen in STS or Eclipse after running the test classes using the **Coverage As** option:

Console Problems Progress Debug Shell Search Terminal Call Hierarchy Coverage

Element	Coverage	Covered Instru...	Missed Instruct...	Total Instructio...
webservice	9.3 %	129	1,251	1,380
src/main/java	5.5 %	73	1,251	1,324
com.bpb.publications.authors.entity	4.6 %	20	411	431
com.bpb.publications.authors.controller	0.0 %	0	252	252
com.bpb.publications.authors.service	12.7 %	26	178	204
AuthorService.java	20.5 %	26	101	127
CustomUserDetailsService.java	0.0 %	0	77	77
com.bpb.publications.authors.config	0.0 %	0	144	144
com.bpb.publications.authors.vo	16.5 %	27	137	164
com.bpb.publications.authors.advice	0.0 %	0	38	38
com.bpb.publications.authors.actuator	0.0 %	0	31	31
com.bpb.publications.authors.security	0.0 %	0	22	22
com.bpb.publications.authors.exception	0.0 %	0	17	17
com.bpb.publications.authors	0.0 %	0	13	13
com.bpb.publications.authors.filters	0.0 %	0	8	8
src/test/java	100.0 %	56	0	56

Figure 11.6: *Coverage in IDE*

Testing RESTFul web services

The preceding test cases were the basic where we tested whether our service was able to hit the mock repository and get the data only at the service level. We can also write the JUnit test for the controllers in a way to test what will be the behavior of the controller method when a specific request comes with a specific set of headers and expect a specific response from the API. Follow these steps to write test case for a RESTFul API:

1. We will write the test case for the **'author/add'** API where we will supply a dummy request body and expect a **200** HTTP status code. The following is the skeleton of the **AuthorControllerTest** class:

```
package com.bpb.publications.authors.controller;
import org.junit.jupiter.api.BeforeEach;
import org.mockito.InjectMocks;
import org.mockito.Mock;
import org.mockito.MockitoAnnotations;
```

```
import org.springframework.test.web.servlet.MockMvc;
import org.springframework.test.web.servlet.setup.MockMvcBuilders;

import com.bpb.publications.authors.service.AuthorService;
class AuthorControllerTest {

    @InjectMocks
    AuthorController authorController;

    @Mock
    AuthorService authorService;


  MockMvc mockMvc;

    @BeforeEach
    void setUp() throws Exception {
        MockitoAnnotations.initMocks(this);
        mockMvc = MockMvcBuilders.standaloneSetup(authorControl-
        ler).build();
    }
}
```

2. The new code which we introduced is the **MockMvc** class. This class is used as the main entry point for the server-side Spring MVC test support. Then, we used the **standaloneSetup()** method of **MockMvcBuilders.** This method takes the controller object for which we had used **@InjectMocks** and registers the controller for creating the **MockMvc** instance. This will take care of all kinds of initializations for controllers and their dependencies which ensure only one controller is active in the test at a time. Next, we will add the following snippet for writing a test case to add the author:

```
@Test
void addAuthorTests() throws Exception {
    mockMvc.perform(MockMvcRequestBuilders.post("/author/add")
            .content("{\"bio\":\"this is my bio\",\"name\": \"John
            Mark\",\"url\": \"www.johnmark.com\"}")
            .contentType(MediaType.APPLICATION_JSON)).andEx-
            pect(status().isOk());
```

```
        Mockito.verify(authorService, Mockito.times(1)).add(anyOb-
        ject());
        Mockito.verifyNoMoreInteractions(authorService);
    }
```

With the help of **mockMvc**, we will try to perform an API request which is of type POST specified using **MockMvcRequestBuilders** which takes the name of the URI on which the required API is hosted. This URI is the same we provided after the localhost and the port. Since this is the POST API, we can also provide the request body by calling the **content()** method as passing a **JSON** string to it. We can also specify the content type of the request body as **APPLICATION_JSON**. Lastly, we expect the API's response as **200** by calling the **isOk()** method.

3. We will later verify that the **add()** method of **authorService** is invoked only once with any type of object being passed using **anyObject()** of the**Matchers** class. This method is static in nature. We can also verify if there should be no more interactions with **authorService** after calling the API by invoking the **verifyNoMoreInteractions()** method.When the API is invoked in the test, it creates an instance of **TestDispatcherServlet** which will have the behavior of **DispatcherServlet**. This will make the overall flow real as if there is a real **DispatcherServlet** sending the requests to the controller. After you run the test, you will be see the following screen:

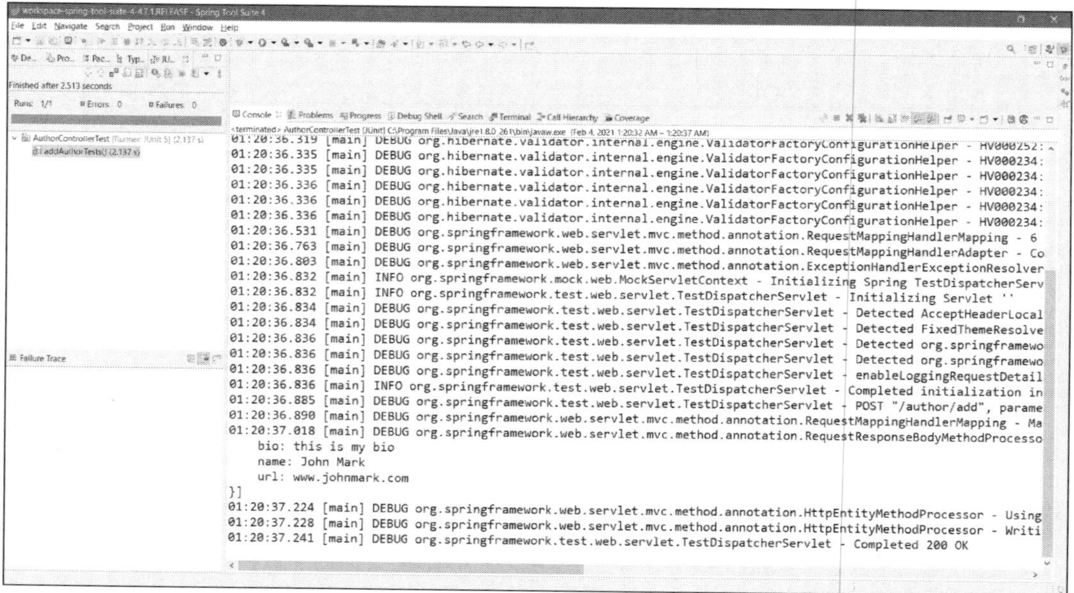

Figure 11.7: Controller test

The console logs show the request body sent and the response received. Let's write another test case where we expect that the API will throw an exception like **NoRecordsException.** The following is the test case for getting the author by providing the query parameter's name and URL to the API:

```
@Test
void getAuthorTest() throws Exception {
    MultiValueMap<String, String> queryParams = new LinkedMultiVal-
    ueMap<>();
    queryParams.add(“name”, “shagun”);
    queryParams.add(“url”, “url”);
    when(authorService.get(anyString(),anyString())).thenThrow(No-
    RecordsException.class);
    mockMvc.perform(MockMvcRequestBuilders.get(“/author”).query-
    Params(queryParams)).andExpect(status().isNotFound());
}
```

4. As we have used the **when()** method to throw an exception of the **NoRecordsException** class when the **get()** method is called from **authorService**, the test will throw an exception as shown in the following screenshot:

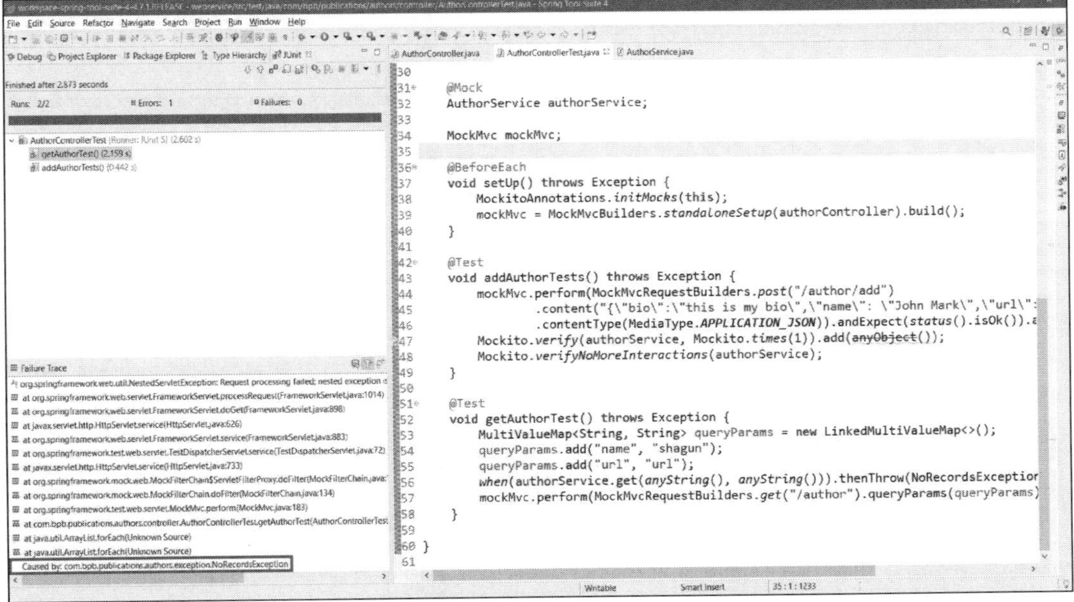

Figure 11.8: Throwing an error

This throws an error which failed the test. Now, *how do we resolve this?*

5. Since we had implemented the **AppControllerAdvice** class using **@ControllerAdvice** on top of the class in *Chapter 6, Building RESTFul Microservices,* we can configure this test class to use that controller advice by changing the configuration to the following code:

```
@InjectMocks
AppControllerAdvice advice;


@BeforeEach
void setUp() throws Exception {
    MockitoAnnotations.initMocks(this);
    mockMvc = MockMvcBuilders.standaloneSetup(authorController).
    setControllerAdvice(advice).build();
}
```

6. Now, if we run the test class again, we will get the error but that will be handled by our **AppControllerAdvice** since we have the exception handler for **NoRecordsException** in the controller advice. To test whether the controller advice handled our exception, you may see this log in the console:

```
10:35:24.857 [main] DEBUG org.springframework.test.web.servlet.
TestDispatcherServlet - GET "/author?name=shagun&url=url",
parameters={masked}

10:35:24.861 [main] DEBUG org.springframework.web.servlet.
mvc.method.annotation.RequestMappingHandlerMapping
- Mapped to com.bpb.publications.authors.controller.
AuthorController#getAuthor(String, String)

10:35:24.909 [main] DEBUG org.springframework.web.servlet.
mvc.method.annotation.ExceptionHandlerExceptionResolver -
Using @ExceptionHandler com.bpb.publications.authors.advice.
AppControllerAdvice#handleNoRecordsException(NoRecordsException)

10:35:24.964 [main] DEBUG org.springframework.web.servlet.mvc.
method.annotation.HttpEntityMethodProcessor - Found 'Content-
Type:application/json' in response

10:35:25.001 [main] DEBUG org.springframework.web.servlet.mvc.
method.annotation.HttpEntityMethodProcessor - Writing [com.bpb.
publications.authors.exception.ErrorMessage@3104f7bd]
```

```
10:35:25.012 [main] DEBUG org.springframework.web.servlet.mvc.
method.annotation.ExceptionHandlerExceptionResolver - Resolved
[com.bpb.publications.authors.exception.NoRecordsException]
10:35:25.012 [main] DEBUG org.springframework.test.web.servlet.
TestDispatcherServlet - Completed 404 NOT_FOUND
```

The log line at *3* and *7* shows the exception handler being used and returns the HTTP status code as we configured it for **`NoRecordsException`**.

Cucumber automation testing

The test cases can also be written in the **Behavior Driven Development** (**BDD**) style, where we can specify three aspects – **`given`**, **`when`**, and **`then`**. **`Mockito`** also provides the same behavior methods by using the **`BDDMockito`** class. The test case for getting all authors is as follows:

```
@Test
void getAllAuthorsTest() throws Exception {
    author = new Author();
    author.setId(1);
    author.setName("Shagun");

    //given
    BDDMockito.given(authorRepository.findAll()).willReturn(Collections.
    singleton(author));

    //when
    List<AuthorVO> response = authorService.getAll();

    //then
    Assertions.assertEquals(1, response.size());
    Assertions.assertEquals("Shagun", response.get(0).getName());
}
```

There is another tool called **Cucumber** which is famous for writing these BDD test cases. It supports automated software tests written in the BDD style. It is written in Ruby language which provides a feature to write test cases in plain English text.

Even business or non-technical stakeholders can understand how to write it. *It's so easy!*

Once these behaviors are drawn, the Cucumber framework converts them into executable test cases written in a language called **Gherkins**. To start executing the test cases while in the build process, we need to start with including the following Cucumber JVM dependency in **pom.xml**:

```
<dependency>
    <groupId>io.cucumber</groupId>
    <artifactId>cucumber-java</artifactId>
    <version>4.2.0</version>
    <scope>test</scope>
</dependency>
```

We can also add JUnit and Cucumber testing dependency as follows:

```
<dependency>
    <groupId>io.cucumber</groupId>
    <artifactId>cucumber-junit</artifactId>
    <version>4.2.0</version>
    <scope>test</scope>
</dependency>
```

Finally, we can add the Spring and Cucumber dependency:

```
<dependency>
    <groupId>io.cucumber</groupId>
    <artifactId>cucumber-spring</artifactId>
    <version>4.2.0</version>
    <scope>test</scope>
</dependency>
```

Now, let us start configuring Cucumber configurations in Java classes. The following is the snippet of the **CucumberTest** class in the **src\test\java** folder with the package name as **com.bpb.publications.authors**:

```
package com.bpb.publications.authors;
import org.junit.runner.RunWith;
import cucumber.api.CucumberOptions;
```

```
import cucumber.api.junit.Cucumber;


@RunWith(Cucumber.class)
@CucumberOptions(features = "classpath:features",
                plugin = { "pretty",
                           "json:target/cucumber-report.json"
                },
                glue = "com.bpb.publications.authors.stepdef")
public class CucumberTest {
}
```

The @CucumberOptions annotation is used to describe the location of feature files and the output plugins. The **glue** attribute defines the package where all our step definitions are stored. Step definitions contain the step-by-step information on how the workflow is for a scenario. The scenario can be a successful login to an application, and step-by-step information could be a user entering the username and password and then clicking on the **Login** button. The same way we will be writing a scenario where a user accesses an application for managing the author information.

Now, we will define the feature file which contains the scenario and the step-by-step process for an API to be executed in plain English text. The following code is the **author.feature** file created in the **src/test/resources/features** package:

```
Feature: Manage Authors
  As a admin
  I want to manage authors information


  Scenario Outline: Call Add Author API
    When the client calls /author/add with name "<name>" , url "<url>"
    and bio "<bio>"
    Then the client receives status code of <status>
  Examples:
    |name      |url                  |bio                    |status|
    |John      |http://johnauthor.com|this is bio for John   |200   |
    |Shagun    |http://shagun.in     |this is bio for Shagun|200   |
```

The preceding file can contain the following keywords:

1. **Feature**: It defines the name of the feature under test.
2. **Scenario Outline**: It describes the test scenario.
3. **Given**: The information or the data setup done before executing specific conditions.
4. **When**: It is the condition which should match in order to execute the next step.
5. **Then**: It defines the outcome when the **WHEN** part is matched.
6. **But**: It provides the logical **OR** condition *N* number of statements that can be used with **GIVEN**, **WHEN,** and **THEN** statements.
7. **And**: It provides the logical **AND** condition *N* number of statements that can be used with **GIVEN**, **WHEN,** and **THEN** statements.
8. **Examples:** It describes the range of data input to be provided on scenario execution and that test scenario will be executed for each of the input provided. The input information is separated by pipe (|).

Similarly, the following scenario is to get the author details by the name and URL that can be placed in the same feature file as this is the part of the same feature, that is, manage author:

```
Scenario Outline: client makes call to GET /author
  When the client calls /author with name "<name>" and url "<url>"
  Then the client receives status code of <status>
Examples:
  |name        |url                 | status|
  |dummy       |http://unknown.com|404     |
  |Shagun      |http://shagun.in  |200     |
  |Shagun      |http://mybook.com |404     |
```

Once the preceding feature is written, the basic idea would be to invoke our REST APIs and provide related fields to act. To do this, we will create a step definition file called **AuthorStepDefinition** in the **com.bpb.publications.authors.stepdef** package under the **src\test\java\com\bpb\publications\authors\stepdef** folder. The contents of the step definition file are listed as follows:

```
package com.bpb.publications.authors.stepdef;
import org.junit.runner.RunWith;
import org.mockito.junit.MockitoJUnitRunner;
import org.springframework.boot.test.autoconfigure.web.servlet.
```

```
AutoConfigureMockMvc;
import org.springframework.boot.test.context.SpringBootTest;
import org.springframework.test.context.ActiveProfiles;

@RunWith(MockitoJUnitRunner.class)
@SpringBootTest
@ActiveProfiles(profiles = "dev")
@AutoConfigureMockMvc
public class AuthorStepDefinition {
}
```

We will use the **`MockitoJUnitRunner`** class to prepare calls to REST APIs by **`MockMvc`**. **`@SpringBootTest`** is responsible for loading the Spring context. We can also specify the profile that needs to be active while running tests. So here, we used **`@ActiveProfiles`** to use **`application-dev.yml`** created in the microservice code.

> **All the features developed will use the live resources like database, REST calls to other APIs, or any unmocked resources. Be assured that the profile you select doesn't harm your running environment. You can also use mock servers while running cucumber tests.**

`@AutoConfigureMockMvc` is again used to configure **`MockMvc`** while invoking an API.

Let us now start providing the step definition information which we declared in the feature file:

1. We will use annotations like **`@When`** and **`@Then`** so that the method will get executed in the order of the scenario. The following is the snippet for calling **ADD API** of **`Author`**:

   ```
   @Autowired
   private MockMvc mvc;

   ResultActions action;

   @When("^the client calls /author/add with name \"([^\"]*)\" , url
   \"([^\"]*)\" and bio \"([^\"]*)\"$")
   public void addAuthor(String name, String url, String bio) throws
   Exception {
   ```

```
        JSONObject jsonObject = new JSONObject();
        jsonObject.put("name", name);
        jsonObject.put("url", url);
        jsonObject.put("bio", bio);
        action = mvc
                .perform(post("/author/add")
                .content(jsonObject.toString()).contentType(MediaType.
                APPLICATION_JSON));
    }

    @Then("^the client receives status code of (-?\\d+)$")
    public void verifyResponseCode(Integer status) throws Exception {
        action.andExpect(status().is(status));
    }
```

2. The annotation takes the value in the form of a regular expression which matches with the condition specified in the feature file. The dynamic values or inputs can be managed by putting the placeholders in parenthesis as shown in the preceding snippet. For execution, first the method annotated with **`@When`** will be executed and the method with **`@Then`** will be executed for a particular scenario. We should not reuse the same scenario again and again but the other methods annotated with any of **`@Given`**, **`@When`**, and **`@Then`** can be repeated as per design. Similarly, we will use the **when** annotation to get the author information by **`name`** and **`url`** as follows:

```
@When("^the client calls /author with name \"([^\"]*)\" and url
\"([^\"]*)\"$")
public void getAuthorNyNameAndUrl (String name, String url) throws
Exception {
    MultiValueMap<String, String> queryParams = new
    LinkedMultiValueMap<>();
    queryParams.add("name", name);
    queryParams.add("url", url);
    action = mvc.perform(get("/author").queryParams(queryParams));
}
```

3. Since we used **then** keyword with the same statement in the feature file, the framework will reuse the method annotation with **`@Then`** which matches the regular expression. Once all the preceding files and codes are in place, you will be seeing the following project structure in **`Project Explorer`**:

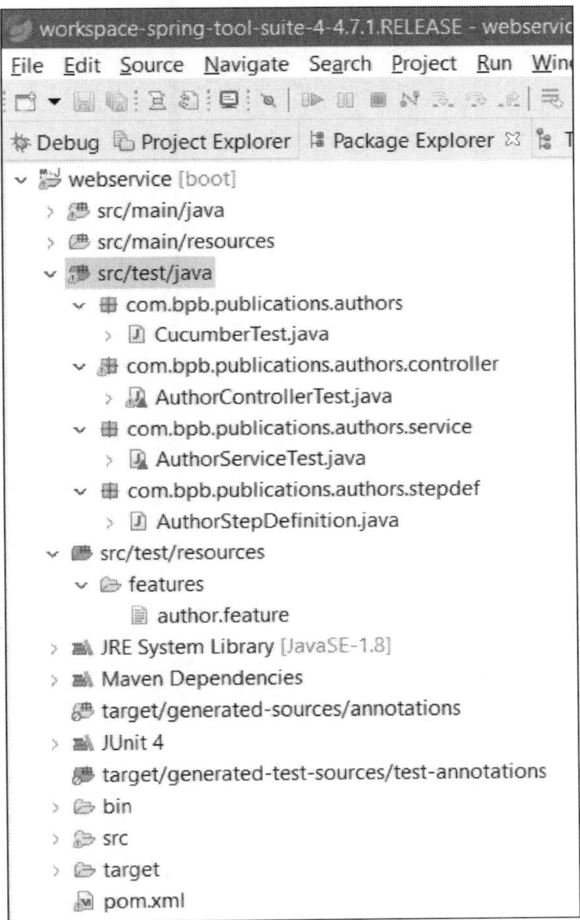

Figure 11.9: *Project Explorer*

4. Now, we are in the last step of completing the test cases. Yes, we will now build the project using the **`mvn clean install`** command on the terminal. You will see several logs, but most likely you will see the following logs which shows the scenario execution as shown in the following screenshot:

```
thor0_ where author0_.name=? and author0_.url=?
Feature: Manage Authors
  As a admin
  I want to manage authors information

  Scenario Outline: client makes call to GET /author/add for adding author information # features/author.feature:5
    When the client calls /author/add with name "<name>" , url "<url>" and bio "<bio>"
    Then the client receives status code of <status>

    Examples:

  Scenario Outline: client makes call to GET /author/add for adding author information                          # features/author.f
eature:10
    When the client calls /author/add with name "John" , url "http://johnauthor.com" and bio "this is bio for John" # AuthorStepDefinit
ion.addAuthor(String,String,String)
    Then the client receives status code of 200                                                                   # AuthorStepDefinit
ion.verifyResponseCode(Integer)

  Scenario Outline: client makes call to GET /author/add for adding author information                         # features/author.fe
ature:11
    When the client calls /author/add with name "Shagun" , url "http://shagun.in" and bio "this is bio for Shagun" # AuthorStepDefiniti
on.addAuthor(String,String,String)
    Then the client receives status code of 200                                                                  # AuthorStepDefiniti
on.verifyResponseCode(Integer)

  Scenario Outline: client makes call to GET /author # features/author.feature:14
    When the client calls /author with name "<name>" and url "<url>"
    Then the client receives status code of <status>

    Examples:

  Scenario Outline: client makes call to GET /author                                 # features/author.feature:19
    When the client calls /author with name "dummy" and url "http://unknown.com" # AuthorStepDefinition.getNameAndUrlofAuthor(String,St
```

Figure 11.10: Console for Cucumber scenarios

5. If the project contains JUnit test cases which we had written in the same project, then a combined test result will be shown in the end as shown in the following screenshot:

```
    When the client calls /author with name "dummy" and url "http://unknown.com" # AuthorStepDefinition.getNameAndUrlofAuthor(String,St
ring)
    Then the client receives status code of 404                                   # AuthorStepDefinition.verifyResponseCode(Integer)

  Scenario Outline: client makes call to GET /author                             # features/author.feature:20
    When the client calls /author with name "Shagun" and url "http://shagun.in" # AuthorStepDefinition.getNameAndUrlofAuthor(String,Str
ing)
    Then the client receives status code of 200                                  # AuthorStepDefinition.verifyResponseCode(Integer)

  Scenario Outline: client makes call to GET /author                               # features/author.feature:21
    When the client calls /author with name "Shagun" and url "http://mybook.com" # AuthorStepDefinition.getNameAndUrlofAuthor(String,St
ring)
    Then the client receives status code of 404                                    # AuthorStepDefinition.verifyResponseCode(Integer)

5 Scenarios (5 passed)
10 Steps (10 passed)
0m34.417s

[INFO] Tests run: 5, Failures: 0, Errors: 0, Skipped: 0, Time elapsed: 32.123 s - in com.bpb.publications.authors.CucumberTest
2021-02-06 21:36:58.735  INFO 1776 --- [extShutdownHook] j.LocalContainerEntityManagerFactoryBean : Closing JPA EntityManagerFactory fo
r persistence unit 'default'
2021-02-06 21:36:58.742  INFO 1776 --- [extShutdownHook] o.s.s.concurrent.ThreadPoolTaskExecutor  : Shutting down ExecutorService 'appl
icationTaskExecutor'
2021-02-06 21:36:58.744  INFO 1776 --- [extShutdownHook] com.zaxxer.hikari.HikariDataSource       : HikariPool-1 - Shutdown initiated..
.
2021-02-06 21:36:58.773  INFO 1776 --- [extShutdownHook] com.zaxxer.hikari.HikariDataSource       : HikariPool-1 - Shutdown completed.
[INFO]
[INFO] Results:
[INFO]
[INFO] Tests run: 9, Failures: 0, Errors: 0, Skipped: 0
[INFO]
[INFO]
[INFO] --- jacoco-maven-plugin:0.8.6:report (report) @ Server ---
```

Figure 11.11: Common logs for JUnit and Cucumber tests

If you have also used the `jacoco` plugin to see the code coverage, then the code coverage metric will be evaluated against JUnits and Cucumber test cases.

Conclusion

We learned most of the Spring Boot development life cycle. We developed a microservice having REST endpoints interacting with the database and other services. In this chapter, we also covered how to write JUnit and Mockito test cases along with Cucumber automation testing. We used several annotations to provide given when and then information for a scenario that can be understood by a non-technical person too! We also measured the code coverage metric using the `jacoco` plugin. In the last chapter of this book, we will learn how to deploy the application to the cloud and hit our APIs from any part of the world via the Internet.

Points to remember

- Writing proper test cases reduces the probability of introducing bugs in the latter part of the SDLC.
- Covering all parts of the code via test cases also makes the developer believe that there is no dead code left behind.
- Use the JUnit 5 framework for writing test cases as it provides many features over and above JUnit 4.
- Cucumber is one of the frameworks to write automation test cases. Mockito is another example.

Questions

1. Why testing is important?
2. How does Maven know this is the method to be put under testing?
3. How to write JUnits test cases?
4. What is the Mockito framework?
5. How do you mock the variables?
6. What are the different methods of initializing mocks?
7. What are assertions?
8. How do you check the code coverage?

CHAPTER 12
Deploying a Spring Boot Application

This chapter explains the basics of Docker and its setup for deploying applications on development or production environments using Docker containers. We will also learn how to use **Heroku Cloud** for deploying our applications in cloud so that the application can be accessed from the Internet.

Structure

In this chapter, we will discuss the following topics:

- Docker and containerization
- Setting up Docker
- Heroku CLI and deployment

Objectives

After studying this unit, you should be able to create Docker images and containerize it. You can access the application API deployed inside a container. You will learn how to deploy an application in Heroku Cloud using the Heroku CLI and understand Heroku provided services.

Docker and containerization

Docker is a software tool that manages the containers into which our application is running. Docker is a **Platform as a Service** (**PaaS**) product that uses the operating system-level virtualization to make the application run in packages or nodes called **containers**. A container is simply another process on your machine that has been isolated from all other processes on the host machine. That isolation leverages kernel **namespaces** and **cgroups** features that have been in Linux for a long time. Docker has worked to make these capabilities approachable and easy to use. There can be multiple containers in a setup that can be isolated from each other to serve the purpose. They communicate with each other via well-defined channels. Those containers may have different configuration files, libraries, and software components. The Docker concept is mainly around developing the application, shipping them into containers, and running anywhere. In some IT industries, this tool is famous as it provides enhanced features and supports to run the application in the cloud environment.

When we run a container, it uses an isolated filesystem that is provided by the container image. This image contains all dependent components and libraries that are required to run an application.

Features

Let us understand the features of Docker and containers:

- Docker reduces the size of the development and allows developers to forget about the environment or infrastructure-related stuff by providing a smaller footprint of the operating system as well as required run-time environments via containers.
- With new containers developed, one can easily work on the development part, whereas the QA or UAT testing can be done on another container which also means another environment.
- Since the containers can be set up for different environments, it can also be scaled up to *n* number of instances.

Setting up Docker

Please perform the following steps to download Docker for Windows:

1. Browse the following website on Chrome:

   https://docs.docker.com/docker-for-windows/install/

   or download it from the following link:

   https://desktop.docker.com/win/stable/Docker%20Desktop%20Installer.exe

2. Open the installation file by double clicking on the file.
3. You will be seeing the following wizard for Docker:

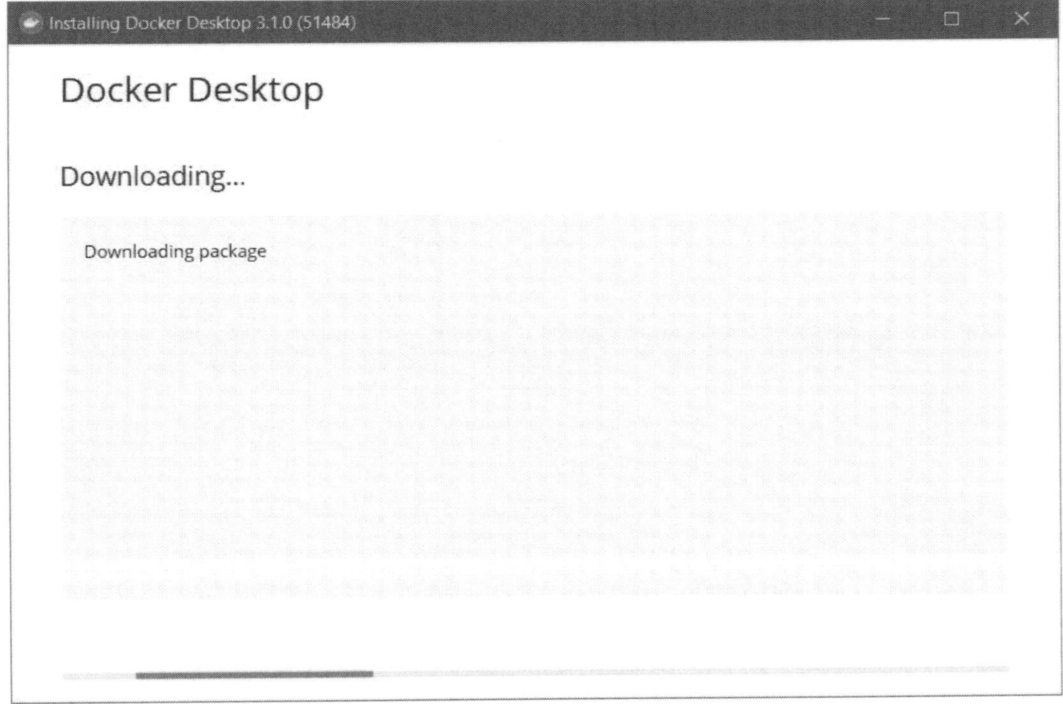

Figure 12.1: *Downloading packages for Docker Desktop*

4. Wait for the installer to complete downloading the packages required on the progress of packages as shown in the following screenshot:

***Figure 12.2:** Unpacking files downloaded from packages*

5. Once all the files are unpacked, you will see the following screen:

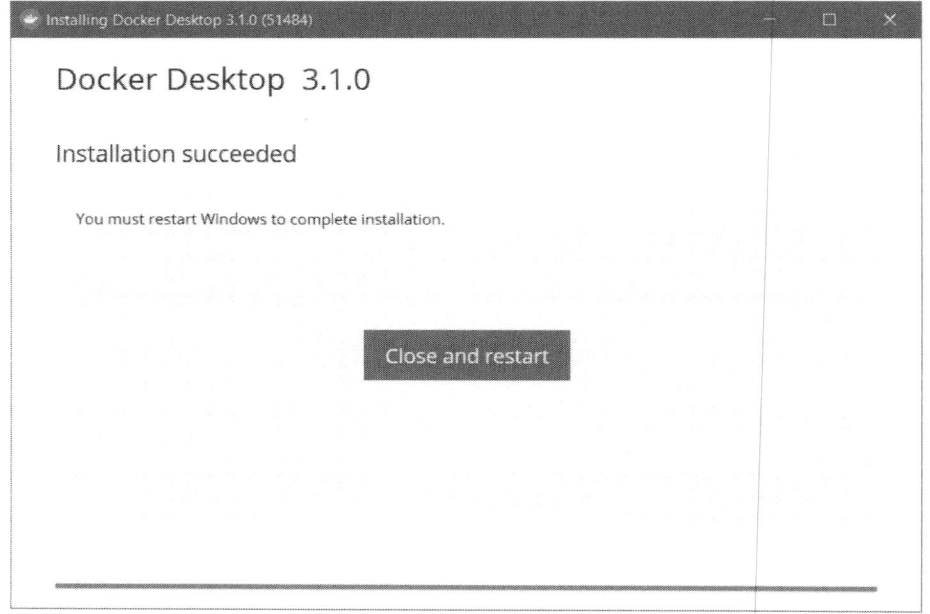

***Figure 12.3**: Installation complete*

6. Click on the **`Close and restart`** button for restarting Windows for completing the registry of software with Windows operating system.

   Once your Docker Desktop setup is completed, you can now open a Command Prompt terminal and verify that Docker is installed successfully by running the: **`docker version`** command. You will see the following screen:

```
C:\WINDOWS\system32\cmd.exe

C:\Users\PCW\Documents\workspace-spring-tool-suite-4-4.7.1.RELEASE\random-number-project>docker version
Client: Docker Engine - Community
 Cloud integration: 1.0.7
 Version:           20.10.2
 API version:       1.41
 Go version:        go1.13.15
 Git commit:        2291f61
 Built:             Mon Dec 28 16:14:16 2020
 OS/Arch:           windows/amd64
 Context:           default
 Experimental:      true

Server: Docker Engine - Community
 Engine:
  Version:          20.10.2
  API version:      1.41 (minimum version 1.12)
  Go version:       go1.13.15
  Git commit:       8891c58
  Built:            Mon Dec 28 16:15:28 2020
  OS/Arch:          linux/amd64
  Experimental:     false
 containerd:
  Version:          1.4.3
  GitCommit:        269548fa27e0089a8b8278fc4fc781d7f65a939b
 runc:
  Version:          1.0.0-rc92
  GitCommit:        ff819c7e9184c13b7c2607fe6c30ae19403a7aff
 docker-init:
  Version:          0.19.0
  GitCommit:        de40ad0

C:\Users\PCW\Documents\workspace-spring-tool-suite-4-4.7.1.RELEASE\random-number-project>
```

Figure 12.4: *Verifying Docker installation*

7. Now, launch the Docker Desktop from the **`Start`** menu to open the dashboard for Docker. If you see the following screen, then we are good to start creating Docker containers:

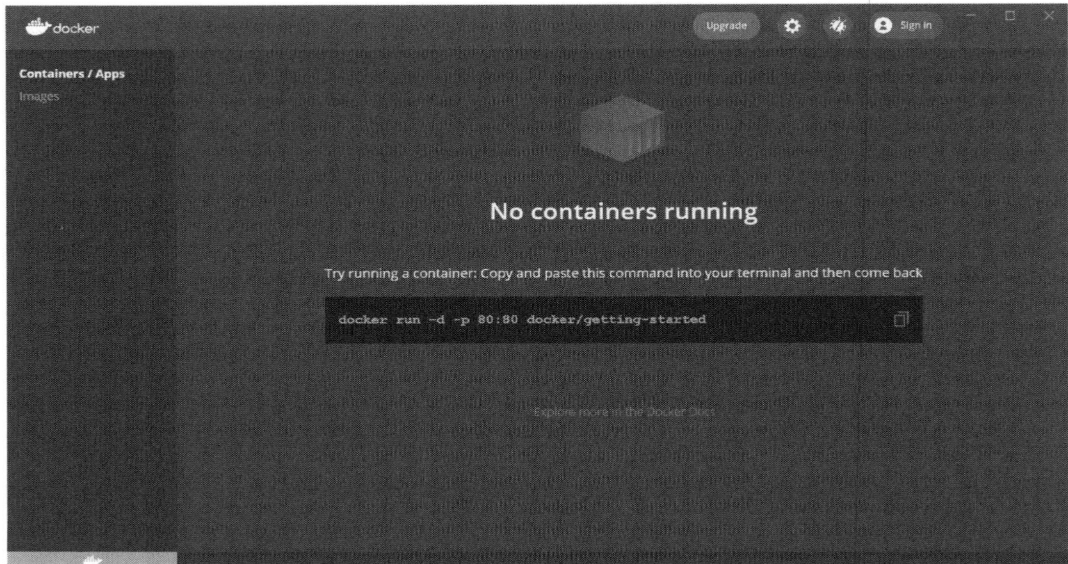

***Figure 12.5**: Docker Desktop dashboard*

To start with creating Docker, we need to create a file named **Dockerfile** which contains the Docker configuration, and we need to place it in the **root** folder of a project which contains **pom.xml**. The following code is the snippet of **Dockerfile**:

```
FROM openjdk:8-jdk-alpine
ARG JAR_FILE=target/*.jar
COPY ${JAR_FILE} app.jar
ENTRYPOINT ["java","-jar","/app.jar"]
```

8. The **Dockerfile** contains the tool information around which it needs to create an image that will be executed inside the container. It specifies the layers of an image. Here, we use **openjdk:8-jdk-alpine flavor** of Java for our runtime environment. After we build the project that generates a **.jar** file, it is placed inside the image with the name **app.jar**.
9. After the preceding configuration is set up, we can now build the project using **mvn clean install**. When the project is successfully built, we can now create a Docker image by running the following command inside the command terminal:

```
docker build -t com.bpb.publications/random-number-project .
```

The output of the preceding command is shown in the following screenshot:

```
C:\Users\PCW\Documents\workspace-spring-tool-suite-4-4.7.1.RELEASE\random-number-project>docker build -t com.bpb.publications/random-nu
mber-project .
[+] Building 58.9s (7/7) FINISHED
 => [internal] load build definition from Dockerfile                                                                    1.0s
 => => transferring dockerfile: 31B                                                                                     0.2s
 => [internal] load .dockerignore                                                                                       0.7s
 => => transferring context: 2B                                                                                         0.0s
 => [internal] load metadata for docker.io/library/openjdk:8-jdk-alpine                                                 5.7s
 => CACHED [1/2] FROM docker.io/library/openjdk:8-jdk-alpine@sha256:94792824df2df33402f201713f932b58cb9de94a0cd524164a0f22833435  0.0s
 => [internal] load build context                                                                                      35.0s
 => => transferring context: 24.77MB                                                                                   33.6s
 => [2/2] COPY target/*.jar app.jar                                                                                    12.5s
 => exporting to image                                                                                                  1.9s
 => => exporting layers                                                                                                 1.4s
 => => writing image sha256:9f5e7133ac677fcbdf6bc085682ba14f7e7d180bf3fac01e1eb91cbc030d2e04                            0.2s
 => => naming to com.bpb.publications/random-number-project                                                             0.1s
```

Figure 12.6: *Building Docker for Spring Boot project*

The preceding command uses the Dockerfile to create a JDK environment where it downloads the files from the Docker repository. Once the files are downloaded, it is exported into the Docker image along-with our **`.jar`** file. Lastly, it places this Docker image inside the new container which is created automatically from the command with the name we provided.

10. Once you see a successful writing image in Docker, open the Docker dashboard and you will see the image just created in the **`Images on disk`** section as shown in the following screenshot:

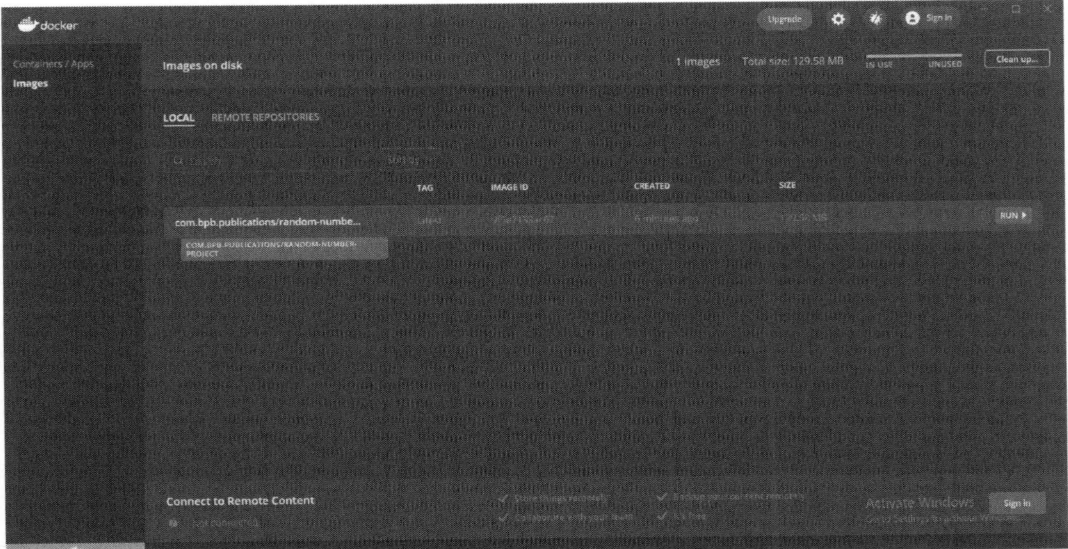

Figure 12.7: *Docker image visible on Docker dashboard*

11. You can also view the image history by just hovering on the list item and clicking on **Inspect** after which you will see all the commands it ran in the background:

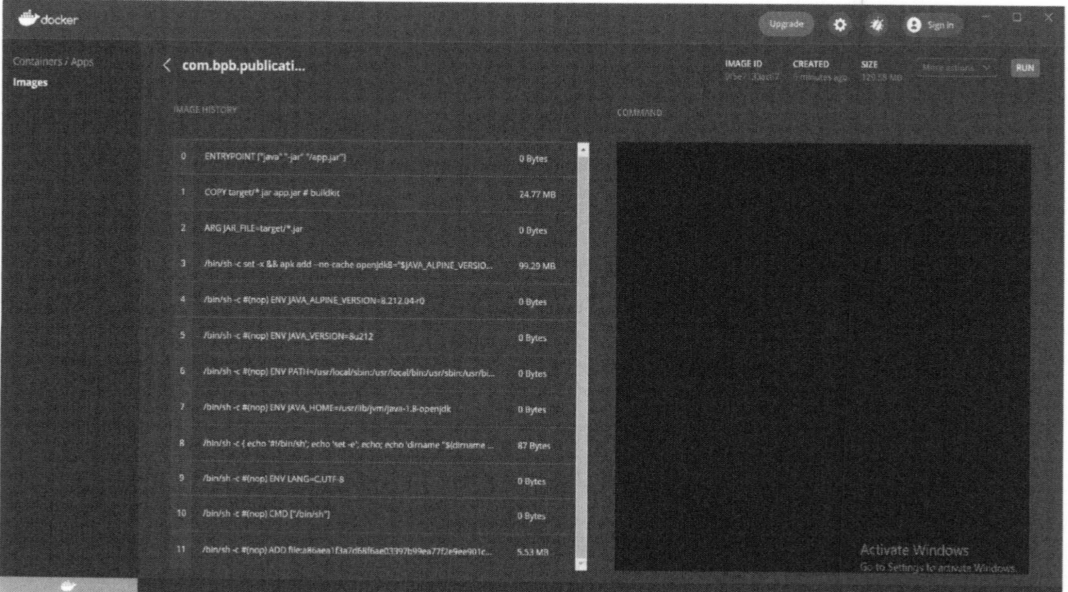

Figure 12.8: *Docker image history*

After we successfully built an image, we need to build a container which is created by running the following command:

```
docker run -e "SPRING_PROFILES_ACTIVE=dev" -p 7003:7003 -t com.
bpb.publications/random-number-project
```

12. As we had different profiles to be selected while running the application, we can provide the environment variable **SPRING_PROFILES_ACTIVE=dev** to the application to run on port **7003**. The **7003** port is published to the container and the host of the application so that the application is accessible on port **7003** for the outside world of Docker. The **-t** option specifies the allocation of pseudo-TTY with the name of the image.

13. The container can be browsed in **Containers / Apps** on the left-hand side of the Docker Desktop dashboard. This is the actual location of the container that can be seen on the Docker dashboard which manages the application lifeline – **stop**, **restart,** or **delete**. Let's see our container which we created automatically as shown in the following screenshot:

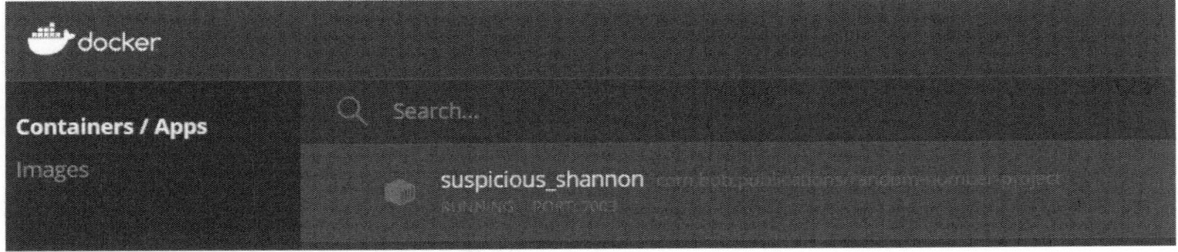

Figure 12.9: Running containers in Docker

As we see it running, we can now access the APIs from the browser or any other REST client by browsing `http://localhost:7003/generate` with a valid access token as the application is security enabled as shown in the following screenshot:

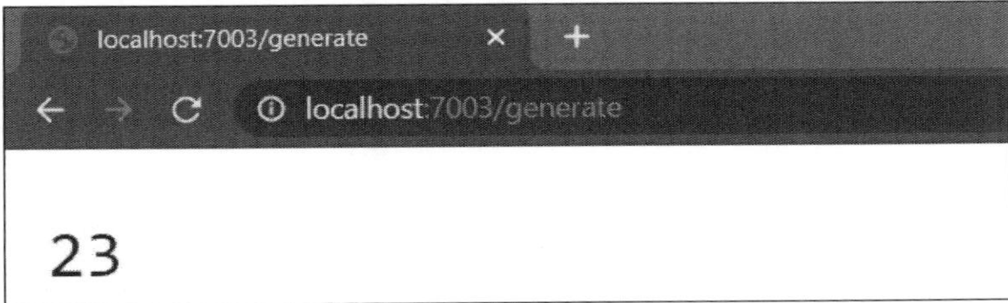

Figure 12.10: Accessing application

> **While running the application inside Docker, the application doesn't understand the resources running in the local workspace. To make it understand to connect to the localhost, we need to provide the value of the connection server as URL: `jdbc:mysql://docker.for.win.localhost:3306/bpb` in connection string of MySQL.**

We have now successfully implemented Docker. Let's now understand how to deploy this application in a public cloud environment using Heroku.

Heroku CLI and deployment

Heroku is a **Platform as a Service** (**PaaS**) that enables developers to build, run, and operate applications entirely in the cloud. It supports applications built-in languages like Java, Scala, Node.js, PHP, Python, Go, Gradle, Clojure, and Ruby. To start using Heroku cloud, follow these steps:

1. We will need to sign up on Heroku if we want to use its cloud features. For this, browse the following website on Chrome:

   https://www.heroku.com

You will see the following screenshot:

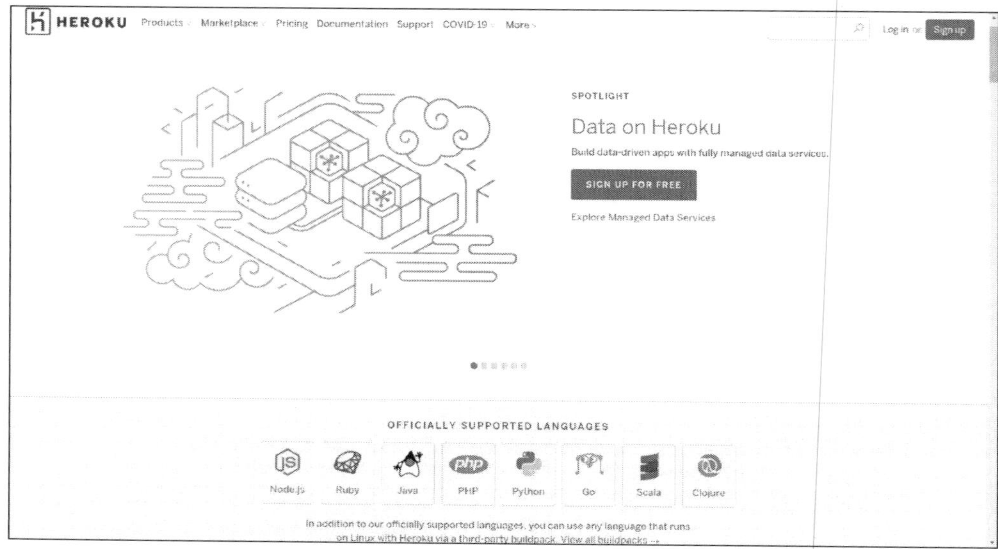

Figure 12.11: Heroku homepage

2. Click on **`SIGN UP FOR FREE`** to create an account on Heroku Cloud. After completing the sign-up process, you will see the following screen where you will see a **`Create new app`** button. Click on the button, and type **`App name`** which should be unique for your application as shown in the following screenshot:

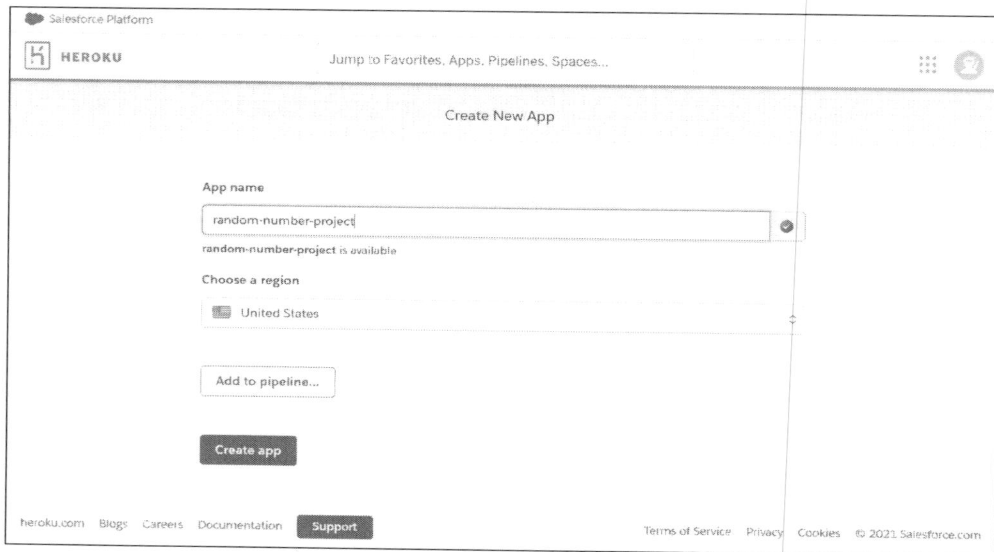

Figure 12.12: Validating app-name

3. Once you see the availability of the app name in *green* color, the application will be created by clicking on the **`Create app`** button. As the next step, you can decide the deployment method from the options available – **`Heroku Git`**, **`GitHub`**, and **`Container Registry`**. For our purposes, the easiest method would be to select **`Heroku Git`** which uses the Heroku CLI. Click on the desired deployment method as shown in the following screenshot:

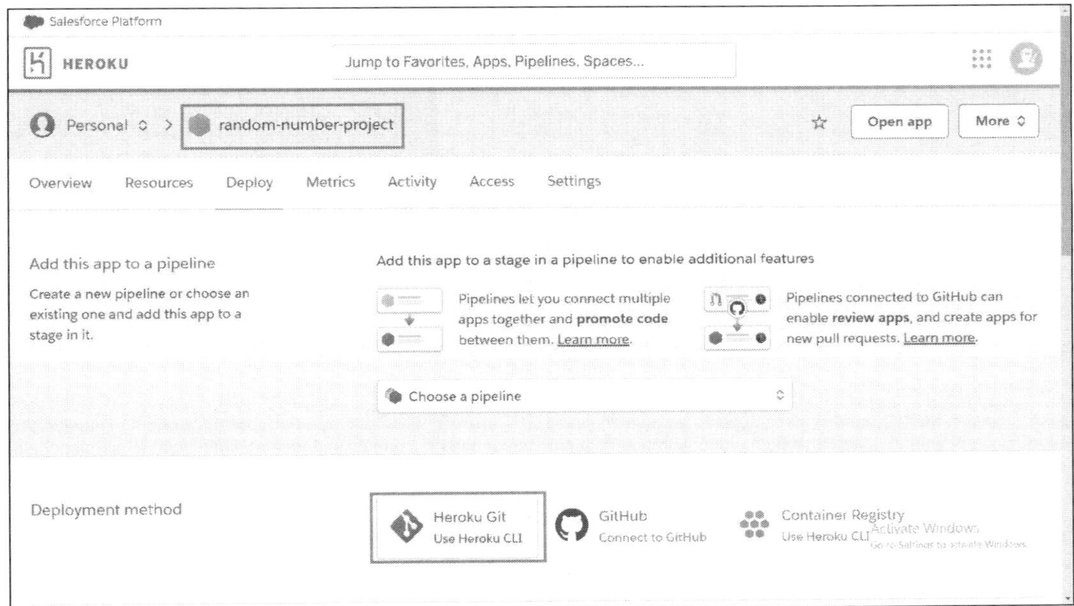

***Figure 12.13**: Selecting deployment method*

4. The Heroku CLI can be downloaded from the following website:

   https://cli-assets.heroku.com/heroku-x64.exe

   Once the installation is completed, you can verify the installation of the Heroku CLI by running the **`heroku`** command in the terminal as shown in the following screenshot:

```
Microsoft Windows [Version 10.0.19041.804]
(c) 2020 Microsoft Corporation. All rights reserved.

C:\Users\PCW>heroku
 »   Warning: Our terms of service have changed: https://dashboard.heroku.com/terms-of-service
CLI to interact with Heroku

VERSION
  heroku/7.49.1 win32-x64 node-v12.16.2

USAGE
  $ heroku [COMMAND]

COMMANDS
  access          manage user access to apps
  addons          tools and services for developing, extending, and operating your app
  apps            manage apps on Heroku
  auth            check 2fa status
  authorizations  OAuth authorizations
  autocomplete    display autocomplete installation instructions
  buildpacks      scripts used to compile apps
  certs           a topic for the ssl plugin
  ci              run an application test suite on Heroku
  clients         OAuth clients on the platform
  config          environment variables of apps
  container       Use containers to build and deploy Heroku apps
  domains         custom domains for apps
  drains          forward logs to syslog or HTTPS
  features        add/remove app features
  git             manage local git repository for app
  help            display help for heroku
  keys            add/remove account ssh keys
  labs            add/remove experimental features
```

Figure 12.14: Verifying installation of Heroku

The preceding command shows the version of CLI installed and helping commands for using the CLI. Now, navigate to the directory which contains the application code. Log in to Heroku Cloud using the **`heroku login`** command as shown in the following screenshot:

```
C:\Users\PCW\Documents\workspace-spring-tool-suite-4-4.7.1.RELEASE\random-number-project>heroku login
heroku: Press any key to open up the browser to login or q to exit:
Opening browser to https://cli-auth.heroku.com/auth/cli/browser/a2fcb4b9-efb7-4c40-b56b-4b4a1487c270?requestor=SFMyNTY.g2gDbQAAAAw0OS4z
Ni40NS4yMjRuBgCGtz7xdwFiAAFRgA.tAHtzHuumT-Vw4Iajlo2GMcYcrCWb3RtHI263AFTmF8
heroku: Waiting for login... |
```

Figure 12.15: Heroku CLI login

5. The browser will automatically open the login URL where you can sign in with your account. The command will halt until there's a successful login. Once the login is successful, you will see the following screen showing the account name through which Heroku will go ahead and deploy the application:

```
C:\Users\PCW\Documents\workspace-spring-tool-suite-4-4.7.1.RELEASE\random-number-project>heroku login
heroku: Press any key to open up the browser to login or q to exit:
Opening browser to https://cli-auth.heroku.com/auth/cli/browser/a2fcb4b9-efb7-4c40-b56b-4b4a1487c270?requestor=SFMyNTY.g2gDbQAAAAw0OS4z
Ni40NS4yMjRuBgCGtz7xdwFiAAFRgA.tAHtzHuumT-Vw4Iajlo2GMcYcrCWb3RtHI263AFTmF8
Logging in... done
Logged in as shagunbakliwal@gmail.com

C:\Users\PCW\Documents\workspace-spring-tool-suite-4-4.7.1.RELEASE\random-number-project>
```

Figure 12.16: Heroku CLI logged in

We will now commit our code into Heroku GIT so that Heroku can take the code from there and process the deployment. To do this, we need to initialize the **`Git repository`** in the folder by using the **`git init`** command. This will create an empty **`Git repository local`**. To create a repository inside Heroku Cloud, we need to execute the **`heroku git:remote -a random-number-project`** command as shown in the following screenshot:

```
C:\Users\PCW\Documents\workspace-spring-tool-suite-4-4.7.1.RELEASE\random-number-project>git init
Initialized empty Git repository in C:/Users/PCW/Documents/workspace-spring-tool-suite-4-4.7.1.RELEASE/random-number-project/.git/

C:\Users\PCW\Documents\workspace-spring-tool-suite-4-4.7.1.RELEASE\random-number-project>heroku git:remote -a random-number-project
set git remote heroku to https://git.heroku.com/random-number-project.git

C:\Users\PCW\Documents\workspace-spring-tool-suite-4-4.7.1.RELEASE\random-number-project>
```

Figure 12.17: *Setting Git repository for Heroku*

6. Add all files in GIT by running the **`git add .`** command and do a commit with the **`git commit -am "Initial Commit"`** command. When all the files are committed, you can push your changes to remote GIT by running the **`git push heroku master`** command. You will see the following logs at the end as shown in the following screenshot:

```
remote:        [INFO] Downloading from central: https://repo.maven.apache.org/maven2/org/codehaus/plexus/plexus-utils/3.0.15/plexus-utils-3.0.15.jar
remote:        [INFO] Downloaded from central: https://repo.maven.apache.org/maven2/org/apache/maven/shared/maven-shared-utils/0.4/maven-shared-utils-0.4.jar (155 kB at 3.7 MB/s)
remote:        [INFO] Downloaded from central: https://repo.maven.apache.org/maven2/commons-codec/commons-codec/1.6/commons-codec-1.6.jar (233 kB at 5.2 MB/s)
remote:        [INFO] Downloaded from central: https://repo.maven.apache.org/maven2/org/codehaus/plexus/plexus-utils/3.0.15/plexus-utils-3.0.15.jar (239 kB at 5.0 MB/s)
remote:        [INFO] Installing /tmp/build_8fc6ea00/target/random-number-project-0.0.1-SNAPSHOT.jar to /tmp/codon/tmp/cache/.m2/repository/com/bpb/publications/random-number-project/0.0.1-SNAPSHOT/random-number-project-0.0.1-SNAPSHOT.jar
remote:        [INFO] Installing /tmp/build_8fc6ea00/pom.xml to /tmp/codon/tmp/cache/.m2/repository/com/bpb/publications/random-number-project/0.0.1-SNAPSHOT/random-number-project-0.0.1-SNAPSHOT.pom
remote:        [INFO] ------------------------------------------------------------------------
remote:        [INFO] BUILD SUCCESS
remote:        [INFO] ------------------------------------------------------------------------
remote:        [INFO] Total time:  15.387 s
remote:        [INFO] Finished at: 2021-03-02T04:49:09Z
remote:        [INFO] ------------------------------------------------------------------------
remote: -----> Discovering process types
remote:        Procfile declares types     -> (none)
remote:        Default types for buildpack -> web
remote:
remote: -----> Compressing...
remote:        Done: 73.1M
remote: -----> Launching...
remote:        Released v3
remote:        https://random-number-project.herokuapp.com/ deployed to Heroku
remote:
remote: Verifying deploy... done.
To https://git.heroku.com/random-number-project.git
 * [new branch]      master -> master

C:\Users\PCW\Documents\workspace-spring-tool-suite-4-4.7.1.RELEASE\random-number-project>
```

Figure 12.18: *Pushing artifact to Heroku*

The preceding logs depict the artifact containing the **`.jar`** file and pom details are pushed to the Heroku repository with the version **`v3`** of the commit. This **`v3`** is derived from the commits which Heroku internally does while creating an app. Lastly, it shows the URL that will route the request to the application when requested. Since we named the application **`random-number-project`**, Heroku created the route as:

https://random-number-project.herokuapp.com

7. *Congratulations!* This was the last step of doing the deployment to Heroku Cloud. Next, the application can be accessed by simply browsing the host API in any of the client like Chrome or by clicking on the **`Open app`** button as shown in the following screenshot:

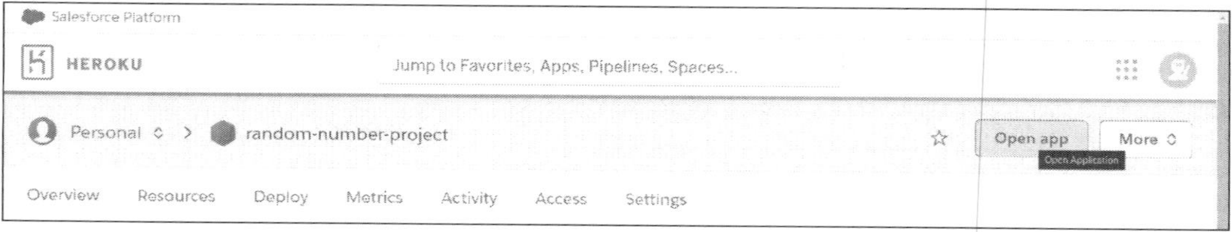

Figure 12.19: *Launching app*

8. You can now access the respective API like which will generate random numbers as per the code which was written earlier in the previous chapters:

   https://random-number-project.herokuapp.com/generate

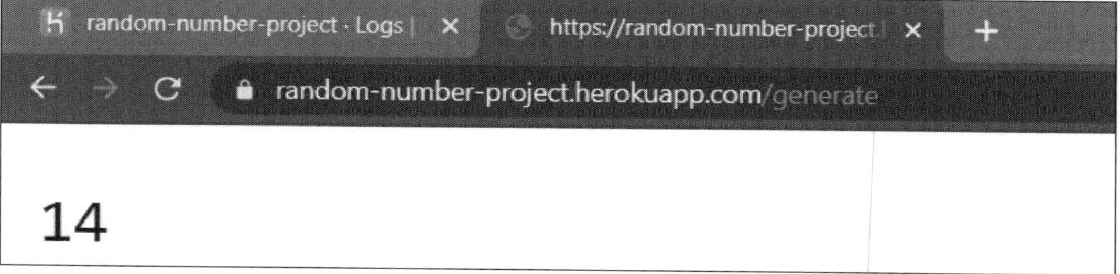

Figure 12.20: *Requesting API*

You can now share the application URL with all your clients who would want to reach out to the application by their HTTP clients (Chrome, **`web-app`**). *How will you check logs?*

9. The application logs can be viewed by clicking on the **`More`** button on the top right-hand corner and selecting **`View logs`**. The logs will be shown in the same way what we used to see in our local workspace as shown in the following screenshot:

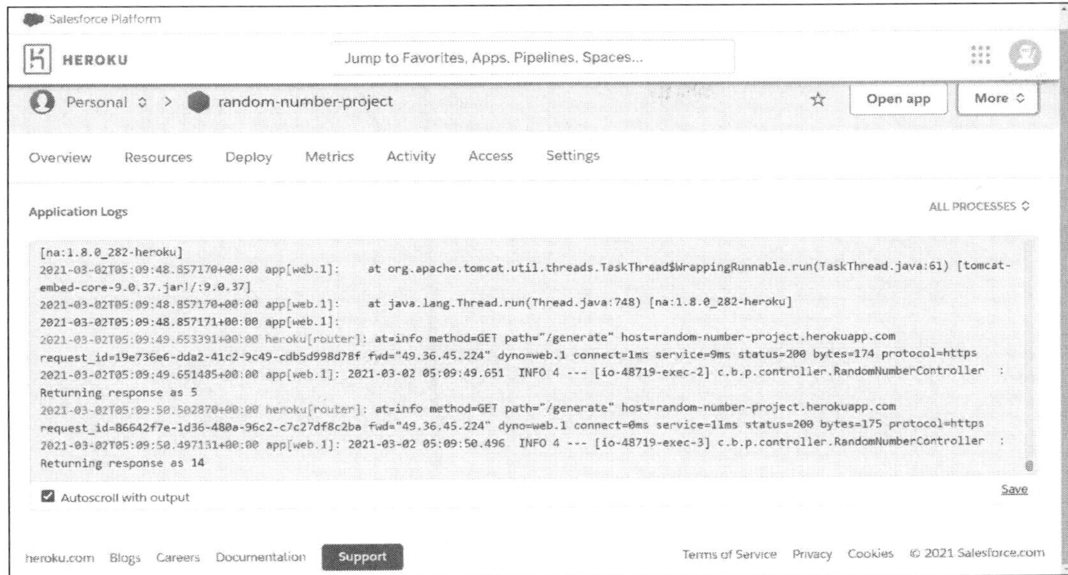

Figure 12.21: *Application logs*

10. You can manage the application by running in different tabs as shown in Heroku. Let's understand that one by one. Starting with the **`Overview`** tab, it shows the activity of the number versions that were pushed to Heroku as shown in the following screenshot:

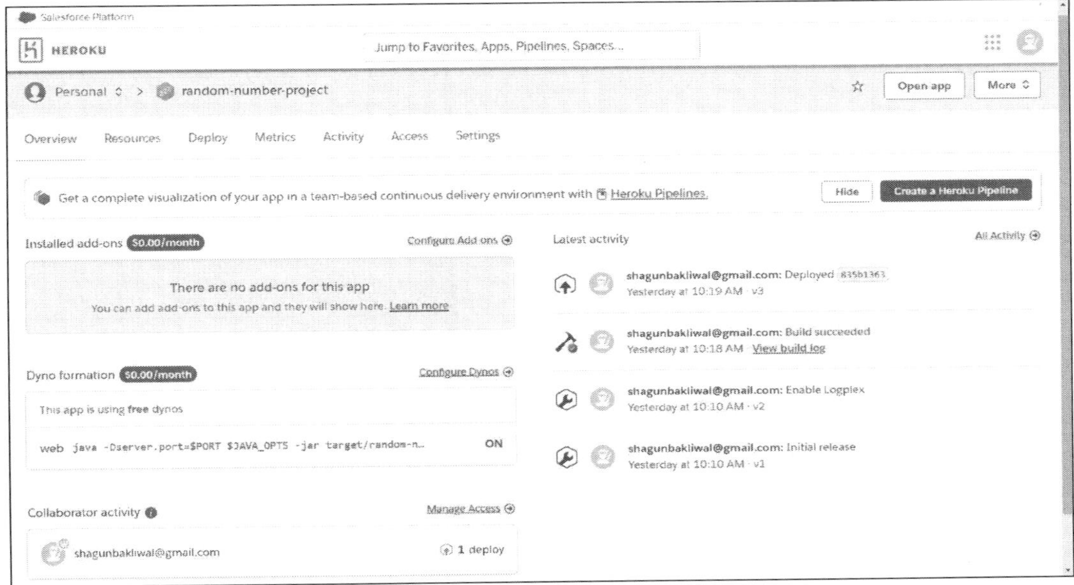

Figure 12.22: *Overview in Heroku*

11. It also shows the add-on installed with this application which incurred **`$0.00/month`** since we haven't selected an add-on pack for our application. The available add-on can be viewed by checking out the following website:

    https://elements.heroku.com/addons

    These add-ons are provided as **Software as a Service** (**SaaS**) where you may be charged from *$0/month* to *$4000/month* and may be beyond that as well depending on the plan you select. For instance, the following screenshot displays the **`for Heroku Postgres`** add-on which starts from *$0/month*:

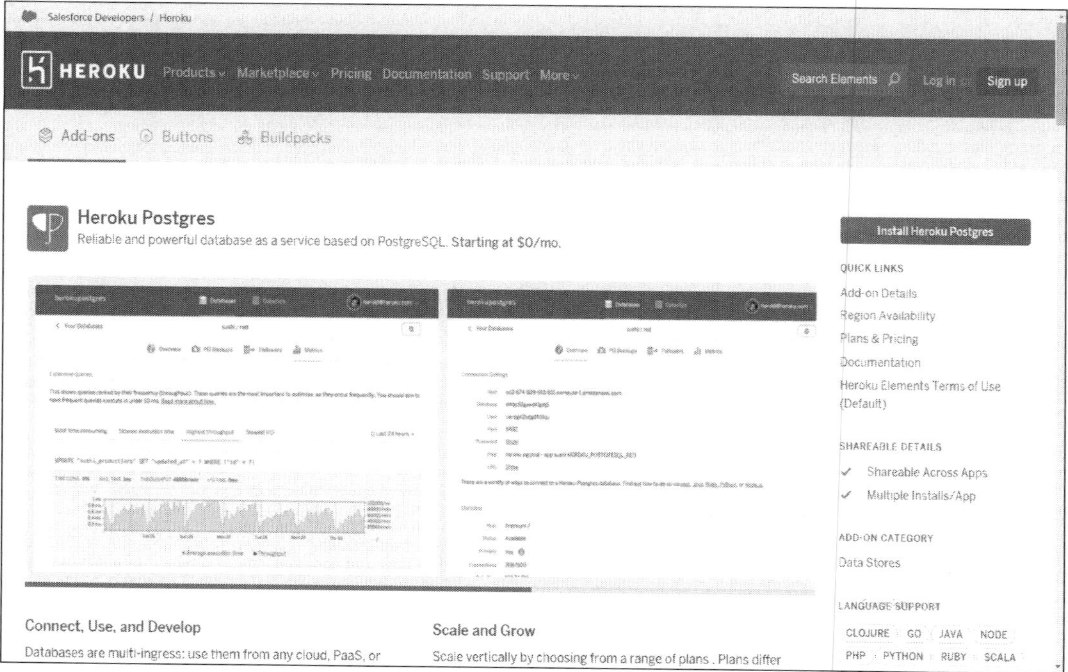

Figure 12.23: *Heroku Postgres service*

12. As we scroll further to any of the add-ons, we will see an extended plan and the pricing section as shown in the following screenshot just like **`Heroku Postgres`**:

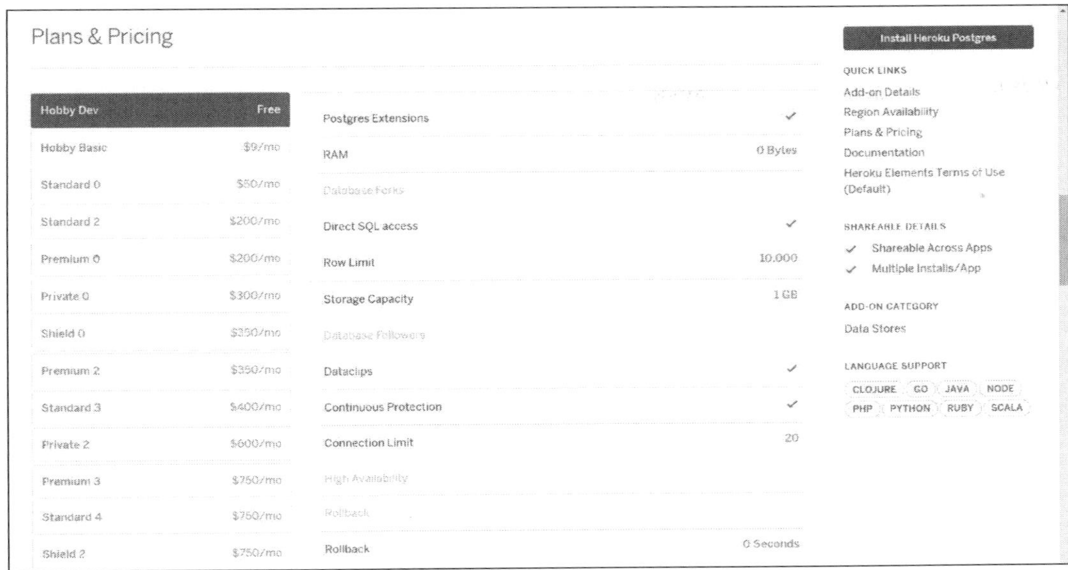

Figure 12.24: *Plans and pricing*

13. Heroku also shows the activity of an application that is deployed by clicking on the `Activity` tab just at the top. This shows all events like creating an application, creating different versions of the applciation that may contain different features for which we need different deployments. A snippet of the activity is shown in the following screenshot:

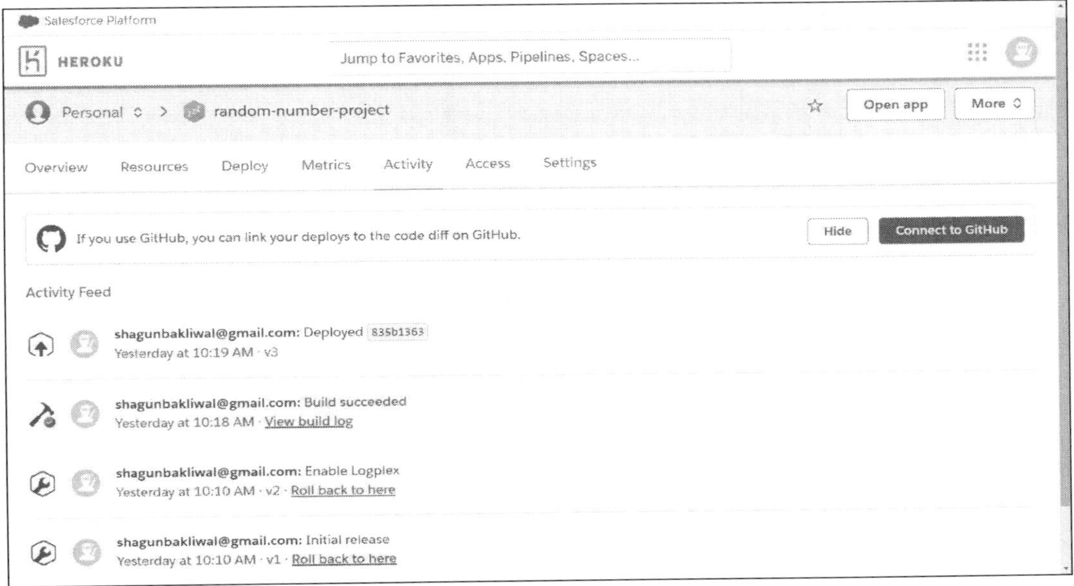

Figure 12.25: *Activity for an application*

Heroku also provides an option to rollback to a particular state or build by clicking on **`Roll back to here`** in the **`Activity`** tab. You can even add different collaborators to the application deployed by clicking on the **`Access`** tab and then clicking on the *Add collaborator* button and providing an email address.

Further, Heroku also provides features like rename the application, delete it, change the build pack, show the memory it acquired, reveal configuration variables, and configure the SSL certificate. If you don't like the URL created, you can also add your domain by changing the settings for the application by clicking on the **`Settings`** button.

These were the basic activities which a developer can configure for his application. More documentation on Heroku can be found on the following link:

https://devcenter.heroku.com

Conclusion

We learned how to set up Docker Desktop in the local system, create Docker images with Java images, and enclose them within the container providing the runtime environment for the application. We also explored the activity on Docker containers and even accessed the application running in the Docker containerized environment. We also learned about Heroku in this chapter. We learned how to create a Git repository, commit and deploy the code, and access the application from the Internet. We also looked at the different add-ons and their pricing plans and other administrative settings which are good to configure applications at the very starting phase of developing and deploying the applications.

Points to Remember

- Docker containers run in an isolated environment to access local resources. You might need to change host details from the localhost to **`docker.for.win.localhost`**.
- Docker images can also be pushed to the Docker hub which acts as a centralized repository for storing all images that can be accessed publicly.
- Signing up on Heroku is free, but remember the services or add-ons are chargeable from *\$0* to *\$1000* per month.
- There is a limit of deploying a maximum of five applications when your account is in the free tier plan.

Questions

1. What are the methods available to execute your application?
2. How can you expose APIs inside a Docker container?
3. How to create Docker images and deploy them?
4. What is containerization?
5. What is the cloud? Explain its features.
6. How many public clouds are available in the market?
7. How can you set up a Heroku application?
8. What are different pricing plans for using Heroku Cloud services?

Index

Symbols

A

B

C

D

E

F

G

H

I

J

L

M

O

P

Q

R

S

T

U

W

Z

Printed in Great Britain
by Amazon

70168207R00199